The Moretonhampstead Branch

A Railway
from Shore to Moor

Immaculately turned-out in lined green livery, 2-6-2T 'large Prairie' No. 4117 takes on water at Moretonhampstead prior to working the 3.15pm train to Newton Abbot on 28th February 1959. Also pictured is the one-road granite engine shed, diminutive signal box and the town's gas works.
Peter W. Gray

Above: A Moreton-bound train hauled by No. 1466 approaches Bovey's fine GW-style wooden bracket 'down home' signal - set for the 'up' platform loop - on 19th February 1959. The level crossing lever cabin (or ground frame) is seen to good effect in this atmospheric picture.
Below: A view of Moretonhampstead on 19th February 1959. 'Large Prairie' No. 4150 is seen detaching a van from its train. *Both, Peter W. Gray*

ISBN 0 946184 88 7   Copyright John Owen & Waterfront   July 2000
Publisher Roger Hardingham
Printed by The Amadeus Press, Cleckheaton, West Yorkshire

The MORETONHAMPSTEAD Branch

A Railway from Shore to Moor

John Owen

Flanked by Heathfield's attractive timber station building and equally delightful rhododendron bushes, Branch 'regular' 0-4-2T No. 1427 brings a Moretonhampstead service beneath the A38 road bridge on its approach to the 'down' platform in late Spring, 1958. The lead-in to Candy's Siding occupies the right-hand foreground. *Colour-Rail*

Published by
Waterfront
A Division of Kingfisher Productions
The Dalesmade Centre, Watershed Mill, Settle, North Yorkshire BD24 9LR

CONTENTS

PART 1 HISTORY & OPERATION

Chapter 1   A Description of the Line 9
Chapter 2   A Line a Long Time in the Making...23
Chapter 3   The Train Services 35
Chapter 4   Locomotives & Rolling Stock...46
Chapter 5   Alarms & Excursions 54
Chapter 6   Signalling & Permanent Way...67

PART 2 STATIONS & LOCATIONS

Chapter 7   Newton Abbot..79
Chapter 8   Teignbridge 89
Chapter 9   Teigngrace..93
Chapter 10   Heathfield 99
Chapter 11   Bovey Sidings 113
Chapter 12   Brimley..117
Chapter 13   Bovey 121
Chapter 14   Hawkmoor/Pullabrook..139
Chapter 15   Lustleigh..143
Chapter 16   Moretonhampstead...151

Postscript: **The Axe and After** 169

ACKNOWLEDGEMENTS

In compiling this work I am indebted to numerous individuals and organisations who have assisted in many ways, and without whom the book would not have been possible. It has been my great good fortune over the past few years to have met, or corresponded with, several former Railway employees who either worked on, or have detailed knowledge of, the Moretonhampstead Branch. It is from them that the inspiration for the book has come, and to whom it is principally dedicated. Especial thanks are due to:
Stan Bickham, David Rouse, Stan Winsor, Stan Dart, Stan Rowe, Wilfred Wright, Stan Griggs, Geoffrey Tanton, Arthur Yendall, Ralph Howard, Ron Tucker, Marjorie Yeoman, Bill Knott, Gordon Vowden, Des Lock and Edna Young.
With the historical and technical research, I should like to acknowledge the assistance afforded by the staffs of the:
GWR Museum, Newton Abbot; Manor House Hotel, North Bovey; National Railway Museum, York; Plymouth and Exeter Reference Libraries; Public Record Office, Kew; Railway Signalling Society; Railway Studies Library, Newton Abbot; and West Country Studies Library, Exeter.
Additionally, considerable informative and interesting material has come from people with local knowledge, and to them I extend my gratitude. In particular:
Mary Adcock, Peter Kay, Wilf Underhay, Mrs. S.G. Camp, Mike Lang, John Westlake, Peter Collier, Pamela Lind, Brian Yeoman, Helena Hawkins, Lance Tregoning, Eric Youlden, Valerie Huish and Kevin Truscott.
My grateful thanks are due to several photographers for so generously supplying prints, and whose contribution has not only been an undoubted asset to the book, but also provided a valuable historical record in itself:

Hugh Ballantyne, David Fereday Glenn, Roger Penny, Ivan Beale, Peter Gray, Richard Riley, Peter Bowles, Geoff Howells, Eric Shepherd, Stan Dickson, Ron Lumber, Ronald Toop; and Miles Barber Glenn for permission to use his late father's photographs.
A special word of thanks goes to Peter Gray. As well as several excellent black and white pictures, Peter has kindly supplied a 'colour supplement', the quality of which, in terms of subject matter, composition and detail, provides a most valuable addition to the book.
For providing pictures from their collections, I wish to thank:
Bovey Tracey Heritage Trust, BR/OPC, Dartington Rural Archive, Herald Express, James Mann, Lens of Sutton, L&GRP, Mid-Devon Advertiser, National Monuments Record Centre-Swindon, National Railway Museum-York, Pamlin Prints, Photomatic Ltd, Real Photographs Co., and WBB-Newton Abbot.
For permission to survey the extant station building and goods shed at Bovey I am grateful to the managements of J. Bibby and Dartmoor National Park respectively, and to John Snow for his tireless help with the arduous task itself.
My sincere appreciation goes to Greg and Maria Reed for graciously providing unlimited access to a word-processor, and for their uncomplaining assistance when my understanding of computer operation failed - as it often did! Sincere thanks too go to Hilary Goodman for assistance with the manuscript, and to Margaret Owen for her unfailing encouragement throughout the research and production stages of the book. Finally, I wish to place on record my appreciation of the endeavours of the publisher, Roger Hardingham, in bringing this project to fruition.

Introduction

From Hingston Rocks, a thousand feet above sea-level, there are exhilarating and wide-ranging views over the north-eastern part of Dartmoor, in the County of Devon. The gorse, heather and bracken of the open moorland stand in marked contrast to the irregular geometry of enclosed pasture and woodland at lower levels. The scene imparts a deep sense of timelessness, enhanced and animated by the endless nuances of light and shade produced by the passing clouds. For almost a hundred years, however, there was a further element in this landscape: the Moretonhampstead Branch steam train.

Gazing down into the broad valley below the breezy moorland heights, a moving white plume of smoke set against heavily wooded slopes defines the distant progress of a train on its journey from the important South Devon railway town of Newton Abbot. Moments later, the rhythmic exhaust beat of a hard-working locomotive drifts up on the wind as it nears the end of its long climb on to the Moor. Soon after, the train itself comes into view, looking rather small amidst the openness of the landscape. In the vicinity of Moretonhampstead Gas Works, the driver shuts off steam for the level run into the station; finally bringing his charge to a stand beneath the wooden train shed at the end of the Line.

Lying near the confluence of the tiny Wadley and Wray Brooks, the small town of Moretonhampstead clusters discreetly around the junction of several roads that link it with the scattered farmsteads and hamlets of the immediate vicinity. Beyond, at higher altitudes, the topography is characterised by broad rolling hills, whose summits are littered with large granite boulders. In general, these rocks display a random distribution, but in places are organised into distinctive block-like protrusions known as tors. Though not far from popular holiday beaches - which enjoy a sheltered aspect and high sunshine totals - rainfall on the Moor is considerably higher, with the correspondingly greater incidence of cloud cover, mist and glowering skies.

The train had, indeed, begun its twelve mile journey in a different world: on tracks laid across reclaimed marshland at the head of the photogenic estuary of the River Teign. Its placid waters and tidal mudflats are flanked by low, rounded hills clothed in the classic South Devon patchwork of lush meadows and rich, red plough-land. Thick hedgerows are commonplace, and trees abound. At Newton Abbot, the track is only a matter of feet above mean sea-level. Indeed, at times when heavy rainfall and/or snowmelt on Dartmoor coincide with high spring tides in the estuary, the River Teign rises perilously close to the Line in the vicinity of the Kingsteignton Road Bridge on the outskirts of the town. In exceptional circumstances, it has actually been known to overwhelm the Line, as well as inundate the low-lying streets near the station. The first six miles of the journey from Newton are relatively easily graded, so that at the halfway stage (at Bovey Tracey) the Line is still only 100 feet above sea level. From this point, however, the nature of the railway changes markedly. In the next six miles the rails have to ascend some 450 feet in order to reach the moorland terminus, this involving long stretches on a rising gradient of 1:49. Thus in just a dozen miles, a train journey on the Moretonhampstead Branch takes the passenger literally from 'Shore to Moor'.

Whilst on the subject of gradients, mention needs to be made of the designation 'up' and 'down' when referring to the direction of travel. Opened in 1866 as the 'Moretonhampstead & South Devon Railway', the Company quite logically assigned the direction of travel to reflect geographical reality: namely, trains from Newton travelled in the 'up' direction, while those from Moreton in the 'down'.

It was customary for Teign Valley trains beginning their journey at Heathfield to leave from the Bay platform. 'Small Prairie' No. 5536 prepares to leave with a stopping train to Exeter, as 0-4-2T No. 1466 heads out of the 'down' loop with its two corridor coaches en route for Moretonhampstead. Passengers could cross the tracks only by means of a boardwalk at the junction end of the station. Due to the 'stagger' of the platforms, this was situated immediately beyond the signal box, and involved the public walking at track level in the confined space between the back of the box and the bay line. Hence the bracket light on the corner of the signal box and the prominent notice with its imperative to 'BEWARE OF TRAINS'. 15.2.58. *Peter W. Gray*

This practice was continued by the South Devon Railway which, though initially operating the services on behalf of the M&SDR, formally took over the Branch in 1872. Also, when that Company was in turn absorbed by the Great Western Railway in 1876, the original nomenclature was retained. However, in 1889 the GWR decided to relate direction of travel to a 'datum' at Paddington: trains travelled 'down' from London to Devon, with the Moreton Branch being a continuation in distance terms - albeit involving a change of trains. This brought about a reversal in the designation. From that time onwards there was the anomalous situation of 'down' trains actually undertaking almost the whole of their journey on rising gradients!

Such idiosyncrasies, though minor in themselves, form part of the widespread appeal that railways seem to possess. In part, this may be explained by a fascination with the sounds, smells and latent power of steam locomotives, or the air of anticipation experienced at stations and on a train journey. In part also, it might be the aesthetic impact of well-proportioned buildings, structures and fittings, or the visual appeal of a steam train moving through the landscape. But in large measure it is also probably due to the fact that railways are about people and people are different both as individuals and in communities. Railways are conceived, planned, financed, built and operated by individuals interacting in a diverse, changing and complex dynamic; while they serve and service communities in a whole variety of ways. In the days before mass road transport, the railway was a vital ingredient in people's lives, directly or indirectly.

While the Moretonhampstead Branch displays many of the 'typical' aspects of Great Western branch lines, it is also very much 'its own line' with its own distinctive hallmarks. It is hoped that in the following pages something of the flavour of this characterful and charming Devonshire branch line might be conveyed, not only as a contribution to the local historical record, but also as a tribute to the men and women to whom it gave employment and through whom many communities were served.

Top: The 10.15am ex-Moreton, in the charge of 'large Prairie' No. 4150, makes a spirited start away from Bovey. This was one of the two 'passenger' (ie. non auto) workings in the last few years, with compartment coaches offering first and second class accommodation. 19.2.59. *Peter W. Gray*

Above: Running-in board. *Peter W. Gray*

Left: Water splashing to the ground from the column indicates that 0-4-2T 1466 has just replenished her tanks and will shortly pull forward with auto coach W241W into the platform prior to working the 3.15pm to Newton Abbot. The brazier, or 'fire-devil', with its tall stove-pipe chimney is seen to good effect in this picture. 25.2.59.
R. A. Lumber

Above: Having crossed Letford Bridge, the regular latter-day pairing of No. 1466 and BR-built auto coach W241W tackles the gradient around the cliff-like southern edge of Knowle Wood, ¼-mile beyond Pullabrook Halt with the 12.50pm from Newton Abbot on 21st February 1959.
Below: Climbing away from the valley of the River Bovey, 1466 raises the echoes as she crosses Knowle Viaduct with the 12.50pm from Newton. Three non-corridor carriages have been provided on this service to accommodate the crowds on the Line's 'last day'.   *Both, Peter W. Gray*

Above: With vegetation already encroaching the disused platform at Lustleigh, colourful bunting and a small group well-wishers greet the southbound post-closure 'Heart of Devon Rambler' - hauled by BR 2-6-2T No. 4174 - on the 6th June 1960.

Below: ' The South Devon Phoenix' ran on the 11th June 1962. The locomotive, ex-GWR 2-6-2T No. 5153, with Train Reporting Number Z17 on its smokebox door, is about to run round its train at Moretonhampstead. The 6-coach special was organised by the South Devon Railway Society as part of its (unsuccessful) campaign to restore passenger services.

Both, Peter W. Gray

Part One
History and Operation

Chapter One
A DESCRIPTION OF THE LINE

Incorporated by Act of Parliament as the 'Moretonhampstead & South Devon Railway', a broadly-defined geographical location is immediately indicated for this line of railway. However, designed to cater for specific interests and communities in this part of the county, it may be appropriate to begin the discourse with a general description of the Line: to provide a sense of place and a context for names and locations mentioned in the main body of the work. This will be attempted by reconstructing a train journey in the mid 1950s from the main line at Newton Abbot to the moorland terminus some twelve miles distant.

Leaving the early afternoon bustle and traffic of Queen Street behind, the intending passenger enters the cool, lofty spaciousness of the booking hall at Newton Abbot station to purchase a 'cheap day return' to Moretonhampstead. Date-stamping both ends of the cardboard ticket, the clerk asks for one shilling and ten pence (nine pence in modern currency). Although the station building is separated from the principal platforms by the 'up through' and 'up main' tracks, it will not be necessary to head towards the recessed double staircase leading to the connecting footbridge, because the Moretonhampstead train will be leaving from its own 'Bay' platform (Number 9) which is set apart from the rest of the station. Walking out to the forecourt on Station Road through one of the two wide doorways, the passenger turns to the right and heads towards the 'Railway Hotel'. This is not to partake of some tasty alcoholic beverage to fortify one for the journey, but because the roadway leading to the Bay is tucked away round the side of that hostelry!

As it is a few minutes past two o'clock, the train - due out at 2.15 - is waiting in the platform. It comprises two of the newly-built, all-steel, open saloon-type carriages known as 'trailers' or 'auto coaches' in railway parlance. At its head is locomotive number 1427. This is one of the delightful, diminutive '1400' class of tank engine widely employed on the West Country branch lines of the old Great Western Railway. Built in 1933, it has for some time been a 'regular' on the Moretonhampstead Branch. A four-coupled engine, with the wheel notation 0-4-2, it is characterised by a tall chimney and huge steam dome. The angular, slab-like side tanks have led many railway enthusiasts and others to give these engines the endearing nickname of 'biscuit tins'. Stepping into the vestibule of one of the trailers

Newton Abbot. Churchward '45xx' class 2-6-2T 'small Prairie' No. 5533 waits with a single trailer in the Bay (Platform 9) with a stopping train for Moretonhampstead in the summer of 1957. In November 1958 the loco was transferred to Truro, from where she was withdrawn in December the following year and scrapped at Swindon Works in January 1960.
G. Howells

MORETONHAMPSTEAD BRANCH ROUTE MAP

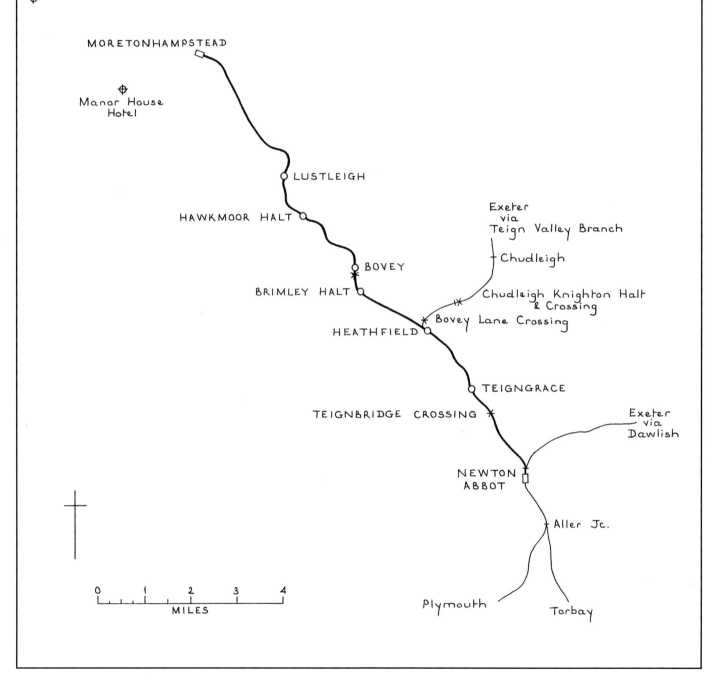

CHAGFORD

MORETONHAMPSTEAD

Manor House Hotel

LUSTLEIGH

HAWKMOOR HALT

BOVEY

BRIMLEY HALT

Exeter via Teign Valley Branch

Chudleigh

Chudleigh Knighton Halt & Crossing

Bovey Lane Crossing

HEATHFIELD

TEIGNGRACE

TEIGNBRIDGE CROSSING

Exeter via Dawlish

NEWTON ABBOT

Aller Jc.

Plymouth   Torbay

0   1   2   3   4
MILES

through the single doorway, there is a choice of seating, though all of it one class. To the left is the small no-smoking section fitted out with conventional transverse seats. These are arranged back-to-back, so that one can either sit facing the direction of travel or with one's 'back to the engine'. On the other side of the vestibule is the much larger smoking saloon, with its mixture of transverse and longitudinal seats. The latter give the passenger the option of sitting facing inwards to the central aisle, above which hang ceiling straps for use by those having to stand at busy times.

Pulling out of the Bay, on time, the Branch train runs parallel with the South Devon main line for a little under a quarter of a mile. With a stopping train for Exeter also due off at the same time, the Moreton service is frequently 'paced' on this length. Over on the left side of travel the passenger cannot fail to notice the impressive bulk of the Teign Road warehouses, used by agriculturally-related industries such as malting, cider making and grain milling. Served by both road and rail, their solid proportions and repeating architectural motifs, executed in rough-hewn pinkish-grey local limestone, give the buildings a pleasing appearance. Towards the end of the long rank, the Line begins its sharp divergence towards the north-west. With a radius of twelve chains (264 yards) this is the most severe curve on the Branch, imposing a maximum speed limit of a mere 15mph. Incorporated into this curve are bridges over, first, the River Lemon and then Whitelake (a man-made channel linking the Stover Canal with the River Teign). Both have three spans, the massive plate girder superstructures being carried on limestone abutments and piers. At a fraction over 80 feet, the central span of Whitelake Bridge is the longest of any on the Branch.

The journey is unavoidably, yet pleasantly, accompanied by the sonorous 'clickety clack' beat rapped out by the wheels as they pass over the narrow gaps between rail lengths. On negotiating the curve by the monumental Newton Abbot East Signal Box this familiar rhythm changes to a less measured metallic clatter as the train trails through three sets of points, enjoined by a degree of squealing from the wheels as their

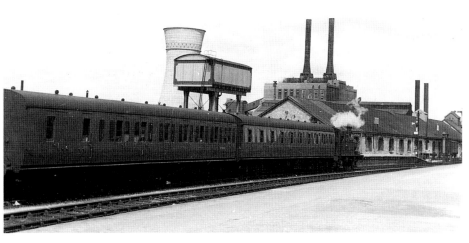

Newton Abbot. The Moretonhampstead Branch train seen from the 'up' island platform on 16th August 1957. Made up of two non-corridor, or 'suburban', coaches of early British Railways vintage, that next to the engine is of 57 feet all-second class standard design, whilst the other (W7390W) is a 63 foot composite brake vehicle. Both are in maroon livery, albeit different shades. The elevated water tank and power station complex, like the train, are now just a memory; but happily the locomotive - Collett 0-4-2 No. 1466 - is preserved in working order at the Great Western Society's Didcot Railway Centre. *R. E. Toop*

flanges impact against the rails. This is followed by a deep percussive rumble as the train crosses the two girder bridges, to begin its journey on the Moretonhampstead Branch proper. Located between these two bridges, on the 'town side' of the track, is the line leading to the 'Electricity Sidings' on Devon Wharf. The huge cooling tower and twin chimneys of the power station dominate the skyline hereabouts. Not a pretty sight!

Gathering speed on the long straight, on a falling gradient of 1:132, the train rattles past Newton Abbot Goods Yard (commonly referred to as the 'New Yard'). What strikes the passenger most, perhaps, is the substantial red brick goods shed and crowded sidings; creating plenty of work for the shunting engine. The Goods Yard is terminated abruptly by the embankment leading to the Kingsteignton Road Bridge, an attractive five-arch masonry structure. The bridge itself marks the lowest point on the Branch, and also the end of the contiguous association with the River Teign, which now swings north to follow a more distant and sinuous course. Immediately beyond the bridge the train passes 'Newton Abbot Clay Siding' (on the right of the direction of travel) with its high loading platform used for the road-to-rail transfer of ball clay.

For the next few miles the railway runs through the centre of what geologists call the Bovey Basin: a flat, 28 square-mile expanse of thick white ball clay deposits, black lignite bands and variously-coloured sands and gravels. The commercial exploitation of the former was largely a consequence of the opening of the Stover Canal in 1790, which the train now crosses on a 46 foot-long plate girder bridge (having just crossed a feeder channel on a similar structure). Moments later, the train reaches Mile Post 1, beyond which the canal comes directly alongside the

Teignbridge. Under a lowering sky, '14xx' class No. 1427 hurries towards the level crossing with the single auto coach assigned to this service; the 2.15pm from Newton Abbot. The wide, raised 'up' side clay loading platform is clearly visible centre left. 19.10.57. *Peter W. Gray*

track. The marshy terrain hereabouts, peppered with flooded worked-out clay pits, may appear somewhat unprepossessing, but the more distant views are much more inspiring. Over to the west is a low but steep ridge, deeply etched into a series of distinct hills: Knowle Hill, Gaze Hill, Daracombe Beacon and Ingsdon Hill. Their bucolic patchwork of ploughed fields, rich grassland and deciduous woodland stands in marked contrast to the matted grass, sedge and scrub of the Bovey Basin.

No sooner has the eye taken in this view, than its contemplation is interrupted by a shrill whistle from the engine. This heralds the approach to Teignbridge Level Crossing, one of only two locations on the Branch where the Line is crossed by a public road. The distant signal, positioned well in advance of the gates, is at 'all clear', but the whistle is to alert the crossing keeper of the train's imminent arrival. Climbing briskly now at 1:97, the train first runs alongside Teignbridge Sidings: one 'loop' siding on either side of the running line for the handling of ball clay traffic. A rake of horizontal-planked mineral wagons are in the process of being loaded with clay from lorries; some are already covered with white 'tented' tarpaulins. The rank of low stone buildings near the east-side loading ramp serves as a reminder of the presence of the disused Stover Canal. The rattle of two sets of points beneath the carriage wheels brings the train momentarily alongside the level crossing gatehouse: a solidly-built, single storey, stone building which until fairly recently had been the keeper's residence, but now serves only as a 'cabin'. Standing beneath the awning next to the lever hut, the keeper exchanges the traditional raised arm greeting with the footplate crew as the train clatters over the roadway.

Smoke drifts past the carriage windows in discontinuous, ragged streamers as the engine comfortably tackles the 1:513 rising gradient at around 40mph. Passing Teignbridge Crossing's 'up' distant signal and Mile Post 2 in quick succession, the Line's gradient steepens to 1:100. Crowning the low ridge over to the left is the prominent landmark of Twelve Oaks Farm, while on the right the train is now alongside the lock gates on the adjacent canal. The distinctive tower of Teigngrace church -a squat grey structure with curious, contrasting red castellations - immediately comes into view, presaging the first stop on the Branch, some two and a quarter miles from Newton Abbot.

Drawing up alongside the gaunt rectangular brick building of Teigngrace Halt, the guard opens the carriage door - which on auto trailers opens inwards - and steps out on to the single, deserted platform. No passengers alight or entrain. With the 'right-away' given to the footplate crew, the train moves off; immediately passing the short single siding with loading bank which comprise the total goods facility. Beyond the siding are the extensive plantations and parkland of the Stover Estate, while by way of a backdrop to the scene is glimpsed the sweeping undulation of Dartmoor with its characteristic, yet individually distinctive, tors crowning the otherwise smooth summits. On the opposite side of the line (the east) a clearer view is had of the part-wooded, part-farmed flanks of the flat-topped Haldon Hills.

The train is now running along an embankment right next to the Stover Canal, on the approach to the collection of buildings that constitute the small settlement of Ventiford, about half a mile to the north. It is here by Ventiford Bridge that the canal ends, on the opposite side of the track to the former Union Inn. Here, just short of 2 ¾ Mile Post 2, a plate girder bridge carried on granite abutments takes the Line over the connecting path, which is accompanied by the Ventiford Brook which drains Stover Lake and flows into the nearby River Teign (and formerly fed the canal). The Inn briefly became the centre of more than local interest in the early days of the Moreton Branch as a result of a well-reported romance between the landlord's daughter and a member of the railway's permanent way gang. It was quite the stuff of romantic novels. Faced with a disapproving father, the couple decided that an elopement was the only way the suitor would get his 'permanent way'. A late-night assignation was arranged, with the determined railwayman turning up complete with ladder to effect an escape through a window - successfully as it turned out!

Having been closed in, briefly, by coppiced woodland, a short climb at 1:70 begins through a shallow clay cutting. With the engine working vigorously, its exhaust is forcibly deflected by the arch of Summerlane Bridge, a few yards beyond Mile Post 3. The train now forges along a level section of track, past the slender tubular steel post of Heathfield's 'down' distant signal - fixed permanently at caution - through open heathland to Shilstone Lane Bridge. The featureless topography of the locality has given no indication that the train has passed from the lower Teign Valley to the lower Bovey Valley, whose small sinuous river remains hidden from view until Bovey itself is reached. From Shilstone Lane the train is accompanied by a mixture of scrubby heath and enclosed mixed woodland until the next road bridge is reached: that carrying the A38 over the Line at Heathfield Station.

A little in advance of the bridge is 'Timber Siding', actually a long loop line on the west side of the track, the name of which reflects the importance of commercial forestry in this part of the Bovey Basin. Even before the train rattles over the southern-most points connecting the siding with the main line, it is slowing down to negotiate the facing points which mark the beginning of a long double track section through the station.

Teigngrace. Moreton Branch 'regular' No. 1427 brings a 'down' train into the tree framed and deserted halt in the summer of 1957. The original platform construction and station building are shown to good effect in this picture, while the disused Stover Canal is just out of shot on the left. *G. Howells*

Heathfield. With the time at quarter to eleven on the morning of 7th July 1956, the presence of three trains produces a 'full house' at the station. The 'down' auto train, hauled by 0-4-2T No. 1427, normally worked through to Moretonhampstead from Paignton but, being a summer Saturday, it had started at Newton Abbot (departing at 10.32). The 'up' train, the 10.15 from Moreton, is in the charge of four year-old British Railways Standard Class 3MT 2-6-2 No. 82001. In contrast with the noisy escape of steam from the safety valves of both 'Moreton engines', Exeter-based 0-6-0 Pannier Tank No. 5412 simmers quietly in the Bay prior to departure with a Teign Valley train at 10.50. It is one of the 25 push-pull fitted '54xx' class of pannier tank, and in this instance is coupled ahead of a single, central vestibule type of auto trailer. *Peter W. Gray*

Coasting gently over the trailing north-end connection with Timber Siding, the familiar wheel noise from the carriage bogies suddenly changes pitch and amplifies as the sound-vibrations are bounced back from the masonry walls of the A38 road bridge, to be followed immediately by a metallic clatter as they encounter the facing points leading to Candy's Siding. The extensive buildings of the pipe and tile works which that siding serves dominate the station area; the great stockpiles of products being a distinctive feature.

Not only is Heathfield the first 'crossing place' on the Branch - allowing trains to pass on an otherwise single track line - but it is also a junction, marking the western end of the Teign Valley Railway from Exeter. The Moretonhampstead Branch is given the classification of 'Main Line', and the Teign Valley that of 'Branch'. Running into the 'down' platform, the train comes alongside another standing on the 'up' line: the 12.47pm from Exeter St. David's. The single auto coach comprising this train is one of the older central vestibule types converted from an earlier steam railmotor. It had been propelled the 17 miles from Devon's county town by another member of the '1400' Class of

0-4-2 tank engine: number 1469, one of Exeter Shed's 'regulars' on the TVR. Arriving in the Bay platform at Heathfield at 1.54pm, passengers had been provided with a connection to Newton Abbot by means of the 1.35pm from Moreton. Having then transferred to the 'up' platform, it will itself continue to Newton three minutes after the Moreton train has left. Due to the staggered nature of the platforms here - made necessary by Candy's Siding - the two trains are not drawn up alongside each other. The signalman, already waiting at the platform end, receives the single line 'electric train token' from the fireman, and hands him in exchange the token for the section ahead to Bovey. As only one token can be issued for a section of single line, it serves as both authority and security to proceed - providing of course that the signals are at 'clear'. Making sure the driver sees that the token is on board, it is hung up in the cab.

Receiving the 'right away' from the guard - answered with a sharp blast on the whistle - the train sets off over the junction, past Mile Post 4 and then sways gently over the points which bring an end to the double track length. Having regained the single line, the driver opens up the regulator and the train is soon scurrying over what is the all-but-level, straight run over the open expanse of Bovey Heath. Immediately beyond the 3-arch masonry bridge which carries the minor road to Little Bovey, the exhaust beat from 1427's tall chimney perceptibly sharpens as the gradient steepens to 1:69 for the short climb to the shallow cutting at the White Hill 'summit', the highest point on the Heath. This was the nominal site of the Civil War's 'Battle of Bovey' of January 1646, in which the Parliamentary forces under the personal leadership of Oliver Cromwell trounced the Royalist troops commanded by Lord Wentworth. From here there is a straight descent at 1:72 to the vicinity of Mile Post 5, the open aspect being replaced by a fringing border of tall trees.

Levelling-off now, the train passes over the facing connection to Granite Siding, with its heavily overgrown loading platform, and shortly reaches Pottery Bridge. This massively-engineered, masonry-built skew bridge carries the Newton to Bovey main road over the Line. The fact that bridges over the railway were built to double track (broad gauge) width, together with the obliquity of the crossing, necessitated the construction of a twin-arched bridge, the Line using the southern-most span. Immediately beyond the bridge, Pottery Siding leads off into the substantial complex of buildings, kilns and clay and lignite pits that comprise Bovey Pottery. This location too, by the 5 ¼ Mile Post 5, sees the beginning of a short but sharp climb at 1:53 to a local 'summit' at Fat Parks: a low ridge of clay and sand utilised by the minor road (Ashburton Road) by which Bovey Tracey is

Above: Bovey Heath. The 4.25pm auto train from Newton Abbot, hauled by No. 1466, shuffles up the 1:69 gradient at White Hill. If the location seems rather exaggeratedly named, it does in fact mark the highest point on the heath and a local summit on the Branch (the Line descending on the other side at 1:72 to the vicinity of Granite Siding). The chimneys of Candy's Tile Works by Heathfield Station are much in evidence centre right. 26.2.59. *Peter W. Gray Below:* Brimley. Situated opposite the 'summit' gradient post in 'Cricket Field Cutting' on the

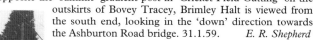

outskirts of Bovey Tracey, Brimley Halt is viewed from the south end, looking in the 'down' direction towards the Ashburton Road bridge. 31.1.59.   *E. R. Shepherd*

linked to the small settlements of Brimley, Liverton and Coldeast. The ease with which these soft materials could be excavated, greatly facilitated the making of a long cutting here, the deepest part of which is marked by a wide, single span, granite-built bridge just a few yards beyond the actual summit. This latter site is marked by Brimley Halt, at which the train now pauses, and a number of people alight. Whereas Teigngrace had formerly been a staffed station downgraded to halt status, Brimley is the first of two purpose-built halts on the Branch, having opened in May 1928. Its short platform and open-fronted wooden waiting shelter represent the height of economy, but the halt is conveniently sited for the housing developments at the west-end of Bovey Tracey, and is well patronised.

A brisk start is made away from Brimley, the gradient now falling at 1:66. After running for a quarter of a mile down the ruler-straight stretch beyond the cutting at Fat Parks allotments, the train comes alongside a cluster of buildings at another delightfully-named location: Pludda (Bovey goes in for some pretty esoteric place names!). Here the gradient ceases, and the track crosses the Manaton Road on the level to enter Bovey Station, just beyond Mile Post 6, the halfway stage on the journey. This must be the chief candidate for the title of most attractive station on the Branch: with its neat, well-proportioned granite station building, sturdy goods shed, tidy platforms and fencing, colourful hanging basket displays and floral border all to delight the eye. For the first six decades of the Line's life, Bovey had been the only crossing place for passenger trains, the second platform at Heathfield not being installed until 1927. That same year, the signalling arrangements at Bovey were altered to allow Moreton-bound trains to run into either 'up' or 'down' platforms. As the former housed the main station building, it was the preferred line when no 'crossing' was to be undertaken. The 2.15pm, however, is booked to 'cross' with the Branch goods train on its return from Moretonhampstead; and as it runs into the station, the latter is standing in the 'up' platform. Today, the dozen or so freight wagons are in the charge of locomotive number 5543: one of Newton Abbot's 'small Prairies' (that is to say, a tank engine of the '45xx' Class with a 2-6-2 wheel arrangement). Running bunker-first, the engine will set about its shunting duties as soon as the passenger train has gone. A one minute stop is allowed the 2.15pm at Bovey; a handful of people leaving the train and a couple getting on. This is not the busiest train of the day!

The hiss of condensing steam escaping from the safety-valve bonnet indicates that 1427 is in good heart for the stiff climb ahead. Having relinquished the electric train token carried from Heathfield, and taken on board that for the section to Moretonhampstead, a storming departure is made in order to get a good run at the imminent and taxing rising gradients. Soon after leaving the station environs, the Line enters upon its most picturesque stretch. Already climbing at 1:61, the train passes over a granite-built bridge; its graceful elliptical skewed arch spanning the swiftly flowing, youthful River Bovey. The embanked Line now curves north-west to enter the Parke Estate. If Bovey is the 'Gateway to Dartmoor', then this is the actual gate. The floodplain of the river narrows appreciably as the hillsides close in beyond the 6 ¼ Mile Post 6 by Southbrook Bridge. A series of cuttings and embankments maintain a straight orientation for the next 800 yards or so; the Line being accompanied for almost all of this distance, on both sides, by thick deciduous woodland, much of it oak. On the right hand side of travel the ground rises steeply into the dense Parke Wood, with its holly and brushwood undergrowth; whilst on the left, occasional glimpses of the River Bovey can be had through the trees. The staccato rhythm of the exhaust from the engine's chimney and the smoke drifting through the foliage add to the appealing ambience of this section. Beyond Mile Post 7 the track takes on a more sinuous course, which imposes a 35mph restriction on all trains between here and Bishopstone Cutting, Lustleigh; a distance of around two and a quarter miles. The gradient on this wooded section is not continually rising as the quarter-mile long graded stretches - all in excess of 1:67 - alternate with level sections of similar length.

A few yards beyond the 7 ¼ Mile Post 7 the train passes over Woolford (or Wilford) Bridge, its plate girder superstructure carried on granite abutments. The minor road beneath links the Moreton and Manaton roads, set back from, and higher than, the railway. A little to the north of the bridge is Plumley, once the residence of William Harris, an active supporter of the

Bovey. 1466 enters the 'down' platform with the 'strengthened' first service of the day from Newton Abbot. A handful of passengers and station master, wait on the other side for the imminent arrival of the first 'up' train, the 7.50am from Moretonhampstead. 28.2.59. *Peter W. Gray*

Bovey. Looking north from the 'up' platform; summer 1949. Straight ahead lies the steeply rising, wooded moorland flank bordering Shaptor Rock, some 700 feet above the elevation of the railway, which now curves to the northwest to utilise the narrowing valley of the River Bovey as far as Hawkmoor (later Pullabrook) Halt. *S. J. Dickson*

Moretonhampstead & South Devon Railway and its predecessor the Newton & Moretonhampstead Railway. Between here and Lustleigh Mill Viaduct, just over a mile distant, the Line passes through a belt of extremely hard metamorphic rock prior to encountering the granite of Dartmoor proper. Its toughness made it one of the most difficult for the engineers to deal with during the Line's construction. Locals refer to this rock as 'shillet', and the engineers found that steel drills had to be used to bore blast holes for the explosives necessary to shatter it: a lengthy and noisy operation in this normally tranquil place. One particular outcrop, at Yeo Farm, additionally contained large masses of hard, fine-grained volcanic 'trap rock'. This, plus the configuration of the land, made any detour around the farm impractical, and both the farm house and its outbuildings had to be demolished and a cutting blasted through. It is near the Moreton end of this feature-known as Yeo Cutting - that the train pulls up at the diminutive Hawkmoor Halt, 7 ¾ miles from

Newton Abbot. That such a scenically delightful and deeply rural location should have a railway halt is remarkable but, as is the case on most services, no passengers leave or join the train. The re-start from the short timber-faced platform is a taxing affair, for the halt is at the beginning of a quarter-mile climb at 1:53.

Letford Bridge, by Mile Post 8, marks the place where the Moreton Branch parts company with the Bovey Valley to follow the course of the tiny Wray Brook for the remainder of the journey. The extreme toughness of the shillet rock at Knowle Hill has greatly constricted the width of the valley between here and Lustleigh. Beyond the curved 3-arch Knowle Viaduct, 40 feet above the bed of the stream, the Line passes through the lengthy Rudge Cutting, the name coming from a nearby residence. At the time the Branch opened, Rudge was the home of James Wills who, until his resignation at the beginning of 1859, had been on the Committee of the N&MR (and one of the many interested parties to have the same surname). The gradient now steepens to 1:50 on the approach to Lustleigh Mill Viaduct. During their preliminary work, the M&SDR engineers had encountered some particularly large granite boulders near the route of the Line, and intended to fragment them by blasting to provide masonry for the viaduct and wing-walls. However, they were such a feature of the locality that residents petitioned the Company to leave them. Sentiment evidently triumphed over economics as their request was granted! The terrain hereabouts presented the railway-builders with their greatest challenge of all, but in the end the variety of engineering works and stone-built structures actually serve to enhance the natural scenic splendour of this charming corner of Devon.

Hawkmoor/Pullabrook. In bright summer sunshine, a 2-coach train pauses at the Halt en route for Moretonhampstead. The fireman leans out of 1427's cab to oversee the pulling forward of the train to bring the rear coach - an auto trailer with guard on board - alongside the short platform. 1957. *G. Howells*

Knowle. Viewed from the slopes below Gradner Rocks, No. 1466 and trailer W241W are dwarfed by the wide-open spaces of the landscape above Pullabrook Halt, whose white-painted waiting shelter is visible far right. The train - the 12.50pm from Newton Abbot - is climbing the 1:53 grade leading away from the Halt, and is approaching the two-arch, granite-built Letford Bridge. The sprinkling of large houses make up the settlement of Lower Knowle. 21.2.59. *Peter W. Gray*

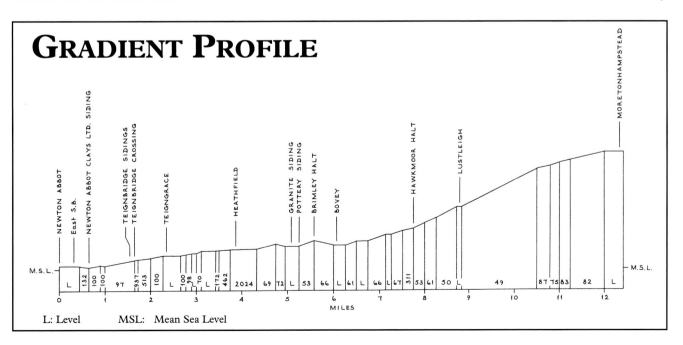

GRADIENT PROFILE

L: Level   MSL: Mean Sea Level

Above: Lustleigh. Accompanied by much escaping steam, 'large Prairie' No. 5183 waits with the 9.20am train from Newton Abbot. A 'station stores' truck is attached to the rear carriage. The notice board advertising the Cheap Day Return fare to Newton Abbot of 1/10 (about 9 pence) is soon to be a meaningless enticement, for in another couple of days the station will be closing its doors to passengers for the very last time. 26.2.59.

Peter W. Gray

Below: Lustleigh. Looking north towards Bishopstone Bridge and beyond to Caseley (or Casely) Wood and, far left, to Elsford Rock, around 945 feet above sea level. The picture is taken from the lineside garden which, in the summer months, formed an attractive complement to the well-kept station. February 1959.

Peter F. Bowles

The sequence of embankment-cutting-embankment in quick succession brings the train past the eastern edge of the picture-postcard village of Lustleigh and into the station beyond. A solitary loaded coal wagon is noticed near the entrance to the single siding that comprises the 'yard' here. It had been detached from the goods train recently passed at Bovey, the absence of a run-round loop making it possible for 'up' freight trains only to shunt traffic. Behind the platform fence another vehicle is seen: an ex-GWR Camping Coach, one of the many dotted around popular holiday locations in the West Country. The single platform, with its granite building and adjacent small wooden goods shed, occupies the only level section on the otherwise continuous climb to Moretonhampstead. Acting as a 'rail-head' for the village and surrounding hamlets and farms, the station is well-used; and several people alight. At Lustleigh the train is well and truly on the Moor, and yet the most challenging section of the Line still lies ahead. Immediately ahead in fact, for beyond Bishopstone Bridge which spans the track near the north end of the platform, there is a climb of over a mile and a half at 1:49 - the steepest on the Branch - with less severe, though still rising, grades beyond. Not surprisingly, therefore, a vigorous start is made away from the station, through the broad rocky cutting beyond the road bridge, past Mile Post 9 and out on to the Kelly Embankment. This last takes its name from nearby residences on the Bovey to Moreton main road ('main road' is something of a misnomer, for although classed as an 'A' road, its narrow and tortuous meanderings put it on a par with a country lane!).

The road keeps relatively close company with the railway for the remainder of the journey, traversing a landscape typified by extensive meadows and thickly wooded slopes sweeping up to open moorland. High above the train a solitary buzzard soars silently and gracefully on rising currents of air: gone are those raucously gregarious and restless seagulls so much in evidence at the coastal end of the Line. The scenery may well be captivating the passengers - though to the 'locals' it is commonplace - but on the footplate the crew have their concentration focused elsewhere. Both loco and locomen have their work cut out on this stretch. The normal quietue of the wide valley of the Wray Brook is broken by the sharp bark of the engine as it pounds up the bank towards East Wray and Mile Post 10. The steepness of the gradient requires the engine to work very hard, smoke billowing into the air as the climb progresses.

At Sanduck Wood the gradient eases to 1:87, but there is no room to relax the effort as there is still a further mile and a half of the ascent left before the final short level run to the terminus. Climbing past Mile Post 11, the speed has dropped to around 15mph, but picks up a little as the train continues to Wray Barton, a substantial farm complex, parts of which date back to Tudor times. Opposite the farm a bridge carries a minor road over the railway. The design of this structure is unusual, for although it is built of the customary Dartmoor granite with a single span sufficient for double track, it carries a double roadway. The wider carriage way is taken by the public road leading to the neighbouring Bovey Valley near Manaton; while

Lustleigh. "Large Prairie' No. 4117 storms away from Lustleigh with the 2.15pm train from Newton Abbot on the last day of passenger services - hence the augmented stock. Having just passed through the short but deep Bishopstone Cutting, containing both blocky and decomposed granite, the train is seen on the long Kelly Embankment. For 1.75 miles between Bishopstone Cutting and Sanduck Wood the train will traverse the most steeply graded section of the Branch, ie. rising to the north at 1:49. 28.2.59. *Peter W. Gray*

Left: Caseley. A timber-built permanent way hut, with brick chimney stack, stands at the southern entrance to Caseley Cutting. Excavated through granite, on a curve of 350 yards radius, the cutting has a maximum depth of 70 feet and stands on the 1:49 northward rising gradient. The half-mile between Bishopstone and Caseley cuttings is the only stretch on the Branch where the accompanying telegraph poles are located on the 'up' side of the track. Summer 1955.
  I.D. Beale

Below: Wray Barton. No. 1466 and trailer W241W form the 2.15pm auto train from Newton Abbot. It has just passed over a mile-long length of experimental track - consisting of steel bull-head rail secured to concrete sleepers by conventional cast iron chairs and wooden keys, a combination not widely used at the time and being given a 'road test' on the Branch. The open nature of the valley of the Wray Brook is clearly revealed in this picture as are the serpentine meanderings of the A382 centre left. 26.2.59. *Peter W. Gray*

to the south side of a thick masonry dividing wall, a narrower 'occupation' track allows for the unimpeded movement of animals between the fields on either side of the Line.

With Hingston Rocks on the skyline straight ahead, the wind first snatches, then deflects and dissipates, the expanding column of smoke as the train hammers up the 1:82 bank towards the girder bridge over the A382 by Steward Farm. A hundred yards or so beyond the highly-skewed bridge, the train passes Moretonhampstead's distant signal. Standing like a sentinel on the embankment, its notched yellow arm fixed resolutely in the horizontal 'caution' position, its presence announces that the journey will soon be over. Passing over the gated but unmanned 'occupation' crossing leading to Budleigh Farm at Boathill, a few yards short of Mile Post 12, the train enters the last, deep granite cutting on the Line. Many passengers begin to gather up coats, bags and the like as the end of the journey is imminent. Soon after passing the mile post the track runs in a straight line, while on leaving the cutting it levels off as well; crossing the road from Bovey on a skew plate girder bridge before coming alongside the gas works and entering the Moretonhampstead Station site. The train gently decelerates as it coasts past the engine shed, the fireman handing the single line token down to the waiting signalman. Finally, the driver brings the train to a stand beneath the wooden train shed which covers both platform and tracks at the moorland terminus: the engine stopping just beyond the roof so as not to fill the space below with smoke. The train is now some 500 feet above the elevation at which it had begun its journey 36 minutes earlier, and in a very different environment.

Although the station's mileage from Newton Abbot is recorded as 12 miles and 28 chains - a measurement centred on the 300' long platform - the tracks continue for a short distance beyond to end at buffer stops six chains (132 yards) from the 'official' terminus. As the passengers file out through the open-arched exit at the end of the train shed, a glance beyond the quietly simmering locomotive leads the eye along the rails that point so expectantly onwards. However, ending emphatically in a low grassy bank, they serve only as a reminder of an extension to Chagford so ardently sought in the days when railway schemes were first mooted. It is to this subject that we now turn.

Top: Wray Barton. On Easter Saturday 1960 'small Prairie' No. 4555, a single coal wagon and an ex-GWR 'Toad' brake van are all that make up the 1.51pm Goods from Moretonhampstead - a very precise departure time given that no other trains used the Branch! By this date, the Goods only ran on Mondays, Wednesdays and Fridays, but as the previous day had been Good Friday, when local freight activity had been suspended, the train ran on the Saturday instead. It is seen here ambling past the 11.25 mile post and about to pass beneath the road bridge opposite Wray Barton. 16.4.60.
The late David Fereday Glenn (Miles Barber Glenn collection)

Above: Boathill. No. 1466 with the 'last day' 12.50pm from Newton Abbot is backed by the wooded slopes which have accompanied the Line for the last three miles or so. The train is nearing the end of the long climb from Bovey, for it will shortly pass over Budleigh Farm 'occupation' level crossing, beyond which the Line continues on the level for just under half a mile to its terminus. Notice the alternating wooden and concrete boundary fence posts, an expedient used quite often along the Branch. 28.2.59. *Peter F. Bowles*

Left: Moretonhampstead. With the end of the Line in sight, the 'Prairie's' fireman hands signalman Wilf Wright the 'electric train token' authorising occupancy of the single line from Bovey. Circa 1958. *Courtesy Valerie Huish*

Above: Moretonhampstead. No. 1466 rolls into the terminus with a single auto coach in tow. The notice boards mounted on the train shed's timber screen advertise sundry cheap day return fares from the station. The white smoke in the distance pinpoints the site of the town's gas works; the manager's house standing out clearly behind the coach. Summer 1957. *G. Howells   Below:* Having arrived with the 2.15pm service from Newton Abbot, No. 1466 faces the buffers at the end of the journey. It is the end of the Line in more ways than one, for the notice board headed 'R.I.P.' advertises a last day, last train 'Special'. The wooden boxes on the platform are stencilled 'THE HOTELS EXECUTIVE, BRITISH TRANSPORT STOCK CELLARS, PADDINGTON'. They were a common sight at Moretonhampstead, being conveyed by road between the station and the Railway's 'Manor House Hotel' out on the moor above North Bovey. 26.2.59. *Peter W. Gray*

Chapter Two

A LINE A LONG TIME IN THE MAKING

PHASE 1: PREPARING THE GROUND

The year 1846 was one of expectation and excitement in the communities around the small Devonshire market town of Newton Abbot: the railway was coming to town! The South Devon Railway Company's line from Exeter was advancing ever westward. Built to the 7' 0¼" or 'broad', gauge favoured by the renowned engineer Isambard Kingdom Brunel, it was open as far as Teignmouth in May and by the end of the year would reach Newton itself. In the heady days of railway speculation nationally at this time, together with the present progress and planned extension of the SDR locally, the desirability of rail link - an artery of communication no less - was widely considered not just an attractive proposition, but de rigueur.

It was against the background of the imminent arrival of trains from Exeter, the advanced state of the 'main line' continuation to Plymouth and preliminary work on the short 'branch' to Torre, that a serious proposal was made for a link between Newton Abbot and Okehampton, via Moretonhampstead. While not traversing a district of high population - far from it in fact - it would pass through areas of significant mineral wealth as well as sink a deep tap root into the heart of the county: with, perhaps, all sorts of possibilities for future expansion.

In the spring of the following year, 1847, the route of the proposed line was surveyed, and preliminary plans and sections were drawn up. From a junction with the South Devon main line a quarter of a mile north of Newton station, it was projected that the line run parallel with the Stover Canal for some two miles from East Golds, near the Kingsteignton road, to its terminal basin at Ventiford. The railway would then continue on the same orientation for a further 2 ¼ miles, this time following the granite setts of George Templer's remarkable Hay Tor Tramway of 1820, to the vicinity of the newly relocated and enlarged Bovey Pottery. The tramway veered off at this point to climb to the granite quarries around Hay Tor, so the line would break fresh ground; running north to Pludda on the Manaton road out of Bovey Tracey. From here it would pick up and follow the valley of the River Bovey - and subsequently its diminutive tributary the Wray Brook - to climb through the picturesque village of Lustleigh to Moretonhampstead. Once on Dartmoor proper, the stream follows the northwest-southeast trend of an ancient geological fault-line: the Sticklepath Fault. Countless millennia of weathering and erosion have etched this out into a distinct 'corridor', albeit irregular in grade, through the north-east corner of the Moor virtually all the way from Bovey to Okehampton. Utilising this natural routeway, the line was planned to continue to the vicinity of Chagford and thence Throwleigh, South Zeal and Okehampton; a total distance from Newton Abbot of approximately 25 miles.

In one of the fascinating, eclectic essays which make up the book 'Small Talk at Wreyland', local gentleman Cecil Torr quotes thus from family correspondence, dated 25th April 1847:

'The surveyors have been from Newton to Okehampton, marking out a new line. They seem to be guided by the stream, and (if it takes place) they will go right up under here. ....I cannot fancy it will take place, for people are a little cooled down, and not so mad for speculation. Had it been projected some little time ago, no doubt it would have taken.'

The sentiment expressed in the letter proved to be correct. A growing sense of commercial realism combined with, and perhaps because of, the severe financial recession of 1849 caused this ambitious scheme to falter even before it could be

Newton Abbot's Globe Hotel, at the junction of Bank Street and Courtenay Street, was the birthplace of the Moretonhampstead & South Devon Railway, being the venue for the majority of meetings connected with the conception and planning of the Branch. August 1945. *Rokeby Collection, courtesy RCHME*

codified into a parliamentary bill. Although this particular scheme soon passed from the general public mind, hopes for a railway to Moretonhampstead and beyond never disappeared completely, as later events were to prove.

PHASE 2: THE NEWTON & MORETONHAMPSTEAD RAILWAY

In some minds at least the idea of a 'moorland railway' remained an attractive and viable proposition. So it was that a group of farmers, entrepreneurs and gentlemen with interests in the locality were galvanised into action by the Rector of Stokeinteignhead, the Reverend John Nutcombe Gould. Just what his interest in the project was is not clear, but he proved to be a most enthusiastic and determined protagonist. In August 1858 advertisements were circulated in connection with a public meeting to be held at the Globe Hotel, Newton Abbot, on Wednesday 18th.

The meeting was presided over by Samuel Trehawke Kekewich, newly elected as one of the MPs for South Devon. Although he lived at Peamore near Exeter, he held the title of Lord of the Manor of Stokeinteignhead, and as such undoubtedly had some sort of contact with the village's Rector. The Rev. Gould moved the first resolution. Not being one to hide his light under a bushel - indeed, his 'enthusiasm' was renowned - the reverend gentleman launched into a glowing promotional exposition, his claims liberally laced with hyperbole. A flavour of his style may be gained from this reported extract published in the 'Exeter Flying Post' of 26th August:

"....(He) did not believe there was another line in England that could be made so cheaply. In the first place the engineering difficulties were comparatively trifling - a first-rate engineer, an ambitious man, would conquer a thousand more difficulties than he would find with this line. Anybody could work it; he could do it himself so far as the head work was concerned. They would have to build no large bridges to throw away their money;

and they would pass through land which had hitherto been of little or no value, but which would be greatly improved the moment the railway passed through it. ....It was said the line would not pay. (He) did not hesitate to assert that the first week the railway was opened the traffic that would go upon it would pay every expense, and give every shareholder a fair and profitable return."

Quite a sales talk! Even allowing for the effulgent optimism, not to say 'clerical errors', the address was well received and the resolution proposing a 'Line of Railway from Newton Abbot to Moretonhampstead through the Bovey Valley' was approved and seconded. After further discussion, an Acting Committee was appointed under the chairmanship of the redoubtable rector, with power to add to their number. Moreton and district was represented by solicitor George Bragg of Forder Street; Rev. William Charles Clack, Rector of St. Andrew's parish church; John Courtier, gentleman (Wray); Elias Cuming, farmer, of Linscott; and Alfred Puddicombe, surgeon, of Cross Street. Messrs. George and Thomas Wills were from the Lustleigh area: Kelly and East Wray respectively. Other 'locals' were John Rowell, a farmer from Teigngrace, and Thomas Hatch from Newton Abbot. However, it was not only people from places on the proposed route who showed an interest. The Committee possessed one member each from nearby Chudleigh and Kingskerswell; while the meeting had been attended by people from as far afield as Ashburton, Exeter and Okehampton. Understandably, however, the proposed railway was essentially a 'local' concern. One person with extensive local concerns and considerable influence was Lord Courtenay. His support was recognised as being invaluable to the success of the scheme. Indeed, a few days previously Mr. Kekewich had discussed the project with 'his lordship', who intimated that he would give it every support if it was deemed to be a practical proposition. Another influential person present was John Divett, senior partner of Bovey Pottery. He proved to be an indefatigable advocate.

The Committee met for the first time the following Wednesday (25th); again at the 'Globe'. Josiah Harris of Bovey Tracey was unanimously voted in as a new member and consented to act as honorary secretary. It was agreed that local landowners and other interested parties be canvassed for support, and to help meet preliminary expenses (estimated at £100). Rev. Gould opened a subscription list with a donation of £5. The task of eliciting subscriptions was devolved upon a sub-committee of eight men. Thomas Whitaker of Exeter gave details of the most viable route for the railway, which was in fact to be essentially that proposed for the southern half of the abortive 1847 scheme.

The next committee meeting took place at the same venue at 2pm on Wednesday 8th September. The endeavours of the subscription sub-committee had been liberally rewarded, although perhaps predictably its members "were requested to continue their exertions". Thomas Whitaker was instructed to survey the route of the line and to prepare all the necessary plans and sections, along with an estimate of the cost of construction (for which he received a fee of £50).

Three weeks elapsed before the next meeting to allow for the survey to be undertaken; but at least events had now been set in motion. Following the presentation of the completed survey (on 29th), Thomas Wills and John Courtier were delegated the task of approaching the landowners or their agents along the route to ascertain their views on the proposed line. At the next meeting, on Wednesday 13th October, it was John Courtier who chaired the proceedings - the first time the Rector of Stokeinteignhead was absent! It was reported that most of the landowners looked favourably on the scheme, and subscriptions were continuing to come in. This was all very encouraging, and the meeting

"Resolved that Lord Courtenay and Mr Kekewich be added to the committee." This would certainly impart 'muscle' to their endeavours. Lord Courtenay - William Reginald Courtenay - was a member of an old county family - headed by the Earl of Devon - going back to the 14th century. In addition to their Powderham Castle estate on the banks of the Exe estuary, the family had numerous and diverse interests in the Newton - Moreton 'corridor'. They owned, for example, extensive tracts of land; had clay workings at Decoy, together with the associated wharf on the Teign at Newton Abbot; and held the title of Lord of the Manor of Moretonhampstead. William Reginald had been one of the MPs for South Devon between 1841 and 1849, and consequently had many useful contacts in addition to family connections. On the death of his father - also called William - in 1859 he succeeded to the title, becoming the 11th Earl of Devon. (The Vicar of Bovey since 1849, incidentally, happened to be a younger brother of the Earl - namely, Charles Leslie Courtenay - and so it was likely that any project would receive good support there.)

The Newton & Moretonhampstead project seemed to be gaining a sound momentum, the protagonists quietly beavering away at their allotted tasks. With Lord Courtenay as an ally they should have no worries about acquiring strips of land from his estates on the moorland section of the route, but they were less certain of the response from another landowner in the Teigngrace area, one Edward Adolphus Seymour, 11th Duke of Somerset. At the meeting on the 3rd November 1858 it was decided that the time had come to make an approach to the Duke, through whose Stover Estate the railway would pass. To complicate matters, the Duke owned the Stover Canal and Hay Tor Tramway, the courses of which the N&MR intended to follow from Newton Abbot to Bovey Pottery, and whose traffic it would subvert. At a meeting held on Wednesday 29th December, the Committee decided to compensate the Duke of Somerset "for the value of his Canal - either by absolute purchase or by a way of annual Rent Charge in the event of his grace assenting to the formation of the intended Railway through his Lands." To help the Committee in their approach to the Duke, both Lord Courtenay and Mr. Kekewich MP sent supporting letters. (This meeting, incidentally, marked the return to the chair of the Rector of Stokeinteignhead after a gap of three months!)

Early in the new year, Lord Courtenay wrote to the Committee explaining that he had "had a very satisfactory interview with the Duke of Somerset." Three days later, on the 14th January 1859, he wrote again; this time unexpectedly suggesting an alteration in the intended route near Bovey Pottery. At the meeting held on Friday 21st January - at the traditional venue of the 'Globe' - it was resolved that George Bragg write to a fellow 'son of Moreton', the famous engineer George Parker Bidder, "to know if he be disposed to render any assistance." Apart from the resignation of James Wills - who had joined the Committee back in September - everything seemed set fair, and the meeting was adjourned until Wednesday 23rd February. That meeting, however, never took place.

Having come so far there was a sudden and unforeseen change in fortunes. Support for the Newton & Moretonhampstead scheme evaporated even more quickly than it had arisen only a matter of months before. Funds were certainly not plentiful and support for the railway was not universal, but the collapse in interest was completely unexpected. It may have been down, but it was certainly not out - not if the ever-enthusiastic Rev. Gould had anything to do with it! The failure of his pet scheme must have come as something of a blow to the clergyman, and for a time we hear nothing of him. Then suddenly he pops up again in the autumn of the following year (1860), convening a meeting of the N&MR

Committee on Wednesday 31st October. After such a long period of quiescence, this was not some odd whim but a response to another proposed railway venture in the area: the Devon Central.

PHASE 3: THE THREAT OF THE 'DEVON CENTRAL'

In July 1860 the London & South Western Railway arrived in Exeter from the east. Even before the first train pulled into the city's Queen Street terminus, the Company was already thinking of extending their influence into the untapped territory of Central Devon. Indeed, they had already secured parliamentary sanction to build a short, steeply inclined line down to the South Devon/Bristol & Exeter station on the floodplain of the River Exe. This acted as the inspiration for a bold assault on broad gauge territory in the form of a 'Devon Central Railways' scheme. A prime-mover and determined advocate of this project was Sir Lawrence Palk of Haldon House, Dunchideock. The intention was to build a standard gauge line (that is 4' 8½") from Queen Street station to Lydford, where it would join with a separate undertaking - the proposed 'Mid Devon & Cornwall Railway' - to provide links with Launceston and Tavistock. From Exeter the line was to run west-southwest to Dunsford Bridge; this necessitating a 780 yard-long tunnel at Perridge Woods. It would then follow the deep, winding, wooded middle section of the Teign Valley to Fingle Bridge, below Drewsteignton and then on to Sandypark, near Chagford. From there it would essentially follow the route past Throwleigh and South Zeal to Okehampton mapped out for the Newton & Okehampton scheme of 1847. Finally, the line would turn south-west to Sourton and Lydford.

Of particular importance to the area under discussion in this book was the inclusion in the Devon Central plan of a standard gauge branch line from Leigh (or Lea) Cross near Dunsford down the Teign Valley by way of Doddiscombsleigh, Christow and Chudleigh to Newton Abbot. Initially, all the Devon Central lines were to be single track, although the Exeter-Dunsford section would be doubled - as would the rest of the 'main line' - if traffic warranted it. The engineer appointed for this undertaking, John Furness Tone, set about drawing up the requisite plans and sections, while Sir Lawrence Palk as chairman of the Provisional Committee began his task of finding allies for the venture. One obvious contact was William Reginald Courtenay, the new Earl of Devon, a man with diverse interests in the area to be served by the projected 'branch'. To the chagrin of his erstwhile broad gauge associates, he agreed to support Palk in the promotion of the Devon Central, becoming a member of the provional Committee.

Events moved quickly during the autumn of 1860. Even before the series of public meetings began, word had spread like wildfire throughout the locality. One criticism was of the inconveniently long distance of the projected line from Moretonhampstead: some three miles from Fingle Bridge or four miles from Sandypark. This led the Company to instruct the engineer to survey a possible route for an additional branch line from Chagford to Moreton, and then on down the valley of the Wray Brook to Lustleigh and Bovey. Not surprisingly, for obvious geographical reasons, this took the same route as those mapped out in the aforementioned schemes of 1847 and 1858.

It was all this high-profile rival activity that had prompted John Gould to call the Newton & Moretonhampstead Railway Committee together on 31st October. The Devon Central

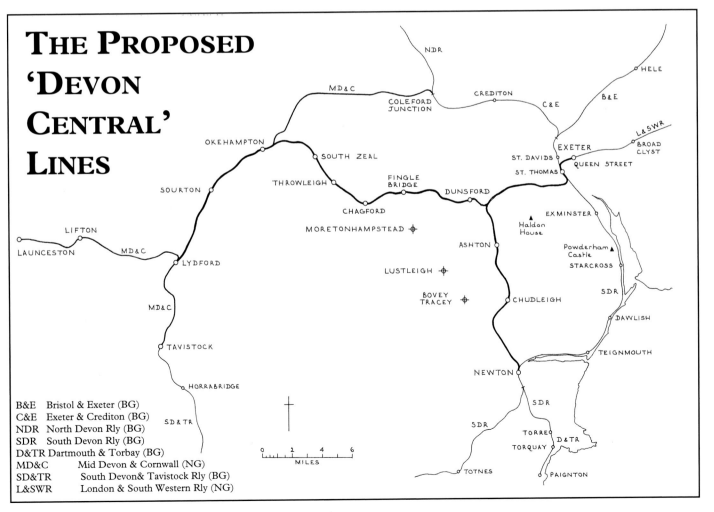

THE PROPOSED 'DEVON CENTRAL' LINES

B&E   Bristol & Exeter (BG)
C&E   Exeter & Crediton (BG)
NDR   North Devon Rly (BG)
SDR   South Devon Rly (BG)
D&TR Dartmouth & Torbay (BG)
MD&C   Mid Devon & Cornwall (NG)
SD&TR   South Devon& Tavistock Rly (BG)
L&SWR   London & South Western Rly (NG)

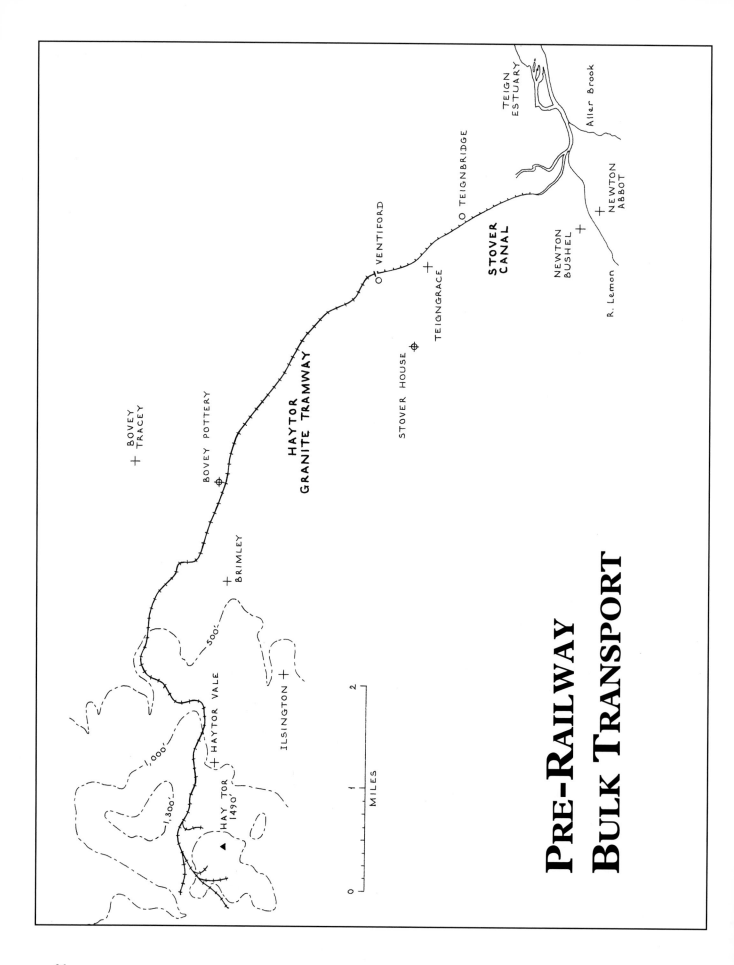

PRE-RAILWAY
BULK TRANSPORT

scheme was viewed with a mixture of apprehension and curiosity, but for the moment it was decided not to oppose it. With the princely sum of £1.13s.0d remaining in the kitty there was not much the members could realistically do by way of rival promotion! Part of their unease was removed when the Devon Central decided to withdraw the branch line option from Chagford to Bovey, due to the paucity of population and perceived lack of commercial possibilities. If the N&MR Committee felt happier, the people of Bovey in particular were not. They wanted a railway. Indeed, they promptly made representations to the Devon Central asking them to consider the possibility of linking the town to the proposed Teign Valley line by means of a short branch instead.

The Devon Central scheme as a whole had elicited a sufficiently positive response to encourage an approach to parliament in the next Session, and a bill was duly drafted. However, the South Devon Railway, along with their close ally the Bristol & Exeter Railway, were alarmed at the prospect of a rival enterprise encroaching on 'their' territory, and registered objections to the proposals. A few landowners also objected. As a consequence of this, when the bill came up for its examination of compliance with Standing Orders (on Thursday 24th January, 1861), the sheer backlog of other hearings awaiting attention, together with the depositions against it, caused its consideration to be deferred until 1st February. Lawrence Palk and his supporters were sufficiently confident of the scheme's basic soundness that they were undeterred by this short delay, and set about advertising a series of public meetings in South Devon even before the revised date.

The first of these promotions was on the afternoon of Tuesday 29th January, at the White Hart Hotel, Moretonhampstead. It was very well attended and enthusiastic in support of the Devon Central. The next afternoon a similar meeting was held at the Globe Hotel, Newton Abbot, and again there was a very large attendance. The chairman on this occasion was the Earl of Devon. The meeting was supportive of the project, although made strong representations of a link to Bovey (and thence to Lustleigh and Moreton if possible). In answer to these requests, it was stated that a survey had been made for a branch line to Bovey (and also to Ashburton). The assistant engineer, Mr. Brown, stated that because Bovey was at a higher level than the valley of the Teign "it would be almost impossible to take a line round to Bovey for this reason" and that "the gradients would be of such a bad nature that a locomotive....could not be worked upon it." The Bovey lobby, however, were not satisfied with this curious explanation, knowing the lie of the land first-hand. After persistent questioning, Mr. Brown admitted that levels had not actually been taken and that his assessment of the severity of the gradients on the western side of the Teign Valley and beyond were purely subjective. The meeting made further strong pleas for a line to Bovey, but also voted in support of the Devon Central scheme as a whole. Another meeting took place at the 'White Hart' in Okehampton the next Saturday (2nd February), while others followed in Exeter and Torquay.

In spite of all this activity, the Devon Central's cause was beginning to run out of steam in Parliament. Continued opposition to the bill was proving a major problem, deterring people from putting up money in support. In a report issued by the South Devon Railway at the end of February, a gloating reference was made to the fact that not one share had been

purchased in the Devon Central to date. It seemed an unavoidable conclusion that the scheme was heading for the buffer-stops. The bill, indeed, was eventually rejected in late May.

This particular project might have failed, but the two chief protagonists - Sir Lawrence Palk and the Earl of Devon - were determined to have a railway. While the former busied himself with new schemes in the Teign Valley, the latter decided to wholeheartedly throw in his lot with the Newton & Moretonhampstead brigade. Although the South Devon Railway had disagreed with the Earl that the Devon Central's recent endeavours had been friendly and afforded mutual advantage, the Courtenay family's long connections with the SDR were valued. The Earl's father had been involved with the SDR from the outset. He had chaired a promotional gathering at Newton Abbot back in October 1843 in support of a railway from Exeter to Plymouth being routed through the town (instead of the rival scheme, which advocated a more direct inland route via Chudleigh and Ashburton). He had also been one of the original SDR directors. Like the title, an enthusiasm for railways seemed to be hereditary!

PHASE 4: THE MORETONHAMPSTEAD & SOUTH DEVON RAILWAY

The interest in, and activity associated with, the Devon Central served to keep the spirit of the Newton & Moretonhampstead project of 1858 alive. In particular, it had revealed a considerable level of support for a railway to serve the communities of the Bovey Basin and north-eastern Dartmoor. If the Devon Central had been on too grand and controversial a scale, perhaps a less ambitious scheme might succeed. The summer of 1861 passed without any signs of a new initiative, but much was going on behind the scenes. This resulted in a convening of the Newton & Moretonhampstead Committee on Wednesday 11th September (at the 'Globe', Newton Abbot). Although our old friend the resilient rector John Nutcombe Gould was present, the chair was taken by the Earl of Devon. This was significant, for it underscored the interest he was now taking personally in getting a line to Moreton built. Another important point was that a number of other influential local people had been invited to attend; men whose business interests and commercial connections carried some weight. These included Edward Snelling Bearne, land steward to the Duke of Somerset; John Divett of Bovey Pottery; Thomas Kitson, on behalf of William Hole of the Parke Estate, Bovey; Thomas Woollcombe, chairman of the SDR; John Hayman Whiteway, clay trader of Newton Abbot; and John Wills, farmer of Higher

Following acquisition of land by the Railway Company, a number of permanent boundary markers were set in place. One such, a granite stone bearing the inscription M & SDR, is seen here beneath the fence alongside the footpath connecting Lustleigh station with the village. 4.8.58.
E. R. Shepherd

Hisley near Lustleigh. Significantly, Mr. Woollcombe offered the Committee "every assistance in carrying out the proposed scheme." As had happened three years before, it was decided to set up another, but this time larger, sub-committee to enlist the support of landowners. Some of these were present at the 'Globe' and immediately indicated their willingness to either give or sell the required land: such as William Harris of Plumley and Thomas Wills of East Wray. The faithful secretary, Josiah Harris, reported that he, along with Peter John Margary of Dawlish (the engineer to the SDR) and a representative of contractors Messrs. Brassey & Ogilvie, had surveyed the proposed route on Tuesday 3rd instant, and was confident that it would be a beneficial undertaking.

Just two weeks after the N&MR Committee meeting referred to above, it was decided at another gathering at the 'Globe' that the time for talking and speculating was over. What was needed was action: a promotional campaign, to fan the embers of interest into a flame. Thus was conceived an intensive publicity drive in the form of public meetings to take place early the following month (October). The first of these was scheduled for midday on Monday 7th at the Three Crowns Inn, Chagford. The Earl of Devon took the chair and opened the proceedings by outlining the aims, perceived commercial advantages and future potential of the line. SDR engineer Peter Margary gave details of the route, stating that the estimated cost of construction would be around £10,000 a mile. Thomas Woollcombe then outlined the terms on which the South Devon Railway would assist. He candidly explained that his Company saw itself in the role of technical and legal consultants in the planning stage, and that on opening they would operate the service on behalf of the new Company in return for 50% of the gross receipts. He strongly hinted that the bulk of the revenue needed to construct the line would have to come from public subscription. Resolutions were passed in support of the scheme. Of especial note was the one which stated that 'the undertaking commenced in 1858 under the title of the Newton & Moreton Hampstead Railway up the Bovey Valley be henceforth designated the Moreton Hampstead and South Devon Railway and a Company be formed to carry the plans into effect." Thus was born the M&SDR.

This was just the beginning of a busy day for the platform party. From Chagford they travelled south-east to Moretonhampstead to hold a meeting at the White Hart Inn. There was a large attendance, including Messrs. Belfield & Froude, directors of the Torbay & Dartmouth Railway. The Earl was once again in the chair. In his introductory remarks, he outlined why he thought the M&SDR would be beneficial to the town - as he had done at the same venue back in January in support of Devon Central. He stressed that an important factor was the link - at the same gauge - with the South Devon coast, which would reduce the transport cost of goods especially coal. It should possible to bring coal from Kingswear at 19 shillings a ton, which would be a reduction of about 30% over current prices. He claimed that the scheme he was presenting now was more realistic and convenient than the Devon Central. Its Moreton Station would be only a quarter of a mile from the town centre instead of the three or four miles under the rival scheme. As at Chagford, the details of the route were outlined by Peter Margary, whose comments were enthusiastically received. The terms and conditions of the SDR's participation were then given by Thomas Woollcombe. The floor carried a unanimous resolution in support of the scheme.

The meeting over, the indefatigable party set out down the narrow, tortuous road to Bovey for their third gathering of the day; arranged for 7pm at the Union Hotel in Fore Street. True to form for the town, the meeting was packed. The local enthusiast for the scheme, John Divett, acted as chairman, speaking eloquently in favour of the railway. Several others

In response to local overtures, the GWR erected a granite slab to commemorate the first directors of the M & SDR, namely: the Earl of Devon, Thomas Wills, William R. Hole, John Divett, Elias Cuming and Thomas Woollcombe. Resembling a grave headstone, it was installed at the bottom of the footpath leading down from Station Road in 1925, and is now held in the National Railway Museum, York. Summer 1957.   *I. D. Beale*

spoke in support, one of whom, William Hole of Parke, said he was ready to take shares to the value of £500 - which brought forth cheers! (He was to become one of the original directors of the M&SDR.) The Earl of Devon in his speech made an interesting and prophetic statement about what we now call 'tourism', stating that the railway would encourage visitors to come and enjoy the "....romantic country in greater numbers, to inhale the fresh and pure air that is so conducive in giving persons vigorous health." Mr. Hole proposed the resolution that "....the meeting has heard with great satisfaction the announcement of the projected Moreton and South Devon Railway, as calculated materially to advance the manufacturing and general interest of this district, and pledge themselves to give the undertaking their united and cordial support." Needless to say this was enthusiastically seconded, and greeted with universal acclamation.

In between the Moreton and Bovey meetings, Thomas Woollcombe managed to rush down to Newton Abbot to address a meeting at the Globe Hotel scheduled for 4pm: no mean feat given the state of the roads in the area at this time. The meeting was well attended, although not to the degree that might have been hoped for due to the short notice given. Mr. Woollcombe was rather more frank about the SDR's involvement: perhaps because he was in 'home territory'. He explained that the South Devon was willing to build and operate the line, but that as his Company was not prepared to commit much in the way of finance, this would doubtless place severe demands on local subscribers (and, unfortunately, there was little interest from outside the immediate area to be served by the line). The SDR, however, would give the new venture advice, technical assistance and credit; and also pay a moderate sum towards preliminary expenses. The chairman at this gathering was William John Watts. Lewis Bearne was also in attendance. These two men were partners in the newly formed Newton based ball clay firm of Watts, Blake, Bearne & Company (WBB), with whom the Railway was later to have dealings. As at the other venues, the meeting voted in support of the scheme. Following the resounding success of Monday's launch, a prospectus was published in the Press two days later, inviting the purchase of shares. There was a capital requirement of £100,000, to be raised in 4,000 shares of £25 each (secured by a deposit of £1 per share). Maps could be examined at, and enquiries addressed to, the Company's Newton Abbot office, where Josiah Harris had been confirmed in the position of secretary.

PHASE 5: PLANNING THE LINE

As a consequence of the public meetings, a 'Moretonhampstead and South Devon Railway Provisional Committee' was set up. As chairman, the Earl of Devon headed the list of 17 members. Some of these had been stalwarts of the former Newton & Moretonhampstead scheme: Elias Cuming of Linscott, Moretonhampstead; John Drew of Peamore, near Exeter; William Harris of Plumley; Charles Langley of Chudleigh; John Rowell of Teigngrace; and Thomas Wills of East Wray. Among the new members with important business interests in the area were: Edward Bearne, William Hole, John Hayman Whiteway and John Wills. The Rev. Gould, once so prominent, now faded from the scene. He was still Rector of Stokeinteignhead, although even here he was to become non-resident, leaving parish duties to a curate-in-charge!

A series of meetings now took place, in which all the usual procedural details and administrative minutiae were dealt with. All of these were held in the 'Globe', an institution that had done well out of the proceedings to date. Its proprietor, John Beazley, incidentally, was the SDR's Newton Abbot agent for the delivery of parcels and small goods, and as such was definitely pro-railway! On Thursday 14th November 1861 provisional agreements hitherto tacitly accepted by the M&SDR and SDR were formalised in a 'Heads of Arrangements'. One of these specified: "The Moreton Company, at their own expense, to make and complete the intended Moreton and South Devon Railway from Moreton Hampstead to Newton (hereinafter called the "New Line"), according to their Act, as a Single Line, with Land and Overbridges for a Double Line, with Double Line where requisite, and all proper and sufficient works and conveniences, including a Junction at Newton with the South Devon Railway; and all to the reasonable satisfaction of the South Devon Company's Engineer."

The main issue left to settle was the question of land acquisition from the Duke of Somerset, along with the future of the Stover Canal and Hay Tor Tramway that the Duke had lumped in with the land deal. The Duke's father, also named Edward Adolphus, had acquired the

estate, canal and tramway from the hopelessly impecunious George Templer in 1829. At this date both modes of transport were doing well, but by the time the 11th Duke inherited the estate in 1855 the tramway was defunct. In the middle of December (1861) a meeting took place with Edward Bearne, the Duke's agent, to discuss the question of land purchase. By this time, the Duke had further moved the goal posts by adding in the sale of his quay at Teignmouth, and requiring the provision of a siding near Bovey Pottery to handle stone from the Hay Tor granite quarries. Speaking on behalf of the M&SDR, Thomas Woollcombe said that the Provisional Committee could not possibly entertain these new proposals, especially the quay sale and £500 per annum canal rental that was being asked. The agent reported back to his employer and another meeting was quickly arranged. The Duke agreed to exclude Teignmouth Quay from the deal, and was prepared to lower the canal rental to the sum of £378 per annum.

The two sides were still some distance apart and although the Duke was agreeable in principle to sell the required land - or rent part of it - he was determined to make some money on the canal as well, again either by sale or rent. After further haggling, a figure of £8,000 was agreed on; this covering land and canal combined. This was drawn up in an outline agreement, with discussion of the precise details covering provision of access, drainage and legal rights being held over until the following year, 1862. (Debate over these details unfortunately became a protracted affair, and the arrangements were not finalised until June.) Meanwhile, a meeting had been set up at Newton Station for Saturday 28th December for discussions between the Provisional Committee and other interested parties on the Duke's estates, notably his tenants and the clay factors Whiteway and WBB.

While negotiations over land purchase continued, the new Company was disappointed at the poor uptake of shares. Contrary to expectations, applications had got off to a slow start. One of the problems was that as a purely 'local' short branch line serving a relatively sparsely populated area, it appeared as something of an economic 'cul-de-sac' to outside

Brimley. With the north-eastern flank of Dartmoor looming ahead, 0-4-2T No. 1439 rounds the curve north of the Halt with the 10.05am through train from Paignton to Moretonhampstead. The auto coaches (trailers 224 and 234) carry the smart carmine and cream livery of the 'early British Railways' period. The engine was withdrawn, from Newton Abbot, in August 1957 and scrapped at Swindon Works the following month. 30.8.54. *R. C. Riley*

investors, who thus failed to respond financially. Also, although a number of the landed and commercial interests in the locality undoubtedly saw the railway as a benefit, they did not have large reserves of capital to invest. Many were members of the county 'squire class' and were not particularly affluent; while Bovey Pottery was the only industry of any size and was currently experiencing hard times.

Undaunted by this disappointment, the M&SDR pressed ahead with the drafting of a bill for submission to Parliament in the forthcoming session. Having the same solicitors as the South Devon Railway, namely Whiteford & Bennett of Plymouth, was a great help; and with the details carefully checked, the document was deposited early in the new year. The first reading in the House of Commons took place on Monday 10th February 1862, the bill proceeding straight away to its second reading. In the absence of objections, its passage to the third reading - and then on to the Lords - was untroubled. In the House of Lords only minor amendments were required to the document.

Excitement grew in the local communities with each report of the bill's progress. When it became known that its final reading in the Lords was included in the business of that House for the afternoon of Friday 27th June, Canon Courtenay, Vicar of Bovey, decided to travel to London to be present at this momentous phase of the Railway's genesis - for with this accomplished, the granting of the Royal Assent was only a formality. Bovey's canon was obviously fired - with enthusiasm that is! The great moment arrived. All went as hoped, although the amendments would have to go back to the Commons for approval. First thing next morning Canon Courtenay set off back to his parish with the good tidings. This was the news for which Bovey had so long waited. Indeed, it was felt that such an historical landmark should be recognised with a special celebration, and this was quickly arranged for the following Tuesday (1st July). The 'Western Morning News' reported the event thus:

"It is felt by the inhabitants of Bovey that the construction of the proposed railway from Newton Abbot to Moretonhampstead would be a great benefit to them and their neighbourhood, and they therefore resolved to celebrate the passing of the bill by a public rejoicing. Arrangements for that purpose having been made, Tuesday was fixed upon as the day. The matter was taken up with spirit, and the little town wore a very gay aspect on Tuesday. Houses were decorated, flags were flying, and in a field belonging to Mr. J.H. Mugford, of the Union Hotel, at 5 o'clock, about 500 persons, including 80 children of the National School, sat down to tea. The following ladies assisted or were present at the tea - Lady Lewin, Miss Ellis, the Misses Lewin (three), Mrs Percy Lepyeatt, Misses Campbell (two), Mrs. Divett and Miss Divett, Mrs. Hole, Mrs. and Miss Manning and the Hon. and Rev. C.L. Courtenay, Dr. Haydon, J.Divett, Esq., and most of the leading inhabitants of the place. In addition to the tea there were a variety of amusements, and some good music was furnished by the Bovey brass band and the Bovey bellringers. The weather was pleasant, and everything passed off most agreeably. The day will long be remembered in Bovey as one of great joy."

The Moretonhampstead & South Devon Railway Company's bill received the Royal Assent on Monday 7th July 1862 (25 & 26 Vic., cap.128). Now an Act, it authorised the Company to raise £105,000 capital through the sale of £10 shares, and to borrow a further £35,000. This was to fund the construction of a broad gauge, single track railway 12 miles and 13 chains in length, from a junction with the South Devon Railway 21 chains (462 yards) north of Newton station. There were to be two intermediate stations - Bovey and Lustleigh - with a crossing loop at the former. There was also an option regarding a possible extension of the Line to Chagford. Running rights over the South Devon main line were granted, and other working arrangements with that Company confirmed: namely, that it would work the Branch on behalf of the M&SDR in return for 50% of the gross receipts, but with rebates allowed on through traffic between the lines of the two companies. (The SDR had only subscribed a miserly £500, this being essentially to qualify for representation on the Board of Directors. In fairness to the Company, though, they had provided loans to help meet preliminary expenses and acted as guarantors on credit in the critical early days.) There were six directors, each of whom had paid a qualification of £300. The chairman of the Company was the Earl of Devon, and the vice-chairman Thomas Woollcombe, town clerk of Devonport and, more importantly, chairman of the South Devon Railway Company (a post which he held from 1849 until 1874). The other directors named in the Act were John Divett, William Hole, Thomas Wills and Elias Cuming.

PHASE 6: BUILDING THE LINE

The first meeting of the newly incorporated Moretonhampstead & South Devon Railway Company was held at the Union Hotel, Bovey Tracey, on Monday 4th August 1862. Thomas Woollcombe chaired the proceedings, which began by confirming the six directors named in the Act. Edward Bowring and Simon Neck were appointed the Company's auditors, for which service they each received an annual fee of £5. Amongst other business, the meeting resolved that "local Committees be formed at Moretonhampstead, North Bovey, Chagford, Lustleigh and Bovey Tracey for the purpose of canvassing additional shares."

After all the excitement of the summer, the next few months were something of an anti-climax. Interest fell to a low level; so much so that when the next half-yearly meeting was called - again at the 'Union' - on Saturday 28th February 1863, there were insufficient members present to form a quorum. Elias Cuming, acting as chairman, adjourned the proceedings until the following Monday at 1pm, to allow time to 'chase up' the errant shareholders. This evidently worked, for they all turned up!

In practice, of course, plans had been proceeding behind the scenes in the interim, even though the Company was strapped for cash. Contact had already been made with Thomas Brassey, of the contractors Messrs. Brassey & Ogilvie, and it was to this firm that the principal contract was now awarded: namely, all the works except the three station buildings and some of the bridges. The contract was to the value of £88,500. Brassey was one of the most successful, respected and wealthy railway contractors of his day. The son of a farmer, he was born in a small village near Nantwich in south Cheshire in November 1805. At the age of 21 he was articled to a land surveyor in Birkenhead, and ten years later started out on his first railway contracts. Initially, these were modest, but his scale of operations grew rapidly, and before long he was undertaking railway building all over the world, as far afield as Canada, India, Argentina and Australia. Although he supervised these far off projects from a base in Britain, when it came to the Moretonhampstead & South Devon Railway he decided to oversee the work personally, taking a house in Torquay (just as Brunel had done some 20 years before during the construction of the South Devon line).

The contractors established their 'base' on the edge of the wood just north of the Stover Canal basin at Ventiford (near the Union Inn). This consisted of workshops, stores and steam mill. Many of the wagons and barrows, as well as some of the plant, used in the building of the Line were constructed here. On fine days in January and February 1863 the figure of Thomas Brassey on horseback could be seen riding over some part or

Typical masonry construction: Lustleigh Mill viaduct 27.12.58 *Peter W. Gray*

other of the route. While the contractors retained overall responsibility for the building of the Line, others were also involved. The agent appointed by Brassey & Ogilvie to superintend the day-to-day work along the route was W. Crosley. To him also was given responsibility for designing all the bridges, including the substantial three-span, wrought iron structures over the River Lemon and Whitelake Channel at Newton Abbot. The engineers employed by the Company were Peter Margary of the SDR, and John Fowler of Queen Square Place, Westminster, along with resident engineer Jonathan Little (who lived in Bovey for the duration).

The six-mile section from Newton Abbot to Bovey presented few serious physical obstacles - other than the two river crossings - although the northern half of the line would be more taxing: especially the 1½ miles on either side of Lustleigh where the terrain was particularly challenging. It soon became evident to Peter Margary that his estimate of gradients no steeper than 1:70 in this vicinity were substantially over-optimistic. There would have to be several stretches between 1:50 and 1:60, and a long section at 1:49. Also, the alignment at Caseley Hill would have to be modified, taking the line through a ridge in a 60-70 foot-deep cutting rather than going round it as previously anticipated (the original plan involving unacceptably sharp curves).

Having plans, sections and elevations on paper was one thing, but in order to execute them a labour force was necessary. The recruit-ment of labourers ('navvies' as they were called) did not prove to be a problem because of the good reputation held by Thomas Brassey in respect of the treatment of the men. Compared with most other forms of labouring work available at the time, the navvies were relatively well paid, so that in addition to the usual itinerant workers, a number of local men found employment on the building of the Branch. Indeed, this became a cause of complaint by many local farmers and landowners, who found themselves faced with a serious manpower shortage as men left to work on the new railway. After months of detailed planning and with the workforce assembled, Mr. Crosley cut the first sod at Heathfield, without ceremony, on Monday 10th August 1863. Initially, the work began slowly, with groups of navvies arriving at various locations to undertake preliminary excavations. They turned up at Lustleigh for example on Monday 9th November. With such a large influx of rough-and-ready men, the date was indelibly etched in the minds of the villagers! The navvies remained in the vicinity for a long time, as the difficult topography dictated a slower rate of progress. The life-style and demeanour of the peripatetic workmen contrasted markedly with those of the settled communities through which they passed. The predictable regime of Victorian country life was disrupted by various incidents, usually involving pilfering, drunkenness and fighting. A lot of people were not amused, but the hostelries did well. Local chronicler Cecil Torr records the experience thus:

"The navvies made things unpleasant here, while the line was building. My grandfather writes to my father on 17 November 1864:- "More than a hundred discharged on Monday, and a pretty row there was: drunk altogether, and fighting altogether, except one couple fought in the meadows for an hour and got badly served, I hear. The same night the villains stole all poor old *****'s fowls. He had them under lock and key, but they broke in and took the whole, young and old....There is not a fowl or egg to be got hereabout." Writing on 29 March 1865, he describes a visit from a drunken navvy the day before - "about as fine a built tall likely a fellow as you ever saw, and nicknamed the Bulldog." He asked for meat and drink, and was sent away empty. "I learnt that he worked Saturday and Monday, and received 5s.6d. for the two days, slept in a barn and spent all his earnings at the public house....Not long after I saw the policeman who belongs to the line - not the Lustleigh man - and he said, 'If anything of the kind occurs again, send for me, and I will soon put all right.' But he spends all his time on the line keeping the navvies in order; and before he can be got mischief may be done." One of the dogs here had been poisoned by meat thrown her by a navvy, 22 September 1864. After that, he kept a revolver."

Although only a single line of rails was to be laid, the route was designed to accomm-odate double track (broad gauge) in the event of future increases in traffic. This obviously pushed up the construction costs, for not only did the 18-foot requisite strip of land have to be wider than for a single line, but the bridges spanning the form-ation had to be of double track width. The remaining bridges/viaducts over roads or rivers, along with cuttings and embankments could be constructed for single track initially, and then widened later if the need arose.

As the work progressed, it was followed with great interest within the locality. The inhabitants of Chagford renewed their campaign to get the line extended to their town, and as a result of their pressure the engineers undertook a new survey from Moreton in the autumn of 1864. By this time it was becoming apparent that the cost of the enterprise was going to exceed the original estimates. Indeed, by the time the Line eventually opened, it was £15,000 over. Against this background, the 'Chagford Extension' had no chance of being built, unless the residents could find some £60,000 themselves to finance it. Thus newly raised hopes were quickly dashed.

Slowly but surely the Line was beginning to take shape. At the fifth half-yearly meeting held in the Company's Newton Abbot headquarters, on Wednesday 24th August 1864, the Engineers' Report stated:

"The Contractors have hitherto chiefly concentrated their men on the works between Bovey Tracey and Moretonhampstead, in consequence of the delay experienced in obtaining the land between the Bovey Heathfield and Newton. That has been settled and the Contractors are now in possession of the land for nearly the whole length of the line. Between Jews Bridge, on the southern borders of the Bovey Heathfield, and Moretonhampstead, the Contractors have made fair progress with the works. Some of the cuttings and embankments are completed, and the masonry of the piers and abutments of several of the bridges have been built, and the arches are being turned. The works are now in full progress between Jews Bridge and Newton."

The 'Jews Bridge' referred to in the Report is that carrying the Exeter-Chudleigh-Ashburton turnpike (now the A38) over the River Bovey close to what later became the site of Heathfield station.

The early part of 1865 was marked by labour trouble. The contractors also had to lay off large numbers of men due to an exceptional period of severe weather, and both these things conspired to slow the work down. At the end of April work was brought to a complete stand due to a dispute amongst the navvies over wages but, fortunately, this was quickly resolved. Tenders were invited for the construction of the station buildings at Bovey, Lustleigh and Moreton. They had already been designed by Peter Margary, and were to be built, in granite, in the Gothic style. Additionally, goods sheds were to be provided at Bovey and Moreton; again executed in granite.

The contract was eventually awarded to Messrs. Call & Pethick of Plymouth; the platforms and building foundations remaining the responsibility of the contractors. Also that spring, the construction of the two river bridges at Newton Abbot was sub-contracted out to Messrs. Hennet & Spink of Bridgwater. These were to be massive 3-span affairs, and would finally allow the presently landlocked branch line to be joined up with the main network at Newton. The bridge nearest the main line junction would carry the Branch over the River Lemon, the other over Whitelake Channel (a stretch of tidal water engineered to link the Stover Canal with the River Teign). With piers and abutments made of local limestone, and wrought iron girders weighing 16-17 tons each, Lemon Bridge was to be provided with spans of 41'3", 68'5" and 45'4"; and Whitelake Bridge ones of 35', 80'2" and 43'.

In the autumn, persistently inclement weather slowed progress again, and presaged even worse to come in the approaching winter. Driving rain was a feature of these months, turning work-sites into seas of mud and misery. To add insult to injury, South Devon was ravaged in January 1866 by what came to be known as the Great Hurricane. Even after the havoc wreaked by its visitation had been cleared up, the rains continued. The Rivers Teign and Bovey, already seriously swollen by prolonged rainfall, were a constant source of worry, especially in the low-lying clay fields between Teignbridge and Newton Abbot. Unless the rain eased and river levels fell before the next high spring tides in the Teign estuary, there was going to be widespread and severe flooding. Unfortunately, the worst-case scenario came to pass, and a major inundation occurred - although the only damage caused was, as might be expected, at Teignbridge. The track here was carried over the floodplain on a low embankment, specifically to keep it above flood level, for inundations were to be expected in this particularly vulnerable area. Into this embankment, just north of the level crossing, were incorporated two wooden bridges, both with flood-relieving side openings. The bridges had to be built on wooden piles due to the softness of the ground here. The surging floodwater first overwhelmed the Stover Canal and then washed up against the railway embankment. At the bridges, water from the river on the one side vied with overflowing field drainage on the other for passage. The bridges eventually yielded to the pressure and they, along with a 400-yard section of embankment, collapsed into the floodwater. The engineers described this difficult time thus in their report of Wednesday 21st February 1866:

"The continuous rains of the last several months have considerably retarded the whole of the works, but they have had the beneficial effect of consolidating the embankments. The late flood which we are informed has been the highest known for the last thirty years only damaged the Line at Teign Bridge road where from being ponded back by the heaps of Potters clay deposited by the side of the Canal and the hedges of the Turnpike road it washed across the Line and scoured away about eighteen chains of the low gravel embankment."

An inevitable delay occurred while the breach was repaired, and the contractors were requested to provide the rebuilt bridges with not only wider openings but an additional span as well. The height of the levee (or earth bund) on the west bank of the Teign was also raised as an extra protection. In the event, the two original flood openings were rebuilt as before and not to the extra width required; while the additional opening was not provided either. The M&SDR directors ordered Brassey & Ogilvie to attend to the task as originally requested, but they simply refused. This became something of a running battle - even after the Line had opened - and in the spring of 1867 the Company ordered them again to carry out their instructions or else be billed for the work put out to another firm. The brinkmanship did not work, however, as the contractors continued to ignore the request and the impecunious Company was reluctant to spend the necessary money or become embroiled in possibly lengthy litigation with all the concomitant expense. The Line was periodically flooded at this same point on subsequent occasions, but fortunately never with the same drastic consequences.

PHASE 7: OPENING THE LINE

By the spring of 1866 the line was all but finished in its essentials. All the engineering work had been completed; the track had been laid and ballasted throughout; and the telegraph wires were in place (although the instruments had yet to be delivered). The finishing touches were being put to Lustleigh and Moretonhampstead stations, although that at Bovey was only half built and the goods sheds were not very far advanced. As almost three years had elapsed since the cutting of the first sod, the Company was anxious to open the Line as soon as possible to bring in much-needed revenue. In order to carry members of the public, sanction had first to be sought from the Board of Trade. This could only be granted following a thorough examination by a member of their Railway Inspectorate. The M&SDR secretary, now one Alexander Lhoyd, wrote to the Board on 26th April to say that the line "will be ready for opening after the expiration of one calendar month from this date." This proved to be somewhat premature, and Lhoyd had to write again on 20th June to say that the line would be "sufficiently completed for the safe conveyance of Passengers" for it to be opened on 2nd July. He requested that an inspection be made in readiness for that date.

The Company was impatient, and rather than wait for the official inspection, decided to organise a Grand Opening at the first opportunity. As a 'Directors Special' could run without the need for official sanction - it would be an entirely a 'private' affair - the Company set about arranging this event for Tuesday 26th June. The excursion was to start from Plymouth, for the benefit of directors and officials of the South Devon Railway, before its great triumphal procession over the new line. Much advance publicity was given to the event, so that by the time the set day dawned, there was huge excitement in the air: more than there had been for the arrival of the SDR twenty years before.

The 'Special' left Plymouth at 9.20am, the immaculate locomotive - one of the SDR's fleet of tank engines - decked out with flags and evergreen laurels and hauling twelve equally clean carriages. As it pulled into Newton station, it was given a rousing welcome by the large crowd that had turned out for the occasion. Their cheers were matched for volume by the strains of the Newton Band, which had been hired for the day and was to travel on the train to Moreton in order to accompany the festivities there. At 11.20am the 'Special' set off once more, amid even louder cheers, because now the great moment had arrived: after so many years of planning, hoping and waiting, the very first passenger carrying train was about to pass over the new branch line and put the communities of Bovey, Lustleigh and Moretonhampstead on the railway map. Hundreds of people were waiting at the long, 5-arch Kingsteignton Road bridge and on its lengthy embanked approaches, eager for a view of the inaugural train. At the sight of the 'Special' rounding the sharp curve over the river bridges, excited cheers, shouts and cries spontaneously erupted from the crowd, which rose to a massive crescendo of acclamation as it steamed beneath the

In this 1909 picture of the Branch's moorland terminus, one of Churchward's recently introduced 'small Prairie' (2-6-2) tank engines arrives with a train from Newton Abbot. The vehicle next to the engine is a non-corridor brake carriage mounted on the distinctive Dean bogie wheels. It is followed by a 6-wheel composite compartment coach with central luggage compartment. Both display a lined-brown livery and are followed by a 4-wheel and 6-wheel compartment coach in 'chocolate and cream' livery. Branch trains at this time still conveyed all three classes of accommodation, although the 2nd class category was soon to be abolished (in 1912).

National Railway Museum

road bridge. All along the Line people turned out to wave and cheer as the train passed by; and at Lustleigh and Moretonhampstead there was a carnival atmosphere as the day was treated as a holiday.

The first station stop made by the 'Special' was Bovey. Unlike the other locations, Bovey did not mark the occasion with a ceremony or festivities, as they planned to hold a celebration of their own on the first day of public service. However, that did not stop crowds turning out to see the inaugural train, with people milling around the station, level crossing and approach roads to get a good view. The air of anticipation grew as the train's arrival was deemed imminent, so that when it finally came into view on the long straight that leads into the station from the south, there was the familiar excited greeting. As the imposing train with its equally imposing passengers stood at the platform, natural curiosity impelled some people to take a closer look by peering into an empty compartment. A few more emboldened souls actually climbed inside to make a more thorough investigation of this new form of transport. However, no sooner had they clambered aboard than the train set off, causing these unwitting passengers to lean out of the windows and frantically call for the 'Special' to stop! As things turned out, Bovey did not get its celebration to mark the formal opening of the railway. The event coincided with the opening of the new Town Hall, an edifice of which the community was proud, and in connection with which a celebration was already planned. Apart from stretching the financial resources of the town to cover two great festivals at more or less the same time, it so happened that a number of the local 'worthies' were away at the beginning of July, and they were the very people who would be expected to put up most of the money.

At Lustleigh a festival had been organised to welcome the railway, and it was attended by most of the people from the village as well as the nearby hamlets and farms. One of the main attractions was a wrestling tournament, for which the area was famous (or infamous?). By all accounts, these were rough affairs at best, and downright violent brawls at worst. From its rousing welcome at Lustleigh, the 'Special' climbed the final 3½ miles to the moorland terminus at Moretonhampstead. Here over a thousand people had gathered to await the arrival of the train, a goodly proportion of these having travelled over from Chagford. A loud and enthusiastic cheer greeted the arrival of the 'Special' and signalled the beginning of several hours of festivities. After the dignitaries had alighted, and been subjected to the inevitable speeches, they adjourned to the town to partake of a celebration lunch. This was held in the schoolroom in Greenhill, by the church, where more speeches and congratulations were made - but accompanied this time by toasts. The townspeople had also determined to mark this very special occasion by organising their own, more frugal, celebration. As the 'Western Morning News' reported:

"In the afternoon various sports were engaged in, and cider was freely, and rather injudiciously, dispensed amongst the men and boys of the town and neighbourhood, several youths who had obtained drink from this or some other source being observed in different parts of the town in a state of intoxication, and lying in the public streets in a perfectly helpless condition. There was also a public tea provided in the streets for women and children. This part of the day's proceedings, under the direction of the ladies of the town, was exceedingly well managed, and the sight was an extremely well managed one. In the evening there was a dinner, and the proceedings passed off most satisfactorily."

A shuttle service operated between Moreton and Newton Abbot to cater for the return arrangements of the guests, with trains leaving the terminus at 3.30, 6.30 and 7.30pm.

The Line had been well and truly welcomed and celebrated, but as yet a public service could not be instituted. This was confidently expected to happen shortly, and on the very next day (Wednesday 27th June) the Board of Trade official arrived to make his inspection. This was undertaken on that, and the succeeding, day by Colonel William Yolland, a man whose association with railway inspection the years 1854 to 1885, after outstanding earlier careers in the Corps of Royal Egineers and Ordnance Survey.. Earthworks, retaining walls, culverts and bridges were all carefully examined, as was the trackwork in general and points in particular. In the case of railway over-bridges this was done by first running the heavier goods locomotives over them at comparative speed, and then requiring them to stand on the structure for some time to test for signs of stress. As soon as he had finished his task on the Thursday (28th), the Colonel set about the very same day compiling his report. After a general preamble, he laid out his observations. These were generally favourable, although he pointed to features which did not satisfy him, as exemplified in the following extract:

"The Line generally is in good order - the Platforms at the Stations are complete, but the whole of the Station buildings are in a very unfinished state - not sufficiently advanced as to be actually useable. I am of the opinion that their Lordships should consider this as an incompleteness of the "works" that fully justifies the postponement of the opening - but they have not hitherto done so - and it would not be fair to Railway Companies to change the practice without due notice. The Turntable is in position at Moretonhampstead but the line leading to it, and over it is not yet in order. This is expected to be done by the end of the week. Starting signals are to be put up for the Passenger and Goods Lines at Moretonhampstead Station interlocking with each other, and the Goods Line is not to be used until this is done. I am of the opinion that their Lordships may sanction the opening of the Line as soon as the Turn Table at Moretonhampstead is in working order - but when the Station buildings are complete. Clocks to face and be seen from the Platforms at the Stations should be provided."

The ever-cautious colonel also expressed uneasiness about the short viaduct at Knowle. He had noticed slight settlements in the massive granite wing-walls on the north side, and recommended that they "...should be pointed up and carefully watched."

The Board acted with their usual rapid dispatch, and notified the M&SDR on Saturday 30th of their willingness to sanction the opening as soon as the recommendations in the Report had been complied with. These were in fact already in hand, and although the Company would like to have commenced the public timetable the following Monday, they felt there was insufficient time for adequate publicity; the notification being received too late for the Saturday papers. Consequently the decision was taken to announce that the formal opening of the Line was to be on Wednesday 4th July.

Compared with the merry-making of the previous week, the first day of public service was something of a tame affair. The first train left Moreton at 9.50am and, being Newton Abbot's market day, its four coaches were well-filled. With only three trains in either direction, the same locomotive and stock handled each working, with the contractors' agent Mr. Crosley riding on the footplate of every journey. This, as the 'Western Morning News' reported the following day, was "....for the double purpose of ascertaining the working of the line, and of informing the engine-driver of the gradient and curves." With all the excitement over, the Line settled into a routine, and set about building up a valued and important association with the communities along its route; an association which lasted for over 92 years.

Chapter Three

THE TRAIN SERVICES

PART 1: PASSENGER SERVICES

Broad Gauge Days

After years of anticipation, the Moretonhampstead Railway was greeted with great excitement and celebration when it finally opened in the summer of 1866. In the early days it enjoyed almost universal good-will, and people commented favourably on the punctuality of the trains and smoothness of the ride. The initial service, however, was sparse in the extreme, so that the affirmation and high expectations began increasingly to turn to disappointment and even annoyance. With only three trains each way on weekdays and two on Sundays, it was a moot point whether or not this constituted a 'service' in the accepted sense. Departures from Moretonhampstead were at 9.50am and 2.20 and 6.40pm (7.30am and 7.15pm Sundays), with an overall journey time of 35 minutes. Trains left Newton Abbot at 11.00am, 3.35 and 8.55pm (8.35am and 8.55pm Sundays), with an extra five minutes being added to the journey time to allow for the predominantly rising nature of the Line. The paucity of the provision soon resulted in complaints to the Moretonhampstead & South Devon Railway Company, who in turn made representations to the South Devon Railway Company who worked the Line on their behalf. True, an additional early morning trip to Newton and back was instituted the following year, but as this only ran on Tuesdays and Wednesdays it was hardly a major improvement! From 1869 it was timetabled to run on all weekdays.

The problem lay in money - or more accurately lack of it. By the end of June 1868 the M&SDR had spent £135,830 on capital projects, and had received an income of £136,694. The latter was mainly derived from shares and loans, the revenue from passengers and freight being disappointingly low: for example, in the half-year ending 31st December 1868 the figure for the whole Branch was only £2,167. While receipts from traffic were increasing, it was at a very slow rate. Thus the takings for the first half of 1868 were only £113 higher than for the corresponding period the previous year. In the six months to August 1870 the Branch had carried 43,400 passengers, and although this was an increase of 2,100 over the same period in 1869, it only yielded an income of £85.17s.5d. This was simply not sufficient to meet expenditure: for by the time all the works had been completed and accounts settled, costs had risen to the £155,000 mark. Given this financial background, the Company found itself locked in a parlous situation. Although the SDR possessed the controlling interest, it was unable or unwilling to actively promote and develop the Line - although a station at Teigngrace was opened in December 1867. While the Branch remained under-capitalised and owed money on loans, prospects for an improved service looked bleak. The obvious and seemingly inevitable outcome was for the M&SDR to merge with the South Devon Railway; an event which took place on Monday 1st July 1872 (whereupon the value of the original M&SDR shares fell by 50%). The new ownership actually made no difference to the frequency of train services, although from 1874 the schedules were relaxed a little: five minutes being added to journeys from Moretonhampstead and three to those from Newton Abbot.

The somewhat casual atmosphere of these early broad gauge years is encapsulated in observations made by one of the residents living near Lustleigh station and related by his grandson, Cecil Torr, in his delightful book 'Small Talk at Wreyland':

"As the trains upon this branch were 'mixed', partly passenger and partly goods, there generally was some shunting to be done; but this caused no delay, as the time-tables allowed for it. If there was no shunting, the train just waited at the station till the specified time was up. The driver of the evening train would often give displays of hooting with the engine whistle while he was stopping here, and would stay over time if the owls were answering back.

The engines on this branch were quite unequal to their work, and there were no effective brakes then. Coming down the incline here, trains often passed the station; and passengers had to walk from where their train had stopped."

History has a habit of repeating itself. On 1st February 1876 it was the turn of the South Devon Railway to be absorbed by a larger neighbouring company, namely the Great Western Railway. This event made no immediate difference to Branch services, although the following year the regular four trains were supplemented by an additional afternoon working in the summer months. This seasonal arrangement continued until 1891, when the summer schedule was boosted by a further train.

Gauge Conversion

The gauge conversion of 1892 was a truly remarkable undertaking. The seven-foot broad gauge to which the Moretonhampstead Branch had been constructed was a legacy of that great engineering genius Isambard Kingdom Brunel's influence in the West Country. Unfortunately, that widely adopted beyond the Great Western network - and increasingly within it - was what the Broad Gauge School referred to as the 'narrow gauge': namely four feet eight and a half inches. This disparity was becoming a serious inconvenience as both the volume of traffic and number of lines grew. Mixed gauge track had reached Exeter in 1876; that is, a formation of three rails which permitted both broad and narrow stock to run over it. However, this was not extended west of that city; the lines here remaining defiantly broad gauge until their continued existence became untenable. As the narrow gauge was inexorably emerging as the national 'standard', it could only be a matter of time before the old South Devon, Cornwall and West Cornwall Railways would have, literally, to come into line.

Following a period of meticulous planning and preliminary engineering, it was announced that the entire broad gauge system in the South West was to be altered over the weekend of 21st/22nd May. Thus the last broad gauge service for Moretonhampstead steamed out of Newton Abbot at 8.35pm on Friday 20th, arriving at the terminus 40 minutes later. Normally the locomotive would have stabled the coaches beneath the train shed on the outer siding before going to the engine shed for the night. On this historic occasion, however, the entire train had to vacate the Branch in order to give the engineering department unhindered possession of the Line. It, along with other 'last trains' in the region, made its way as 'empty carriage stock' to Exeter initially, and then on to the extensive holding sidings at Swindon. As all broad gauge stock was to be at, or beyond, Exeter by midnight, careful timetabling was necessary to prevent congestion and delays, especially at junctions. Thus the 'path' plotted for the Branch train involved departing from Moreton at 10pm. The progress of the train back to Newton marked the end of an era, but also held out new possibilities for the future.

BROAD GAUGE TRAIN SERVICES

Table 1. June 1867. MORETONHAMPSTEAD & SOUTH DEVON RAILWAY

Up Trains		Week Days					Sundays	
- -	**Newton**	8W30	10. 55	3. 55	7. 45	9G00	8. 35	8. 55
6m 06ch	Bovey	8W45	11. 10	4. 10	8. 00	9G25	8. 50	9. 10
8m 66ch	Lustleigh	8W55	11. 20	4. 20	8. 10	-	9. 00	9. 20
12m 28ch	**Moretonhampstead**	9W10	11. 35	4. 35	8. 25	-	9. 15	9. 35

Down Trains	Week Days					Sundays	
Moretonhampstead	7W25	10. 00	2. 15	6. 10	-	7. 30	7. 15
Lustleigh	7W37	10. 12	2. 27	6. 22	-	7. 42	7. 27
Bovey	7W46	10. 21	2. 36	6. 31	9G50	7. 51	7. 36
Newton	8W00	10. 35	2. 50	6. 45	10G15	8. 05	7. 50

W - Runs Tuesdays & Wednesdays only   G - Goods train

Table 2. March 1875. MORETONHAMPSTEAD BRANCH : SOUTH DEVON RAILWAY

Up Trains		Week Days					Sundays	
- -	**Newton**	8. 25	11. 40	4. 15	5G00	8. 05	8. 35	9. 05
2m 28ch	Teigngrace	8. 32	11. 47	4. 22	5. 10	8. 12	8. 42	9. 12
3m 70ch	Chudleigh Road	8. 37	11. 52	4. 27	5. 15	8. 17	8. 47	9. 17
6m 06ch	Bovey	8. 43	11. 58	4. 33	5G25	8. 23	8. 53	9. 23
8m 66ch	Lustleigh	8. 53	12. 08	4. 43	_	8. 33	9. 03	9. 33
12m 28ch	**Moretonhampstead**	9. 08	12. 23	4. 58	_	8. 48	9. 18	9. 48

Down Trains	Week Days					Sundays	
Moretonhampstead	7. 15	10. 40	1. 20	-	7. 05	7. 25	7. 10
Lustleigh	7. 27	10. 52	1. 32	-	7. 17	7. 37	7. 22
Bovey	7. 36	11. 01	1. 41	6G00	7. 26	7. 46	7. 31
Chudleigh Road	7. 42	11. 07	1. 47	6. 45	7. 32	7. 52	7. 37
Teigngrace	7. 47	11. 12	1. 52	CR	7. 37	7. 57	7. 42
Newton	7. 55	11. 20	2. 00	7G15	7. 45	8. 05	7. 50

Table 3. June 1890. MORETONHAMPSTEAD BRANCH : GREAT WESTERN RAILWAY.

Down Trains			Week Days						Sundays	
- -	**Newton Abbot**	dep	8. 27	11. 57	1G30	3. 18	5. 30	8. 33	8. 30	7. 46
2m 28ch	Teigngrace	dep	8. 33	12. 03	CR	3. 24	5. 36	8. 39	8. 36	7. 52
3m 70ch	Heathfield	arr	8. 37	12. 07	1G42	3. 28	5. 40	8. 43	8. 40	7. 56
		dep	8. 39	12. 09	2G13	3. 29	5. 42	8. 45	8. 41	7. 57
6m 06ch	Bovey	arr	8. 44	12. 14	2X23	3. 34	5X47	8. 50	8. 46	8. 02
		dep	8. 46	12. 16	2G55	3. 36	5X49	8. 52	8. 47	8. 03
8m 66ch	Lustleigh	dep	8. 56	12.26	CR	3. 45	5. 59	9. 02	8. 57	8. 13
12m 28ch	**Moretonhampstead**	arr	9. 09	12. 39	3G20	3. 57	6. 12	9. 15	9. 10	8. 26

Up Trains			Week Days						Sundays	
Moretonhampstead		dep	7. 15	10. 45	2. 05	4. 10	4G30	7. 05	7. 40	6. 47
Lustleigh		dep	7. 25	10. 55	2. 15	4. 20	CR	7. 15	7. 50	6. 57
Bovey		arr	7. 32	11. 02	2X22	4. 26	4X55	7. 22	7. 55	7. 04
		dep	7. 34	11. 04	2X24	4. 27	5X55	7. 24	7. 58	7. 05
Heathfield		arr	7. 39	11. 09	2. 29	4. 31	6G10	7. 29	8. 03	7. 10
		dep	7. 41	11. 11	2. 31	4. 32	6G50	7. 31	8. 04	7. 11
Teigngrace		dep	7. 46	11. 16	2. 36	4. 37	CR	7. 36	8. 09	7. 16
Newton Abbot		arr	7. 53	11. 23	2. 42	4. 43	7G10	7. 43	8. 16	7. 23

CR - Calls when required.   X - Trains cross each other on a single line.   G - Goods train.

Table 4. Summer 1905
MORETONHAMPSTEAD BRANCH
Single Line, worked by Electric Train Staff. The Crossing Stations are Moretonhampstead
Junction, Bovey and Moretonhampstead. The Staff Stations are Moretonhampstead Junction,
Heathfield, Bovey and Moretonhampstead.

Down Trains		Week Days									
Stations		Pass	Pass	Pass	Gds	Pass	Gds	Gds	Pass	Pass	Pass
Newton Abbot	dep	8. 15	9. 52	12. 02	1. 15	2. 50	4R00	4R45	5. 47	7U15	9. 00
Moreton'stead Junction		CS	CS	CS	CS	CS	CS	CS	CS	CS	CS
Teign Bridge Siding		-	-	-	-	-	-	4R55	-	-	-
Teigngrace	arr	8. 20	9. 57	12. 07	CR	2. 55	-	-	5. 52	7U20	9. 05
	dep	8. 21	9. 58	12. 08	CR	2. 56	-	-	5. 53	7U21	9. 06
Heathfield	arr	8. 25	10. 02	12. 12	1. 37	3. 00	4X15	-	5X57	7U25	9. 10
	dep	8. 27	10. 04	12. 14	1. 55	3. 02	-	-	5X59	7U27	9. 12
Bovey	arr	8. 32	10X09	12. 19	2X03	3. 07	-	-	6. 04	7X32	9. 17
	dep	8. 34	10X11	12. 21	2. 40	3. 09	-	-	6. 06	7X34	9. 19
Lustleigh	arr	8. 43	10. 20	12. 30	CR	3. 18	-	-	6. 15	7U43	9. 28
	dep	8. 44	10. 21	12. 31	CR	3. 19	-	-	6. 16	7U44	9. 29
Moretonh'stead	arr	8. 57	10. 34	12. 44	3. 05	3. 32	-	-	6. 29	7U57	9. 42

Up Trains		Week Days									
		Pass	Pass	Pass	Pass	Pass	Gds	Gds	Gds	Pass	Pass
Moretonh'stead	dep	7. 10	9. 52	10. 45	1. 50	4. 05	-	-	4P25	7. 15	8U20
Lustleigh	arr	7. 18	10. 00	10. 53	1. 58	4. 13	-	-	4. 37	7. 23	8U28
	dep	7. 19	10. 01	10. 54	1. 59	4. 14	-	-	4Q45	7. 24	8U29
Bovey	arr	7. 25	10X07	11. 00	2X05	4. 20	-	-	4. 55	7X30	8U35
	dep	7. 27	10X10	11. 02	2X07	4. 22	-	-	5Q07	7X33	8U36
Pottery Siding		-	-	-	-	-	-	-	CR	-	-
Granite Siding		-	-	-	-	-	-	-	CR	-	-
Heathfield	arr	7. 32	10. 15	11. 07	2. 12	4X27	-	-	5X32	7. 38	8U41
	dep	7. 36	10. 17	11. 09	2. 15	4X29	-	4R50	7W10	7. 39	8U42
Teigngrace	arr	7. 40	10. 21	11. 13	2. 19	4. 33	-	CR	CR	7. 43	8U46
	dep	7. 41	10. 22	11. 14	2. 20	4. 34	-	CR	CR	7. 44	8U47
Teign Bridge Siding		-	-	-	-	-	5R15	CR	CR	-	-
Moreton'stead Junction		CS	CS	CS	CS	CS	CS	CS	CS	CS	CS
Newton Abbot	arr	7. 47	10. 28	11. 20	2. 26	4V43	5R25	5R35	7. 30	7. 50	8U53

Mileage		Sundays							
- -	**Newton Abbot**	dep	8. 55	7. 52		**Moretonhampstead**	dep	8. 00	6. 45
2 28	Teigngrace	dep	9. 01	7. 58		Lustleigh	dep	8. 09	6. 54
3 70	Heathfield	dep	9. 06	8. 03		Bovey	dep	8. 16	7. 01
6 06	Bovey	dep	9. 12	8. 09		Heathfield	dep	8. 22	7. 07
8 66	Lustleigh	dep	9. 22	8. 19		Teigngrace	dep	8. 27	7. 13
12 28	**Moretonhampstead**	arr	9. 35	8. 32		**Newton Abbot**	arr	8. 33	7. 20

Pass - Passenger train
Gds - Goods train
CR - Calls when required
CS - Calls for Train Staff purposes only
P - Stops at Mile Post 12 between 4. 26 and 4. 28pm to pin down wagon brakes.
Q - Trucks taken on at Lustleigh & Bovey to be marshalled at Heathfield
R - Runs when required

U - Runs Mondays, Wednesdays and Saturdays only & until September 9th
V - 3 minutes allowed for signal checks at Newton Abbot
W - To leave Heathfield at 7. 50pm MWSO up to September 9th, and arrive at Newton Abbot at 8. 10pm
X - Indicates points at which trains are booked to cross each other on a single line

Somewhere in the order of 5,000 workmen were brought into the region by special trains in readiness for the big weekend; being accommodated in station buildings or tents for the duration. A special train, originating in Bristol, arrived at Moreton with the Branch contingent at 4.45pm on Thursday 19th.

The Moretonhampstead & South Devon Railway had been built using 18' and 24' lengths of bridge rail weighing 60lbs per yard. These were bolted directly on to 12" x 6" timber sleepers (called longitudinal sleepers as they ran beneath the rails and not at right angles to them). To maintain the required gauge and impart rigidity to the formation, 6" x 4" hardwood transverse sleepers - or transoms - were fixed across the gap between the rails every 12 feet (11 on curves). The whole formation was bedded in ballast of broken stone and gravel. To narrow the gauge, one line of rails would be left in situ and the other closed up by the requisite amount - this being achieved by freeing the longitudinal sleepers of the line to be moved from the transoms, the surplus ends of which were then sawn off. The line could then be closed up and rejoined to the shortened cross-ties. Rather more exacting effort was required in converting the siding and loop points. In spite of the scale of the operation, on Monday morning, 23rd May, the first standard gauge train made its way out to Moretonhampstead, consisting of four 6-wheeled coaches: two 1st and 2nd class composites and two brake-3rds. The workmen's 'special' left the terminus at 6.40am the following day.

While Branch trains had taken on a most definite 'Great Western' look following gauge conversion, the level of service remained basic. Although there were still only four trains each way on winter weekdays, there now appeared a useful 'market day' service. Running every Wednesday and fourth Tuesday, it catered for the livestock markets at Newton Abbot and Moretonhampstead respectively (one train undertook a round trip in the morning and the other in the afternoon). Six trains ran during the summer, while the traditional single morning and evening Sunday working operated throughout the year. Further improvements took place during the Edwardian era. During the winter months five trains were provided each way on Mondays to Fridays, rising to seven on Saturdays, while the two market day 'specials' also continued to feature. The summer-time provision remained at six on all weekdays, although was increased to seven from 1908. The two Sunday trains continued to follow their time-honoured routine.

The Years of Promise & Prosperity

The summer of 1910 marked the beginning of an improvement in the level of passenger services on the Line. Eight trains were now running each way on weekdays, with one extra on Wednesdays. The tourist potential of the Branch seemed at last to be getting through to Paddington. For 45 years trains had simply shuttled to and fro between Shore and Moor, with no 'off-line' workings. Then suddenly and incredibly it was decided to provide a through coach between London and Moretonhampstead. This was instituted on 1st June 1911; namely the 11.50am from Paddington. The Torquay-bound express arrived at Newton Abbot at 3.22pm, where the coach was detached and transferred to the Branch train. This subsequently departed at 3.45pm, reaching Moreton 50 minutes later. In the reverse direction, the coach was conveyed by the 10.45am from Moreton, with ten minutes allowed for the transfer at Newton (11.20-11.30am). Sadly the operating economies made necessary by the First World War put paid to this summer-time facility, and it was never restored. Wartime exigencies also brought about a reduction in the number of weekdays trains: from eight in 1914, to six the following year; then five in 1916 and 17, and finally down to only four in 1918.

Another casualty of that desperately tragic conflict was the Sunday service. Withdrawn at the end of 1916, this was the first time in the Line's life that it ceased to be a seven-day operation.

Post-war recovery was slow. Not least among the reasons was a chronic manpower shortage. It was not until 1922 that the level of service returned to that pertaining at the outbreak of the war, with Sunday trains also being reinstated (although then, as thereafter, for the summer months only). However, it was during this post-war low point, in 1920, that an interesting development took place; namely, the institution of through workings between Moretonhampstead and local 'off-line' locations. Initially restricted to Kingswear and Paignton, there was a subsequent broadening out to include Plymouth and, less intensively, Churston, Goodrington Sands, Torquay and Totnes. Unlike the erstwhile London endeavour, the entire train ran to and/or from these places, and through-working remained a feature of Branch timetables until the withdrawal of passenger services in 1959. In terms of the variety, the peak years were 1921-1928; the latter being the last time Plymouth featured. In terms of the number of through workings, the equivalent dates were 1923-1928; with 40-50% of the winter services continuing 'off-line', rising to between 70 and 85% in the summer months. These, like the other Branch services, were the preserve of the '45xx' 'Prairies'. Although Totnes rarely featured in the 1920s regime, it was to become one of the most enduring links. Between 1931 and 1959 the first advertised 'down' service train of the day commenced its journey there, always departing at 7.25am.

In addition to these innovations, the inter-war years played host to the summer-time Bovey shuttle. Hitherto, all passenger trains had run the full length of the Branch, but in 1922 two intermediate services were provided between Newton Abbot and Bovey. One of these was a through working from Paignton which, uniquely in the history of the Line, did not stop at Newton. Leaving the resort at 10.15am, it had a three-minute stop at both Torquay and Torre before continuing non-stop to Bovey. Run in conjunction with 'road motor tours' to Dartmoor, a return service for Paignton left Bovey at 5.45pm, running initially non-stop to Newton Abbot (where it called between 5.59 and 6.03pm) before proceeding to the Torbay resorts. By 1927 the number of these intermediate workings had risen to seven. All the 'up' trains terminated at Newton, while

A rake of neat, short-wheelbase 'chocolate and cream' compartment coaches stands in the platform at Moretonhampstead in this 1913 view. Nearest the camera is the brake vehicle, with its guard's lookout ducket. Notice the station name inscribed on the backrest of the seat by the goods shed wall. *L&GRP*

Table 5. Summer 1928

MORETONHAMPSTEAD BRANCH

Single Line, worked by Electric Train Staff. Heathfield and Bovey are Crossing Stations.
The Staff Stations are Newton Abbot, Heathfield, Bovey and Moretonhampstead.

Down Trains			Week Days								
Dist. m ch	Stations		Gds TV	Pass	Pass TP	Pass TP	Pass TP	Auto	Gds	Auto -	Pass TP
- -	**Newton Abbot**	dep	6. 30	8. 08	8. 45	9X20	10. 20	11. 00	11. 10	12. 00	12X47
1 45	Teign Bridge Sdg	arr	6. 36	-	-	-	-	-	CR	-	-
		dep	6. 55	-	-	-	-	-	CR	-	-
1 51	Teign Bridge Crossing		-	-	-	-	-	-	-	-	-
2 28	Teigngrace	dep	-	8. 13	8. 50	9. 25	-	11. 05	-	12. 05	-
3 70	Heathfield	arr	7. 02	8X16	8. 53	9X29	10. 27	11. 08	11. 25	12. 08	12X53
		dep	8. 40	8X21	8. 54	9X31	10. 28	11. 09	11X45	12. 09	12X55
5 06	Granite Siding		-	-	-	-	-	-	CR	-	-
5 19	Pottery Siding		-	-	-	-	-	-	CR	-	-
5 46	Brimley Halt	dep	-	8. 26	-	9. 36	-	11. 14	-	12. 14	-
6 06	Bovey	arr	-	8. 27	8. 59	9. 37	10X33	11. 15	11. 53	12X15	1. 01
		dep	-	8. 28	-	9. 38	10X36	-	12X23	-	1. 03
8 66	Lustleigh	arr	-	8. 36	-	9. 46	10. 44	-	CR	-	1. 11
		dep	-	8. 39	-	9. 49	10. 47	-	ST	-	1. 14
12 28	**Moreton'stead**	arr	-	8. 50	-	10. 00	10. 58	-	12. 52	-	1. 25

Down Trains			Week Days									
			Auto	Auto	Pass TK	Auto	Auto	LE	Pas TK	Pass TK	Auto	Auto
Newton Abbot	dep		1. 00	2. 00	2X47	3. 00	4. 00	4. 10	5. 00	6X00	6X18	7. 00
Teigngrace	dep		1. 05	2. 05	-	3. 05	4. 05	-	-	-	6. 23	7. 05
Heathfield	arr		1X08	2X09	2. 53	3. 08	4. 08	4X20	5X06	6X06	6. 26	7. 08
	dep		1X09	2X11	2. 53	3. 09	4. 09	-	5X08	6X10	6. 27	7. 09
Brimley Halt	dep		1. 14	2. 16	-	3. 14	4. 14	-	5. 13	6. 15	-	7. 14
Bovey	arr		1. 13	2. 17	3. 00	3. 15	4X15	-	5X14	6. 16	6. 32	7X08
	dep		-	-	3. 03	-	-	-	5X15	6. 17	-	7X15
Lustleigh	arr		-	-	3. 11	-	-	-	5. 23	6. 25	-	-
	dep		-	-	3. 14	-	-	-	5. 25	6. 28	-	-
Moretonhampstead	arr		-	-	3. 25	-	-	-	5. 36	6. 39	-	-

Down Trains			Week Days					Sundays					
			Pass	Auto	Auto	Pass TK		Auto	Auto	Auto	Auto	Auto	Auto
Newton Abbot	dep		7X30	8. 00	9. 30	9. 45		9. 00	10. 40	2. 05	3. 00	5. 30	7. 23
Teigngrace	dep		-	8. 05	-	-		-	-	-	-	-	-
Heathfield	arr		7X36	8X08	9. 38	9X52		9. 07	10. 47	2. 12	3. 07	5. 37	7. 30
	dep		7X39	8X09	-	9X54		9. 08	10. 48	2. 13	3. 08	5. 38	7. 31
Brimley Halt	dep		-	8. 14	-	-		9. 13	10. 53	2. 18	3. 13	5. 43	7. 36
Bovey	arr		7. 44	8X15	-	9. 59		9. 14	10. 54	2. 19	3. 14	5. 44	7. 37
	dep		7. 45	-	-	10. 01		9. 15	10. 55	-	3. 15	5. 45	7. 38
Lustleigh	arr		7. 53	-	-	10. 09		9. 23	11. 03	-	3. 23	5. 53	7. 46
	dep		7. 56	-	-	10. 12		9. 26	11. 06	-	3. 26	5. 56	7. 49
Moreton'stead	arr		8. 07	-	-	10. 23		9. 37	11. 17	-	3. 37	6. 07	8. 00

Up Trains — Week Days

Stations		Pass	Pass TH	Pass TS	Pass TP	Auto	Pass TK	Auto	Gds TV	Auto	Pass
Moreton'stead	dep	7. 55	-	9. 05	10. 15	-	12. 05	-	-	-	1. 45
Lustleigh	arr	8. 03	-	9. 13	10. 23	-	12. 13	-	-	-	1. 53
	dep	8. 04	-	9. 14	10. 24	-	12. 14	-	-	-	1. 54
Bovey	arr	8. 10	-	9. 20	10X30	-	12X20	-	-	-	2. 00
	dep	8. 11	9. 05	9. 21	10X35	11. 35	12X21	12. 30	-	1. 30	2. 03
Brimley Halt	dep	8. 14	-	9. 24	10. 38	11. 38	-	12. 32	-	1. 33	-
Heathfield	arr	8X18	9. 10	9X28	10. 42	11X42	12. 26	12. 36	12. 38	1. 37	2X09
	dep	8X20	9. 12	9X31	10. 43	11X44	12. 27	12. 37	1X15	1. 38	2X12
Teigngrace	dep	8. 25	-	-	10. 48	11. 49	-	12. 41	-	1. 43	-
Teign Bridge Siding		-	-	-	-	-	-	-	CR	-	-
Newton Abbot	arr	8. 30	9X20	9. 39	10. 53	11. 54	12. 35	12X46	1. 27	1. 48	2. 20

Up Trains — Week Days

Stations		Auto	Auto	Pass	Auto	Gds	Gds	Pass TP	Auto	Pass TK	Auto
Moreton'stead	dep	-	-	4. 00	-	-	4P 20	5. 45	-	6. 55	-
Lustleigh	arr	-	-	4. 08	-	-	4. 32	5. 53	-	7. 03	-
	dep	-	-	4. 09	-	-	4. 45	5. 54	-	7. 04	-
Bovey	arr	-	-	4X16	-	-	4P56	6. 00	-	7X 10	-
	dep	2. 25	3. 30	4X19	5. 00	-	5X 20	6. 02	6. 35	7X16	7. 30
Brimley Halt	dep	2. 28	3. 33	-	5. 03	-	-	-	6. 38	-	7. 33
Pottery Siding		-	-	-	-	-	CR	-	-	-	-
Granite Siding		-	-	-	-	-	CR	-	-	-	-
Heathfield	arr	2. 32	3. 37	4X24	5X07	-	5. 50	-	6. 42	7. 21	7X37
	dep	2. 33	3. 38	4X26	5X08	5. 20	-	6X08	6. 43	7. 22	7X38
Teigngrace	dep	2. 38	3. 43	4. 31	-	-	-	-	6. 48	-	7. 43
Teign Br. Sdg	arr	-	-	-	5. 26	-	-	-	-	-	-
	dep	-	-	-	5. 50	-	-	-	-	-	-
Newton Abbot	arr	2X43	3. 48	4..35	5. 16	5X55	-	6X15	6. 53	7X28	7. 48

Up Trains

Stations		Week Days				Sundays					
		Gds	Pass TP	Auto	Auto	Auto	Auto	Auto	Auto	Auto	Auto
Moreton'stead	dep	-	8. 20	-	-	10. 00	12. 00	-	4. 30	6. 30	8. 30
Lustleigh	arr	-	8. 28	-	-	10. 08	12. 08	-	4. 38	6. 38	8. 38
	dep	-	8. 29	-	-	10. 09	12. 09	-	4. 39	6. 39	8. 39
Bovey	arr	-	8X35	-	-	10. 15	12. 15	-	4. 45	6. 45	8. 45
	dep	-	8X 36	9. 00	-	10. 16	12. 16	2. 30	4. 46	6 46	8. 46
Brimley Halt	dep	-	-	9. 03	-	10. 19	12. 19	2. 33	4. 49	6. 49	8. 49
Heathfield	arr	-	8. 41	9. 07	-	10. 23	12. 23	2. 37	4. 53	6. 53	8. 53
	dep	8X15	8. 42	9. 08	9X55	10. 24	12. 24	2. 38	4. 54	6. 54	8. 54
Teigngrace	dep	-	-	9. 13	-	-	-	-	-	-	-
Newton Abbot	arr	8. 30	8. 50	9. 18	10. 05	10 .32	12. 32	2. 46	5. 02	7. 02	9 02

Auto - Push-pull train, third class only
CR - Calls when required
LE - Light engine
P - Stops only to pin down or pick up wagon brakes:
    Stop Board at Mile Post 12   4. 21/23
    Stop Board 6m 15½ch   4. 53/55
ST - Calls for Station Truck purposes only

T - Through trains to or from :

H - Plymouth
K - Kingswear
P - Paignton
S - Totnes
V - Teign Valley Line

Above: One of the original batch of 'small Prairies', No. 2178, pauses at Lustleigh with a train for Moretonhampstead in 1912. The bogie vehicle behind the engine is a passenger full brake coach. Next come a couple of 6-wheeled non-corridor coaches of the type widely used on the Branch from the 1892 gauge conversion. Bringing up the rear are two of William Dean's bogie clerestory coaches, the last a brake vehicle. *National Railway Museum*

Right: A break with small coach tradition began around the turn of the century when William Dean's clerestory bogie coaches began to appear on the Branch, as here on a 'down' train at Bovey in the mid 1920s. They are still in the all-over brown livery of earlier years. *Lens of Sutton*

five of the return workings began there. Of the other two, one originated in Plymouth and one in Kingswear.

In terms of the level of service, the peak years were from 1927 to 1939. Typically, nine trains ran the full length of the Branch all year round (often with an additional working on Saturday evening). This increased to ten or eleven in the summer months of the mid and late '30s, during which time the Sunday provision rose from five to eight. Traffic volumes were significantly boosted over the southern half of the Line by virtue of the six to eight intermediate journeys made by the Newton Abbot - Bovey 'shuttle' on weekdays. In 1933 one of these auto train (push-pull) workings was extended to Lustleigh.

The Last Years: 1939 -1959

The tense and melancholic months prior to the outbreak of the Second World War (in September 1939) saw certain changes in the modus operandi of the Branch. The weekday level of service between Newton Abbot and Moretonhampstead continued, as in previous years, with eleven trains each way.

The difference lay in the ratio of conventionally loco-hauled carriage stock to the push-pull auto trains. On Saturdays the latter accounted for the entire operation, and on Mondays to Fridays for all but two of the services. With the exception of the 7.25am from Totnes, the auto trains were confined entirely to the Branch, so that there was a consequent and severe diminution in 'off line' workings. In the 'up' direction there was only one through train: the 9.51am from Moreton to Goodrington Sands; while in the other there were two: the 9.55am from Kingswear and the 4.47pm from Paignton. On Sundays, six of the eight trains were timetabled as 'auto'; none of them running 'off line'. The weekday service was supplemented by the Newton to Bovey 'shuttle', although with four auto trains each way, this was a reduction by two from the previous season.

Table 6. Summer 1955

MORETONHAMPSTEAD BRANCH

Single Line, worked by Electric Train Token or Train Staff. Auxiliary Token instruments on Platform Nos. 5 and 9 at Newton Abbot. Intermediate Token instrument at Newton Abbot end of the Up Loop at Heathfield. Heathfield and Bovey are Crossing Stations. The Token or Staff Stations are Newton Abbot, Heathfield, Bovey and Moretonhampstead.

Down Trains			Week Days							
Dist m ch	Stations		LE	Gds TThS	Auto TT	Pass 3rd	Auto TP	Gds	Auto	Auto
- -	**Newton Abbot**	dep	6. 45	7. 00	7. 50	9. 20	10. 32	11. 15	12. 45	2. 15
1 45	Teign Br.Sdg	arr	-	7. 06	-	-	-	CR	-	-
		dep	-	7. 20	-	-	-	CR	-	-
2 28	Teigngrace Halt	dep	-	-	7. 55	9. 25	10. 36½	-	12. 49½	2. 19½
3 70	Heathfield	arr	-	7. 27	7. 58½	9. 28½	10X40	11. 25	12. 53	2X23
		dep	-	8. 40	8. 00	9. 30	10X43	11. 40	12. 54	2X24
5 46	Brimley Halt	dep	-	TV	8. 04½	9. 34	10. 47½	-	12. 58	2. 28
6 06	Bovey	arr	-	-	8X06	9. 36	10. 49	11X47	1. 00	2. 30
		dep	-	-	8X11	9. 37	10. 51	12. 20	1. 01	2. 31
7 61	Pullabrook Halt	dep	-	-	8. 16	9. 42	10. 56	-	1. 06	2. 36
8 66	Lustleigh	dep	-	-	8. 20	9. 46	11. 00	-	1g10	2. 40
12 28	**Moreton'stead**	arr	7. 15	-	8. 31	9. 57	11. 11	12. 48	1. 21	2. 51

Down Trains		Week Days					Sundays			
Stations		Auto SS	Auto	Auto S	Auto	Pass 3rd	Pass	Pass TG	Pass	Pass TG
Newton Abbot	dep	3¶05	3. 30	4. 30	6. 05	8. 15	9. 00	11. 40	3. 55	7. 48
Teigngrace Halt	dep	3. 10	3. 34½	4. 34½	6. 09½	8. 20	9. 04½	11. 44½	3. 59½	7. 52½
Heathfield	arr	3. 14	3X38	4X38	6. 13	8. 23½	9. 08	11. 48	4. 03	7. 56
	dep	3. 15	3X39	4X39	6. 14	8. 24½	9. 09	11. 49	4. 04	7. 57
Brimley Halt	dep	TV	3. 43	4. 43	6. 18½	8. 29	9. 13	11. 53	4. 08	8. 01
Bovey	arr	-	3. 45	4. 45	6. 20	8. 30½	9. 15	11. 55	4. 10	8. 03
	dep	-	3. 46	4. 46	6. 21	8. 32	9. 16	11. 56	4. 11	8. 04
Pullabrook Halt	dep	-	3. 51	4. 51	6. 26	8. 37	9. 21	12. 01	4. 16	8. 09
Lustleigh	dep	-	3. 55	4. 55	6g30	8g41	9. 25	12. 05	4. 20	8. 13
Moreton'stead	arr	-	4. 06	5. 06	6. 41	8. 52	9. 36	12. 16	4. 31	8. 24

Up Trains		Week Days								
Stations		Pass 3rd	Auto TP	Pass 3rd	Auto	Gds TThS	Auto	Auto TV	Gds	Auto
Moreton'stead	dep	7. 50	8. 40	10. 15	11. 35		1. 35		1. 51	3. 15
Stop Board 12m.p.		-	-	-	-	-	-	-	1P53	-
Lustleigh	dep	7. 59	8. 48½	10. 23½	11. 44	-	1. 44		2b11	3. 23½
Pullabrook Halt	dep	8. 01	8. 50	10. 26	11. 46	-	1. 46		-	3. 25½
Stop Board 6m. 15½ ch		-	-	-	-	-	-	-	2P20	-
Bovey	arr	8X05	8. 54	10. 30	11X50	-	1. 50		2X22	3. 29½
	dep	8X08	8. 55	10. 32	11X52	-	1. 51		2. 45	3. 30½
Brimley Halt	dep	8. 11	8. 58	10. 35	11. 55	-	1. 54		-	3. 33
Pottery Siding		-	-	-	-	-	-	-	CR	-
Granite Siding		-	-	-	-	TV	-	-	CR	-
Heathfield	arr	8. 15	9. 02	10X39	11. 59	11. 52	1. 58	1X54	3. 15	3X37
	dep	8. 16	9. 03	10X42	12. 00	12. 15	1. 59	2X27	5. 00	3X40
Teigngrace Halt	dep	8. 20	9. 07	10. 45½	12. 04	CR	2. 02½	2. 31	-	3. 44
Teign Br.Sdg	arr	-	-	-	-	CR	-	-	5. 08	-
	dep	-	-	-	-	CR	-	-	5. 19	-
Newton Abbot	arr	8. 25	9. 12	10. 50	12. 09	12. 33	2. 07	2‡36	5. 25	3. 49

Up Trains		Week Days					Sundays			
Stations		Auto	Auto S	Auto	LE	Auto SO	Pass TG	Pass	Pass TG	Pass
Moreton'stead	dep	4. 15	5. 15	7. 00	9. 00	-	9. 50	1. 25	4. 40	8. 30
Lustleigh	dep	4. 23½	5. 23½	7g09	-	-	9. 59	1. 34	4. 49	8. 39
Pullabrook Halt	dep	4. 25½	5. 25½	7. 11	-	-	10. 01	1. 36	4. 51	8. 41
Bovey	arr	4. 29½	5. 29½	7. 15	-	-	10. 05	1. 40	4. 55	8. 45
	dep	4. 30½	5. 30½	7. 17	-	-	10. 06	1. 42	4. 56	8. 46
Brimley Halt	dep	4. 33	5. 33	7. 20	-	TV	10. 09	1. 45	4. 59	8. 49
Heathfield	arr	4X37	5. 37	7. 24	-	10. 26	10. 13	1. 49	5. 03	8. 53
	dep	4X45	5. 38	7. 25	-	10. 27	10. 14	1. 51	5. 04	8. 54
Teigngrace Halt	dep	4 49	5. 41½	7. 29	-	10. 31	10. 18	1. 55	5. 08	8. 58
Newton Abbot	arr	4†54	5. 46	7. 34	9. 35	10. 36	10. 23	2*00	5. 13	9. 03

b -	Arrive 7 minutes earlier	S -	Runs 5 minutes later on Saturdays
g -	Guard to collect tickets	SS -	Runs 10 minutes later on Saturdays
CR -	Calls when required	SO -	Saturdays only
3rd -	Third class only	TThS -	Tuesdays, Thursdays & Saturdays only
P -	Stops to pin down/pick up wagon brakes	T -	Through train to or from
* -	Advertised in public timetables as 2. 02pm	G :	Goodrington Sands Halt
‡ -	Advertised in public timetables as 2. 40pm	P :	Paignton
¶ -	Advertised in public timetables as 3. 00pm	T :	Totnes
† -	Advertised in public timetables as 4. 56pm	V :	Teign Valley Line

Table 7.   **TEIGN VALLEY SERVICES : HEATHFIELD**

		Arrivals			Departures	
1890	7. 35 -	Passenger	(7. 05 Ashton)	8. 42 -	Passenger	Ashton
	11. 06 -	Mixed	(10. 30 Ashton)	12. 12 -	Passenger	Ashton
	2. 25 -	Passenger	(1. 55 Ashton)	3. 35 -	Passenger	Chudleigh
	4. 27 -	Passenger	(4. 18 Chudleigh)	5. 45 -	Mixed	Ashton
	7. 25 -	Passenger	(6. 55 Ashton)	8. 48 -	Passenger	Ashton
1905	7. 33 -	Passenger	(6. 35 Exeter)	8. 32 -	Passenger	Exeter
	11. 00 -	Passenger	(9. 45 Exeter)	12X20 -	Passenger	Exeter
	12X15 -	Goods	(9. 20 Exeter)	3. 10 -	Passenger	Exeter
	2. 10 -	Passenger	(1. 12 Exeter)	4X25 -	Goods	Exeter
	4X18 -	Passenger	(3. 06 Exeter)	6. 10 -	Passenger	Exeter
	7. 23 -	Passenger	(5. 01 Dulverton)	9. 20 -	Passenger	Exeter
1928	8. 12 -	Rail Motor	(7. 10 Exeter)	8. 23 -	Motor	Exeter
	10. 33 -	Rail Motor	(9. 30 Exeter)	8. 40 -	Goods	Exeter (ex N. Abbot)
	11. 41 -	Rail Motor	(10. 35 Exeter)	10. 45 -	Motor	Exeter
	12. 38 -	Goods	(6. 35 Exeter), to N. Abbot	1. 00 -	Motor	Exeter
	2. 01 -	Rail Motor	(12. 55 Exeter)	2. 57 -	Motor	Exeter
	4. 57 -	Rail Motor	(4. 30 Christow)	5. 10 -	Motor	Exeter
	7. 19 -	Rail Motor	(6. 15 Exeter)	7. 40 -	Motor	Exeter
	9. 47 -	Rail Motor	(8. 45 Exeter)	9. 55 -	Motor	Exeter
	10. 50 -	SO. Auto	(9. 45 Exeter)	10. 55 -	SO. Motor	Exeter
1955	7. 57 -	Auto	(7. 00 Exeter)	8. 05 -	Auto	Exeter
	10. 38 -	Auto	(9. 46 Exeter)	8. 40 -	TThS Gds	Christow (ex NA)
	11. 52 -	TThS. Gds	(10. 45 Christow)	10. 45 -	Auto	Exeter
	12. 53 -	SO. Auto	(12. 06 Alphington Halt)	1. 04 -	SO. Auto	Exeter
	1. 54 -	Auto	(12. 47 Exeter)	3. 15 -	Auto	Exeter (ex NA)
	5. 24 -	Auto	(4. 25 Exeter). Later SO	6. 20 -	Auto	Exeter
	7. 07 -	Auto	(6. 05 Exeter)	8. 30 -	Auto	Exeter
	10. 26 -	SO. Auto	(9. 30 Exeter), to N. Abbot			

The war years saw a much-reduced service of six or seven trains in operation. From 1940 all the passenger duties were scheduled as auto workings - in theory at least. That year also saw the withdrawal of the summer Sunday service and 'Bovey Shuttle'. The ending of hostilities in 1945 brought only a slow recovery. General economic exhaustion and depletion in manpower, exacerbated by a serious coal shortage, militated against services resuming the level and diversity of the 1930s. The summer Sunday trains were not reinstated until 1949, while the 'Bovey Shuttle' had gone for good. It was against this background of austerity that Britain's railway network was nationalised: on 1st January 1948.

Passenger services in the Western Region days of British Railways showed little variation in number, timing, origin and destination of Branch trains. Typically, eight trains ran on weekdays between mid September and mid June, being joined by an additional mid-afternoon working for the summer peak: the 3.30pm from Newton Abbot/4.15 return from Moreton. After the summer of 1955 this particular train was pruned from the schedules, so that from then until closure, eight trains ran all year round: four in the morning and four in the afternoon/evening. From the early '50s, the first 'down' service of the day - the 7.25am auto train from Totnes - continued its turn of duty with a trip from Moreton to Paignton and back, departing at 8.40 and 10.05 respectively. Down to the autumn of 1953, all services were timetabled to be worked by auto trains, but from that date a few 'passenger' (that is, non-auto) workings were included; notably the 7.50, 10.15 and 4.15 from Moretonhampstead, and 9.20, 3.30 and 8.15 from Newton Abbot. Periodic shortages of auto coaches (trailers), especially in the summer, saw the impromptu substitution of other carriage stock, both corridor and non-corridor. Of the four summer Sunday trains, two ran through to Torbay: either both to Goodrington Sands Halt, or sometimes with one continuing to Kingswear.

The inflexibility of the timetable in these years became increasingly at odds with the needs of a growing body of local commuters, while connections with main line trains at Newton were often less than obliging. Even so, the withdrawal of passenger services at the end of February 1959 was a severe inconvenience to many.

PART 2 : GOODS SERVICES

Goods services began on Monday 8th October 1866, three months after the Line had opened for passengers. The delay was caused by the unfinished state of the goods sheds at Bovey and Moretonhampstead. Initially, goods vehicles were attached as required to passenger trains, which thus frequently ran as 'mixed' services. From the spring of the following year, 1867, a separate goods train was introduced between Newton Abbot and Bovey. For the first few years of its existence, it left Newton at 9pm, after the day's passenger operation had finished. With a journey time of 25 minutes, and a further 25 minutes allowed for shunting at Bovey, it arrived back at Newton at 10.15pm. From 1875 it was re-timed to run substantially earlier, typically 4.45pm from Newton. Traffic for Lustleigh and Moreton continued to be conveyed as required by passenger trains, and it was not until 1882 that the daily goods train was extended to run the full length of the Branch. This now left Newton Abbot in the early afternoon, its timings varying only by a few minutes over the next 40 years: between 1.05 and 1.30pm.

Throughout these years, the train began its 'diagram', or turn of duty, at Newton Abbot Goods Yard, a cramped location occupying a narrow strip of land bounded by Moretonhampstead Junction, Teign Road and the passenger station. The headshunt for the sidings ended near the top of the embankment leading to Lemon Bridge. Twelve months or so

after the 1892 narrowing of gauge, the bridge was widened to take a second track, thus allowing the headshunt to be extended as far as Whitelake Bridge, where a connection with the Branch was put in. By the early 1900s the yard had become severely congested and totally inadequate for the traffic with which it was expected to deal. As a consequence, the GWR decided not only to expand the provision, but also to segregate the town's goods station from the wider 'marshalling' function performed at Newton. The former was to be relocated to an extensive low-lying wedge of marsh between the Branch and Whitelake Channel. The considerable task of preparing the site was phased to coincide with the doubling of the line between Torquay and Paignton, as the preliminary excavations - in particular the opening out of the 133 yard long Livermead Tunnel - would provide the requisite overburden. The first train of 22 earth-filled ballast wagons arrived from Torquay on 1st March 1909, and by the time the work had been completed, approximately 58,320 cubic yards of material had been transported. The land-fill operation on the extensive new marshalling yard in Hackney Marshes began on 1st July 1910. With the goods yard site preparation completed a fortnight later, the engineering trains switched to Hackney, until the Torbay endeavour was completed on 8th October. Supplementary hard-core in the form of quarry refuse was railed in from Trusham on the Teign Valley line. Altogether, an estimated 30,649 cubic yards of 'filler' was used.

The new goods yard opened for traffic on 12th June 1911, and Hackney sidings six months later. The goods yard was generally referred to by railwaymen as 'New Yard', and was able to accommodate up to 464 wagons; a vast increase over its antecedent. It was dominated by a huge red-brick goods shed, built by Hunt of High Wycombe, while cattle pens and end-loading facilities were also provided, along with a new stable block. In association with the works here, Whitelake Bridge was widened - between February and May - so that shunting movements between old and new sidings could take place without interfering with trains on the Branch.

Although New Yard was the starting place for the Moretonhampstead goods train, both yards featured in its working. The train was first assembled at Hackney. This complex consisted of an 'up' and 'down' running loop, 6 reception loop lines and 14 dead-end sorting, or marshalling, sidings (in May 1943 the outermost of these was extended, and joined by two more). The yard was a busy place, requiring the continuous attendance of two shunting engines (known as 'pilots'): one to cover the east end and one the west. Only for a few hours on a Sunday did shunting operations cease. On weekdays during the mid 1950s, around forty goods trains arrived in the yard, almost half of them in the night shift (10pm to 6am). Traffic for the Moreton Branch was transferred from the main line services to one of the sorting sidings specifically set aside for them, the pilot assembling the wagons in the order required by the schedule of work to be performed en route. Once the train had been formed, it was ready for the short 'transfer' trip over to New Yard. Depending on the time and loading, and to minimise the number of transfers, traffic for the Teign Valley freight and/or Newton Abbot goods yard might additionally be coupled to the train.

The transfer was the responsibility of the New Yard, or No.1, pilot. In the early and mid 1950s, '57xx' 0-6-0 Pannier Tanks were the engines regularly assigned to this duty. 'Ex-Works' locomotives were also pressed into service sometimes, while on rare occasions a '94xx' 0-6-0 might be seen performing the work. The severity of the gradients on the northern half of the Line reduced the number of wagons which the Branch goods train was permitted to convey beyond Bovey, with the consequence that it was often made up to 'full load'. This proved somewhat taxing for the ubiquitous and workaday Pannier Tanks that were increasingly allocated to the duty after 1945. These engines had to work very hard just to keep the train moving; and on misty days especially this gave rise to a spectacular exhaust display. The blast from the chimney greatly increased the draught through the boiler tubes, so that not only were ash and cinders drawn from the firebox, but pieces of burning coal as well. These shot out through the chimney to add a pyrotechnic display to the already noisily impressive progress of the train. With heavy regulator work by the driver, heavy demands were made on the fireman, who found his fire disappearing all too fast: indeed, live coal was expelled almost as fast as he could shovel it in! In times of drought when the grass was tinder dry, it was by no means uncommon for trains to start line-side fires.

Utilising a lull in the busy routine of Newton Abbot East signal box, the pilot picked its way over the complicated trackwork to collect the waiting wagons. This move was performed without a brake van, although the 4-wheeled vehicle used by the shunters, and nicknamed the 'chariot', was sometimes attached to the formation. As the yard points by Whitelake Bridge faced trains from the station, once they and the junction points had been set, the trucks could be propelled in a single movement directly into New Yard: generally into one of the two long sidings between the Branch running line and goods shed. Extending to Kingsteignton Road bridge, that nearest the Branch was known as 'Back Siding No.1', and was able to hold up to 35 wagons. That next to the goods shed was 'Back Siding No.2'.

Up until 1922 the Moretonhampstead goods train always set out from Newton in the early afternoon, but in the years which followed it moved to the late morning: invariably leaving between 10.45 and 11.15am - the latter applying from the Second World War. As departure time drew closer, the pilot left off its general shunting duties to once more attend to the Branch train, initially attaching a brake van to the rear. In Great Western days, the Line had its own 'dedicated' van, but after nationalisation it was more usual to see a standard BR vehicle on the train. This was often changed week by week, or even day by day, depending on availability. The guard meanwhile had booked on duty at the guards' room on the 'up' platform at the station, and walked over to the yard. His first task was to make a note of the details on the wagon labels in order to compute the loading of the train, which he communicated to the driver prior to departure. This had to fall within the limits set down for the Branch. In the 'down' direction these followed a tripartite division reflecting the changing ruling gradient: Newton Abbot to Teigngrace; Teigngrace to Bovey; and, most dramatically, Bovey to Moretonhampstead. In the 'up' direction there were only two sections, with Heathfield as the 'fulcrum'. The maximum loads permitted over these sections depended on the nature, or class, of the traffic and the power classification of the locomotive assigned. Entering all the relevant details in his journal, the guard was joined by a travelling shunter, who would accompany the train throughout its journey.

As a long turn of duty (or roster) for the enginemen, the locomotive was got ready by one of the motive power depot's preparation gangs. Around 15 minutes or so before the time of departure, and with the junction clear of traffic, the engine made its way over to New Yard; the East Box signalman having already informed the yard shunter by telephone that the manoeuvre was about to take place. Passing the signal by Lemon Bridge, the loco sounded a whistle 'crow' to alert personnel in the vicinity that it was approaching. The engine generally ran into whichever of the back siding 'roads' was unoccupied. Once clear of the points, the shunter changed them to the siding on which the pilot and Branch wagons were

waiting. As soon as the ground signal covering the exit from the yard changed to the 'off' position, the shunter pressed a plunger on the Klaxon horn located by the river bridge. This was the signal for the pilot to draw the train out on to the Branch in the direction of the station, the signalman having 'set the road' for the Bay platform line. When the wagons were well clear of the yard points, the pilot was uncoupled and retreated further along the line. The Klaxon sounded again and now the 'train engine' backed out of the yard to couple to the head of the formation (locomotives invariably worked 'chimney first' to Moreton; bunker first on the return). The yard points were changed back to the running line, the fireman collected the single line token from the signalman, and the train set off along the Branch. After a short pause for signals, the pilot dutifully returned to the yard to continue its busy round of shunting which, as at Hackney, was continuous for all but a short respite on Sundays. In addition to its goods yard duties, No.1 pilot also shunted 'Electricity Siding' and 'Newton Abbot Clay Siding'.

A significant proportion of the freight handled on the Branch fell into the category of small goods, or 'smalls' for short. The upper weight limit for individual items was 3cwt; the lower, half a hundredweight (below that the goods were classed as 'passenger parcels'). Generally insufficient in quantity to make up a full truck-load at any one location, the enormous variety of merchandise was loaded into general-purpose box vans, known as 'station trucks', which were included in the formation of the daily 'pick-up goods'. At major depots like Newton Abbot there was much sorting and transfer of smalls for forwarding to the receiving station or other depots. This procedure, though effective, was cumbersome and slow due to the manhandling and transhipment involved. Indeed, if there were insufficient items to make up a full truck, there might be a delay of a day or two.

These factors, combined with growing road competition, prompted the GWR to institute a Goods Zoning Scheme. Its aim was to modify the way in which small goods were handled in such a manner as to speed up transit. It was to apply to the whole of the Great Western network, which was accordingly divided into districts, or zones, based on important and/or strategic rail centres. The plethora of small goods was to be fed to these zonal depots, where full loads could be made up and railed on to other such depots. Less important, though still significant, freight centres were identified within the zones under the designation of 'sub-depots'. Thus from the main centre, goods were either transferred for direct road delivery to customers, or for subsequent forwarding by rail to the sub-depots (and thence by GWR road vehicle to customers within their catchment area). The reduction in handling should, ideally, give a service - on weekdays at least - to any part of the Company's system, however remote. The penalty paid was that smaller locations lost their general small goods 'station truck' facility, although full loads - such as minerals and bulk freight - were not affected by this scheme.

The Exeter Zone came into operation on 1st February 1947, to be followed on 1st March by the Newton Abbot Zone. It was a measure of the amount of small freight carried by the Branch that both Bovey and Moretonhampstead were designated as sub-depots. The latter had always covered a large geographical area by virtue of its moorland location, and its sphere of influence remained intact (including as it did the sizeable traffic from Chagford). The Bovey catchment was expanded to take in Lustleigh and district, while Heathfield was covered by the Newton-based zone (or 'trunk') lorry. Thus appeared the familiar 'Collection & Delivery' vehicles which, following nationalisation, came to be painted in crimson and cream, with the distinctive British Railways banner motif on the cream uppers.

Chapter Four

LOCOMOTIVES & ROLLING STOCK

Broad Gauge Days

As the M&SDR possessed no locomotives or rolling stock of its own, they were provided by the South Devon Railway, whose tally of engines at the time the Branch opened in 1866 stood at 40: all saddle tanks. Of these, 28 were 4-4-0s, predominantly for passenger work; that is, four-coupled engines with leading bogie. The remaining 12 were 0-6-0, or six-coupled, locomotives designed to cover goods duties. Of the former, 12 were 'Comet' class engines with 5' 9" diameter driving wheels, and 16 'Hawk' class - essentially the same design as the 'Comets' but with driving wheels three inches smaller in diameter. These were joined just weeks after the Branch opened by six more 4-4-0 saddle tanks; namely the 'Pluto' class - the same genus as the other four-coupled locos but with 5' 8" diameter driving wheels and inside plate frames. It is not known which of these worked the inaugural, and subsequent, trains, although one was 'dedicated' to the Branch, being shedded overnight at Moreton (and changed as required by the 'parent' shed of Newton Abbot). To the modern eye, the cab-less 4-4-0 passenger engine with its slab-fronted smoke-box, tall chimney and enormous convex saddle tank appears wonderfully antique; not so much Heath Robinson as Minimalist! Turned out in a dark green livery - which included the wheels - the only lining was restricted to the low coal bunker: a broad black band with thinner white edging (the edging being changed in later years to red). Hand-rails, safety-valve bonnet and nameplate were in brass. All South Devon engines were named rather than numbered; the nameplate being centred on the tank sides.

It was only after the Great Western Railway took over the Branch, on 1st February 1876, that the locomotives began to acquire numbers. By this date the South Devon stock had risen to 85 engines, these eventually being given the number sequence 2096-2180. The direct involvement of the GWR increased the variety of motive power on the lines west of Exeter, but brought about no immediate change in the level of service. Of particular interest to the Moreton Branch was the decision the following year (1877) to modify ten of the 'Hawthorn' class of Great Western 2-4-0 engines for use specifically in South Devon and Cornwall. Having been built in 1865/6 as tender engines with six-foot diameter driving wheels,

they went through a transmogrification to emerge as saddle tanks with five-foot coupled wheels and larger cylinders. Although it is not easy to establish with certainty which of these were allocated to the Branch, it is very probable that 'Cerberus', 'Hedley', 'Melling', 'Penn' and 'Pollux' undertook spells of duty as the 'Moretonhampstead Engine' in later broad gauge days.

Throughout this period, all Branch passenger trains provided first, second and third class accommodation: typically in six-wheeled, four-compartment carriages. Of box-like wooden construction, emphasised by small rectangular windows and a roof with merely the slightest elliptical curvature, the coaches were uncompromisingly angular in appearance. This was further enhanced by the pronounced overhanging of the underframe beyond the slender spoked wheels. The only embellishment - if one can call it that - was provided by the rather ugly projecting cylindrical lids/ventilators for the smoky, malodorous oil lamps, which inadequately lit the unheated compartments. However, what these plain brown-liveried carriages lacked in aesthetics, they made up for in smooth riding and durability.

Branch goods trains at this time were hauled by 0-6-0 saddle tank locomotives; indeed, the Company's working timetables specified six-coupled engines as the motive power for them. They also laid down the maximum loadings permitted on the Branch; these reflecting the very different ruling gradients on the southern and northern halves of the Line. Thus from Newton Abbot to Bovey a train could be made up to a maximum of 27 'ordinary' wagons, or 18 coal trucks, or 35 empties.

From Bovey to Moreton the respective numbers were 15, 12 and 25. In practice, trains invariably ran with a mixture of all three classes of traffic, so that loadings had to be computed accordingly. With two engines, double loads were permitted, but there was an upper limit of 40 wagons.

Standard Procedure

Gauge conversion produced no change in the pattern of train services on the Branch, which continued to be somewhat sparse until the first decade of the twentieth century. It did, however, give rise to an increasing variety of locomotives and rolling stock. To begin with, motive power for both passenger and goods trains was almost exclusively the preserve of 0-6-0 saddle tanks; these having a less austere appearance than their broad gauge predecessors. Their near monopoly, however, was soon to be challenged by other classes of engine. The Armstrong-designed, Wolverhampton-built '517' class of 0-4-2 standard gauge tank engine was produced between 1868 and 1885. The 'narrowing' exercise of 1892 brought some of these to Newton Abbot, and they appeared occasionally on Branch passenger services for a few years on either side of the turn of the century (and again from 1928 when auto trains were introduced between Newton and Bovey). These attractive little 40-ton engines, with

Armstrong '517' class 0-4-2T No. 829. Built in October 1873 it was originally provided with a half-cab and rear spectacle plate. Contemporary engines Nos. 830 and 831 were shedded at Newton Abbot at the end of 1935. The loco behind No. 829 is fitted with condensing apparatus for working through the Metropolitan Line tunnels. *Photomatic Ltd*

their angular side tanks, marked the beginning of a move away from the long reign of the saddle tanks.

In the early years of the new century, 2-4-0 'Metropolitan' tank engines could also sometimes be seen on Moretonhampstead Branch passenger trains, albeit on an irregular basis. In their original form these engines were cabless, the only protection for the crew being a narrow front-only weather-board cum spectacle plate. Use of a tarpaulin gave a little more protection when running forwards, but one shudders to imagine the misery of working bunker-first in inclement winter weather, especially when an icy, sleety wind was whipping up on to Dartmoor from the east. The name of this class comes from their association with London's 'Metropolitan Line', for which the locos were fitted with condensing apparatus for working through the smoky tunnels of the capital. Later, around forty of this class were provided with the necessary equipment to allow push-pull (or auto) working, and engines 3581, 3587 and 3590 worked on the Branch in the early years of the Second World War. This was virtually at the end of their working lives, as the last two were taken out of service (from Taunton) in 1944, and the former from St. Blazey in Cornwall in November the following year.

All three classes of locomotive described above displayed the by-now standard Great Western accoutrements: tall chimney with copper band at its top; large brass steam dome; tapered brass safety-valve casing; and prominent tool-box. They hauled an assortment of GWR 4 and 6-wheeled non-corridor compartment coaches; all the services continuing to offer first, second and third class accommodation. These vehicles were soon joined by newer, longer wheel-base carriages designed by William Dean, the Great Western Locomotive, Carriage & Wagon Superintendent between 1877 and 1902. He favoured vehicles with the distinctive clerestory type of roof, and built several versions; their wood-panelled superstructures being mounted on bogie wheels of his own design. While the older stock retained the traditional Great Western 'chocolate and cream' livery first employed in 1864, the newer vehicles displayed the lined-brown livery which enjoyed a short-lived vogue between, approximately, 1908 and 1912 (when it was succeeded by a rich plum-red for the next ten years or so). It was in the latter year that the 'second class' category was abolished.

If the service provision remained unimaginative, innovations in the motive power scene at least added variety to the few trains that were running, and acted as a precursor to the expansion that was so eagerly desired. A break with the Line's 'small-engine' tradition came about in the first decade of the twentieth century; namely, the appearance of the six-coupled 'Prairie' tank engines (a name derived from the wheel notation 2-6-2: one leading pony wheel, three driving wheels, and one trailing pony wheel per side). Indeed, from the end of the decade the Branch was very much the preserve of these engines, for both passenger and goods trains. This was particularly appropriate, as this class was designed by 'local lad' George Jackson Churchward. Born at Rowes Farm, Stoke Gabriel, in January 1857 he was educated at Totnes Grammar School before beginning an apprenticeship, at the age of 16, at Newton Abbot Locomotive Works. His mentor there was John Wright, the Locomotive Superintendent of the South Devon Railway; a post which also carried responsibility for the motive power on the Cornwall and West Cornwall Railways. When the Great Western Railway took over the operation of these lines in February 1876, George was transferred to the much bigger enterprise at Swindon, to continue his training initially under Joseph Armstrong and then his successor William Dean. Completing his 'time' in 1877, he moved up steadily through the ranks, gaining a breadth of experience in a number of

An unidentified 2-4-0 'Metro' tank engine stands in the Bay at Newton Abbot with a Moretonhampstead train. Fitted for auto working, and with the 820 gallon tanks of the 'medium' sub-group of the once numerous class, her pay-load consists of a single central vestibule type trailer. Engine 1415 was at Newton Shed in the mid 1930s until withdrawn from service in April 1938. She was succeeded by three younger representatives - of 1899 vintage - with larger tanks. No. 3587 was still to be seen at work on the Branch until late 1942. Undated. *Rokeby Collection, courtesy RCHME*

departments. So it was, twenty years later, that he became chief assistant to the renowned William Dean. When that worthy gentleman retired, George was the obvious candidate for the job; a man of ideas and vision, and yet at the same time grounded firmly in practicality. He remained in the prestigious post of Locomotive, Carriage & Wagon Superintendent (a title which was changed in 1916 to that Chief Mechanical Engineer) between June 1902 and December 1921. (Sadly, G.J. Churchward met an untimely end when, several years after his retirement, he was hit and killed by a Paddington to Fishguard express whilst out on one of his regular walks alongside the track at his beloved Swindon.)

The first batch of 'Prairies' was built between 1906 and 1910; these excellent machines carrying the numbers 2161-90 for a few years before inheriting the familiar '45xx' classification. They had an innovative coned boiler and top-feed apparatus - for better steaming - along with inside steam pipes, but continued to display many of the already classic Great Western features, such as the copper chimney band and brass safety-valve bonnet. Following the success of the first 30 of these versatile and competent locomotives, a further 25 were built between 1913 and 1915 (nos. 4530-54). These displayed a few modifications from the earlier batch, although the differences were in details rather than basics, albeit visually significant: the introduction of outside steam pipes to the cylinders; support struts to the smokebox; considerably-raised water inlet covers; and a curved interface between the front and side running plates. In January 1922 Charles Benjamin Collett succeeded Churchward as Chief Mechanical Engineer. Not only did he continue to produce the 'Prairies' but greatly expanded the building programme. In 1924 a further 20 of the 1,000-gallon, square tank versions left Swindon Works (nos. 4555-74). Between 1927 and 1929 a hundred more came off the production line, these possessing larger 1,300-gallon water tanks, the leading edges of which had been tapered to improve visibility from the cab. Weighing 61 tons, they were four tons heavier than their predecessors, but otherwise were virtually identical. The first 25 of the 1927 batch continued in the 4500 number series (4575-99); the remainder being enumerated 5500-74 (although all were classified generically as '45xx').

Above: Churchward '45xx' 'small Prairie' No. 4547 - of the 1914 batch - is seen in immaculate 'ex-Works' condition in the Bay platform at Newton Abbot, having just arrived with a two coach train from Moretonhampstead. Although the engine was allocated to Penzance in the year of the photograph, she had been sent to Newton Abbot for a scheduled overhaul, following which she was pressed into service on the Moreton Branch before returning to Cornwall. Withdrawn from St. Blazey shed in February 1960, she was briefly stored at Barry Docks until broken up at John Cashmore Ltd's scrapyard, Newport, in May. (The carmine and cream corridor coach on the left belongs to an earlier Teign Valley arrival.) 20.4.57. *The late David Fereday Glenn (Miles Barber Glenn collection)*

Left: This picture shows to good effect one of the 1928 2-6-2s, No. 5536. Carrying a shed plate for Exeter (83C), is waiting in the Bay at Heathfield with a Teign Valley service in 1957.
Hugh Ballantyne

Built in 1908, Rail Motor No. 96 was to be seen 25 years later at work on the Teign Valley Branch. With a length of 70 feet and seating for 61 - which included nine 'overspill' flap-seats in the luggage compartment next to the cab - it was one of the last batch of steam rail motors to be built. In 1934 it was converted into an auto trailer (No. 213), which increased the seating capacity to 77.   *Real Photographs*

For a few months in 1927/8, steam railmotors made an appearance on the Branch. Consisting of an integrated vertical-boiler engine and open-plan saloon-type coach, with a driving compartment at either end, they were unlike anything else on the Great Western system at the time. Perhaps for reasons of novelty or aesthetics, the GWR went to great lengths to conceal the engine, for not only was it encased within, and looked like, the carriage body, but the chimney barely protruded above the roof (creating problems with smoke clearance). These interesting contraptions had been at work on the Teign Valley Line since the beginning of the decade. Then, in the summer of 1927, having worked over that line to Heathfield from Exeter, one of these vehicles was timetabled to travel the two miles to Bovey. Arriving at 7.31pm, and departing for Newton Abbot 24 minutes later, it subsequently returned to Exeter via the Teign Valley (8.30 from Newton). In the autumn and through the spring of 1928 this working continued, although was re-timed to run in the afternoon: calling at Bovey between 2.15 and 2.30pm. Thereafter, the railmotors retreated to their usual Teign Valley route, where they virtually monopolised the services until 1935.

When the Bovey shuttle resumed for 1928's summer season, the number of trains each way had risen to nine. Of greater significance than the increased provision, perhaps, was the appearance on this service of auto trains (or 'push-pull' trains). Indeed, dealing exclusively with this service, this was the first time such trains had been used on the Moretonhampstead Branch. Six years later, they ran over the full length of the Line, although the majority of these workings remained the province of the 'Prairies'. At the outset, motive power for the auto trains was provided by the Armstrong '517' class of 0-4-2 tank engine. Since their earlier appearance on the Branch they had undergone various modifications, to take on an even more 'standard' Great Western look. Most obviously, this included a full cab, increased capacity coal bunker, reduced chimney height, and a changing over in the positions of the tool box and tank flaps. The whistles were also more prominent: one giving a long blast, and one a short.

A small number of '517s' were shedded at Newton Abbot during these years: such as Nos. 530, 838, 847, 1162 and 1443. The three present for the summer of 1935 were Nos. 830, 831 and 1487. Their withdrawal, between December that year and the following August, was timed to coincide with the arrival of the Collett 0-4-2s, which took over their role on the Moreton/Bovey push-pull trains. Introduced as the '4800' class, these incomparable little engines, weighing in at 41 tons 6cwt, had a strong generic link with their Armstrong predecessors; being an updated version rather than a new design. With coupled driving wheels of 5' 2" in diameter and single trailing wheel of 3' 8" (the same as the '517s'), they had a coal capacity of 2 tons 13cwt and side tanks able to hold 800 gallons of water. Numbers 4866 and 4868, built in February 1936, were delivered directly 'ex-Works' to Newton Abbot; to be joined in very short order by 4870. Although 4868 was soon transferred to Exeter, the arrival by January 1938 of Nos. 4829 and 4865 boosted the stock (the latter having been allocated 'new' to the sub-shed at Ashburton almost two years previously). In 1946 the designation '4800' class was changed to '1400' class, with the locomotives being renumbered accordingly: thus 4866 became 1466 and so on.

The great operating and time saving advantage of auto trains was that the engine remained at one end of the train: there being a driver's compartment at the front of the coach (a vehicle generally referred to as a 'trailer'). Thus an auto-fitted locomotive could either pull or push its train, avoiding the need to run the engine round at the end of the journey. This was made possible by replicating all the essential controls in the trailer's driving compartment. The regulator handle mounted above the centre window of the compartment was connected to that in the engine's cab by means of a transmission rod running beneath the coach. Some men preferred to stand for part or all of a journey, though a tip-up seat was provided on the right side of the compartment - on which were the other controls - so maintaining the Great Western tradition of right-hand drive. The driver was able to progressively apply the train's brakes by working the short 'brake application valve' handle. There was also a large floor-mounted ratchet-type hand brake at the front-centre of the compartment. When a train was in 'push' mode - the engine propelling the trailer(s) - the fireman was left in splendid isolation on the footplate. However, a system of electric bell codes permitted communication between the guard's vestibule, driver's compartment and footplate (using seven recognised codes). Being at the head of the train, it was important for the driver to be able to use the loco's whistle. This was achieved by means of a steel wire that ran from the front of the cab, through the trailer(s) in a cylindrical housing, to a chain

Two representatives of the '1400' 0-4-2 class of tank engine are seen in the Bay platform at Newton Abbot. The 6.15pm stopping train to Exeter via the Teign Valley waits at the back of the Bay (Platform 9) headed by No. 1468 (one of the class fitted with top-feed apparatus). Sister engine 1472 has just taken on water prior to working the 6.05 Moreton service, which will leave from the Bay also. The 'Castle' class loco (5053 *Earl Cairns*) is standing in Platform 5, having arrived with a freight from Goodrington Yard, Paignton (the final leg of the 'diagram' for the loco which earlier had hauled the 'down' 'Torbay Express' to Kingswear). Platforms 7 and 8 are occupied by 4-6-0 No. 6938 *Corndean Hall* and Standard 4-6-0 Class 5 No. 73029 with the 2pm Penzance to Crewe 'Perishables'. 6.8.57.   *Peter W. Gray*

draped above the right-hand window of the driver's compartment. A gong was fitted to the upper 'off-side' face of the trailer as an additional means of warning when the train was being propelled. It was activated by a foot-operated pedal just to the right of centre, between the handbrake and sanding lever. Gravity-fed sanding equipment was provided for 'coach-first' running (a facility that required the fitting of guard-irons to protect the leading bogie wheel). One very marked feature of the trailers was their large oval buffers, their size being necessary to offset any possibility of buffer-locking on tight branch line curves.

The only passenger access to the coach was via a single door. This opened into the guard's vestibule, which separated the smoking and non-smoking saloons; closed off from both by sliding doors. The walls of the vestibule were festooned with all manner of items: a large tin first aid cabinet; two conical flag holders; two coat hooks; two hinged wooden ticket boxes; a rack for destination boards; and a letter rack for inter-station correspondence. There was also a tip-up seat and light-switch housing, along with an electric bell-push which permitted coded communication between the guard and locomen. Retractable steps for use at low platforms or from rail level were manually operated by levers just inside the doors. When giving the 'right away' from stations, the Company's rule book instructed guards to so inform the driver only by means of the bell communication and not the whistle and green flag normally used on other trains. To do this, he gave a single ring on the bell-push (meaning 'Start'), which repeated in the driver's compartment.

In terms of seating, the trailers in use in Great Western days showed more in the way of variety. The open-plan saloons were third class only, and fitted with both transverse and longitudinal seats. The differences lay in the relative proportions allocated to the type of accommodation, and in the location of the guard's vestibule. Some trailers had a greater emphasis on transverse rather than longitudinal seats; other had smaller smoking saloons; and others still were fitted with hinged seat-backs, so that it was always possible for the passenger to face the direction of travel. Ceiling straps were provided between the longitudinal seats for standing passengers, as the central aisle was wider there.

The open plan nature of the saloons was clearly a great benefit to the guard, giving him an immediate over-view of the whole carriage and direct access to the passengers. Regulations required him to "announce the names of stations and halts to the passengers in the cars in a CLEAR AND DISTINCT VOICE just before reaching the stations or halts." This accessibility was of course mutual, something for which one person at least was grateful. At Heathfield, connections could be made between the Moreton Branch and Teign Valley line to Exeter. On one occasion, as the Branch train began to move off, an elderly lady asked the guard what time it was expected to reach Exeter. "Oh, my dear, you'm in the wrong train" he replied. Rushing to the window in the vestibule, he yelled out to the Teign Valley train - which was also leaving - to stop; which it promptly did. Both trains then backed up, and the lady duly transferred. On many auto-worked lines, guards issued tickets to passengers joining trains at halts and unstaffed stations. On the Moreton Branch, this was not the case; a notice displayed in the trailers stating that: "Passengers joining Rail Motor Cars and trains at Stations must obtain tickets at the booking office." However, to cover the eventuality of a passenger leaving a train without a ticket where no platform staff were in attendance, guards were provided with an Excess Fares pad, on which details of the fare were made out: there was no such thing as a free ride! Monies collected in this way were paid in at the booking office at Moretonhampstead, this station being the guards' 'base'.

An interesting variation on the push-pull theme was found on the Branch from the early 1930s to mid '40s; namely, the use of a 'Clifton Down' two-carriage set. The low-roofed, square-ended coaches had been adapted for auto working from existing non-corridor stock. As the first of the ten sets so modified was put to work on the Clifton Down Line between Bristol and Avonmouth, that location gave its name to the arrangement. Whereas all conventional trailers were provided with a driver's compartment - to allow them to be run singly or in pairs - the Clifton Down type ran as a two-set in a fixed relationship. The 50 foot-long, 8-compartment composite (ie 1st and 3rd class) non-driving coach was marshalled next to the engine. The other vehicle was a 51 foot-long brake all-third coach, containing five compartments. These were succeeded by the guard's vestibule, adjoining which was the luggage compartment, and finally that for the driver. Although the coaches were shorter than the saloon type, their non-corridor, or suburban, design gave a higher seating capacity. The set which was regularly used on the Branch consisted of non-driving coach number 3275 and brake coach, with driving compartment, number 3331.

The Last Years: 1939 - 1959

The outbreak of war marked the end of the long domination of the '45xx' 2-6-2s on Branch passenger trains in favour of auto-fitted locomotives. The period 1939-43 saw the reappearance, and swan-song, of the 2-4-0 'Metropolitan' tank engines: in particular numbers 3581, 3582, 3587 and 3590 (all of 1899 vintage). Working alongside the recently-built Collett 0-4-2s - notably numbers 4827 and 4839 - the motive power of these years was truly "ancient and modern". With a substantial military presence in the locality, the normal carriage allocation of Branch trains was frequently augmented to deal with the increased numbers of passengers. On a number of occasions between 1941 and 1944 it was common to see coaches 3275 and 3331 of the Clifton Down set combined with a conventional auto trailer, with the engine in between. As trailers, or auto cars, moved widely around the system, many and varied were the ones that saw service on the Branch. Some stayed longer than others to become 'regulars' for a few years. In the late 1940s and early '50s this was the case with numbers 148 and 155. Both were conversions from earlier steam railmotors. Dating from 1927, they were 70 feet long with seating for 82 and 77 respectively. For the greater part of the 1950s, trailers 224 and 234 were often to be seen, these 64-foot, 66 seater all-steel versions having been purpose-built in 1951. Their place was taken right at the end of the Line's life by numbers 240 and 241 of the 1953 series. Depending on the availability of locomotives, it sometimes happened that non auto-fitted engines were assigned to the Branch. In such circumstances, trailers had to be treated as conventional coaching stock for operational purposes: that is, loco-hauled in both 'up' and 'down' directions.

The nationalisation of the railways saw the progressive introduction of new liveries on the Branch as locomotives and coaching stock went in for repainting. During the second half of the war, the rather basic Great Western roundel (or 'shirt button') monogram had been replaced by the initials 'GWR' on the tank sides of the green-liveried locomotives. These now came back 'ex-Works' in plain black and displaying the new 'Hungry Lion' crest. Consisting of a golden lion standing astride a red wheel and black banner proclaiming in white letters BRITISH RAILWAYS, this logo was more popularly nicknamed the 'lion on wheel' or, more tongue in cheek, the 'ferret and dartboard'. The auto trailers displayed either an all-over maroon of the early war years, or the traditional two-tone livery, which for so long had been their hallmark: but this was not the familiar chocolate and cream of the GWR, but carmine and cream (below and above the waist respectively). This colour scheme was more graphically described by some as 'strawberry and cream' or more irreverently by others as 'blood and custard'. In either format, the roof was painted grey (in pre-war days it had been white, but was toned down to be less conspicuous).

The exclusive use of auto trains continued well beyond nationalisation, although the legacy of the railmotors was still to be seen in railway working timetables, where push-pull trains were frequently referred to as 'Motor' or 'Rail Motor'. It was only from the autumn of 1953 that what the timetables denoted as 'passenger' workings were insinuated into the regime: namely, non auto-fitted compartment coaches, which ruled out the push-pull mode of operation. Sometimes these trains were made up of all-third class accommodation, while at other times a composite coach (1st /3rd) was substituted for one of the thirds. The formation could either be made up of two 'brake ends', or one non-gangwayed 'compartment' and one 'brake'; while in the last few years, corridor vehicles also occasionally appeared. These last, like the trailers, carried the new carmine and cream livery. The non-gangwayed stock, both ex GWR and British Railways standard types, were painted maroon; again with grey roofs.

Just as a few of the standard corridor coaches turned up on the Branch in the last years, so too did one class of BR's standard locomotives. Built to a Swindon design, the Class 3 lined-black mixed traffic tank engines were introduced in 1952. A number of these 74-ton 2-6-2s were allocated to Newton Abbot in 1955/6. Indeed, eleven of them were present during the operation of 1955's summer timetable: numbers 82001/2/4/5/6 and 9; and 82031/32/33/34 and 38. They were principally employed on the main line, covering stopping trains to Exeter and Paignton/Kingswear, as well as some of the Torbay portions of up-country expresses. Additionally, some found their way on to the Moretonhampstead Branch. When run in conjunction with the trailers, the non auto-fitted 2-6-2s had to run round the coaches at both ends of the journey. Much less frequently, the Standards appeared on the Branch 'pick-up' goods train, as did 82009 on 1st August for example - on which day (Bank Holiday Monday) the passenger trains were worked by 82002 and 82034. The latter, along with sister engine 82033, had the longest of an otherwise brief sojourn of the class at Newton Abbot; being allocated new to the depot in January 1955 and remaining until the autumn of the following year. While 82034 was one of the four Standards subsequently sent to Wellington in Shropshire, 82033 was one of the five despatched to Treherbert in the Rhondda Valley, and among the last to go. By way of exchange, Newton Abbot received from South Wales a few of the '51xx' class of 2-6-2 tank engines.

Like the '45xx' 2-6-2s described earlier in the chapter, the '51xx' class was also designed by G.J. Churchward and introduced in 1906. At 78 tons 9 hundredweight, they were

Completed in November 1936 'large Prairie' No. 4117 was initially assigned to Newton Abbot Shed, although would not have worked on the Branch at that time. The engine's principal association, however, was with Taunton shed. Brief spells of duty at Exeter prior to, and after, her short latter-day appearance at Newton saw her back in Taunton in August 1960, from where she was withdrawn in September the following year. In this picture she is seen approaching the road overbridge at Wray Barton, approximately midway between Lustleigh and Moretonhampstead on the last day of passenger trains on the Branch. 28.2.59.

Peter F. Bowles

significantly heavier than their '45xx' cousins; and with generally greater dimensions were distinguished from them by the appellation: 'large Prairie'. Though looking similar, there were sufficient variations within the 'large Prairie' family of engines to warrant a sub-division into four classes: 31xx, 51xx, 61xx, and 81xx (to further complicate matters, the designation '51xx' also included the 41xx number series: 4100-4179!). These Class 4 mixed traffic engines were by no means strangers to Newton Abbot, its shed having an allocation of eight or nine in the late 1940s/early '50s. They were used on some of the 'local' passenger services between Exeter and Kingswear, as well as for banking purposes at Aller Junction and Totnes. Their first appearance on the Branch - north of Heathfield at least - did not take place until the first day of the winter timetable of 1956/7: Monday 17th September. On that day, the passenger services were worked by 5174 and 5196; while a few days later it was the turn of 4176 and 5183 to share the duties with an 0-4-2 auto engine. They continued to feature until the passenger service was withdrawn.

The year 1956 also saw developments in the rolling stock scene. In June, after a gap of approximately fifty years, the second class category of carriage accommodation was reintroduced and third class abolished. In more egalitarian times, a 1st/2nd classification was deemed more appropriate than 1st/3rd. Following this came changes in livery. Most notably, this brought about the demise of the erstwhile carmine and cream of the early British Railways period in favour of a lined maroon livery (on newer main line vehicles it also saw a

return to the traditional chocolate and cream of Great Western days). This was only a gradual transition, however, as stock went into the Works for their scheduled overhaul; and the 'early BR' colour scheme could still be seen on the Branch right up to the end. The plain maroon non-corridor (or suburban) coaches were neatly lined-out with yellow bands above and below the windows, this simple cosmetic expedient smartening them up considerably. So it was that by the late 1950s all sorts and conditions of coaches could be seen on the Branch, especially on summer Sundays and bank holidays when more substantial trains were run.

Along with the livery changes came a new emblem. The now familiar 'Hungry Lion' was replaced by a more discreet beast and wheel. The same elements were indeed incorporated, along with the addition of a crown; but the overall effect seemed less eye-catching. Unruffled by all the motive power and rolling stock changes of the British Railways era, the pattern of services remained remarkably constant. But this predictability was soon to be rudely shattered. As a sign of things to come, regular travellers on the Branch became disquietingly conscious of the withdrawal of the Teign Valley passenger trains in June 1958. Could their Line be next? Many also noticed the appearance, the following month, of a 350 horsepower 0-6-0 diesel shunter in the New Yard at Newton Abbot - a hint that the days of steam were numbered. As it sadly turned out, this was indeed to be the last summer for the Moretonhampstead Branch passenger trains, and thus they remained the preserve of steam to the end.

BR Standard Class 3 No. 82034 2-6-2 tank engine on an 'up' train at Bovey. The loco was delivered 'new' to Newton Abbot in January 1955 and remained until September the following year.

Hugh Ballantyne

Chapter Five

ALARMS AND EXCURSIONS

A familiar inter-war scene every summer at Bovey. The GWR's own fleet of charabancs, which the Company referred to as 'Road Motor Cars', are waiting for the next train from Newton Abbot. On the right, XY 2110 advertises 'Bovey, Becky Falls & Manaton', T 7692 'Haytor Rocks' and the vehicle behind it 'Princetown'. The corrugated iron waiting shelter for the use of bus passengers is behind vehicle L 6307. In the centre of the scene, keeping a supervisory eye on proceedings, is station master George Haywood. Circa 1925.   *Photomatic Ltd*

PART 1: ALARMS

Interspersed with the normally uneventful daily routine, the Branch had its moments of drama and excitement. Some of the incidents were due to human or mechanical failings and others to the vagaries of the elements.

Runaways

As far as human error was concerned, one such example occurred almost at the very outset of the Line's life. On Saturday 9th March 1867 came the first recorded runaway - one of several in the early years. The mixed passenger and goods trains of the time were generally lightly loaded, but the pulling power and braking ability of the tank engines provided by the South Devon Railway were severely tested on the 1½ mile climb at 1:49 north of Lustleigh. The rolling stock of the 3.35pm from Newton Abbot on that day consisted of two carriages, two goods wagons and a brake van. Leaving Lustleigh on time (4pm) the loco laboured up the gradient with increasing

difficulty. It finally ground to a halt on the stretch of line opposite East Wray. The footplate crew were unable to build up a sufficient head of steam to move the train forwards, and consequently decided to lighten the load. As the goods vehicles were at the rear of the train, the men resolved to uncouple them and leave them behind while they continued with the coaches the remaining two miles to Moretonhampstead, and then come back for them. Unfortunately, the brakes on the trucks were not applied sufficiently beforehand, and as soon as they were uncoupled began to run back down the grade, gaining speed all the time. They clattered through Lustleigh station at an estimated speed of around 40 mph, the clerk-in-charge hurriedly telegraphing Bovey to alert the staff there to open the level crossing gates. At least, with only one locomotive in service on the Line, there would be no danger of a collision with another train, but no-one could predict where the wagons might come to a stop, or even if they would hold the track. Hold the track they did, however, and duly rattled through Bovey.

Immediately beyond the level crossing, the gradient changed

to 1:66 up - the first rising gradient encountered by the runaway. This certainly slowed it down, but not sufficiently to prevent it reaching and cresting the summit by the Ashburton Road bridge. The renewed descent was only brief, and another rise beyond Granite Siding helped reduce speed once more. Even so, the vehicles only finally came to a halt at Teigngrace, eight miles from where their 'release' had begun. The hapless train crew, meanwhile, dismayed at the sight of half their charge disappearing from view, had been powerless to do anything about it. All they could do was to continue with the two carriages to the terminus. At this date, there was no intermediate telegraphic communication between Bovey and Teignbridge level crossing - the stations at Heathfield and Teigngrace had yet to open. Having ascertained that the runaway had gone through Bovey, the crew set off 'light engine' to find out just how far beyond that place the wagons had managed to get. Seeing the wagons standing at Teigngrace must have come as a great relief to the pursuing enginemen, who had doubtless imagined all sorts of possible horrific consequences - for themselves as much as the wagons! With the two reunited, the loco set off once more for Moretonhampstead.

The usual reason for these early-day runaways was the mode of shunting carried out at Lustleigh. With almost all of that place's goods traffic originating from the south, trains from Newton Abbot were called upon frequently to either put off vehicles in the siding or allow for unloading at the platform (on which was the small goods shed). The former operation was not a straightforward affair, for the yard was served by a single dead-end siding facing trains from Newton. Incoming traffic was marshalled next to the engine on leaving Bovey, and on arrival at Lustleigh the driver brought the train to a stand in advance of the siding points. The brake in the guard's van was screwed down to secure the wagons before the inward vehicle/s were detached from the rest of the formation. In the absence of a run-round facility, the engine could not enter the siding as it would be trapped there, so it was uncoupled from the trucks and attached instead by a long rope. The loco then drew forwards over the points, taking up the extensive slack in the rope, until the trucks also began to move forwards. Once the engine was clear of the points, they were switched for the yard, the loco continuing until the taut rope drew the wagons into the siding. Their brakes were then applied, the rope detached, and the points changed back to the main line. The loco now set back until it was clear of the points, which were then reset, and it entered the siding to propel the wagons as far along it as required before rejoining the rest of the train out on the main line.

This all seems fine in theory until one considers the conditions on the ground. Although the station and siding were conveniently on the level, the gradient changed to 1:50 down at the south end of the layout, so that the security of the rest of the train out on the main line depended upon the ability of the brake van to hold it. On one celebrated occasion, the guard failed to apply his brake adequately, so that while the engine was going through the procedure described above, the rest of the train began to roll backwards down the bank. An urgent message was telegraphed to Bovey to warn them of the runaway. A member of the permanent way staff there, possibly recalling the earlier incident, realised that although the wagons would come through the station at some speed, they would be slowed as they traversed the rise beyond. He hurried along the Line towards the Ashburton Road bridge to await the runaway, and as the wagons trundled past, displayed remarkable foresight and presence of mind in pinning down as many of the brake handles as possible as the wagons rattled past him. In this way, the runaway was actually brought to a stand before the last vehicle had cleared the bridge, and thus prevented possibly serious consequences further along the line. After this incident, shunting manoeuvres in the yard at Lustleigh were confined solely to 'up' trains - that is, those travelling from Moreton - with the only exception to this being if a banker was employed on a 'down' freight.

The Lost Train

One evening early in March 1953 the last scheduled service of the day - a 'down' passenger train from Newton Abbot to Moretonhampstead - pulled away from Bovey, on time, at 8.31pm. As its red tail-light curved away towards the river bridge, the signalman sent two beats on his block instrument to inform his colleague at Moreton that the train was 'entering section'. It was due at the terminus at 8.52, with the locomotive booked to leave again eight minutes later to return 'light' to the motive power depot at Newton. Given the steepness of the climb beyond Lustleigh, railwaymen would not be surprised if a train was a little late reaching its destination, but when the 'train out of section' bell had not been received from Moreton after an unusually long time had elapsed, it gave rise to some concern. The signalmen conferred by telephone. Time passed; but still no train. As Lustleigh station was unstaffed in the evening, there was no way of knowing whether the train was on the Bovey side or the moorland section beyond. It was decided to inform the two station masters. On arriving at the Bovey station master's house at 9.30pm, the flustered signalman was told that Mr. Yendall was at his brother's helping with wall-papering, and was directed there. Preoccupied with such matter-of-fact domestic chores, the last thing Arthur expected that evening was to go chasing around darkened country lanes looking for a lost train!

With the train somewhere north of Bovey, the problem was how to locate it. Given the long association of the Railway with the nearby taxi firm of Moir & Davie, Arthur asked Reg Moir if he would drive him along the route in one of his cars to search for the train. He agreed. By now it was 9.50pm and still no word had been received from the train crew as to their whereabouts. The only option was to follow the Line as closely as possible. Thus Messrs. Yendall and Moir set off along the pitch-black, narrow, hedge-lined lanes to Hawkmoor Halt. Arriving at the remote platform, they found that the single oil lamp had been turned out, indicating that the train must have called. Continuing along the lanes north of the halt, seeking to gain glimpses of the Line wherever possible, they eventually arrived at Lustleigh - to be met by the same darkened, empty scene there. However, they were able to ascertain from residents that the train had called at the usual time, and departed for Moreton. Once out on the A382, their task was made easier as the road ran close to, or at least within sight of, the railway. It was on this moorland section that the train was eventually spotted amongst some trees, the carriage lights shining out of the darkness. Armed only with a small cycle lamp for illumination, Arthur set off across the fields, to find to his dismay that a wide stream interrupted his mission; creating a rather soggy end to his adventure. Arriving at the stricken train, he was soon joined by his colleague from Moreton who had walked the line from the terminus.

The 1:49 rising gradient had proved too much for the 0-4-2 tank engine. It had been experiencing problems with free-steaming earlier in the day, and the steep bank had over-taxed it, causing a complete failure. When it became obvious that the locomotive was not going to be able to move, the fireman set off on the long walk to Moretonhampstead to arrange for a relief engine to be sent from Newton Abbot to assist the stranded train. The guard walked back along the line to place detonators to protect the rear of the train; while the driver was out with his flare lamp looking around the engine to see what might be wrong, and "to see that nobody pinched it" as he rather irritably put it when asked what he had been doing. With no likelihood of an early rescue, the passengers decided to make their own way to Moreton, walking or, more accurately, stumbling along the track in the darkness until they reached the road. From this point, going under foot was much easier, and fortunately they were soon picked up by motor vehicles sent out from Moreton.

Snow

The exceptionally dry month of February 1891 might have lulled Devonians into thinking that they were getting off lightly that winter. The settled, if cold, anticyclonic conditions proved to be the calm before the storm, for the very next month the West of England was hit by what came to be known as the 'Great Blizzard'. Dartmoor is noted for its periodically heavy falls of snow, whipped into drifts by strong winds howling across the open, undulating topography. This time, low-lying areas received a battering as well. Drifting snow blocked the lanes up to hedge-height, becoming compacted and turning into ice. In the numerous locations where sunken lanes were a feature, the easiest way was to walk along the hedge tops, as the snow was thinnest there! If conditions were difficult for road users, so they were also for the Branch trains. Snow piled up underneath the road overbridges, presenting an impenetrable white 'plug'. A snowplough engine was sent out from Newton Abbot in an attempt to clear the Branch, but it became stuck in the drift that had accumulated beneath the bridge at Heathfield station. Unable to move either backwards or forwards, a second engine had to be despatched to pull it clear. Old-fashioned muscle-power had to be used, with men in the permanent way gangs using shovels to dig out the deeper drifts before the snowplough could work through to shallower patches. It took almost a week to clear the full length of the Branch and enable the resumption of normal services. Many of the settlements in the upper Bovey Valley were cut off for up to two weeks, and even then could only be reached with difficulty. Snow lingered on the higher expanses of the Moor until June.

The next serious stoppage due to snow was in 1947. Snow began falling in the last week of January, and although amounts on the Moor were fairly large, the lower ground on the fringe got off lightly. Light snow showers by day alternated with very hard frosts at night, bringing about a slow but progressive accumulation. Trains ran with no real problems, other than icy rails first thing in the morning, causing footplatemen to resort to a liberal use of the loco's sanding apparatus.

Then in the early hours of Thursday 30th, a strong easterly wind ushered in the worst blizzards since 1891. The heavy snowfall continued all morning, the biting wind piling up drifts three to four feet high. So heavy was it, that in just two hours all bus services in the area were withdrawn as roads became impassable, and although the Branch trains continued to run, the timetable increasingly suffered severe disruption. Later in the day the snow stopped and the last service train managed to leave Newton Abbot at 8.10pm as usual. Unfortunately it had begun snowing again, and on the higher, exposed moorland section of the Branch in particular, conditions quickly began to deteriorate. Instead of arriving at Moretonhampstead at the scheduled time of 8.55, the train did not turn up at the terminus until half-past midnight. The single auto coach was stabled on the 'engine release road' and the locomotive belatedly went 'on shed' for the night. Conditions were now so atrocious that the station was cut off from the outside world, forcing the train crew and signalman to spend the night at Station Master Tooley's house.

The men awoke to a scene of complete white-out. Lying snow was level with the top of the platform, while the auto coach was totally buried by a huge snow-drift. Even when points were dug out, it was so cold that when defrosted by steam they immediately froze again. Any notion of a train service was out of the question, so driver, fireman, guard and signalman settled down to playing cards to await the arrival of the snowplough engine. The only snowplough available in the area was at Newton Abbot, and as it was needed in the first instance on the main line, the card-game developed into a marathon session lasting some twelve hours, at the end of which, the snowplough had still not arrived. With the main line services between Newton Abbot and Exeter almost back to normal by the evening, it was only then that the snowplough could turn its attention to the Branch. It was not until 6am the following morning that the Line was clear throughout, although there was still much to do before services could resume. Throughout this time, the station site remained cut off from the town, and it was to be three days before the train crew and signalman were relieved. The footpath connecting the station master's house with the station itself was cleared or, more accurately, excavated. As Bob Tooley was a man of quite short stature, he could only be seen on the path by dint of his hat moving along the top of the trench! By the weekend, supplies of food at the house were beginning to run low, the inhabitants having to rely principally on stored potatoes for food and melted snow for water (the mains supply having frozen).

Conditions elsewhere on the Branch were not much better. At Lustleigh for example, the snow was also level with the top of the platform. Station staff and permanent way gangs had much arduous hand-and-foot-numbing work to do to clear platforms and approach roads, while frozen points and buried tracks at goods yards all continued to pose problems. Despite this, trains were soon running as normal; reflecting great credit on the dedication and professionalism of the personnel. Away from the Line, some moorland villages remained cut off as deep drifts blocked the lanes. As the blizzards had been nation-wide, there was wholesale disruption to long distance traffic. This gave the parcels office staff at Newton Abbot a literal headache when a consignment of twelve dozen day-old chicks travelling from Yorkshire to Moretonhampstead were delayed up-country by the bad weather. They had been due to arrive on Saturday 1st February, but in the event did not turn up until the Sunday evening, and consequently had an enforced ten-hour wait for a Branch train. Judging by the noise they were making, the chicks were none too pleased. The staff placed the boxes on racks near the hot water pipes, but although they might be kept reasonably warm they had not been fed for some time - a fact which resulted in an ever-growing an even louder protest. But that was not the only problem in the parcels office that night, for it was already playing host to eight boxes of rabbits, a crate of ducks and a pig, all similarly marooned and all hungry!

A sudden rise in temperature on Monday 3rd caused a rapid melting of snow on Dartmoor, with the result that flooding now occurred. However, this milder weather proved to be nothing but a brief respite in the Arctic phase, with more snow falling just two days later, to be followed by severe frost. The disruption to trains though was minimal, with services running more or less as normal - which was more than could be said for the buses, as the Newton Abbot to Chagford service had to terminate at Bovey due to the state of the road beyond. Snow showers, punctuated by periodic blizzards, continued into early March, and although the Newton Abbot snowplough was pressed into service on these occasions, the Branch trains managed to keep running - if not always to the published timetable. The next severe blizzards to afflict the locality came in the 'big freeze' of the winter of 1963/4. By this time, passenger trains on the Line had been withdrawn, but with the bus services in chaos, many people were caused to reflect with regret on the loss of their Railway.

Flood

The low-lying Bovey Basin lies in the rain shadow of the main Dartmoor massif. However, the two principal rivers draining the area, the Bovey and the Teign, rise at 1,400 feet or more on an expanse of moorland receiving about twice the average annual rainfall near sea level. Although the peat at the highest levels is able to absorb large quantities of water, the ground runoff into the head-streams has a quick response to rainstorms once it has become saturated. Thus, after long periods of wet weather, the short time lag between storm and river discharge means that river levels rise dramatically, with a consequent risk of flooding on low ground. Shallow flooding could be coped with, providing that trains proceeded with caution; but when the floodwater surged over the track with force, there was a possibility that ballast would be disturbed or even washed away, making the line unsafe.

The first disruption caused by floods occurred very early in the Line's history. Prolonged, heavy rain on Saturday 23rd March 1867 caused the level of the River Teign to rise with alarming rapidity. It was not long before the swollen river burst its banks along its lower course. The low-lying parts of the Line were inundated, with ballast being washed away in a number of places. The most seriously affected location was Teignbridge. The extent and depth of the floodwater delayed the departure of the last train of the day: the 7.45pm from Newton Abbot. It was not until 9pm that it pulled out of the station, Driver Marsh proceeding with great caution. On reaching the level crossing, the gate-keeper stopped the train and warned the driver not to continue. The water beyond the crossing was so deep that to carry on would have been imprudent, dangerous even, and so the train set back to Newton, where the two dozen or so passengers had to spend the night. This course of action, though inconvenient, proved to be the right one, for when the muddy water subsided, a section of track exceeding twenty yards in length just north of the crossing had been completely washed away by the force of the flood. On Sunday 24th, a large gang of workmen under the direction of M&SDR engineer Peter Margary began repairs to the line, enabling train services to be resumed the following Tuesday.

The most vulnerable place of all on the Moretonhampstead Branch is at the Kingsteignton Road bridge on the edge of Newton Abbot. South of here the Line runs alongside the River Teign which, although a little way inland from the heavily silted head of the estuary, is still tidal. The bridge marks the lowest point on the Branch, as the track dips below the road in order to avoid the latter being excessively embanked to give the necessary clearance (about 23 feet from rail level to the head of the arch). The substantial structure, built of limestone masonry with granite chippings, is specifically designed to allow for the possibility of flooding; there being two semi-circular lateral flood arches with spans of 14' 9" in addition to the three main 28' 6" arches (with the Line going through the central one). Whilst the bridge might be able to relieve the problem of flooding, it could not prevent it. The combination of high spring tides in the estuary and the River Teign in spate is a recipe for trouble, as the track lies only eight or nine feet above the high water mark of average tides. Minor flooding was commonplace near Newton Abbot, but occasionally conditions conspired to produce a major inundation, with the Branch line and adjoining goods yard awash to a considerable depth.

Serious inundations at Newton Abbot occurred in the winter of 1864/5 when the Line was under construction; in the spring of 1898; in December 1929; February 1938; October 1960 and December 1979. The 1960 flood was particularly serious. The autumn equinox is generally characterised by gales and high tides, and that year it occurred at a time of exceptionally wet and unsettled weather. The West Country generally was lashed by days of heavy rain. Almost 7½" fell on the eastern flanks of Dartmoor during September; this being almost a quarter of the average total for the whole year. Rivers dramatically rose to dangerously high levels, and on Saturday 1st October the Teign was no longer able to contain itself, and spectacularly overflowed its banks. At Teignbridge the turgid, swirling floodwater washed out a section of ballast north of the level crossing, causing

Situated on the floodplain of the nearby river, the layout at Bovey station was liable to periodic inundation. As a rule, the water depth was not very great - as here in December 1929 - although could disrupt services while the Permanent Way Gang checked the integrity of the ballast and ensured that the track itself was clear of obstruction.   *James Mann Collection*

a minor subsidence in the track. The crossing keeper found himself marooned as the waters rose around his cabin, and he had to be rescued by tractor. Much worse happened further downstream. In the East Gold Marshes, near the Kingsteignton Road bridge, the angry, debris-laden water surged into a large open-cast excavation belonging to Newton Abbot Clays Ltd. Situated alongside the Branch, and 100 feet deep in places, the force of the torrent was such that the side of the pit caved in, taking a hundred-yard stretch of the railway line and embankment with it. This severed both the Moreton Branch and surviving stub of the Teign Valley Line from the rest of the network, trapping 0-6-0 Pannier Tank number 3659 on the Heathfield side, where it had been in charge of the morning goods to Christow. Even with permanent way staff working round the clock, such major damage was going to take a long time to repair. Hundreds of tons of rubble were tipped into the breach to recreate and consolidate the track bed. It was planned to use 3659 to bring some of this material from Trusham, but by 15th October the engine was to be seen 'out of steam' in the

57

bay platform at Heathfield. It was not until Friday 4th November that the Line reopened for traffic - goods only at this date. The clay pit on the other hand was so severely affected that it never worked again - expensive machinery and equipment having to be abandoned in the flooded pit.

Another area vulnerable to ordeal by water was in the vicinity of Bovey Station. While tides were no longer a consideration here, the station occupied a low-lying site, so that when the River Bovey burst its banks, the resultant flooding could be extensive. The most serious instance during the Line's life was that of 1898. An earlier period of snow on the Moor turned to rain as the temperature rose. Combined snow-melt and continuing rainfall saw the River Bovey and its tributaries quickly rise on the moorland stretch above Lustleigh Cleave. So rapid was it in fact that it produced a surge down the narrow wooded valley, which then burst out across the floodplain near Bovey Bridge, north of the station. The force of the water was such that it caused damage to buildings in Station Road and flooded the ground to a depth of around three feet. At the station, water was up to the top of the platforms and train services were suspended until the level subsided. The 'Railway Hotel' (later renamed 'Dartmoor Hotel') provided accommodation for people in that part of town who were stranded. The river overflowed its banks on a number of subsequent occasions, but the resultant flooding was generally only shallow, although in 1938 the station layout was under about four feet of water. Trains were subject to delay while the ganger checked the track, but the disruption was never on the scale of the great 1898 inundation.

Diversions

The Heathfield to Newton Abbot section of the Branch was used, in conjunction with the Teign Valley line, as a diversionary route for trains south of Exeter when the main line via the coast was blocked for some reason or other. This useful function had been made possible by the remodelling of the junction layout at Heathfield in October 1916, although it was another five years before the facility was called upon. Just before midday on 22nd September 1921 an 'up' express from Plymouth overran the 'up home' signal at Dawlish and ran into the local Exeter to Hackney goods train which was making its way over the crossover at the western end of the station. Fortunately the collision took place at low speed, and although no-one was hurt, the main line was blocked for around eight hours. Torquay Line trains were diverted over the Teign Valley/Moreton Branch, while those for Plymouth and Cornwall ran over the London & South Western Line via Okehampton.

Mercifully, accidents on the main line were extremely rare; it was 'acts of nature' that caused trains to be diverted on subsequent occasions. The soft, red, variegated sandstone cliffs backing the railway between Dawlish Warren and Teignmouth may form an attractive accompaniment to a train journey, but their very nature makes them notoriously unstable. There were a number of landslips on this section in the inter-war years, the most serious of which took place in March 1923. A cliff fall between Parson's Tunnel and Sprey Point on the morning of Monday 12th necessitated the diverting of trains in the manner described above until a little after midday on Wednesday. After this time, single line working for some of the passenger services was introduced, with goods trains continuing to run over the diversionary route until the main line was fully reopened on Thursday 22nd. During this period, the Teign Valley signal boxes - along with Heathfield and Teignbridge Crossing - were kept open 24 hours a day (except on the Sunday). Some of the other, less serious, landslips also required the Teign Valley route to be pressed into service, though for shorter periods of time.

Just as unpredictable as the terrestrial incidents on the coastal section were storms at sea. The main line was particularly vulnerable during south-easterly gales, when the largest waves experienced on this stretch of coastline were generated. Heavy seas on Christmas Eve 1929 made it necessary to introduce single line working here, but this proved to be only a forerunner of worse to come. Late in the evening of Saturday 4th January, a severe gale began to batter the line to such an extent that the sea wall at Dawlish was dangerously undermined, causing trains to be diverted via the Teign Valley and 'Southern' routes for the next three days. Another major storm on Monday 10th February 1936 was so severe that it whipped up the otherwise calm waters of the Exe estuary normally protected by the sand spit of Dawlish Warren. This proved too much for the low river wall at Powderham, which suffered a serious breach. Amazingly, the sea wall remained intact during this prolonged battering. Late in 1945 the estuary was afflicted once more. On 18th December both 'up' and 'down' tracks were damaged at Starcross, causing trains to be diverted over the usual two routes: between 8.30pm and 2.30pm the next day. The weather was in an angry mood, and just two days later, heavy seas damaged the wall at Starcross again and also at Dawlish., requiring the customary diversions to be made: between 8.45am and 6pm that day. The closure (in June 1958) and prompt lifting of the Teign Valley Branch north of Christow meant that when the main line was next closed - due to track and platform damage at Dawlish by a heavy storm on Wednesday 7th March 1962 - the Western Region of British Railways no longer had recourse to this useful facility.

War

The two world wars impressed themselves on the life of the Railway, and the communities it served, by the frequent coming and going of people in uniform: of joyous home-comings and sad farewells. As a rural branch line with no strategic significance, it fortunately escaped any physical damage, although during the Second World War did have a few close calls. The first of these was at Bovey in 1940 when a land mine was dropped near St. Mary's Church, the blast shattering windows both there and in the town. Another came in 1942 when an enemy bomber returning home jettisoned a large number of incendiary bombs as it flew over the railway. These fell to the ground some two miles west of Bovey station - in Yarner Wood - where they caused serious fire damage to an area of great commercial value and arboreal interest (the latter being recognised when the woodland became a nature reserve in 1952). On another occasion, a German plane fired its canon in the direction of the railway, but with no injurious consequences other than superficial damage to the notice boards near the level crossing caused by falling shell cases. Further north, the Moretonhampstead ganger was not a little perturbed when walking his length one morning to find an unexploded bomb in Caseley Cutting near Lustleigh. Doubtless jettisoned by an aircraft desiring a quick get-away, it disrupted train services for a time while the Army was called in to deal with it.

More seriously, was the damage and disruption caused at Newton Abbot. Two German bombers attacked the railway layout here just before 6.45 pm on the evening of August 20th 1940. In addition to track damage, all the buildings on the 'down' island platform were destroyed and those on the 'up' side damaged, notably the refreshment room. There was also slight damage to 'West' signal box. Tragically, four railwaymen and ten members of the public were killed. Train services on both the main line and Moreton Branch were disrupted as a result of this attack. Another air raid took place on 25th April 1942. Although there was serious damage in the town and around nearby Devon Square and Torquay Road, the only problem suffered by the Railway was broken windows in 'East' signal box, the goods shed and buildings in Hackney Yard.

During the war years, the Branch locomotive was still

shedded overnight at Moretonhampstead, although it was customary to fill up the coal bunker at Newton Abbot prior to leaving with the last 'down' train of the day. However, on one evening an air raid alert sounded, so it was decided to despatch the train straight away without coaling the engine. Not only was the loco's reserve of coal already very low, but that particular day its normal load was increased - albeit slightly - by dint of a box van attached to the coaching stock. The journey to Bovey was uneventful, but with the steep climb ahead, the footplatemen knew they would have their work cut out. Pulling away from Lustleigh, it became clear that they were in for trouble. By the time they reached Caseley Cutting the already struggling tank engine slipped herself to a standstill, sending sparks cascading into the inky blackness of the night sky. With the probability of enemy aircraft about, the crew were worried that their train was a sitting duck, while the fireman gloomily reported that there was not enough coal for them to continue much further. After further bouts of slipping, with all the accompanying worrying pyrotechnics and painfully slow progress, Driver Sam Pearce was forced to capitulate, and brought the train to a stand on the embankment beyond the cutting. Explaining the predicament to the guard and the mere handful of passengers on the train that night, it was resolved that more fuel had to be found. Presaging a sequence in an Ealing Comedy film, they all scrambled down the embankment and went into the nearby woods to collect brushwood, branches and saplings - anything in fact that would burn - to supplement the almost non-existent coal supply. Fuel was taken back to the engine and flung into the firebox. Gradually the needle on the steam pressure gauge began to rise, until Sam judged that it was high enough to attempt to restart the train: an undertaking which was not made any easier by being stuck on the steepest section of the entire Branch. To everyone's delight and relief, the loco held her feet and slowly but surely moved onwards and upwards towards the terminus, where its long overdue arrival had been giving Station Master Hawkes considerable anxiety.

The prudence of having an alternative route for main line trains between Exeter and Newton Abbot saw the Teign Valley line and Moreton Branch south of Heathfield kept open 24 hours a day from 1941 until the end of the war. In order to accommodate the longer trains - by Branch standards - which might be expected to divert over the route, the platform loops at Heathfield station were lengthened, while a double-track junction was installed (May 1943).

As the war progressed, the Armed Forces developed a significant presence in the area. Several large properties were requisitioned for military use: such as the Manor House Hotel near Moretonhampstead; Parke House at Bovey; Ugbrooke House near Chudleigh; and Stover House near Teigngrace. Virtual towns of Nissen huts sprang up in the Heathfield-Knighton Heath area, with a fuel dump at the latter being provided with sidings at the direction of the Ministry of Works (in August 1943) and connected to the Teign Valley line. A huge American military hospital was built at Ilford on the Stover Estate, and in the months following D-Day (June 1944), ambulance trains became an all too familiar feature. Those from the east travelled via the Teign Valley, often at night. Waiting ambulances conveyed the wounded men either from Chudleigh or Heathfield stations the short distance to Ilford, while the empty carriage stock of these trains continued to Newton.

As was to be expected at such a time of upheaval, there were several reasons why people needed to travel - even if posters posed the question as to whether or not a journey was really necessary. Every station on the Branch saw an upturn in the number of passengers using the trains during the years of the conflict. Not only were there more journeys, but the average distances travelled also increased. This was reflected in the higher revenue engendered. With such a large military presence in the Heathfield area, this station's accounts exemplify the wartime situation in relation to its pre-war context. Taking two respective years with almost the same number of ticket sales (excluding 'seasons'), the revenue produced during the war years was almost double. Thus 1935 saw 20,739 tickets sold, with a value of £714, while in 1944 the figures were 20,818 and £1,345. The number of season tickets in the latter year showed a five-fold increase, and reflected the increase in regular, largely short-distance commuting.

On many occasions during these years, Branch trains would be made up to three or four coaches. It was, perhaps, the arrival of the Americans that made the biggest impact of all in the locality. Troops from the United States were much in evidence in Moretonhampstead from the summer of 1942. Their compliment soon numbered some 2,000 men. The white troops were billeted in the town, while their coloured compatriots were housed in an extensive, less comfortable and distinctly breezy camp on Mardon Down to the north-east. The fear of antagonism between the two groups went beyond the segregated accommodation; even the 'nights on the town' followed a racially-determined, mutually-exclusive rota. On these nights all the pubs were packed, and it even produced revenue for the Railway. Numbers of women travelled out to Moreton in the evening, picked up a serviceman or two (or three), spent the night in the town and travelled back home the next morning. The greatly unbalanced male-female ratio occasionally caused disputes to break out, which generally ended in a fight, and once even in a stabbing (when one man was knifed in the back). This activity was frowned upon by many residents - especially when the same ladies returned again on the other group's night out.

PART 2 : EXCURSIONS

To the Victorian travel writer, Dartmoor was a wild and romantic place. Paintings and engravings frequently show exaggerated dimensions or perspectives, with heightened elemental forces often thrown in for good measure! One work on the Moor, published in 1888, was actually entitled 'Amid Devonia's Alps': sub-titled 'Wanderings & Adventures on Dartmoor'. This had been written by William Crossing, who also wrote 'Dartmoor'; 'Dartmoor Worker'; and 'A Hundred Years on Dartmoor'. These, together with works by Worth and others, helped to make the Moor known nationally. There had been a certain amount of tourism as early as the 1860s, but it was on a very small scale. The appearance of a growing number of books about the Moor made it all the more alluring, and the number of visitors began to increase. The early tourists were people with a sufficiency of time and money, or those to whom bleak, lonely and mysterious places had great appeal. The scenery of the Moor is indeed impressive, particularly for the scale and nature of the contrasts it offers: from the bleak, rolling heights with their rocky tor-crowned summits, to the wooded almost secretive valleys on the margin. The Moretonhampstead Branch made all this accessible.

As descriptions of the Moor became more widespread, so more people were enticed to see it for themselves; and the whole scenario became mutually reinforcing. The series of annual publications known as the 'Homeland Handbooks', which contained information for visitors to various parts of Britain, first appeared in 1897, with No. 8 in the series dealing with 'Dartmoor with its Surroundings'. Trips over the Moor in open horse-drawn coaches became popular from the late 1890s. By 1900 Bovey had become known as the 'Gateway to Dartmoor' and Chagford either as the 'Capital of Dartmoor' or the 'Torquay of Dartmoor' (the latter presumably an allusion to its having become a place of excursion for the well-to-do).

The new century saw the pace quicken. Neither the South Devon Railway nor the Great Western Railway had shown any understanding of, or interest in, the possibilities of the Moretonhampstead Branch as a tourist artery, feeding visitors to the Moor. However, recognition was beginning to dawn somewhere in 'headquarters' at Paddington, and was suddenly given impetus when, in June 1903, the rival London & South Western Railway inaugurated their own motor bus service between Chagford and Exeter, whence connections were made with Waterloo expresses. In spite of this threat, it took the GWR a little longer to get their act together, and it was not until 1906 that they provided a Company omnibus to run between Chagford and Moretonhampstead, connecting with the Branch trains. Three years later, they started a service across the Moor to Princetown. This was quite adventurous for the time, the laden bus crawling its way up the long hill out of Moreton to give its intrepid occupants a bone-shaking ride over the rough moorland roads of the day.

It was about this time also that day-tripping began in earnest, catering for ever-widening classes of people. Day trips from Torquay were particularly popular, with a number of beauty spots in close proximity to Branch stations. The walk to Lustleigh Cleave from the village was a favourite; alternatively, carriages could be taken from Bovey up to Haytor Rocks; or the bus from Moreton to Chagford. There was even an incredibly ambitious scheme put forward in 1905-6 to reopen the old Haytor Granite Tramway between the outskirts of Bovey and Haytor Rocks and run it as an electric tramway. The plan involved replacing the old stone setts with iron rails, and installing catenary wires. At the time, this was not considered as far fetched as it might seem now, for in the early years of the century some experimental work had been done to produce electricity from burning lignite to produce gas, which in turn

was used to convert water into steam to power turbines, and so produce electricity. There was a plentiful supply of both the requisite raw materials. For several decades attempts had been made to make commercial use of lignite ('Bovey Coal'); while in the case of the water supply, a leat had long been bringing water from above Becky Falls to Bovey Pottery pond, which was then drawn off to power the waterwheels. It was an exciting scheme and undoubtedly would have been a 'hit' with visitors, but it never got off the drawing board.

Once the GWR decided to promote the South West of England, it really got the bit between its teeth. It embarked on a series of publicity-style publications, which were to grow in scope and be joined later by wall posters and railway carriage picture displays. Thus, in 1906, the Company launched their 'Holiday Haunts', which continued until nationalisation over forty years later. It was in this, in 1908, that the slogan 'G.W.R. - The Holiday Line' first appeared (six years later this was imperiously modified to: 'G.W.R. The Nation's Holiday Line'). A number of travel books followed in 1912, although Devon was not initially included. In the years immediately before the Great War, the GWR put on a through-carriage service between Paddington and Moretonhampstead (as described in Chapter 3), and was also offering 'tourist tickets' from London to Dartmoor - a gloriously huge destination! These could be of the 'day return' variety, which included breakfast on the express from London. On arrival at Newton Abbot, Company transports were waiting to take the trippers for a short tour prior to stopping at one of the moorland hotels near Haytor for lunch. This was followed by an excursion around the famous sites, and included a stop for afternoon tea before returning to Newton. An evening meal was served on the journey back to London. By

All dressed up for a day at the seaside. Members of Bovey Tracey Baptist Church Sunday School congregate beneath the newly installed platform canopy in 1910 for their Anniversary outing. The diamond-shaped plaque bearing a capital letter T by the booking hall doorway indicates that the services of the S & T Department telegraph lineman are required.

Bovey Tracey Heritage Trust

way of an alternative, the ticket holder was given the option of a rail trip from Newton Abbot to either Bovey or Moretonhampstead, with a road tour starting from there. For those wishing to spend more than a day in the area, it was possible to make breaks of journey at specified locations. The tourist traffic now passing through Bovey was reflected in the building of the 'Refreshment Rooms' (later 'Tor Vue Cafe') by the level crossing.

The war years put a brake on tourist development, but then in 1923 the GWR began an expanded series of daily road excursions from Bovey and Moretonhampstead, using their own fleet of 'Road Motor' vehicles: largely Daimler-built charabancs. The most enduring venues were those operating from Bovey: the shuttle service to Haytor Rocks, and a circular tour taking in Haytor, Widecombe and Manaton - including a stop to view the scenery at Becky (or Becka) Falls. At the height of their popularity, trips were run as far afield as Tavistock, taking in the remains of the Bronze Age settlement at Grimspound and including a stop at Princetown. Another ran to Princetown via Lustleigh, Moretonhampstead and Two Bridges. The Company omnibuses continued to ply between Moreton and Chagford, with a summer-time addition to Postbridge and Two Bridges: both with their placid, boulder-strewn rivers and convenient hostelries set in the open expanse of central Dartmoor.

The Great Western's road motors brought in considerable revenue during these years, as the following examples from station accounts may suffice to show. In the first year for which records are available (1925) these vehicles carried 19,696 passengers from Bovey and 24,446 from Moretonhampstead/Chagford; earning £2,179 and £643 respectively. The volume increased at Bovey until the peak of 1928, when 30,817 people boarded the buses and paid a total of £2,352. Contrariwise, at Moreton/Chagford the numbers fell progressively, although there was an upward turn to 19,473 in 1929. From this year, numbers at Bovey also fell away sharply; sinking to 20,216 in 1932 - a figure that is still higher than 1925 but, significantly, only yielded a revenue of £715. To make matters worse, the road motors were now experiencing growing competition from charabancs running from some of the hotels in Bovey, as well as road tours direct from Newton Abbot, which cut out the need to travel on the Branch at all. Private motoring and expanding bus services were other factors in the decline. Thus 1932 proved to be the last year of the GWR's direct participation in the road motor venture, while it had sold the Chagford franchise to the Western National Omnibus Company three years before.

But this was by no means the end of the tourist contribution to the life of the Branch. Some of the routes formerly run by the Great Western vehicles were now taken over by private operators, notably Western National and J. Potter & Sons of Haytor Vale. As before, the vehicles would be parked on the station approach road at Bovey awaiting the arrival of trains from Newton Abbot - for which privilege their operators paid an annual concessionary fee to the Railway. The Western National Company pulled out of the Bovey venue after a few years, leaving only J. Potter to keep the tradition alive here. Potter's 'Tor Bus Service' was arranged as far as possible to dove-tail with the trains. There was no real problem in this regard when meeting 'down' trains, and passengers found the buses waiting on the approach road. If the latter were running late, the passengers had the use of a substantial corrugated iron waiting shelter, built specifically for the use of the earlier Road Motor

---

SPECIAL HOLIDAY SEASON TICKETS ARE ISSUED AT STATIONS IN THE WEST, AS SHEWN BELOW.

PASSENGERS :

Holders of Tourist Tickets and holders of Excursion Tickets available for one week or longer on presenting the backward portions of their Tickets at the Stations for which they were issued—as named in the first column below—can obtain for holiday purposes during their visit Special Holiday Season Tickets, available for as many journeys as desired between the Stations the Season Tickets embrace, as under :—

N.B.—Special Holiday Season Tickets are also issued for holiday purposes to Tourists with Tickets for places beyond, breaking the journey at the Stations shown as issuing these Special Tickets.

FARES FOR TOUR (No. 3.)

Monthly Fares.		Fortnightly Fares. (14 days)		Weekly Fares. (7 days)	
1st	3rd	1st	3rd	1st	3rd
36/-	21/-	24/-	14/-	16/-	10/-

Holders of TOURIST TICKETS and holders of EXCURSION TICKETS available for a week or longer to | DISTRICT COVERED BY HOLIDAY SEASON TICKET.

ASHBURTON	TORQUAY	STARCROSS
BOVEY	TORRE	TEIGNGRACE
BRIXHAM	PAIGNTON	HEATHFIELD
DARTMOUTH	CHURSTON	BOVEY
DAWLISH	BRIXHAM	LUSTLEIGH
MORETONHAMPSTEAD	KINGSWEAR	MORETONHAMPSTEAD
NEWTON ABBOT	DARTMOUTH	TOTNES
PAIGNTON	KINGSKERSWELL	STAVERTON
TEIGNMOUTH	NEWTON ABBOT	BUCKFASTLEIGH
TORQUAY †	TEIGNMOUTH	ASHBURTON
TOTNES	DAWLISH	

† Torquay Tourists can also obtain Holiday Season Tickets at Torre Station.

FARES FOR TOUR (No. 4.)

Monthly Fares.		Fortnightly Fares. (14 days)		Weekly Fares. (7 days)	
1st	3rd	1st	3rd	1st	3rd
26/-	15/-	18/-	10/-	12/-	7/-

TOURISTS AND EXCURSIONISTS (whose Tickets are available for a week or longer) to | DISTRICT COVERED BY HOLIDAY SEASON TICKET.

	TOTNES	GARA BRIDGE
	BRENT	LODDISWELL
ASHBURTON	WRANGATON	KINGSBRIDGE
KINGSBRIDGE	IVYBRIDGE	STAVERTON
TOTNES	CORNWOOD	BUCKFASTLEIGH
	PLYMPTON	ASHBURTON
	AVONWICK	

CYCLES :

Holders of the Special Holiday Season Tickets are permitted to take with them a Bicycle or Tricycle, for all journeys they make in the District, covered by the Holiday Season Tickets at the following charges (except on certain dates by the Cornish Riviera Limited Express Trains, particulars of which will be found in the Company's Time Books and Notices) :—

		Monthly Rate.		Fortnightly Rate.		Weekly Rate.	
		Bicycle.	Tricycle.	Bicycle.	Tricycle.	Bicycle.	Tricycle.
Tour 3	...	5/-	7/6	3/6	5/-	2/6	3/6
Tour 4	...	3/6	5/6	2/6	4/-	2/-	3/-

RAIL, RIVER & COACH EXCURSIONS.

NOTE.

In the following pages short particulars are given of a few of the Circular and other Trips, by Rail, River and Coach, that are available in the Shire of the Sea Kings.

Limited space does not admit of more than a brief summary of these trips being set out, but full information, and particulars of the many other delightful excursions run by or in conjunction with the Great Western Railway, are furnished in pamphlets which may be obtained at any of the Company's Stations and Offices.

COACHING EXCURSIONS ON DARTMOOR.

COACHES FROM BOVEY AND NEWTON ABBOT STATIONS.

Combined Rail and Coach Tickets are issued every week-day, May to October inclusive, at the following Stations for Bovey and Newton Abbot, from which places Coaching Excursions are run daily at the inclusive fares shewn :—

FROM			Inclusive fare for Rail and Coach Trip. s. d.	FROM			Inclusive fare for Rail and Coach Trip. s. d.
Brent	...	...	6 9	Kingswear	...	...	6 6
Brixham	...	...	6 6	Newton Abbot	...	...	5 0
Churston	...	...	6 0	Paignton	...	...	6 0
Dartmouth	...	...	6 6	Plymouth (Millbay)	...	...	7 0
Dawlish	...	...	6 0	,, (North Road)	...	...	7 0
Devonport	...	...	7 0	,, (Mutley)	...	...	7 0
Exeter (St. David's)	...	...	6 6	Starcross	...	...	6 0
,, (St. Thomas)	...	...	6 6	Teignmouth	...	...	5 6
Ivybridge	...	...	7 0	Tiverton	...	...	7 0
Keyham	...	...	7 0	Torquay	...	...	5 6
Kingsbridge	...	...	7 0	Torre	...	...	5 6
Kingskerswell	...	...	5 6	Totnes	...	...	6 3

Different routes over some of the most delightful parts of Dartmoor are covered daily, and, amongst other places, the following well known features of interest are visited :—BECKY FALLS, MANATON, HAYTOR ROCKS, BUCKLAND WOODS, HOLNE CHASE, etc., etc.

Tickets at the same fares as those shewn against Exeter, Torquay and Plymouth can be previously obtained at the G.W. Offices at 97, Queen Street, Exeter ; Vaughan Parade, Torquay ; 107, Old Town Street, Plymouth ; and 96, Fore Street, Devonport.

Proprietors of Coaches from Bovey Station—Messrs. HELLIER & LEE.

Proprietors of Coaches from Newton Abbot Station—

Messrs. THE NEWTON ABBOT COACHING CO.

For full particulars apply for Programme of Rail, River and Coach Trips obtainable free of charge at the Stations, or post free from the Superintendent of the Line, Paddington Station, W.

Table 9. G.W.R. ROAD MOTOR SERVICES : Summer 1914

In connection with the Company's Trains, Road Motor Cars are run between the places mentioned below : -

MORETONHAMPSTEAD STATION AND CHAGFORD (G.W.R. Office).
Passing Halfway House, Easton Cross (for Fingle Bridge), and Rock House.

WEEK DAYS ONLY

Moretonhampstead (Station)	9. 00	10. 40	12. 55	3. 50	4. 40	5W50	6. 40
Half Way House	9. 17	10. 57	1. 12	4. 07	4. 57	6W07	6. 57
Easton Cross	9. 23	11. 03	1. 18	4. 13	5. 03	6W13	7. 03
Chagford Moor Park Hotel	9. 35	11. 15	1. 30	4. 25	5. 15	6W25	7. 15
G.W. Office, Rock House	9. 37	11. 17	1. 32	4. 27	5. 17	6W27	7. 17

Chagford G.W. Office, Rock Hse	9. 00	9. 50	12. 10	3. 05	5. 05	6. 00	7W10
Moor Park Hotel	9. 02	9. 52	12. 12	3. 07	5. 07	6. 02	7W12
Easton Cross	9. 12	10. 02	12. 22	3. 17	5. 17	6. 12	7W22
Half Way House	9. 18	10. 08	12. 28	3. 23	5. 23	6. 18	7W28
Moretonhampstead (Station)	9. 40	10. 30	12. 50	3. 45	5. 45	6. 35	7W50

W : Will not run after September 12th

Single fares from Moretonhampstead Station to:

Sloncombe Lane	...	3d	Easton Cross ...	...	6d
Half Way House	...	5d	Chagford	...	9d

Daily during the Summer, Dartmoor Coaching Trips are run by Mr. H. J. Osborne, Rock House, Chagford, in connection with Motor Cars, leaving Rock House after arrival of Car due at 11. 17am.

Table 10. TOR BUS SERVICE : Operated by J. Potter & Sons, Tor Garage, Haytor.

SUMMER TIME TABLE (July 8th to September 29th, 1935)

BOVEY TRACEY - MANATON									
		Week Days					Sundays		
		am	pm	Pm	pm	pm	Am	pm	pm
BOVEY	dep	11. 00	1. 10	3. 10	4. 30	6. 25	11. 05	2. 40	4. 35
BECKY FALLS	arr	11. 20	1. 30	3. 30	4. 50	6. 40	11. 20	3. 00	4. 55
MANATON	arr	11. 25	1. 35	3. 35	4. 55	6. 50	11. 25	3. 05	5. 00

MANATON	dep	11. 45	2. 00	3. 40	5. 30	6. 50	11. 25	3. 15	5. 05
BECKY FALLS	dep	11. 50	2. 05	3. 45	5. 35	6. 55	11. 30	3. 20	5. 10
BOVEY	arr	12. 10	2. 25	4. 05	5. 55	7. 15	11. 45	3. 40	5. 30

BOVEY TRACEY - HAYTOR - WIDECOMBE										
Week Days										
BOVEY	10. 10	11. 00	11. 50	12. 45	1. 10	2. 35	3. 10	5. 20	6. 30	7. 20	7. 50
HAYTOR	10. 30	11. 20	12. 10	1. 05	1. 30	2. 55	3. 30	5. 40	6. 50	7. 40	8. 05
WIDECOMBE	10. 50	11. 37	-	-	1. 50	-	3. 45	-	-	-	-

WIDECOMBE	-	-	10. 50	11. 40	-	-	1. 15	1. 55	4. 45	5. 10	-
HAYTOR	9. 50	10. 35	11. 30	12. 00	-	12. 30	1. 30	2. 15	5. 00	5. 30	6. 50
BOVEY	10. 05	10. 50	11. 45	12. 15	-	12. 45	1. 45	2. 30	5. 15	5. 50	7. 10

Sundays										
BOVEY	11. 10	2. 40	3. 45	5. 40	7. 55	**W'COMBE**	-	1. 15	3. 50	5. 00	-
HAYTOR	11. 30	3. 00	4. 15	6. 00	8. 15	**HAYTOR**	10. 10	2. 15	4. 10	5. 20	6. 40
WIDECOMBE	-	3. 15	4. 30	-	-	**BOVEY**	10. 25	2. 30	4. 25	5. 35	7. 00

customers. Situated on the south side of the main station building, it was fitted out with wooden benches. It was less easy to guarantee a connection on the return journey. The train was generally on time, but the road vehicles could be subject to all manner of delays. On the occasions when the Tor Bus was running late, it would come racing down the road from Manaton or Haytor only to find all too often that the level crossing gates were closed across the road and the train already signalled out. Almost before the bus had come to a halt at the crossing, anxious passengers scrambled off and made a dash for the station, being funnelled through the narrow pedestrian wicket gate like sand through an hour-glass. However, they need not have worried, for once the bus had been spotted coming past Parke Lodge, the station staff would hold the train to allow the connection to be made.

If the reality of the motor vehicle was inescapable by the early 1930s, the GWR remained tireless in its campaign to attract passengers. Their promotional literature continued, including the famous 'Glorious Devon' poster. An interesting example of local initiative also occurred. Recognising the artistic talent of one of the parcels clerks at Torre station, the man was encouraged to paint colourful, eye-catching posters to publicise the Moretonhampstead and Teign Valley Branches. One such was of Haytor Rocks, with golden rays of sun in the background and the caption "HAYTOR CALLS YOU. Cheap day tickets to Bovey". (The artist was Arthur Yendall, later to become station master at Bovey.) Torbay was still a lucrative recruiting ground for day-trippers, and the Ward Lock Guide Books to Torquay in the mid 1930s described the Moreton Branch as the 'moorland railway'. A few of the Branch trains worked through from the Branch to Kingswear and back, making the trip as straightforward as possible by cutting out the delay caused by changing trains at Newton Abbot. Combined rail and road tours were popular at this time, one such in the summer of 1933 exemplifying the nature of these excursions. The adult fare for this particular tripartite tour was 3/3d (around 16 pence in modern currency):

Combined Rail and Road Tours from Torbay

Tour No. 11

Rail	-	Starting Station to Moretonhampstead
Road	-	Moretonhampstead to Easton Cross
Walk	-	Easton Cross to Fingle Bridge and back
Road	-	Easton Cross to Moretonhampstead
Rail	-	Moretonhampstead to Starting Station

Organised in association with the
Western National Omnibus Company

In addition to carrying people to a wide variety of holiday destinations, the Great Western Railway became involved in an even more direct way with the tourist/leisure industry. One element of this was the concept of the Camping Coach (or Camp Coach as they were initially referred to). It was in the summer of 1934 that one of these vehicles was first installed in the goods siding at Lustleigh - along with other attractive locations in the region. This novel form of holidaymaking is discussed in more detail in Chapter 15.

Overnight accommodation in a railway carriage in a very different league to the humble camping coach was provided by the Royal Train, which made three visits to the Branch; rather more than most rural lines could normally boast. The first of these was in 1937, in connection with King George VI's tour of Duchy of Cornwall property. Two locomotives were allocated to this substantial train: the 'train-engine' being 'Dean Goods' 0-6-0 tender engine No. 2327, and the assisting engine 'small Prairie' 4542. The train was berthed on the night of 31st

October/1st November in the secluded, easily-guarded cutting just north of the road over-bridge at Wray Barton. In the morning, it moved on to the terminus at Moretonhampstead, where the king met members of the parish council before being driven off over the Moor to Princetown. The next visit was made in the summer of 1969. Having reviewed the Fleet in Tor Bay on 27th July, Queen Elizabeth spent that night aboard the Royal Train at Heathfield. The last excursion, in 1983, involved the Prince and Princess of Wales, who spent the night of 8th/9th March on the train just south of Teigngrace. The eight-coach, maroon-liveried train was hauled from Newton Abbot by Class 47 No. 47500 *Great Western*. In the morning, the train moved the short distance to Teigngrace Halt, arriving at 9.35. Long disused, and now devoid of its station building, the place had been smartened-up for the occasion: vegetation had been cut back, the platform edge cleared and part of its surface covered with gravel, on to which Prince Charles alighted. Before moving on to Heathfield, and a separate engagement for Princess Diana, a Class 31 locomotive ran 'light engine' from Newton to couple to the rear of the train. The formation then moved off - with motive power being provided solely by 'Great Western' - to arrive at Heathfield just before 10.25. Here the princess alighted, to be welcomed by a reception party before being driven off to visit the Bovey Tracey Toddlers' Playgroup. The train meanwhile departed (at 10.30am), to return 'empty carriage stock' to Newton Abbot, hauled by the Class 31 - and with 47500 still attached to the other end.

An important, long-term and distinguished feature of the local tourist scene was the Manor House Hotel. Conceived and built as a grand private residence, ownership eventually passed to the Great Western Railway, largely as a result of one of those sets of chance events with which history abounds. In June 1825 William Henry Smith was born in Duke Street, off Grosvenor Square, London - the same street in which the Earl of Devon had his 'town house'. At the age of 16, his father (also named William Henry) put him to work in his successful newsagency business in the Strand. This was very much against young William's will, but he buckled down to the work and proved to have considerable business acumen. Indeed, on reaching his

King George VI is the focus of attention of both the official welcoming party and locals alike. He has alighted from the double doors at the end of one of the two 12-wheel Pullman-style saloons which form the centrepiece of the Royal Train. Built by the London & North Western Railway in 1903, they possess a smart purple-lake and 'spilt milk' livery, and are accompanied by nine other 'support' carriages. Notice that the platform name board at this date is double-sided. 1.12.37. *Dartington Rural Archive*

majority in 1846, he became junior partner in the firm, which came thereafter to be known as 'W.H. Smith & Son'. The business went from strength to strength. Although railways were still in their infancy, it occurred to William that potential might exist for selling books and newspapers to the travelling public. He first approached the London & North Western Railway, not only with a view to securing the Euston franchise, but also a monopoly throughout their entire system. This bore fruit, and the first station bookstalls opened in 1851. The reputation of the stalls and the ambition of William meant that by 1862 the firm had secured similar agreements with all the major railway companies. By this time, the firm was extremely prosperous, and although his father died in 1865, William resolved to continue the expansion.

Success in business brought wealth and prestige. In 1868 William became M.P. for Westminster, and a burgeoning political career followed. So far, all his business endeavours had been linked to the family firm, with its power-base in London. Then in 1880 he decided to buy 5,000 acres of moorland in the parish of North Bovey. Whatever long-term plans he might have had for his acquisition they came to nought, for on 6th October

the house was built in the Tudor style, with much oak panelling in the lofty, spacious principal rooms; the banqueting hall being provided with an impressive Jacobean-style carved stone chimney-piece. The work was completed in 1907, and the 'Manor House' was born.

Despite the opulence of the house and attractive, expansive grounds, the Second Viscount made only occasional visits. As head of the family business, he was largely detained in London, but his times in residence were noteworthy events in the locality. The family travelled down from their home in Henley-on-Thames, not only with enormous quantities of baggage, but also their own domestic staff. The Manor House's coach and pair was despatched to Moreton station to meet the train and convey the gentry on the three mile journey to their moorland retreat. These visitations were interrupted by the First World War, when the house was pressed into service as a convalescent home for troops. After the war, it was returned to the family, and the excursions resumed. On the death of Lord Hambledon in 1928, it was decided to sell the estate, but as its total value was so high, it was divided into 132 lots. The sale took place by auction at Newton Abbot's Globe Hotel on 8th November 1928. As Lot 67, the house and grounds were billed as "That Dignified Country Seat. Distinguished as "North Bovey Manor", Moretonhampstead, South Devon, occupying a magnificent position in the midst of Park and Pasture Lands of singular charm. It is approached by a Drive intersecting the Estate for ¾ mile, guarded at each end by a Lodge." In spite of this up-market billing, and its undoubted magnificence, bids failed to reach the minimum threshold price, and it was withdrawn. Eager to be rid of the property, however, it was sold shortly afterwards by private treaty to a Mr Bartlett of Bideford, who the following year (1929) re-sold it to the Great Western Railway.

Designed in the style of a Tudor Mansion by the renowned architect Walter Edward Mills and built, at enormous expense, by Lewis Bearne of Newton Abbot, Lord Hambledon's Manor House was completed in 1907. The extensive grounds were maintained by four gardeners, while the small number of permanent domestic staff was augmented by the Smith family's own personnel during the times they were resident. The house is seen here in its original form before acquisition and enlargement by the GWR (in 1929 and 1935/6 respectively). *Dartington Rural Archive*

The GWR promptly set about converting the house into a hotel, retaining as much of the character of the interior as possible. Early in 1930 an 18-hole golf course was laid out north of the house, and the 'Manor House Hotel' opened for business. To begin with, many of the guests travelled to Moretonhampstead by train, being conveyed from the station by the hotel's own taxi. As time went on, a growing percentage began to arrive by car, but whichever

1891 he died. This was just at the very time his services to commerce and politics were about to be recognised with the granting of the title of the first Viscount Hambledon (although the following month, his widow was created Viscountess).

A new personality now entered the stage: William's eldest son, the 23 year-old William Frederick Danvers Smith. Realising that the title would eventually pass to him, he began to think about developing the Dartmoor estate. In 1900 he purchased the title of 'Lord of the Manor of Moretonhampstead' from the Earl of Devon, and decided to build a house on the estate that would be in keeping with his newly-acquired status. On a 193-acre site south of the Moretonhampstead to Two Bridges road the house, together with the grounds, were to be on a truly grand scale, with no expense spared - thanks to the family fortune. The exterior of

way they made their way to the Moor, a substantial amount of traffic connected with the hotel was handled by the Branch. The splendour of both the hotel and its surroundings made it extremely popular; so much so that the accommodation was increased in an expansion programme executed in 1935/6. In addition to golf, other recreational activities now on offer were tennis (on both hard and grass courts), badminton, squash, croquet, swimming and trout and salmon fishing. All this came to an abrupt end at the outbreak of the Second World War, when the hotel was requisitioned by the Army as a military hospital for British, American and Canadian officers. This also brought much traffic to the Branch, though sadly of a different kind.

In 1946 the Manor House was returned to the GWR, who restored and reopened it as quickly as possible. Once again, the

Company set about promoting the hotel, as for example in two of their publications for 1947: namely, 'Walks Around Manor House Hotel, Near Moretonhampstead, Devon', and 'Motoring from Manor House Hotel' (both priced sixpence). As it turned out, that was to be the last year of the Great Western Railway itself, for on 1st January 1948 the railways were nationalised. Under the new regime, the British Transport Commission - through the 'Hotels Executive' - took responsibility for the 44 'railway hotels', 400 or so station refreshment rooms and train restaurant/buffet cars. Business at the Manor House continued to prosper, and the golf course was remodelled and extended in 1956. Countless travellers on British Railways Western Region must have noticed the presence of the hotel on the old GWR route maps which were still a common feature of the compartment rolling stock for many years after nationalisation.

The hotel continued in Railway ownership long after passenger services on the Branch were withdrawn (February 1959). In 1963 the Hotels Executive became 'British Transport Hotels', but the local administration continued as before - and the facilities were expanded to include a conference room. The magnificent building was also enjoyed by employees of BR, when staff dances and functions were occasionally held there. The slimmed-down railway operation which had emerged by the beginning of the 1980s presaged a change in attitude towards railway-owned hotels. In 1983 British Transport Hotels sold the Manor House to private owners, and thereby ended the association between the Railway and a building which itself had resulted from a Railway-inspired family firm.

If the Manor House Hotel put the town and the Branch on the map nationally, an event that drew in crowds locally was the annual Moretonhampstead Carnival. This was a feature of the Line right up until closure. In 1957, for example, it was held on Thursday 22nd August. Cheap half-day excursion tickets were offered on the 12.44, 2.15, 4.30 and 6.05pm trains from Newton Abbot; with returns from Moreton at 7.00 and 9.30pm. The last departure of the day - at 9pm - was normally an 'empty carriage' working, but for the carnival ran at the later time as an advertised service, calling at all stations (with the proviso that "If the event is cancelled, postponed or abandoned, this Special Train will not apply"). The following year, special cheap day tickets were being offered on any train after 9.30 in the morning: 1/10d from Newton Abbot for example, instead of the usual 3/3d. Over 500 people travelled on the Branch that day to attend the event. Until the First World War, another regular event in the town was the monthly livestock market, held on the fourth Tuesday of the month. For a few years on either side of the turn of the century, the GWR ran an extra train to and from Moreton to cater for the increased patronage.

The Branch also continued its popularity to the very end with the folks of the Torbay towns. On fine bank holidays and summer Sundays, trains were well-filled, often crowded. Thus for example on Easter Monday 1954 (19th April) the mid-morning through train from Paignton to Moretonhampstead - consisting of 0-4-2 No. 1439 and saloon trailers 224 and 234 - was absolutely packed to the doors by the time it left Torre. Elsewhere in the county, Sunday School outings generally went to the coast, but for those who already lived there it was a treat to go somewhere inland. When large numbers were arranged for in advance, extra seating could be provided.

So far, all the discussion has been about bringing visitors into the locality. What about traffic the other way: outward-bound excursions and cheap tickets for 'locals'? In broad gauge days and into the First World War, the Company provided an additional morning 'market day' train from Moretonhampstead to Newton Abbot on Wednesdays. This was soon joined by a further service on Saturdays, but these trains fulfilled a local rather than excursion function. Only from the late 1920s did

some trains continue beyond Newton to provide 'Branch residents' with a direct service to the resort towns of Torbay (see Chapter 3). Off-line travel was encouraged by the advent of 'cheap day' tickets. A 1954 sample of third class cheap day returns, available by any train from Moretonhampstead, is as follows:

Dartmouth	6s 6d	Paignton	4s 9d
Dawlish	4s 9d	Teignmouth	4s 0d
Exeter (via Ide)	5s 9d	Torquay	4s 3d
Exeter (via Newton Abbot)	7s 3d	Torre	4s 0d
Goodrington Sands Halt	5s 0d	Totnes	5s 0d

Other, cheaper than normal, Excursion Bookings were a feature of the Branch from the early years of the century. An interesting example from the summer of 1912 involved three transport modes, to make up what must have been a really appealing day out. It began by taking the train to Totnes - changing at Newton Abbot - from where a steamer trip was made down the River Dart to Dartmouth. From there, excursionists were taken on by road motor coach to Kingsbridge by way of Torcross. The return from Kingsbridge was by rail; involving a change of trains at Brent and Newton Abbot. The inclusive third-class fare was 6/- (30p) from Moretonhampstead and Lustleigh, and 5/6 from Bovey. There were also cheaper combined rail and river trips on offer at 3/9d. These combined trips continued to be a feature of summer seasons into the 1950s, as were special cheap day returns to a variety of destinations. In the last summer that passenger trains ran on the Branch, one such location so promoted was Plymouth; the second class return fare from Moretonhampstead being 6/3d, from Lustleigh 6/-, Bovey 5/3d and Heathfield 4/9d. (The second class category was reintroduced in June 1956, in parallel with the abolition of third class.) After a period of stability, fares were increased in October 1957. Thus for example, a penny was put on the cheap day return fare from Moreton to Lustleigh and Bovey, making it 1/- and 1/9d respectively; and 3d on that to Heathfield and Newton: to 2/3d and 3/3d respectively.

In addition to the 'cheap day returns', special Seaside Excursions were a feature of the post-war years. On Thursday 28th July 1955 for example, one such 'cheap excursion' was put on from Moreton to the Torbay resorts. Leaving the terminus at 9.30am, it ran non-stop to Torquay before continuing to Paignton and Goodrington Sands. The third class return fares on this 'Special' were substantially lower than the normal cheap day returns, as quoted above: 2/6d to Torquay, 2/9d to Paignton and 3/- to Goodrington. The return excursion arrived back at Moreton at 8.30pm, having given the day-trippers something like nine hours to enjoy the beaches and savour the other tourist delights.

One important and enduring excursion feature of the Branch from the turn of the century was the Sunday School Special. These heavily-laden trains were generally destined for the nearby resorts of Teignmouth or Torbay, and were looked forward to with great eagerness by local children. These 'Specials' actually continued to run even after regular passenger services over the Branch were withdrawn at the end of February 1959. Thus a few months later, on Tuesday 18th August, a train of five non-corridor coaches in the charge of 'large Prairie' 5164 carried a payload of 100 pupils and 200 adults from Moretonhampstead non-stop to Paignton and Goodrington Sands. Leaving at 8.50am, it was required to travel over the Branch at a sedate 15 miles per hour. The following August the Special ran to the same destinations, but this time calling at Lustleigh as well. Again there were five non-corridor coaches, with 'small Prairie' 5573 providing the motive power.

The excursion arranged for Thursday 10th August 1961 was on a bigger scale. The train was scheduled to consist of the customary five carriages, but in the event was made up to eight, with additional stops arranged for Bovey, Heathfield and Teigngrace. Leaving Moretonhampstead at 8.45am the Special collected the excited scholars and accompanying adults for the pilgrimage to the resorts of Paignton and Goodrington Sands. Unfortunately, the day turned out to be very wet, and more than spirits were dampened as the hours passed - for the return journey was not scheduled to leave Goodrington until 7.10pm. Calling briefly at Paignton to pick up the remainder of the excursionists, the train then ran non-stop to Teigngrace. A two-minute pause was made here, as at Heathfield and Bovey, before the taxing climb on to the Moor began. Very soon the locomotive began to struggle; for not only was its load much heavier than expected, but the rain had made the rails greasy. Leaving Lustleigh, the footplate crew became very concerned at the low level of water in the gauge glass. Not having stopped at Newton Abbot, there had been no chance of topping up the tanks. Although the excursion had now been divested of a high proportion of its passengers, it seemed increasingly likely that the engine would be unable to make it to the terminus. There may have been water in abundance all around that evening, but there was little of it in the loco's tanks, so the driver took the drastic, but unavoidable, decision to stop the train, uncouple and continue 'light engine' to Moretonhampstead to take on water. Having been disappointed by the dreadful weather, even the natural resilience of the children was tested by the tedious wait for the engine to return. The train eventually arrived at the

terminus with its tired and fractious passengers at around 9.45pm, over an hour late. It had certainly been a memorable day, though not for the usual reasons.

The outing of 1962 was to be different in a number of ways. Firstly, the destination was to be Teignmouth rather than Torbay, and secondly, the train was to be made up to the exceptional number of ten non-corridor coaches (and given the excursion number 1Z11). Thirdly, and sadly, this was to be the last of the long line of Sunday School Specials to run over the Branch. The empty carriage stock arrived at the terminus from Newton Abbot at 8.10 am on Thursday 16th August. Leaving at 8.35am, it sauntered back to the main line at the enforced post-closure maximum speed of 15 miles per hour, calling at Lustleigh, Bovey, Heathfield and Teigngrace. An unadvertised stop of ten minutes was made at Newton for the engine to change ends before continuing to Teignmouth, where it arrived at 9.58am. As soon as the passengers had alighted, the empty stock set off for the sidings at Exminster, where the loco stabled the carriages and collected the guard before continuing 'light engine' to Exeter (St. David's). In the reverse direction, the engine left Exeter at 6.10pm, with departure from Teignmouth scheduled for 7.19pm. Unbeknown to those travelling on the train, not only was this to be the last Sunday School Special, but also the very last passenger train to run north of Bovey. It finally arrived back at Moretonhampstead at 8.42pm, its departure for Newton fourteen minutes later marking the end of an era.

Morning coffee to Moreton? Well, not quite! The return leg of the 8.40am through working between Moretonhampstead and Paignton was used to convey a cafeteria coach from the Torbay resort to Newton Abbot on 10th May 1958. This through train was inaugurated in 1943 and ran to virtually identical timings almost every year until the Branch closed, though generally excluding summer Saturdays when the main line was at saturation point dealing with holiday traffic. The train, the 10.05 from Paignton, is here seen leaving Torre station behind No. 1427. Notice the signalman's 'sighting mirror' behind the cafeteria coach.

Peter W. Gray

SIGNALLING & PERMANENT WAY

etails of signalling on the Moretonhampstead Branch in its early, broad gauge, days are few and sketchy. There is a scattering of references in contemporary reports and correspondence, but little of any substance. For example, in relation to the junction with the main line, the Railway Inspector, Colonel Yolland, noted in his report of Thursday 28th June 1866 to the Board of Trade that he understood the temporary single line connection with the South Devon Railway was "....to be replaced by a double Junction complete with signals that will lock the points at the entrance to the Newton Station Yard from the East in the course of two months". In regard to the terminus, he stated: "Starting signals are to be put up for the Passenger Lines at Moretonhampstead Station interlocking with each other - and the Goods Line is not to be used until this is done." There are no records as to whether the public level crossings at Teignbridge and Bovey were protected by signals (which elsewhere in the West of England were of the disc-and-crossbar type).

At the outset, the Line was worked by the South Devon Block Telegraph. Details of train movements were telegraphed on to the next station. With the sparse service appertaining in these early years, trains were operating on a 'one engine in steam' principle: that is, one locomotive working all the services in a series of out-and-back shuttles. In such circumstances, telegraphic communication was perfectly adequate; with the instruments housed in the stations' booking office. Points were switched by means of adjoining capstans, connected to which were swivel-type 'point signals': metal discs - painted black with a white peripheral ring - which were turned to face the direction in which the point was set to indicate 'all clear'.

Although built as a single-track railway, trains were able to pass each other - or 'cross' in railway parlance - at Bovey, this being the halfway point on the Line. This provision was not called upon in the early years, for until 1875 the Newton Abbot to Bovey goods train ran late in the evening, after the Moreton-based passenger 'shuttle' had finished for the day. But then it moved to the afternoon, which broke the simple 'one engine' system; while from 1882 a separate goods train ran the full length of the Branch. However, with the meagre service of the time, and providing trains adhered rigidly to the timetable, this presented no problem, with the crossing arrangements being printed in the Company's working timetables. Thus in the publication for the summer of 1884, for example, we read that the 1pm goods train from Newton Abbot was to cross the 2.15pm passenger train from Moretonhampstead; with the returning goods (4.50pm from Moreton) crossing with the 5.33 passenger train from Newton. When unscheduled movements were necessary, such as the running of 'specials', any requisite 'crossing orders'

were telegraphed in advance from Newton.

The block telegraph remained the sole method of signalling until 1889, when the Train Staff and Ticket system was introduced. The staff was a wooden baton about twelve inches long and three and a half inches thick, with a metal hoop at one end - for hanging up in the station office or locomotive cab - and a keyed attachment at the other, for unlocking the ticket box. To aid identification, that used between Newton Abbot and Bovey was square in section, while that from Bovey to Moretonhampstead was round. The names of the locations at either end of the section were inscribed on a brass plate attached to one side of the staff. Possession of the staff gave a driver authority to enter a single line section in complete safety, for there was only one staff per section, and he was not permitted to proceed without it. The limitation of using the train staff by itself was that it had always to be at the end of the section where it was next required. This was fine when a straightforward out-and-back mode was in operation, but would obviously pose problems when successive trains were to be run in any one direction. Greater flexibility was made possible by using a ticket in association with the train staff (although the staff alone could always be used). The large paper tickets were kept in a locked box in the station office: those from Bovey to Newton being red in colour, and from Bovey to Moreton blue. As the box could only be unlocked by the key on the staff, it was impossible for tickets to be issued simultaneously at either end of the section. Prior to issue, the relevant details were filled out in the pre-printed spaces, and the ticket then given to the driver, who would also be shown the staff. The train could now proceed to the next 'block post', its progress being communicated by the block telegraph instrument. Once it had cleared the section, another train could be authorised to follow, and so on as necessary, until the staff was required at the other end of the section in order to send a train or trains in the reverse direction.

The gauge conversion made over the weekend of 21st/22nd May 1892 seemed to prompt the Great Western Railway into updating its method of signalling on the Branch. A brick-and-timber 25-lever signal box built to a 'Teign Valley' design had existed at Heathfield since that standard gauge line's opening in 1882, but its principal sphere of operation was with that railway,

The mighty Newton Abbot East Signal Box seen not long before closure. The Moretonhampstead Branch curves away behind the box, far left. The intensity of the traffic, along with the complexity of the track layout, meant that its operation called for both physical and mental agility. When any of the regular top-grade signalmen were away, the work was covered by the 'Special' class of 'Newton Abbot Relief' signalmen, who also covered West Box and Aller Junction.
Roger Penny

and it did not function as a block post on the Moreton Branch. That situation now changed, and it was brought into the 'staff and ticket system'. The Branch was thus divided into three lengths, or 'block sections', with the signal boxes controlling entry into the sections being referred to as 'block posts': namely, Newton Abbot East, Heathfield, Bovey and Moretonhampstead. There was still only one staff per section, the designations now being: square staff/red tickets from Newton to Heathfield; semi-circular staff/blue tickets from Heathfield to Bovey; round staff/green tickets from Bovey to Moreton. Orders were placed for signal boxes at Bovey and Lustleigh in June 1892, and presumably also for Teigngrace and Moreton; for within the next few months they were all up and running (the boxes at Teigngrace and Lustleigh were not block posts, and of brief duration; see Chapters 9 & 15 respectively). This permitted all point switching to be controlled from one place, although at Bovey the level crossing needed on-site supervision, so was provided with a 'ground frame' worked in conjunction with the signal box.

Additionally, the layout at each place was fully signalled, with standard lower-quadrant GWR semaphore signals being introduced, including 'working' distant signals. Only when all the 'stop' signals had been operated - or 'pulled off' in railwaymen's jargon - could the distant arm be lowered to the 'all clear' position. This even applied on the approach to the dead-end at the terminus, but gave the driver the assurance that the line ahead was clear right through

The Webb Thompson 'Electric Train Staff' machine, with generous compliment of staffs in the 'stem' magazine and 'ringing key' top right.

British Rail

to the buffer stops. If on a train's approach the signal arm remained in the horizontal (or 'on') position, it acted by way of a caution to the driver that he did not have a 'clear road' ahead and must be prepared to stop at the next signal. This useful function at all the locations on the Branch was ended about 1907 when all the distant signals were fixed at 'caution', irrespective of the 'state of the road' ahead.

The existence of only one through platform at Heathfield imposed a limitation on passenger train timetabling, and offset the benefit of the new system. On 14th November 1901 the Electric Train Staff system of signalling superseded the Train Staff and Ticket on the Branch. It represented a considerable refinement of the former arrangement, allowing much greater flexibility. As a matter of interest, the system had been tried out on the single-track section of the South Devon main line between Dawlish and Parson's Tunnel ten years previously. The central feature of the new system was the Webb-Thompson instrument. This had a magazine that was able to store several long metal staffs, and was connected electrically with the machine in the neighbouring signal box. The iron ETS was about twice the length of the old wooden train staff, and

weighed 3½lbs. Each staff possessed a series of raised rings towards one end, the spacing of which ensured that they only matched the corresponding grooves in the instrument to which they belonged. Not only did this prevent them from falling out of the machine, but also made it impossible for a wrong staff to be inserted. The other end of the staff carried the inscribed names of the two 'Staff Stations' to which it applied and ended in a key-like attachment, which was used to unlock, or 'release', ground frame lever stages. The instrument could only be operated by the two signalmen working in conjunction with each other by means of set procedures and co-ordinated bell codes (a tab-like 'ringing key' was provided on the machine, with the bell itself mounted on the instrument shelf above the levers). The action of drawing a staff from one instrument locked both it and its counterpart, making it impossible for either signalman to draw another until it was replaced in the instrument at the end of the journey through the section. A large wooden cabinet next to the signal box contained upwards of 40 batteries used in connection with these instruments and associated 'circuit' telephones. At Bovey it was fixed to the side of the goods shed, and at Moretonhampstead to the engine shed wall. The introduction of the ETS saw the demise of the two non-block posts of Teigngrace and Lustleigh; the siding points at these places now being released by the key on the staff.

Collecting a heavy metal staff from a moving train demanded circumspection on the part of a signalman. As all trains stopped at all stations on the Branch, this was not a problem, but at Moretonhampstead Junction - controlled by Newton Abbot East Signal Box - trains were booked to run past (although signal stops were by no means uncommon here due to conflicting movements on the main line). On 11th April 1912 a 'setting-down' post was installed at the rear of the 73-lever East box. It consisted of a 'cow horn' style catching arm projecting from a wooden post, and was backed by an oil lamp to indicate its position at night. The catcher projected through a heavy-duty rope safety net, which served to deaden the swing of the staff as the fireman dropped its hooped attachment over the arm, or directed it straight to the ground in the event of a 'miss'. It removed the need for a signalman to be in attendance to receive the staff by hand, leaving him free to leave the box at a more convenient time at this busy location. Although there was a speed limit of 15mph at the junction, trains often ran by the post at speeds of 20mph or more. This, plus the sharp curve of the track, made life difficult for the fireman. Trying to keep a firm grip on the cab side or handrail with one hand, he was forced to lean far out of the cab with the staff in the other, trying to keep it steady.

At Newton Abbot movements from the 'up' running lines to the Branch were signalled from the fine gantry at the north end of the station. The first, fourth and sixth signals, from left to right, relate to the 'through', 'main' and 'relief' lines respectively. The motor operated main line 'distant' signals were worked from Hackney signal box, while the short-posted 'stop' signals relate to the engine sidings/loops. Although 6022 *King Edward III* is bringing the 'Cornish Riviera Express' into the station from the Moreton Branch, all is not what it seems! Sunday engineering work is in progress at the opposite end of the station, and the express had run into Newton on the 'down' main line as usual and then reversed onto the Branch before drawing forwards to the 'up through' and thereby travelling 'wrong line' to by-pass the works. 4.12.55. *Peter W. Gray*

Although a direct junction between the Moreton and Teign Valley Branches had been put in at Heathfield in October 1916, there was still only one through platform line. Prior to the introduction of a more intensive passenger service on the Branch, in 1927, it was decided not only to install a second platform line, but also to introduce reversible (two-way) working over both the 'loops' that this addition created. At the same time, reversible working was introduced over the 'up' platform line at Bovey. Thus at the latter, the 'down home' signal in advance of the level crossing was provided with a bracket-mounted arm, signalling a 'down' train from 'main to up platform' (worked by lever number 4); while an 'up platform to main' starting signal was installed near the north end of the platform (No. 5). Ever safety-conscious, this two-way working prompted the introduction of additional precautions. The mechanical locking of the levers was organised in such a way that if the new bracket signal was lowered to 'all clear', the 'up home' signal was locked at 'stop'. The reverse, of course, also applied. At Heathfield the same, though more extensive, precautions were made.

As part of this exercise, track circuits were installed to the lines affected by reversible working. At Bovey, the length of track through the 'up' platform between the two starting signals

was thus provided; and at Heathfield, both the through platform lines. All the gaps between the rails were welded to provide a continuous steel strip into which a weak electric current was passed. When a train moved along, or stood on, this length its wheels short-circuited the current, and a dial on the instrument shelf in the signal box showed the legend 'TRACK OCCUPIED'. As soon as the train moved off the wired length, the circuit was restored and the dial changed to 'TRACK CLEAR'. Train crews were informed of the existence of these circuits by the attachment of a white diamond-shaped plate to the posts of the signals to which they related. This gave them exemption from 'Rule 55': whereby if a train was held at a signal for more than two minutes, the fireman had to walk to the signal box to make sure the signalman was aware of their presence and thereby ensure the protection of the train from possible conflicting movements. Following the necessary inspection, the new arrangements were commissioned on 9th June and 22nd July at Heathfield and Bovey respectively.

The expansion programme at Newton Abbot of the mid 1920s brought about the complete remodelling of Moretonhampstead Junction. In addition to working to and from the 'through' platforms at the rebuilt station (numbers 1-8), Branch trains could also run into their own dead-end, or

NEWTON ABBOT EAST BOX - 1895

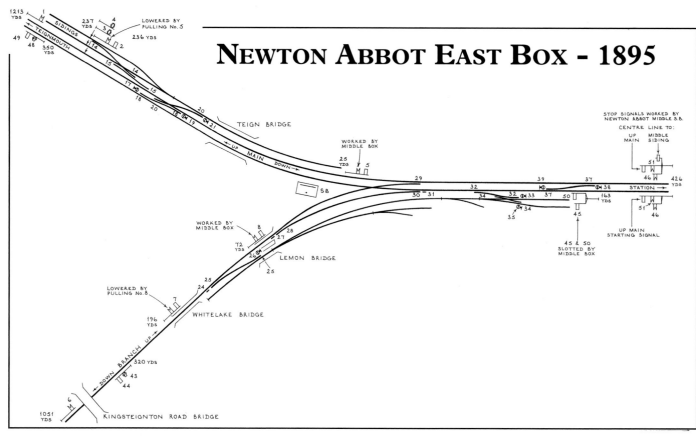

1955

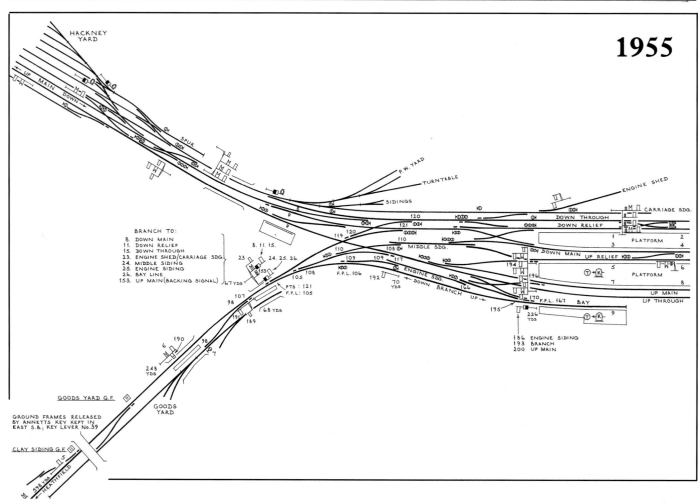

'bay', platform (No. 9) without the need to occupy any part of the main line. The major revision of the track layout required a new, very much larger Newton Abbot East Signal Box, the third to occupy the site. Earlier track modifications at the junction (in 1893) had been accompanied by the building of a new signal box. This brick-built box was, like its SDR predecessor, located in the angle of land between the Branch and main line. Its 34-foot by 12-foot operating floor stood 10' 10" above rail level and contained a 51-lever frame. Expansion of the layout in connection with Hackney Sidings and the new Goods Yard in 1911, saw the box fitted with a new frame of 73 levers (with 3-bar vertical tappet interlocking between points and signals). It was brought into use on 7th May that year. The extensive works of the next decade dictated that a completely new signal box be built. A truly enormous wooden structure, its floor area measured 79' 8" by 14' 2", and was 14 feet above rail level. With 5-bar vertical tappet interlocking, the frame contained 177 operational levers, numbered from 1 to 206 - the 2 'spares' and 27 spaces to allow for possible future expansion. This made it far and away the largest manually operated Great Western signal box in the West of England. An additional 'electric train staff' setting-down post was installed at the junction for use by trains working into the new bay line, while a 'picking-up' post was also provided next to it. Open continuously, its size - along with the volume of train, light engine and shunting movements within its limits - meant that it required a staff of two signalmen and a 'booking boy' on each shift (only in its last years was one of the night-shift signalmen dispensed with). One man dealt with the 'up' part of the frame and the other the 'down' on an alternating daily basis, while the booking boy was responsible for logging train times and details in the Train Register, and also acted as a 'runner' for the signalmen.

The commissioning of the new East box on 25th April 1926 brought to an end the short life of another Moreton Branch signal box at Newton; namely, Newton Abbot Goods Yard Signal Box. A small, ground level structure, its nameplate was almost longer than the box itself! It was situated on the 'up' side of the Branch, between the running line and River Teign, about 80 yards on the Newton side of the Kingsteignton Road bridge (at 49 chains from the station; 28 from the junction). With an operating floor measuring 17' 6" by 11', it housed a 12-lever stud frame, with switch. Its sole function was to control a single set of points - facing to 'down' trains - at the road bridge end of the new Newton Abbot Goods Yard of 1911: the box itself opening on 10th May that year. It was open for about ten hours a day, generally from 8.15am to 6.15pm. Outside these hours, it was 'switched out'; that is, all the 'up' and 'down' signals were lowered into the 'clear' (or 'off') position. The presence of the box divided the otherwise long block section to Heathfield, so to give train crews a tangible indication as to whether 'long' or 'short' sections were in operation, the single line apparatus varied. When open, the sections on either side of the signal box were worked by the electric train staff, but when it was closed, the long section from East box to Heathfield was worked by tablet. Closing on the same day that the enlarged East box opened, its role was taken over by that place, even though it was too far to be worked mechanically. The limitations of point rods put the outer limit on manual operation at 200 yards from a signal box, and although this was later raised to 350 yards, it was still too far. Thus the two-lever 'Goods Yard Ground Frame' was released by the Annetts Key kept at Newton Abbot East (and described in Chapter 7 in connection with Newton Abbot Clay Siding). Converted to hand-operated points following the abandonment of conventional signalling on the Branch in October 1965, the crossover remained for a further seven years.

The next significant development took place during the Second World War. Not only was Heathfield's track layout revised, but also the Electric Train Token made its first appearance on the Branch. The same in principle as the train staff mode of operation, it was a light-weight and less cumbersome extension of it. Made of aluminium and weighing only eight ounces, one face of the token was inscribed with the names of the signal boxes at either end of the section to which it applied. An integrated, and individually-machined, key-like extension at one end ensured that a token could only be inserted into the designated signal box instruments. Additionally, it could unlock the release lever at intermediate ground frames. To facilitate ease of handling - it was barely eight inches long - it was clipped securely into a stout holder, complete with a large metal hooped 'catcher'.

On 25th July 1943 the token replaced the staff on the Newton Abbot to Heathfield section. The requirements of, and increases in, traffic in the war years saw the two platform loops at the latter extended by eight chains in the Newton direction, giving them a length of 1,721 feet. A trailing crossover was installed by the road bridge and, significantly, a double-track junction with the Teign Valley Line provided, bringing about conventional, mutually-exclusive 'up' and 'down' signalling. In the bay platform, the engine-release crossover was removed. These changes gave the layout a sense of spaciousness quite unusual for a branch line junction, and brought about a re-ordering of lever functions in Heathfield Signal Box. The box dated from the layout changes effected during the First World War, and replaced the smaller 'Teign Valley' cabin of 1882. Of standard Great Western design, it was built of local brick, with a hipped slate roof. Its operating floor measured 33' 6" by 12', was 9 feet above rail level, and housed a 3-bar vertical tappet interlocking frame of 42 levers set at 4½"centres. It was brought into use on 2nd October 1916.

The expansion of June 1927 saw the box fitted with a new, 58-lever frame, comprising 5-bar vertical tappet interlocking and levers set at 4-inch centres. The alterations of May 1943 saw the retention of this frame, which now contained 44 working levers, with 14 spaces. The south-end points were too far removed from the box to be worked manually, so were fitted with an electric motor. This distance led to the provision of an Auxiliary Token Machine by the 'up advanced starting' signal to obviate the delay and inconvenience of a long walk with the token for a train waiting at the signal for 'line clear'. The extended loops, together with a 200-yard stretch of single line beyond, were provided with track circuits - four in all - which were indicated on the illuminated diagram above the instrument shelf in the signal box. Just in case men became over-reliant on the diagram, the GWR issued the following stricture: "The use of the illuminated diagram is intended as an aid to signalmen, but does not relieve them of the duty of observing, as far as practicable, the movements of points and signals as laid down in the Rules, and watching trains in accordance with the Block Telegraph Regulations."

In January 1945 the electric train token was extended to the Bovey to Moretonhampstead section; the ground frame lever stage at Lustleigh being adapted accordingly. At the end of April the following year, auxiliary token instruments were installed on Platforms 5 and 9 at Newton Abbot, enabling trains to leave with the device already on board rather than having to collect it by hand from the line-side picking-up post. Only the Heathfield - Bovey section continued with the electric train staff, but early in 1952 the ETT was substituted there also.

Matters relating to signalling were the responsibility of the Signal & Telegraph Department linemen, who travelled on the Branch regularly. The signal lineman dealt with the mechanical side of the work, with all the paraphernalia linked with points and signals: facing point locks, point rods, slide bars, signal wires and so forth. The telegraph lineman attended to telegraph/telephone equipment and signal box instruments,

Heathfield Signal Box

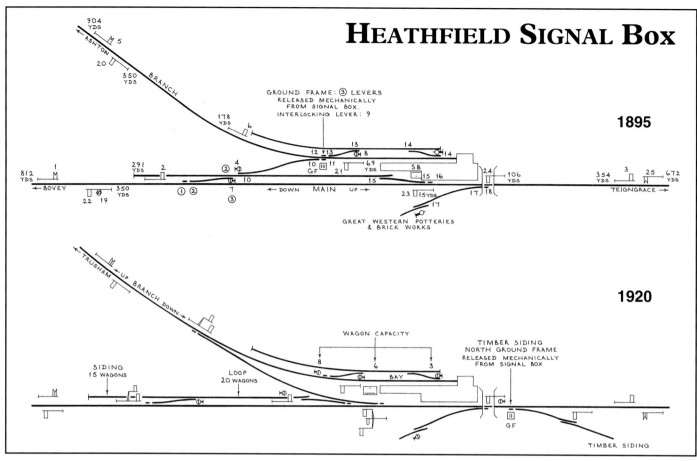

1895

GROUND FRAME: ③ LEVERS
RELEASED MECHANICALLY
FROM SIGNAL BOX.
INTERLOCKING LEVER: 9

904 YDS

ASHTON BRANCH

M 5

20

350 YDS

178 YDS   6

12 13   13   14

10   11   8   14

812 YDS   1   291 YDS   2   ② ④   10   69   SB   24   106 YDS   354 YDS   3   25   672 YDS

BOVEY   350 YDS   ① ②   7   DOWN   MAIN   UP   15   15 16   23 15YDS   17 18   TEIGNGRACE

22 19   ③   GF   21   17

GREAT WESTERN POTTERIES
& BRICK WORKS

1920

TRUSHAM   M   UP BRANCH DOWN

WAGON CAPACITY

TIMBER SIDING
NORTH GROUND FRAME
RELEASED MECHANICALLY
FROM SIGNAL BOX

SIDING
15 WAGONS

LOOP
20 WAGONS

8   6   3

BAY

GF

TIMBER SIDING

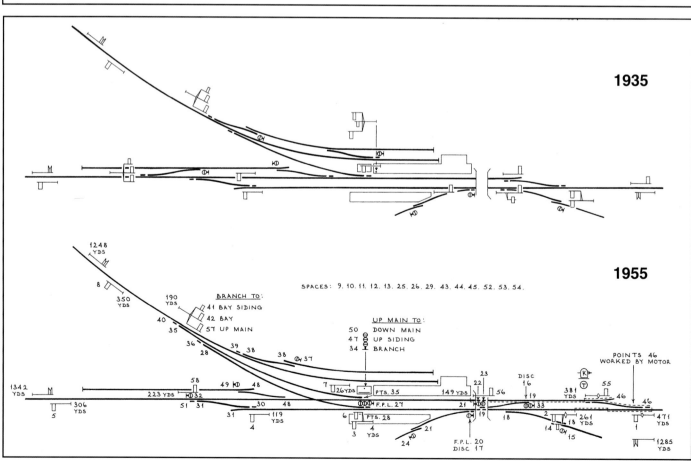

1935

M

1955

1248 YDS

8   350 YDS

190 YDS   BRANCH TO:
41 BAY SIDING
42 BAY
57 UP MAIN

40
35

36   39 38

28   38   37

UP MAIN TO:
50 DOWN MAIN
47 UP SIDING
34 BRANCH

SPACES: 9. 10. 11. 12. 13. 25. 26. 29. 43. 44. 45. 52. 53. 54.

58   49   48

1342 YDS   M   223 YDS   32   7   26YDS   PTS. 35   149 YDS   23   DISC 16   381 YDS   55   POINTS 46
WORKED BY MOTOR

306 YDS   51 31   30 48   22   19   56   46   46

5   31   119 YDS   6   F.P.L. 27   21   33   2   261 YDS   471 YDS

4   PTS. 28   19   18   14 18   1

3 4 YDS   21   F.P.L. 20   15   1285 YDS

24   DISC 17

The track layout and associated signalling at Heathfield changed appreciably over the years. A new layout at the junction was commissioned in October 1916, and with it the sizeable standard brick-built GWR Type 7D Class 3 signal box seen here. Notice the triple ground signal, which covers reverse movements from the 'up' platform. The bottom disc, in the 'off' position, signalled access to the Teign Valley Branch; the centre disc to the 'up' siding; and the top disc to the Moretonhampstead Line. Having made a connection with a train from Newton Abbot to Moreton, No. 1429 is about to depart for Exeter. The corrugated iron weighbridge house alongside the 'up' siding stands out clearly to the right of the 'up' main home' signal. 13.8.57.   *R. E. Toop*

Below: The platform-mounted GWR Type 6, Class 4 signal box at Bovey. Measuring 15 feet x 8 foot 6 inches, much of the structure is of timber construction, although the back wall, chimney stack and those parts of the end elevations above and including the plinth are of brick. Its stud-locking design of frame housed 17 levers set at 5¼" centres. Circa 1961. *Lens of Sutton*

including the staff/token machines. While the S&T's engineering headquarters was in Reading, the linemen's local 'depot station' was Teignmouth. Placed under the supervision of an inspector, the depot covered a huge stretch of the main line: from, but excluding, Burlescombe near the Somerset border to Brent on the southern fringe of Dartmoor. It also took in the Tiverton, Culm Valley, Teign Valley, Moretonhampstead, Kingswear and Brixham branches.

After the war, the general pattern of signalling remained unchanged until the withdrawal of passenger services at the end of February 1959. The only alterations in detail were at Bovey. The small timber-built, platform-mounted Bovey Signal Box of 1892 vintage contained a 17-lever frame, containing 14 working levers, with spaces for three more should the need arise in the future (as it happened, the 'fixing' of the distant signals early in the century, reduced the former category by two). When the station opened, only one siding had been provided, this serving the goods shed and loading dock. Passing behind the 'up' platform, it crossed the 'up' line on a diamond crossing and trailed into the 'down' line near the north end of the loop. A second, much-needed 'back siding' was added just before the turn of the century, and as they converged very near the 'diamond', both were provided with right-hand catch points

BOVEY SIGNAL BOX

1895
1920

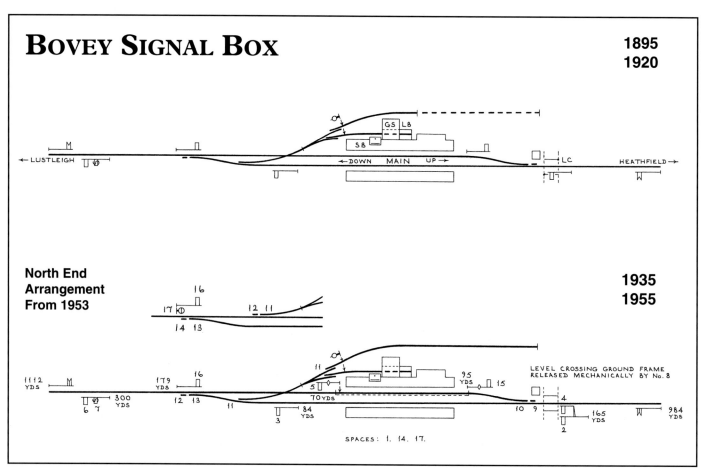

**North End
Arrangement
From 1953**

1935
1955

SPACES: 1. 14. 17.

MORETONHAMPSTEAD SIGNAL BOX

1895

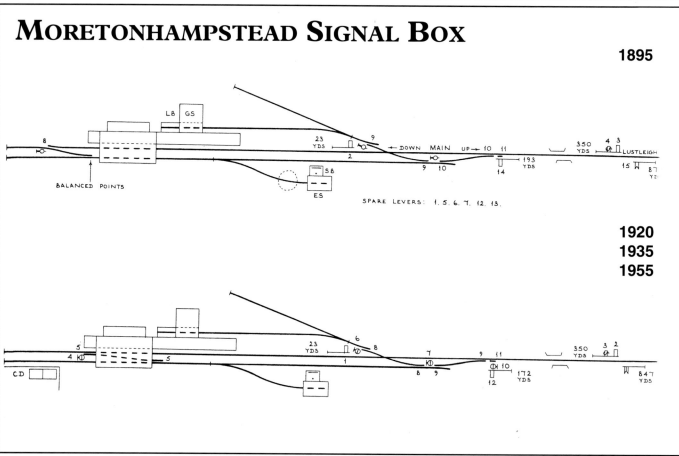

1920
1935
1955

A token gesture at Bovey. Signalman Tom Booth exchanges single line tokens with the fireman of 'large Prairie' No. 5183 on the 9.20am from Newton Abbot. Bovey retained its aesthetically pleasing square-sectioned, pine-post signals until the end. The white 'Rule 55 Exemption' plate - or 'diamond' - attached to the post of the signal in the 'off' position for the train indicates to the crew that the line through the platform is track-circuited. 26.2.59.   *Peter W. Gray*

(the purpose of which was to deflect runaway wagons from the main line). The catch points were operated from the signal box, but the required siding was set by a hand-operated point lever at the actual junction. One swivel-type ground-mounted 'point disc' covered the exit from both lines. Essentially, this comprised a lamp-case attached by a transverse length of point rodding to the catch points blades. In its 'normal' position it showed a rectangular red plate and centre light to the front. When the points were switched over, the lamp casing swivelled through a right-angle to show a green circular disc and centre light.

In connection with the two-way signalling scheme of 1927, the signal box was provided with a new stud-type frame, replacing what is thought to have been a double-twist type earlier version. As before, there were 14 operational levers with 3 spaces. The track layout at Bovey remained unchanged for decades. Then, in 1953, it was decided to take advantage of track relaying at the station to alter the connection with the goods yard sidings. The diamond crossing and trailing point were removed and replaced by a 'facing' connection with the

'up' line. The permanent way aspect of the work was supervised by the Divisional Engineer from Taunton, while the signalling matters went to Reading for approval (this being granted on 25th February). It was now that the three spaces in the signal box frame came in useful, for with the addition of a new facing point lock and two 'independent' disc-type ground signals, three new levers were needed. The engineering work was completed by the end of August, while the disc signals were in place by mid September.

Moretonhampstead Signal Box was of non-standard design, given its rather confined and unusual location squeezed in between the engine release line and north wall of the engine shed. Built of brick and timber, its operating floor was at rail height, and measured 17'3" by 8'. It was originally provided with a frame of 15 levers, of which nine were operational and six 'spare'. The spare levers were painted white, their number being joined by a seventh (number 15) when the distant signal was fixed at caution circa 1907 - and contemporaneously moved a couple of dozen yards nearer the station. Round about 1920 a new stud-type frame of 12 levers - all working - was installed.

Above: Moretonhampstead signal box seen in the summer of 1957. A Class 5, non-standard brick-and-timber box, the levers in its stud frame were set at 5¼" centres. Signalman Dave Evans waits with the token by the engine shed, which at this date was in use as a coal store by the local Co-operative Society. *G. Howells*
Below: Changed days! In September 1985 Class 50 No. 50025 *Invincible* is framed by a signal gantry heavily pruned as a consequence of track rationalisation at Moretonhampstead Junction. The only surviving connection between the main line and Branch is a single track trailing into the 'down' line by the fourth carriage.

Hugh Ballantyne

This event saw the old non-independent swivel-type 'point discs' replaced by standard disc-type ground signals controlled independently of the points. Moreton may by this time only have had three working signals, but in later years they were all different! The 'starting' signal was provided with a metal lattice post - a feature more at home on the Southern Railway - while the 'home' signal's post was of pierced concrete, a type first used during the First World War. The last of the GWR tapered, square-sectioned wooden posts - that of the 'advanced starting' signal - was removed in the early 1950s, to be replaced by a slender tubular steel version with pressed steel arm. The 'shunt' signal below the original wooden arm of the advanced starter was not replaced, so reducing by one the signal box's tally of working levers.

On receiving the 2-1 'train out of section' bell code on the late evening of Saturday 28th February 1959, Moretonhampstead and Bovey signal boxes closed for the very last time. Before the goods train made its run over the Branch the following week, various modifications had to be carried out. Two-lever ground frames were installed at the three sets of points previously worked from Bovey box, while the level

crossing gates were provided with padlocks. At Moreton, only the points at the east end of the layout were linked to a ground frame; all the others being changed to hand operation. Signal arms were removed from both locations. Although the electric train token was retained between Newton Abbot and Heathfield - along with the crossing keeper at Teignbridge - the Branch north of Heathfield was converted to 'one engine in steam' operation. In connection with this, a single wooden 'Train Staff ('D' pattern)' was used. The key on this staff was the means by which the new ground frames were unlocked - as well as the existing lever stages at Granite Siding and Lustleigh, which had been appropriately modified.

Despite these changes, the layout at Heathfield remained fully signalled, although a single shift now sufficed to cover the freight workings on the Branch and surviving remnant of the Teign Valley Line, which had closed to passengers the previous year. On weekdays, the box was more or less an 'office hours' affair, and was also open for about four hours on a Saturday morning for a Teign Valley working. In June 1961 the auxiliary token instrument was removed from Platform 5 at Newton Abbot, and by the summer of the following year, Heathfield signal box was only open as required. This arrangement continued until October 1965 when it was decided that the box could be dispensed with. It closed on and from Tuesday 12th, the Line thereafter being treated as a long siding, with all points being operated by hand-levers.

Even the mighty Newton Abbot East Signal Box was eventually swept away by the inexorably advancing tide of rationalisation. Periodic culls of the trackwork simplified the layout at Moretonhampstead Junction, and from January 1966 the only direct link with the Branch was by means of a trailing connection with the 'down' main line. Further pruning concomitant with the Exeter-based multiple-aspect colour-light resignalling scheme transferred the junction from 'down' to 'up'; from 'trailing' to 'facing'; and from the traditional site to the north end of the 'up' platform. From 2nd May 1987 the greatly reduced work here was subsumed into that controlled by the panel in the new power box. (One of the men operating Newton Abbot East at the time of its demise was Derek Aggett. He had also been one of the last two signalmen at Bovey when the box there closed almost three decades previously. Employment in Cullompton, Hackney, Dainton and Teignmouth signal boxes culminated in his return to East Box, the very place where his railway career had begun as a 15 year-old booking boy in 1952.) Access to the Branch was - and still is at the time of writing in 1999 - signalled by a stencil-illuminated indicator (a small rectangular box) to the left of signal E11 near the platform end.

PERMANENT WAY DEPARTMENT

For permanent way purposes, the Moretonhampstead Branch was divided into three 'lengths', each covered by its own set, or 'gang', of men: ganger, sub-ganger and lengthmen. The latter were widely known as 'packers' on this, and other, West Country lines, while the sub-ganger was usually referred to as the 'second man'. The gangs came under the supervision of an inspector based at Newton Abbot, the sidings and assorted buildings of the permanent way depot occupying the piece of land between the main line and Marsh Road. The breakdown crane which was kept there was for use on the main line between Starcross and Wrangaton, and the various branches in between (including the Teign Valley as far as, but excluding, Christow).

The southernmost part of the Branch was designated as extending between the distances of 25 chains (ie. 550 yards) from the station - to the rear of Newton Abbot East Signal Box - and the 3¾ mile post: near Heathfield's 'up advanced starting' signal. This was covered by the Newton Abbot Branch Gang.

The Bovey Gang then took over as far as, but excluding, Hawkmoor/Pullabrook Halt at the 7¾ mile post. The final 4 miles and 54 chains were the responsibility of the Moretonhampstead Gang.

In addition to looking after the track - rails, sleepers and ballast - the gangs had to ensure the good order of everything between, and including, the boundary fences. This brought in a wide range of work, from cutting back vegetation, cleaning out ditches and snow-clearing, to keeping a 'watching brief' on the physical state of station/halt platforms and public access roads and paths. More specialised work relating to bridges and viaducts was beyond their remit, and was referred to the Divisional bridge inspector at Taunton. Passengers might well catch a glimpse of the gang cutting grass or mending fences, or simply standing back from their work on the track to allow the train to pass. The approaching engine's whistle and the acknowledging wave from the gang was not just some quaint rural branch line exchange of greetings between colleagues, but principally a safety procedure: if the whistle was not acknowledged, it meant that the men were not aware of the train's presence and therefore in danger. The whistle would be repeated; the driver being ready to make a brake application if necessary.

Heavier work often involved the use of a small, low-slung four-wheel wooden trolley to carry the materials: such as sleepers, rail chairs, fence posts and wire. When the trolley was taken to a job, it was essential that it had sole occupation of the single line. While in effect treated as a train, the ganger was not issued with the usual authorisation (staff or token), but with the ganger's occupation key: a large brass key with the inscribed names of the signal boxes at either end of the section. The action of withdrawing this from the key instrument in the signal box locked the electric train instruments in both boxes, and thus ensured that no conflicting train movements could take place. Such was the nature of the work, that men might spend a considerable time within the signalling section, so that a means had to be devised whereby the instruments could be unlocked to allow trains to safely pass the work site. Thus, on arriving at the location, the trolley was lifted off the track as soon as practicable, while the ganger walked to the nearest occupation hut. There were thirteen of these on the Branch, situated roughly every three-quarters of a mile. Inside was the 'ganger's occupation key instrument'. By inserting and turning the brass key, the instruments in the signal boxes on either side were 'released'; while an accompanying telephone allowed communication with the signalmen.

In addition to the 'key huts', other cabins existed to fulfil the conventional role of store-cum-refuge, without the key function. Widely referred to as 'packers' or 'platelayers' huts, they were commonly built of old sleepers, with a brick chimney-stack and single shuttered window. A wooden bench and small fire-grate constituted the only 'furniture'. Minor architectural structures they might have been, but showed a variety of building materials, for in addition to the usual timber construction, the Branch sported examples in brick, stone and prefabricated concrete panels.

The condition of the permanent way in all three 'lengths' was always exemplary. The gangs took pride in their work, and would be aghast at the weed-infested, dishevelled ballast and unkempt line-side vegetation which is so often the order of the day on the modern railway. Keeping the track-bed in such good order was aided by the visitation of the weed-killing train. Generally consisting of three old locomotive tenders - collectively holding around 10,000 gallons of water - a 2,000-gallon concentrated-chemical tank wagon and a brake van, this trundled along the Branch once a year. As the work was physically demanding, some men as they got older transferred to other grades. Not only was the work heavy, but also unrelenting. In addition to the regular weekday work, the gang

was additionally required to assist when necessary on Sundays with track relaying either on the Branch or, more usually, main line. After long hours in all weathers, men returned home exuding an all-pervading aura of creosote from much handling of Baltic Redwood sleepers.

The nature of the duties undertaken by the gang gave the men, over the years, an intimate knowledge of their section of line and the territory adjoining it. Although fences were well maintained, there was always the possibility of a problem at user-operated farm occupation crossings. At one such near Moretonhampstead the gate leading to a field of cattle was inadvertently left open on one occasion, and a particularly valuable animal strayed on to the line. It was subsequently struck and killed by a train. The desire to apportion, and/or avoid, blame caused the ensuing compensation debate to run on for many weeks. The scenic stretch through the Parke Estate at Bovey was one where game, notably pheasants, untrammelled by such things as boundary fences, frequently met an untimely end. The permanent way team kept an eye out for such trespassers - and it was not unknown for the means of disposal to be by way of certain kitchen tables.

One essential task that had to be performed by the ganger or second man every day that trains were running, was to walk the length. This solitary duty was periodically enlivened by conversation with other railwaymen, or by events taking place near the line. Thus on one occasion, one of the men was sitting in the line-side hut near Letford Bridge enjoying a short break, when the sound of animated female voices wafted into the room. A group of ladies on an outing decided, collectively, that the call of nature required answering - and urgently. A hedgerow hereabouts seemed to be the ideal place. Though effectively concealed from the road, as propriety demanded, the chosen site happened to be in full view of the permanent way hut. Its occupant could not resist a wicked practical joke, so instead of ignoring them, decided to wait awhile, and then in his best stentorian tone yelled out a single "Oi!" Instead of feeling considerable relief, the ladies' nonchalant chatter turned to screams and cries of dismay, followed by a hasty retreat to the road in obvious confusion and consternation as to the origin of the disembodied voice!

In its sylvan setting near Woolford/Wilford Bridge, this rustic platelayers' hut looks as if it would be more at home in the pages of a children's story book! Railways were required by statute to mark out their lines with mileage posts at quarter-mile intervals, and those seen here date back to Broad Gauge days (as does the hut). From the mid 1930s the GWR began replacing these aesthetically pleasing cast iron posts with squat, plain double-sided concrete versions. The hut is quite close to the present 7¼ mile post, and it seems that during the change over, the old posts were taken the short distance and left behind the hut; where they remained hidden until brought out and posed for this picture. 27.2.59. *Peter W. Gray*

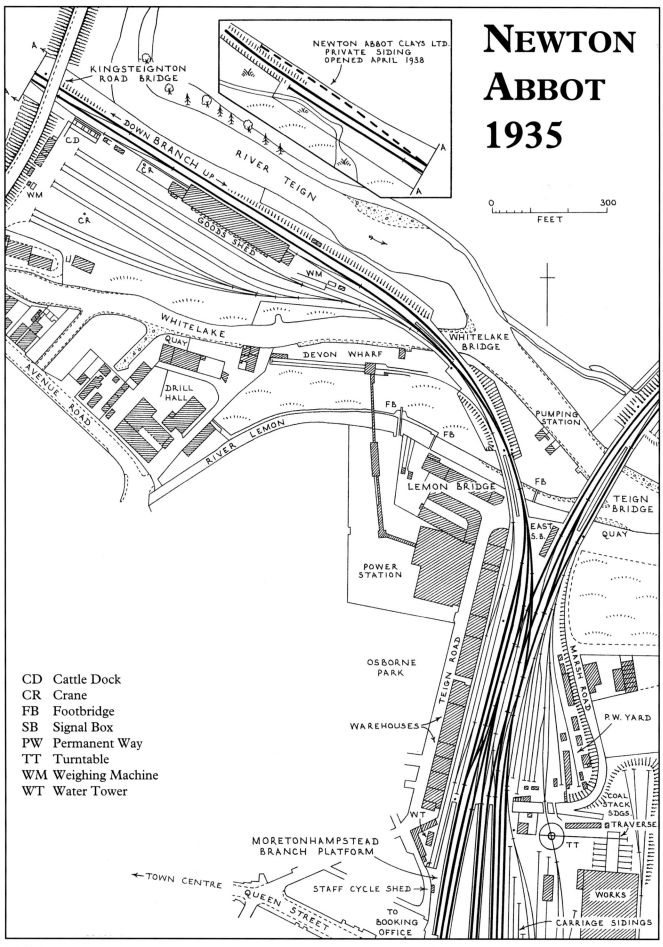

NEWTON ABBOT 1935

NEWTON ABBOT CLAYS LTD.
PRIVATE SIDING
OPENED APRIL 1938

A

KINGSTEIGNTON
ROAD BRIDGE

RIVER TEIGN

CD

CR

WM

CR

DOWN BRANCH UP

GOODS SHED

WM

0   300
FEET

WHITELAKE
QUAY

DRILL
HALL

DEVON WHARF

WHITELAKE
BRIDGE

AVENUE ROAD

RIVER LEMON

FB

FB

PUMPING
STATION

LEMON BRIDGE

FB

EAST
S.B.

TEIGN
BRIDGE
QUAY

POWER
STATION

OSBORNE
PARK

TEIGN ROAD

MARSH ROAD

P.W. YARD

WAREHOUSES

CD Cattle Dock
CR Crane
FB Footbridge
SB Signal Box
PW Permanent Way
TT Turntable
WM Weighing Machine
WT Water Tower

COAL
STACK
SDGS.

TRAVERSE

TT

WT

MORETONHAMPSTEAD
BRANCH PLATFORM

← TOWN CENTRE

QUEEN STREET

STAFF CYCLE SHED →

TO
BOOKING
OFFICE

WORKS

CARRIAGE SIDINGS

PART 2

Chapter Seven

STATIONS & LOCATIONS

NEWTON ABBOT

When the Moretonhampstead & South Devon Railway opened their line to Newton Abbot in 1866, this market town and commercial centre was already well on the way to becoming, in addition, a 'railway town'. The main line from Exeter had arrived twenty years previously, with its continuation to Plymouth and a branch line to Torre (and subsequently Paignton and Kingswear) following in quick succession. The twin 13th century settlements of Newton Abbot and Newton Bushel, separated only by the tiny River Lemon and civic exclusivity, lay some distance west of the damp, low-lying, flood-prone area utilised by the railway. Although the two small towns - little more than overgrown villages - had amalgamated under the name of Newton Abbot, the station had originally been named simply 'Newton': perhaps out of deference to both places! This situation remained until March 1877 when the suffix 'Abbot' was added.

Conversely, from Newton's perspective, the Branch contributed only a small part of the work performed at this extremely busy location (over 900 people were employed by the GWR here in the mid 1920s, with around 750,000 passengers using the station every year). A detailed exposition of the full railway scene in the town, therefore, is beyond the scope of this book, and so it is principally only those aspects relating to the Moretonhampstead Branch that will be dealt with in this chapter. Whether or not passengers on the main line knew of the Branch, its existence certainly impressed itself on them as their carriages clattered and swayed over the tangle of points at the junction near the Teign river bridge. While the final approaches to Newton were made on a curve, the station itself was on a more-or-less straight north-south orientation: although the Great Western Railway preferred the respective appellations 'east' and 'west' (that is, related to mileage from Paddington).

The original South Devon Railway Company's station was of

Dating from the 1858-61 rebuilding, the rather undistinguished street frontage of Newton Abbot station is seen in October 1924, just before major reconstruction work began.   *National Railway Museum*

The addition of the 'Moorland Railway', as the Moreton Branch was often called, reinforced the role of the town as a railway junction. Indeed, throughout the 'Steam Age' Newton Abbot was a major railway centre in the West of England. This may be illustrated by an oft-told family anecdote. A year or so after the Great War, my grandfather was returning home to Devon after a visit to Huddersfield; a journey which involved changing trains at Crewe. In the days before public address systems, passengers relied on route-indicator boards or members of staff for information. Amid the bustle occasioned by the approach of a southbound express, he enquired of a porter whether it was the right train; to which he got the reply: "Exeter. Yes. Change at Newton Abbot." To a Devonian this naturally caused some quiet amusement; but if the porter's geography was at fault, it at least showed his clear understanding of the town's importance on the railway network!

As the place where the Moretonhampstead Branch 'plugged in' to the rest of the rail system, Newton Abbot featured prominently in the life and times of the Moorland Railway.

the 'Brunelian' one-sided type, the platform being divided into 'up' and 'down' portions, with a train shed (or overall roof) for each. A physically separate platform and train shed was added following the opening of the branch to Torre (December 1848). The operational inconvenience of this arrangement was progressively removed by a programme of reconstruction between 1858 and 1861, which provided three parallel running lines through the station, each separated by a platform: 'up', 'centre' and 'down'. The Moretonhampstead Branch of 1866 made a junction with the main line near the confluence of the rivers Lemon and Teign a quarter of a mile north of the station. The layout here was controlled by Newton Abbot East Signal Box - initially called Newton East Cabin - although the location was referred to officially as Moretonhampstead Junction. Branch trains ran over the main line metals between the junction and the station and could work into either the 'down' or 'centre' roads; the latter permitting both arrivals and departures. Later track alterations in connection with the quadrupling of the line from Aller Junction meant that all down

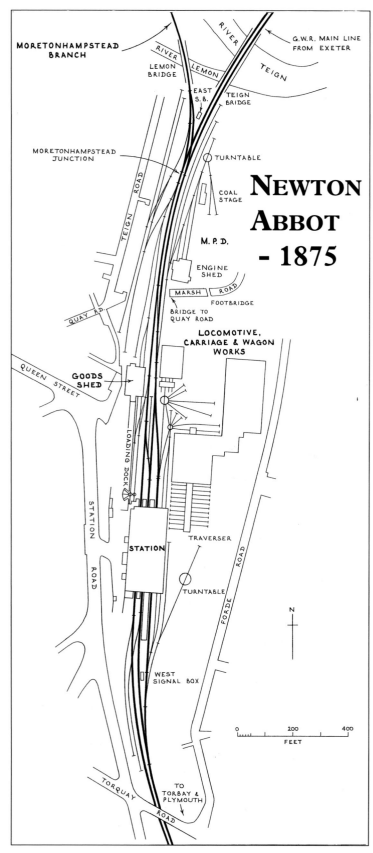

main line, and incoming Branch, trains were obliged to work into the 'down' platform only (although Branch departures were still able to use the centre line). The station became very congested at times, and with only three platforms there was much shunting of stock to keep the running lines clear. The layout as a whole was becoming cramped, and although plans for expansion were mooted in 1906, nothing was to happen on the passenger scene for many more years: except for the lengthening of the 'up' and 'centre' platforms by 70 feet and 88 feet respectively (October/November 1913). Platform lengths were now: 'up' 596 feet; 'centre' 675 feet; 'down' 676 feet.

The most significant development for both main line and Branch services took place in the mid 1920s. The station was entirely rebuilt and the track layout extensively remodelled. This truly massive undertaking began in November 1924 and went on in planned phases for the next three years. The work was of necessity protracted in order to keep interference with train services to a minimum and permit continued passenger use of the station facilities. The new, wide platforms were of such length (1,375 feet) that they were sub-divided. A paired numbering sequence was instituted - from 1 to 8 - with the lower numbers at the north end: 1 and 2 on the 'down relief' line; 3 and 4 on the 'down main'; 5 and 6 'up relief'; and 7 and 8 'up main'. The midway separation was marked by 'scissors' crossovers on both the outer faces - 'down relief' and 'up main' - and a 'trailing' crossover on the inner. This allowed considerable operational flexibility, especially when dividing or joining trains to and from Plymouth and Torbay.

The solid bulk of the new red brick station building was erected to the north of its 'low rise', rather plain, predecessor. It consisted of booking office, booking hall and parcels office on the ground floor, the former being partitioned in April 1945 to create a separate section for enquiries. On the first floor was a dining/tea-room occupying 1,250 square feet. With independent access to the street, it was available for public hire. Above that, on the top floor, were various offices: notably those of the Divisional locomotive superintendent and chief clerk, but also handling administration, wages/accounts and general correspondence. What would have been an otherwise undistinguished rectangular block was relieved by a liberal incorporation of white, marble-like Portland limestone, a prominent central triforum - with clock donated by the townspeople - and an impressive Mansard roof. The contract for the building had been awarded to A.N. Coles Ltd. of London & Plymouth in October 1925, with work commencing the following January. It opened for public use on 8th February 1927, although the official opening ceremony for the whole complex did not take place until Monday 11th April. The general expansion of facilities brought the new building much closer to the street than previously, making for a somewhat cramped forecourt.

The Moretonhampstead Bay

The junction layout at Newton Abbot East became considerably more complex as a result of the expansion programme. In addition to the main line connections, Branch trains originating or terminating at Newton were now able to use their own 'Bay' platform, parallel with, and independent of, the running lines through the rest of the station. The new Bay was built on the site of the old South Devon Railway goods yard, the goods shed here having been superseded by a very much larger structure in the 'New Yard' of 1911 (alongside the Moreton Branch). The platform, 320 feet long, was physically separate from the rest of the station, and was reached by way of a gentle ramp leading from the roadway on the north elevation of the main station building, opposite the parcels office. Facilities for passengers were sparse in the extreme: there was

Above: Newton Abbot station as seen from the Torquay Road bridge at the south end of the layout, circa 1908. The large, glazed train shed covering the 'up' and 'centre' platforms is clearly seen, together with the subsidiary overall roofs on the east side (covering the 'down' main line and carriage sidings, the latter subsequently being removed). The original West signal box was situated between the 'down main' and centre lines, but moved to this elevated position in 1893 following the expansion of the track layout at this end of the station. Notice the mixture of coaching stock: the short wheelbase vehicles, far left, being of the type still widely in use on the Moretonhampstead Branch. *Photomatic Ltd*

Right: Looking north from the footbridge beneath the train shed covering the 'up' main and middle running lines. The centre island platform was used by Moretonhampstead Branch departures, these being controlled by the small 23-lever 'Newton Abbot Middle Signal Box'. 'Down' main line trains and Branch arrivals used the outer face of the island platform on the far right of the picture. *National Railway Museum*

Above: In the autumn of 1924 work began on reconstructing the station. This view, taken from 'Middle Signal Box' on 15th January 1925, shows the north end of the new 'up' island platform. A start has yet to be made on the Moretonhampstead Branch/Parcels Bays, the access ramp to which will adjoin Phillips' 'Railway Hotel', whose gable end is just visible top left. *National Railway Museum   Below:* The new station building, seen not long after its opening in 1927. Among the architectural details of note are the shallow pilasters on the front elevation, a prominent dentil course below the roof and in the pediment, and the extensive, inscribed canopy. The Moretonhampstead Bay platform lies off-picture left, opposite the Parcels Office entrance.   *Lens of Sutton*

79774. NEWTON ABBOT, GREAT WESTERN STATION.

Above: Looking south from the soon to be replaced East Signal Box. The layout remodelling is in an advanced state, while the Moreton Bay is complete (seen to the right of the new main line island platforms). Roof inscriptions on the Teign Road warehouses were a long-standing feature. At this period, the more distant one advertises HENLEY'S FAMOUS CYDER, and the nearer EDWIN TUCKER & SONS LTD. MALTSTERS & SEED MERCHANTS. 5.3.26. *Below:* Moretonhampstead Junction, with the Branch and Lemon Bridge left, and South Devon main line and Teign Bridge right. The days of the 1893 signal box are numbered as the trackwork nears completion (although a trailing crossover was added in front of the enormous new East Box a short time after its commissioning). 5.3.26. *Both, National Railway Museum*

Viewed from the north end of the Bay, 0-6-0 Pannier Tank No. 3606 waits with two carmine and cream 'high-waist' Collett corridor coaches for departure at 4.35pm with a Teign Valley service, the 4.25 Moretonhampstead train having just left from the same platform. Though not advertised in public timetables, the 4.35 continued beyond its nominal destination of Exeter with an Exe Valley working to Dulverton. Platform 7 is playing host to 4-6-0 No. 4980 *Wrottesley Hall* with the 3.35pm relief train from Plymouth to Cardiff. 27.5.58.   *R. A. Lumber*

no canopy or awning of any kind and, initially, no waiting shelter. However, on 10th January 1947 a capacious brick-built waiting room was opened on the widest part of the platform. Passengers were not able to enjoy this new-found and welcome spaciousness for too long though, because in February 1955 the room was subdivided to provide a small office for the payment of wages. From the late 1950s the waiting accommodation was also used in connection with, first, the 'Car Tourist' service from London and later by various 'Motorail' services which used the Bay for loading the cars (a ramp having been built at

the buffer stop end). Long after this traffic had ceased, and the shelter had fallen into disuse, it continued to sport a 1979 'Motorail' poster on one of the walls well into the '90s! Its forwardly-sloping corrugated iron roof was extended on the north side to provide cover for a large wooden-gated lock-up shed. Abutting the opposite (south) wing was a substantial open-fronted corrugated iron bicycle shed, with space for motorcycles next to the waiting room. Appended to the end elevations of this tripartite arrangement was a small hut. Measuring approximately 12' x 7' they were built of reconstituted stone blocks - resembling conglomeritic breeze blocks - mounted on a shallow brick plinth and with a backwardly-sloping corrugated iron roof.

For nearly half its length, the outer (west) face of the platform was used as a Parcels Bay but, unlike the inner, had no direct access to the main line. Egress from the Moretonhampstead Bay, indeed, could be on any of three lines of travel. Although the 'Bay starting' signal at the end of the platform possessed only a single arm, the route to be taken was revealed in the indicator box beneath, namely: BRANCH, ENGINE SIDING, UP MAIN (black capital lettering on a white background; illuminated by a backlight at night). The 'Engine Siding' (actually a 'loop') was used as a 'refuge' or holding siding for the pilot engines coming off expresses up from Plymouth, having given much-needed assistance in tackling the ferocious gradients on this line. The siding was also used in connection with loco-hauled (that is, non push-pull or auto) Branch passenger trains. The absence of an 'engine release' crossover in the Bay itself, dictated a certain modus operandi. As the locomotive of a train that had arrived in the

Earnest conversation momentarily halts the loading of the 3.10pm Moretonhampstead auto train in Platform 9. Ahead of it is the 2.55 Teign Valley auto train to Exeter, its carmine and cream trailer being one of the converted steam rail motors with central vestibule. Motive power for both services is provided by a Collett 0-4-2 '14xx' tank engine. 1947.   *G. W. A. Shepherd*

Bay was trapped at the wrong end of the carriages for a return journey, it first propelled the coaching stock out along the Branch until clear of the points at the end of the platform. Having uncoupled, the engine returned to the Bay, where it could take on water at the column if necessary. It then 'ran round' the carriages by way of the engine siding, the driver finally easing the train back into the platform.

As the main station building was separated from the platforms by two running lines, access was by means of a footbridge, the stairs to which led out from the rear of the booking hall. Near the staircase end of the footbridge was the ticket barrier, making it impossible to reach or leave the platforms without showing one's ticket. The Moretonhampstead Bay, being a separate entity, was free from this inspection. The Railway Authorities, ever-concerned to circumvent fare-dodging, made sure that the Bay was not excluded from scrutiny! Just before a train was due in from the Branch, a porter walked out to the platform, to wait by the gate at the entrance. As passengers filed through the exit, he inspected/collected their tickets and in case anyone was found to be without, he was armed with an 'Excess Fares' pad to enable them to purchase one then and there. Passengers joining a Branch train at Newton had their tickets checked/collected at their destination, so could walk straight on to the Bay platform unchallenged. The guard would invariably be standing by his train prior to departure, and knew many of the 'regulars' by sight if not by name. If the coaching stock consisted of non-corridor vehicles, and if the guard did not recognise a traveller and/or know their destination, he would politely enquire. If they were bound for Brimley or Hawkmoor Halts, with their very short platforms, they would be directed into a compartment near that of the guard to ensure they would be able to alight. The guards and many of the passengers put in 'long service' on the Moreton Branch, which created something of an esprit de corps.

Motive Power Depot

No description of the Branch would be complete without at least some reference to the motive power depot at Newton Abbot, of which Moretonhampstead's tiny one-track granite engine-house was a sub-shed. In broad gauge days the Branch was very much self-contained as far as passenger traffic was concerned. As 'parent' shed, Newton provided the Branch Locomotive, which undertook all the duties and remained overnight at the moorland terminus. Only the goods service was covered by a loco and crew from the main line depot: itself only a modest twin-track shed with a handful of engines. Even after gauge conversion and the construction of a much larger six-road shed on a new site (in 1893), direct involvement with the Branch was minimal until the institution of a more intensive service in the late 1920s (especially in the summer months). The Moreton-based engine made periodic visits to the parent shed for routine maintenance: such a boiler washing, tube-cleaning or fire-bar replacement - some of which could be done overnight - or for more general overhaul or repairs to the Works, during which time the depot supplied another loco, generally of the same class. As there was a good deal of interchange between the motive power depot and its sub-sheds - Ashburton, Brixham and Kingswear also featured at various times - the same engines turned up at regular intervals on Branch services. It was only from November 1947 that all the work devolved on Newton Abbot in toto following the closure of the shed at Moretonhampstead.

The closure of the engine shed at Moretonhampstead coincided almost exactly with the end of the Great Western Railway. On the 1st January 1948 nationalisation saw the creation of British Railways, at which time Newton Abbot's

motive power depot had an allocation of 74 locomotives. On weekday mornings three of these had to be got ready for duties on the Moreton Branch: two 'passenger' and one 'goods'. The work of preparing engines at the beginning of a turn of duty (or 'diagram') and 'disposing' them at the end was largely performed by shed staff rather than footplate crew. These were the 'preparation gangs', made up of pairings of drivers and firemen from the depot's 'relief link'. They worked in a series of overlapping eight-hour shifts, the pattern of which reflected the busier times at the shed, the duty being referred to by its starting and finishing times: such as the 'Six to two Prep.' (namely 6am to 2pm). Other than on Monday mornings, the Branch engines did not need to be prepared from 'cold' having been kept in 'light steam' overnight from previous turns of duty. The fire needed periodic attention, while boiler pressure and water level were checked. This was the responsibility of the fireman. The driver moved the engine around the depot as necessary: to take on water and coal; to position the loco in the correct running order for duty; and/or to make room for incoming engines requiring disposal. When everything was ready for the Branch crew, the loco was left nicely simmering, and the details were chalked up on the shed notice board for the attention of the locomen. However, depending on the nature and/or duration of the roster, some loco crews were obliged to do some of this work themselves, as was the case with the first 'down' Branch working of the day. The engine had been kept in 'light steam' overnight, with one of the preparation gangs keeping an eye on it at intervals during their shift; so the crew really only had to make the final preparations in getting their charge ready 'ready for the road'. In the case of tank engines, as used exclusively on the Branch, an allowance of 45 minutes was given in the men's rosters for this work (it was an hour in the case of tender engines), with a further ten minutes to move off shed. At the end of their shift, the crew had 15 minutes for 'disposal', which included 'ticket time': filling out the details of work done. In the case of the 'late turn' Branch roster - only one loco was needed to cover the afternoon and evening passenger diagrams - the men were required to service the engine before booking off. When it was to be used the next day, it was necessary only to 'clean' the fire rather than 'drop' it completely.

The routine of booking on and off duty took place in the time office. When reporting in, men consulted the roster boards to see which loco had been assigned, along with the names of the other personnel in the 'set': a set comprising driver, fireman and guard. (The guards booked on in their own room in the suite of staff offices on the 'up' island platform at the station.) The experience of both driver and fireman counted for a great deal in ensuring a problem-free journey. However, the individual 'character' of the engine was also a factor. Branch locomen had their favourites and their pet aversions. Of the '1400' class Collett 0-4-2 tank engines, No. 1439 was particularly disliked. It had a reputation for poor steaming, and educed comments such as: "You had a job with just one coach on", and "it was a pig of an engine". Number 1466 on the other hand was the most highly favoured. For most of its life a 'Newton Abbot engine', it was really looked after by both shed staff and footplate crews, and was invariably turned out in excellent order. Much of its time was spent on the Ashburton Branch, but it made regular appearances at Moreton as well. The Churchward 2-6-2 'small Prairies' were generally popular engines, performing particularly well on the demanding goods duty. Of the more powerful and much heavier 'large Prairies', No. 4150 was considered the best of the bunch; although these engines were confined to passenger services due to restrictions on their use at certain sidings. While no such restrictions were placed on the Standard Class 3's, they were considered to be

A six-road structure, measuring 150 feet' x 100 feet, Newton Abbot engine shed (83A) had an allocation of around 70 locomotives in the decade following nationalisation. In this 1956 view, the line-up includes, from left to right: 4089 'Donnington Castle', 'large Prairie' No. 5108, Modified Hall No. 6988 'Swithland Hall', and 'large Prairies' 5154 and 4145. The elevated 47,000 gallon water tank is seen beyond the 'Castle', while behind the coal stack rise the chimneys belonging to the power station on Teign Road. The shed closed to steam in 1962, a new diesel-only depot opening in October of that year.   *Hugh Ballantyne*

poor substitutes for the admirable 'small Prairies'. Firemen especially disliked them due to their voracious appetite for coal on the climb north from Bovey, during which the enclosed cab became uncomfortably hot. The fireman had to keep busy with the shovel, for if the boiler pressure was not kept right up to the mark, the ejector failed to maintain the vacuum and the brakes started dragging on. When this happened, there was every likelihood that the train would grind to a halt on the long haul above Lustleigh.

The variety and volume of work performed at the motive power depot demanded a highly structured and planned regime, coupled with competent execution. In overall charge was the Divisional Locomotive Superintendent. For well over two decades this post was held by the renowned A.W.H. Christison. Having worked his way up from the shop floor, he was a 'railwayman's railwayman': well respected and always formally addressed as "Mister Christison" - at least to his face! From the elevated position - in more ways than one - of his office in the main station building, he liked to spend time watching the trains

below. He had a reputation as a fair-minded man, although woe-betide any driver who allowed his engine to make black smoke in the station! About once a month he made a tour of inspection of the depot, wearing that traditional badge of office: a bowler hat. His 'reign' lasted into early British Railways days, when his job description became that of District Motive Power Superintendent. Following retirement, he would occasionally return to his former stomping ground from his local station, Totnes, on the footplate of one of the banking engines returning to shed after a turn of duty assisting goods trains on the taxing gradients on either side of the Dart Valley.

The busy daily routine of the shed was overseen by a day foreman, who worked 'office hours', with duty foremen covering the shift work. They were based in the suite of staff rooms and offices situated on the easternmost part of the site, near Forde Road. The accommodation comprised, in sequence: chargeman cleaner's hut; day foreman's office; duty foremen's office; time office; stores; locomen's messroom; cleaners' cabin; and fitters'/boilersmiths' cabin. A short distance beyond was the wash house. Finally, there was the sand furnace, used to provide dry sand to combat slipping on greasy or icy rails - of which the Moretonhampstead Branch had its fair share on the steep section north of Bovey.

The proximity of the rooms was undoubtedly a convenient arrangement for the staff, although it was regretted on one celebrated occasion by a young cleaner. Newton Abbot shed was noted for the exemplary condition of its locomotives. This was due to the sterling efforts of the cleaners. Coming under the direction of a foreman cleaner, they were organised in small groups and assigned a number of locomotives. (Additionally, it was the duty of one of the men on the night shift to clean the offices on the top floor of the main station building.) Understandably, men felt aggrieved if one of their number was not thought to be pulling his weight. A youngster who had recently joined up was just one such case. He seemed to be permanently tired, and as soon as one loco was finished he would slope off. A search would invariably find him asleep in the cleaners' cabin. He came in for a lot of stick from his colleagues, but it did not make any difference. One night they decided to make their protest more forcibly. One of them climbed on the cabin roof and draped a damp cloth over the chimney. Not long afterwards, the youngster came out of the smoke-filled room coughing and spluttering, and angrily shouting "I'll get you" - to the great amusement of his workmates.

It was a few days later that he decided to exact revenge. The cleaners were allowed a short meal break during their shift, in which they retired to the warmth of their cabin. It was during this time that the errant cleaner decided to act. Obtaining a detonator, he clambered on to the roof of the staff rooms with the intention of dropping it down the cabin chimney. The heat of the fire would do the rest, and this time it would be the others who would get a rude awakening. Unfortunately, he chose the wrong chimney, and despatched the detonator into the stove of the drivers' cabin next door. Unaware of this, the cleaners were enjoying a chat over their sandwiches, when there was an almighty explosion nearby. Instinctively they rushed outside, to be joined by men converging from all around the depot to see what had happened. One can imagine their quizzical amazement at the sight of several drivers rapidly emerging from their cabin absolutely plastered with ash and coal dust. They were deafened and obviously shaken but, while dusting themselves down, and in between bouts of coughing, managed to make their displeasure evident by a colourful and comprehensive range of expletives. Although they cut a comical picture to the observers, it was a great indignity to men who were at the pinnacle of their profession - especially the 'Top Link' men, who were referred to at Newton Abbot as the 'OO Link' or 'Glory Boys'. Not surprisingly, the young cleaner, convicted of the recklessness of his action, kept a very low profile for a long time afterwards!

Newton Abbot Clay Siding

Beyond the Kingsteignton Road bridge, two-thirds of a mile from the station, was 'Newton Abbot Clay Siding'. Situated between the East Gold and West Gold Marshes, the bleakness of terrain, with its liability to flooding, is compensated for by the presence of commercially valuable ball clay deposits: a variant of china clay, for which Cornwall is so renowned. It was in the West Gold Marshes in 1932 that the Devon & Courtenay Clay Company purchased land for exploitation. The Company - owned by Candy & Co. of Heathfield - immediately approached the Great Western Railway with regard to the provision of a siding (on 23rd November). The GWR's Traffic Committee agreed to the request. The scheme, however, fell into abeyance, and when the Railway was next approached for a siding here it

was by Newton Abbot Clays Limited - which had operations on the other side of the Branch, in the East Gold Marshes. A 'Private Siding Agreement' between the two Companies was signed in August 1937 for the installation of a siding and loading dock on the 'up' side of the running line, facing trains from Newton. It opened to traffic on 7th April the following year.

As a single siding with no 'run-around' facility, it could only be shunted by an 'up' goods train. To obviate this inconvenience, an arrangement was designed whereby it could be attended from Newton Abbot. It was thus permissible for empty wagons to be propelled out to the siding, and loaded ones drawn back. There was no need for a brake van. As the siding was just inside the 'Branch outer home' signal, and so within the limits of East Box, it could be treated as a local shunting manoeuvre. This removed the need for the signalman to issue the 'electric train staff' (later, 'token') which gave authority to enter a single-track line of railway. The points which linked the siding to the running line were much too far away to be manually operated from the signal box by conventional point rodding. To overcome this, a line-side lever-stage, or 'ground frame', was employed. It possessed two levers: a blue-painted 'facing point lock' and a black-painted point lever. Normally held immovable in the frame for obvious security reasons, they were released by means of a special key - the Annetts Key - that was kept in an instrument in the signal box. Safety is paramount in railway operation, so the key could not be casually withdrawn from the machine; it was locked in place. To obtain it, the signalman first pulled a 'release lever' (No. 39). This unlocked the instrument and allowed him to turn and withdraw the key. The main block instrument was now locked by dint of this procedure, so that it was impossible for another train to occupy the section. The same key was used to unlock the nearby 'Newton Abbot Goods Ground Frame' - the lever stage there having replaced the small, ground-mounted 'Newton Abbot Goods Yard Signal Box' of 1911-1926.

In 1969 Newton Abbot Clays Ltd., along with the siding, were acquired by another Newton-based clay firm: Watts, Blake, Bearne & Co. (WBB). The siding continued in use, even though by this date the Branch passenger trains had been absent from the scene for ten years. At this time, the Line was experiencing something of a goods renaissance. Indeed, in later years the dock at the Clay Siding was revamped, incorporating an overhead gantry-style loading facility. The massive track rationalisation at Newton Abbot in 1985 associated with the Exeter-based multiple-aspect signalling scheme meant that the siding was worked by 'up' trains only, with inward 'empties' having to make the round trip to and from Heathfield. Clay continued to be despatched - principally conveyed in four-wheeled PGA wagons - to a variety of destination;s one consignment, for example, on 10th January 1991 going to a firm in Warrington. As it turned out, this was approaching the end of the siding's working life, for by the middle of the decade it was out of use.

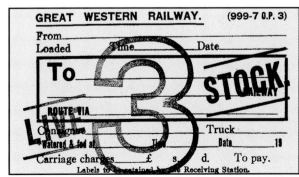

TEIGNBRIDGE

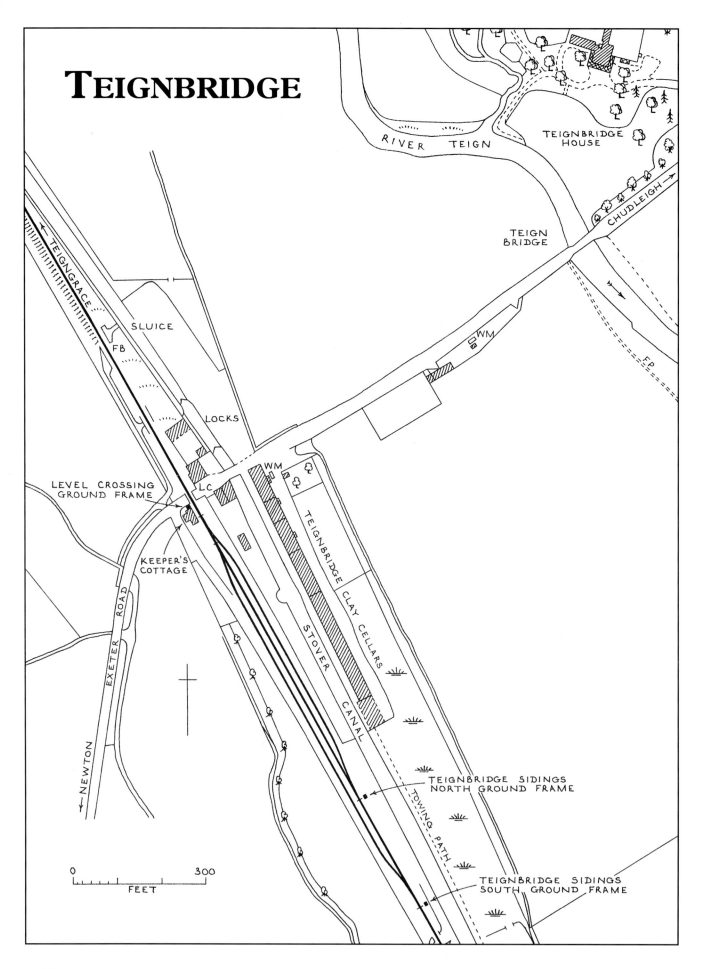

RIVER TEIGN

TEIGNBRIDGE HOUSE

CHUDLEIGH

TEIGN BRIDGE

TEIGNGRACE

SLUICE

FB

WM

LOCKS

WM

LEVEL CROSSING GROUND FRAME

LC

KEEPER'S COTTAGE

TEIGNBRIDGE CLAY CELLARS

STOVER CANAL

EXETER ROAD

NEWTON

TOWING PATH

TEIGNBRIDGE SIDINGS NORTH GROUND FRAME

TEIGNBRIDGE SIDINGS SOUTH GROUND FRAME

FP

0   300
FEET

Chapter Eight

TEIGNBRIDGE

From the plate girder bridge carrying the railway over the canal at Stover Locks in the East Gold Marshes, both transport modes keep close company across the alluvial flats of the lower Teign floodplain. Heading now in a north-westerly direction, their line of travel is intersected by a minor road linking the parishes of Kingsteignton and Highweek. This crosses the nearby river by means of the eponymous Teign Bridge, which had for a long time been the lowest bridging-point on the river (the railway track here being only about 15 feet above mean sea level). A minor road it might be, but it is also very old - dating back to Roman times - and was once the main Exeter to Newton Abbot 'highway'. By the early 1860s the amount of traffic using the road was much reduced, vehicles preferring the Kingsteignton Bridge route. This, together with the unconsolidated, poor load-bearing terrain, permitted the Moretonhampstead & South Devon Railway Company to set aside the normal requirements for a bridge, and instead allow the road to cross on the level: 1 mile 51 chains from Newton Abbot.

Teignbridge Level Crossing

The narrowness of the road meant that a single hand-operated gate on either side of the track sufficed. To ensure the safety of those using the crossing, and to open the gates, a resident gatekeeper was employed, his residence adjoining the west (Highweek) side of the track and south of the road. Built to an L-shaped plan, the single storey cottage with its ashlar walls was also provided with a small garden. The house was 'tied' to the Company, and the keeper was certainly tied to the job:

having to be in attendance during the hours that trains were running. One week's holiday a year was the only 'long' break the keeper received in Great Western days (the work then being covered by a 'relief' signalman). Understandably, it became the practice to appoint a person to the post whose partner could help out. It was quite common to find wives of railwaymen installed as keepers, deputing their husbands to cover the duties for brief absences, as for shopping or other essential expeditions. In 1947 this tradition came to an end when the GWR decided that the condition of the cottage had deteriorated to such an extent that it was no longer fit for habitation, and on 19th September condemned it as a dwelling house. The building was retained, however, as a 'cabin' for the keeper. Although he had to commute to work now, at least he had the benefit of a spacious refuge in between trains, otherwise he would have been confined to the cramped interior of the wooden lever cabin. This cabin was grandiosely described by its nameplate as TEIGNBRIDGE CROSSING BOX. While technically it was a 'ground frame' rather than a signal box, the term 'box' just about summed up its size in respect of floor space!

Prior to the introduction of the electric train staff mode of operation in 1901, signalling communication on the Branch had been by 'South Devon Block Telegraph Instruments'. By this means, the keeper was informed as to when a train was 'on line', and thus attend to the gates. The lever cabin was probably provided in association with, or soon after, the ETS system. Of lap-board construction, it was attached to the cottage by a simple awning, to provide shelter for the keeper as he watched trains pass over the road. He was in fact required to keep the

Teignbridge level crossing viewed from the 'up' side of the track. The lever cabin, situated between the keeper's house and level crossing, is timber-built, the walls being of shiplap construction. The ridge tiles of the slate-clad roof are of a pronounced round-topped, saddle-back type. The crossing keeper maintains a watchful eye on the photographer as the 12.45pm Teign Valley train to Newton Abbot hurries over the road, hauled by one of Exeter Shed's 0-6-0 Pannier Tanks No. 3677. 19.10.57.   *Peter W. Gray*

crossing under observation, because although the gates were locked against road traffic, the pedestrian (or 'wicket') gates adjoining them - next to the cabin - could not be locked, and consequently it was important to make sure that no-one tried to dash across the line just before the passage of a train. As an added precaution, the wicket gates opened away from the track. The 'crossing indicator' instrument on the shelf above the levers in the cabin informed the keeper of the direction of travel of an approaching train. In addition, an 'extension bell' was fixed to the centre of the front wall of the house. In this position it could be heard from inside the cottage, cabin or immediate vicinity. It repeated the bell codes sent between the signalmen in the boxes at either end of the section: Newton Abbot East and Heathfield. When the bell emitted two rings - which were repeated by way of acknowledgement - it meant that a train had entered the section. The indicator responded to the working of the block instrument in Heathfield signal box, showing whether it was an 'up' or 'down' service. This took the form of a display in capital letters in a 'window' in the face of the wooden crossing indicator instrument. The lever cabin also doubled as permanent way 'Occupation Hut No.2', housing all the accoutrements connected therewith: the 'ganger's key' instrument and telephone; the telephone and code card for the Newton Abbot to Moretonhampstead circuit; and associated batteries.

The heavy wooden gates were hinged to the right-hand stanchions - as viewed from the road - with the locking mechanism being worked by lever No.2 in the cabin. The interlocking mechanism of the ground frame was such that the keeper was not able to pull the lever to lower the appropriate distant signal until the gates were locked (or 'bolted' in Railway parlance) across the road. The 'down' distant signal was 614 yards from the cabin, and the 'up' 605 yards. Train crews kept a sharp lookout for them, for if they were still in the 'on' position (caution) as they passed, it would be necessary to reduce speed in anticipation of the gates still being against them. There were no 'stop' signals at Teignbridge, red-painted lamp cases centred on the top bar of the gates fulfilling this role. These were filled with paraffin to show a red light at night. Approaching a distant signal at 'caution', the engine driver would 'whistle up' to warn the keeper of the train's presence, and would continue to whistle at frequent intervals until he could see either the signal arm lower to the 'off' ('clear') position or that the gates had been opened. The locomotives were fitted with two whistles: one giving a shrill 'warning' blast, and the other - the brake whistle - having an altogether deeper sound; and it was this latter that drivers used to alert both the keeper and the guard. As the train passed, the driver and keeper invariably exchanged salutes in the time-honoured raised arm fashion: as much to indicate that all was well as a greeting.

Teignbridge Level Crossing came under the jurisdiction of Newton Abbot, which was responsible for paying the keeper's wages. Although the keeper undertook the periodic topping-up of the paraffin gate lamps, a signal lamp-man from Newton attended to the distant signal lamps and necessary maintenance. Following the withdrawal of passenger services in 1959, the keeper was retained for a time. In the signalling changes of 1965, which saw the end of traditional block instrument working on the Branch, the level crossing ground frame was taken out of use (12th October). The locking mechanism was disconnected and the gates padlocked across the track in between trains. Shortly afterwards, red 'targets' were fitted to the gate centres to fulfil the role of 'stop' signals, and as the freight trains were now running during daylight hours only, the lamps were removed. Additionally, 'Stop Boards' were placed a few yards in advance of the crossing, with the (hopefully!) superfluous instruction to the train crew to "Stop. Open crossing gates before proceeding." The shunter who

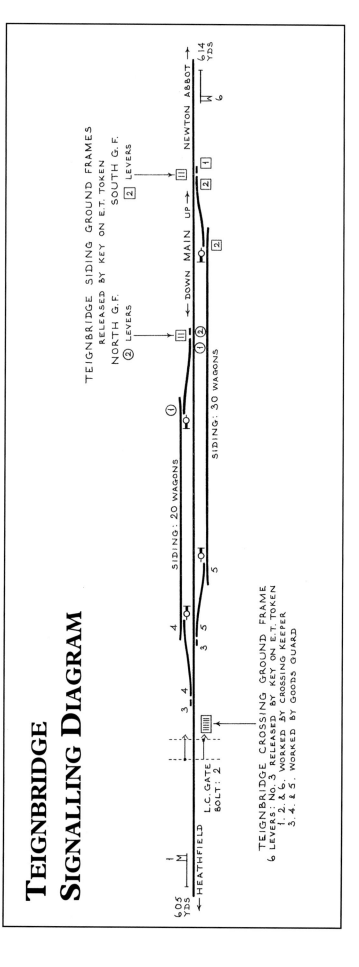

Teignbridge Signalling Diagram

90

accompanied the trains had responsibility for dealing with the gates.

Teignbridge Siding

It was off the road to the east of the level crossing that clay storage/loading facilities, known as clay cellars, were provided on the Stover Canal. The stone-built cellars were still in active use when the Branch opened, but no attempt was made to set up a rail-served facility (the Railway Company being the owners of the canal at this time). The desire to open a 'clay siding' first surfaced in 1892, the year the Branch was 'narrowed' from the 7-foot broad gauge to the 4' 8½" standard. Following an approach to the Great Western Railway by William Herbert Whiteway-Wilkinson, representing the local clay firm of Whiteway & Co., a siding agreement was signed in mid June. However, it was not until 1st May 1896 that such a facility was opened: 'Teign Bridge Siding', centred at 1 mile 45 chains from Newton Abbot station. It was installed on the 'up' side of the running line, nearest the canal, and was able to hold twenty standard-length wagons. For a little over half its length it was accompanied by a wide loading platform, with a ramp at the level crossing end. Access to the site was through a wide gateway adjoining the crossing. Being on the canal side of the railway, as were the clay pits, it did not increase the volume of road traffic needing to cross the line. For the first few years, 'down' trains only were booked to call 'as required'; the goods train at this period leaving Newton at 1.15pm. This arrangement entailed railing loaded trucks on to Heathfield for collection on the return leg; the ball clay going principally to Teignmouth Quay for export. Early in the new century, traffic was sufficiently constant to warrant the 1.15 to make a scheduled stop each weekday on the outward journey, and to call 'as required' on the return.

As the requirements of the clay industry changed, so the method of servicing the siding was adapted to meet the new needs. The variations are too numerous in detail and frequent in occurrence to enumerate fully, involving permutations of scheduled and request stops for Moreton, Heathfield and Teign Valley Services, in 'up', 'down', or both directions! Of particular note was the institution, in 1904, of a request service dedicated solely to the siding. The train left Newton Abbot at 4.45pm and was booked to arrive at Teignbridge a generous ten minutes later. It returned at 5.15 (advanced to 5.20 in 1906). This now caused the Moreton Goods to be timetabled to call as required on both legs of the journey. In addition, there was also

a local request trip to Heathfield and back. Booked to leave Newton at 4pm, it ran non-stop to Heathfield, arriving 15 minutes later. The return journey began at 4.50, with provision for stops at Teigngrace and Teignbridge if required; with arrival back at Newton scheduled for 5.35pm. Only one of these 'trip' workings would be run on any given day due to the operational constraints imposed by the fact that the Line was single track. The coverage of the siding by these services removed the need for the Moreton Goods to call. In the Company's working timetables for the years before the First World War, these trains were identified by the initials RR - 'runs as required' - in relation to which the following instruction was issued:

"Heathfield to advise Newton Abbot by 2pm whether 4pm or 4.45 train is required. On occasions when the 4.0 or 4.45pm RR train is run the 4.24pm Goods ex Moretonhampstead will not call at Teign Bridge, but the work at that place will be done by the RR train."

As traffic grew, it was decided to provide a second siding and clay loading dock. This was installed on the other ('down') side of the running line, and brought use on 22nd January 1914. Road vehicles reached the dock by means of a gated trackway leading off Exeter Road, to the rear of the crossing keeper's cottage. It was the responsibility of the keeper to ensure that this gate, like the one for the original siding, was kept closed after any work had been completed. The opportunity was taken to put in a longer length of track to allow for any future expansion: the new siding being able to accommodate thirty standard wagons. As a 'loop', it was connected to the running line at both ends. The Newton-end point turnout was operated by a lever stage (or ground frame) 'released' by the keyed attachment at the end, initially, of the electric train staff, and from July 1943 the electric train token. The same arrangement applied to the other siding. Both loops were operated at the level crossing end from the ground frame in the lever cabin.

Despite the presence of a second loop line, official railway publications continued to refer to the location in the singular: Teign Bridge Siding. Later, and on the lever cabin nameplate, the location was identified as 'Teignbridge'. The regime for servicing sidings continued to show variations over short periods of time. Only from the mid 1930s did a fairly constant pattern emerge, which continued for the next twenty or so years. In the 'down' direction this involved the scheduled calling of the first train of the day - the Teign Valley Goods - generally between 7.06 and 7.25am; followed by a request stop by the Moreton Goods in the late morning. In the 'up' direction, the roles were

'Small Prairie' No. 5530 - with the larger, sloping tanks - rattles over the north end points of Teignbridge Siding on the last leg of its return journey with the Moretonhampstead Goods. The engine was one of the eight '45xx' 2-6-2 tank engines shedded at Newton Abbot in its last days under GWR ownership, but later found service at Gloucester, whose shed plate (85B) she still carries. Withdrawn from Newton Abbot in January 1960 and taken into storage at Swindon, she met her end at Buttigieg's scrapyard, Newport, in May that year. The buildings to the right of the loco are part of the former clay cellars (covered stores) alongside the Stover Canal. 19.10.57. *Peter W. Gray*

reversed: the early afternoon Teign Valley Goods calling by request only, with the returning Moreton Goods making a booked stop for about eleven minutes in the late afternoon.

If additional shunting was necessary, or a consignment of clay needed urgent despatch, provision was made to cover the work from Newton Abbot. The 1934 Working Appendix of the timetable, for example, states that:

"Whenever necessary, a brake-van may be propelled from Newton Abbot East for the purpose of picking up loaded traffic at Teignbridge Sidings. The Guard must ride in the brake-van, keep a sharp look-out, and be prepared to hand-signal to the Driver. The loaded train must return to Newton Abbot East with brake-van at rear."

This arrangement permitted the layout to be shunted from the south end without interfering with the public road at the level crossing, and also saved a little time as there was no need to run the engine round. The driver had to be in possession of electric train staff for the section to Heathfield, the Newton East signalman sending the 'blocking back' code to the former (which was cancelled when the train arrived back at Newton).

The ball clay industry was subjected to fluctuations in production due to market forces and then to the disruption of the Second World War. Soon after the war the fortunes of one group at least began to revive markedly both in terms of output and productivity: the Newton-based firm of Watts, Blake, Bearne & Co. In 1947 the Company constructed a new clay loading platform alongside the original, shorter siding. In return for the Railway's agreeing to the installation, WBB undertook to meet all costs and, additionally, to avoid any accusations of self-interest, generously permitted its use by other operators. Underpinned by a framework of steel girders, the new platform had a surface of transverse metal plates edged with raised timber baulks against which lorries could back prior to tipping their contents into the waiting trucks. The track in front of, and

slightly beyond, the platform was embedded in concrete up to the top of the sleepers, to facilitate the easy hosing away of any clay spillage into a drain which ran along the outside edge of the 'apron'. In 1950 the loading dock on the longer 'down' siding was renewed. The crossing keeper was required to prepare a list of all the wagons dealt with at the sidings, and notify the goods agent at Newton Abbot. It may be worth mentioning en passant that the firm with whom the original Siding Agreement had been made - Whiteway & Co. - was acquired by WBB in 1964.

The withdrawal of passenger services on the last day of February 1959 brought about a revision in the freight schedules. The sidings were now attended by a 'through' train in both directions on all six weekdays, with an additional 'request' out-and-back 'trip' working from Newton Abbot on Mondays to Fridays. Of especial significance to the post Steam Age history of Teignbridge was the introduction of a vacuum-fitted 'Clayliner' service to Stoke-on-Trent. Open, plank-sided wagons were used, most of these being of the standard 13-ton BR type, although a few of pre-nationalisation vintage were also pressed into service. All were painted in red bauxite livery, with the directive "FOR CHINA CLAY TRAFFIC ONLY" picked out in white inside a black panel. The train commenced its journey at St Blazey (near Par) in Cornwall, and ran on Mondays to Fridays, with any ball clay from Teignbridge being taken the short distance to Newton Abbot by a local 'trip' working to pick up the Clayliner there. Traffic for the North of England and Scotland was subsequently forwarded from the Potteries. The first consignment connected with this service left Teignbridge on Thursday 18th November 1965.

Five weeks previously the Branch had been reduced in status in effect to a goods siding, following the closure of Heathfield signal box. The point rodding from the ground frames at Teignbridge had been disconnected, and replaced by pivot-action hand levers. The tarpaulin-covered wagons continued their regular visits for some years, generally using the shorter 'up' side loading platform. The wagon-labelling and other work connected with this traffic was sufficient to warrant a continued staff presence, so that the post of 'checker' replaced that of crossing keeper (the title of 'leading railman' being further substituted in 1967/8). When the sole surviving post at Heathfield was abolished on 5th June 1972, the work at that place transferred to Teignbridge, whose leading railman consequently had the distinction of being the very last member of staff employed on the Branch - but not for long. Ball clay was still being despatched at the beginning of the 1980s, but by the middle of the decade the rusty and overgrown condition of both sidings pointed to the fact that they had fallen into disuse. With the decision to introduce new, higher capacity, air-braked rolling stock from 1987, and with the surviving giant clay firms of WBB and ECC opting to install new facilities at Newton Abbot and Heathfield respectively, the end had finally come for Teignbridge. By the summer of the following year, the sidings were officially out of use, and although they remained in situ, their connections with the running line had been either clipped or severed. Within the next few years both sidings had been lifted and the connections removed, while the former crossing keeper's cottage by this time was displaying an air of serious dilapidation.

Top: Teignbridge Sidings are pictured from the down-side loading platform in the mid to late 1960s. The uncovered wagons are awaiting their cargo before the assemblage can be taken to Newton Abbot to pick up the 'Clayliner' train. Given the viscous nature of ball clay and its susceptibility to discolouration, tarpaulins were essential to eliminate the risk of contact with water. The thick vegetation behind the loading platform is evidence of the advanced state of dereliction into which the adjacent Stover Canal has fallen, having seen no traffic for the last thirty years or so. *Below:* About twenty years before the previous picture was taken, the newly rebuilt clay loading platform plays host to one of Watts, Blake, Bearne & Co.'s lorries, seen about to discharge its load into one of the waiting wagons. *Both, WBB*

Chapter Nine

Teigngrace

Just beyond the 2¼ mile post the Branch came along side a former wharf on the Stover Canal, which was reached by means of an 'occupation' style level crossing over the railway (the gates being opened by the user). On the west side of the Line, a trackway led to the village of Teigngrace. The term 'village' is probably too generous, for the 1861 census showed a population of just 172. Even then, that figure was for the whole parish; an area comprised in the main of tracts of wood and heath - notably the Teigngrace Heathfield - and the extensive grounds of the Stover Estate. Apart from the tiny village, the only other settlements consisted of a few scattered houses and farms. Indeed, when the Line opened in 1866, the paucity of the population did not warrant the provision of a station. This situation was soon to change, for what the village lacked in size, it made up for in influence: both social and economic.

The Lower Lodge of the Stover Estate was situated on the edge of the village, at the end of a long drive down from Stover House, the residence of Edward Adolphus Seymour, Duke of Somerset (and Lord-lieutenant of Devon!). His agent, Edward Snelling Bearne, lived in the village, while the Rector of the church of St. Peter and St. Paul was an appointee of the Duke. As one of the conditions of selling the requisite land to the Moretonhampstead & South Devon Railway, the Duke had

secured the right to stop any train at Teigngrace whenever he wished to travel. Given these considerations, it seemed only logical, politic and practical to provide a station, and the work was soon put in hand.

Teigngrace Station opened on Monday 16th December 1867, with the official distance of 2 miles 28 chains from Newton Abbot. It was reached by way of a wide, straight, tree-lined drive from the public road at the north-end of the village. The facilities were fairly basic, consisting of a single 200 foot-long platform with a plain, centrally-positioned red-brick building. With a symmetrical arrangement about an open-fronted waiting alcove, the accommodation consisted of a booking-cum-parcels office on one side (south) and lavatory block on the other. Apart from an apron of non-slip ironstone tiles in front of the station building, the platform surface was of rolled, broken stone and gravel. Faced with masonry blocks and edged with stone flags - later replaced in part by concrete slabs - it was backed by wooden palings. During Victorian and Edwardian times, these were adorned with several enamel advertisement boards. Its importance was considered sufficient to justify the appointment of a station master, Benjamin Taylor, as well as a porter.

Easter Saturday morning 1957 was damp and grey when 'large Prairie' No. 4105 arrived with a train from Moretonhampstead. Being an unstaffed halt, it is the guard's responsibility to ensure that passengers have entrained/alighted and that all doors are secure before giving the 'right away'.

The late David Fereday Glenn (Miles Barber Glenn collection)

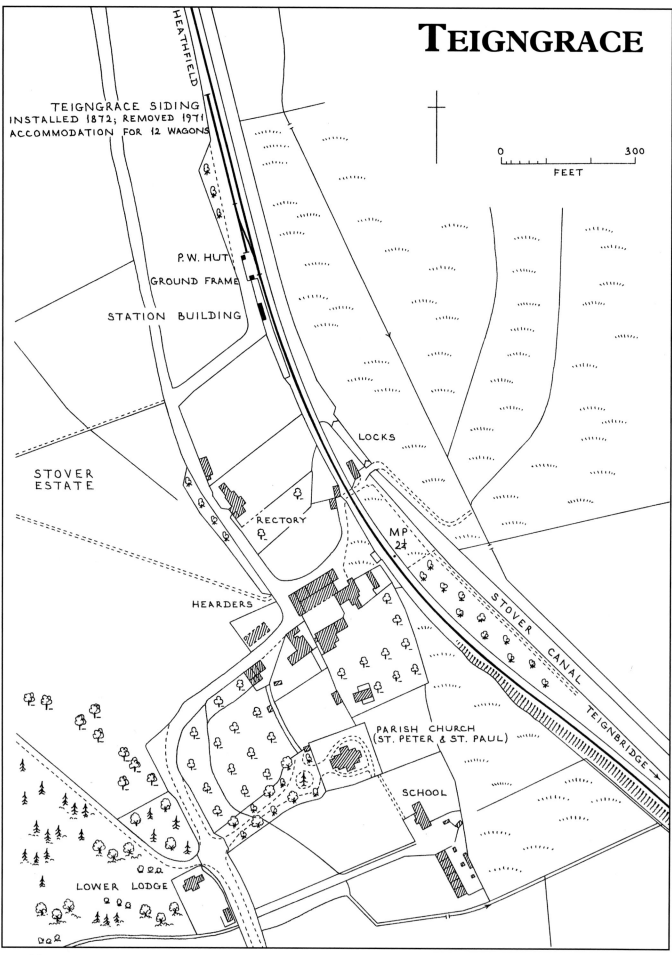

TEIGNGRACE

TEIGNGRACE SIDING
INSTALLED 1872; REMOVED 1971
ACCOMMODATION FOR 12 WAGONS

HEATHFIELD

P.W. HUT

GROUND FRAME

STATION BUILDING

0   300
FEET

LOCKS

STOVER
ESTATE

RECTORY

MP
27

HEARDERS

STOVER CANAL

TEIGNBRIDGE →

PARISH CHURCH
(ST. PETER & ST. PAUL)

SCHOOL

LOWER LODGE

A 1921 view of Teigngrace station, looking north towards Heathfield. The lamp post nearest the camera marks the southern end of the original 200 foot platform, whilst the wooden palings backing the 52 foot extension of 1892 carry various advertisements. At the far end of the platform, standing on the site of the short-lived signal box, is the white-painted wooden cabin, or 'ground frame', from which the siding points were operated. *L&GRP*

There were also economic factors promoting the provision of a station here. During the years that the Line was under construction, iron ore was being sent away by barge from the wharf at Teigngrace. It was brought on a long and slow journey from the mine at Smallacombe, in Haytor Vale, and was stockpiled on the canal side by the bridge. On the opening of the railway, this traffic understandably switched to the more conveniently located Bovey station, but there remained the possibility of developing ball clay, gravel and lignite deposits on the Duke's land. To cater for this expected traffic, plans were drawn up for a siding to be put in immediately to the north of Teigngrace station. An estimate of £260 for this work was submitted to the M&SDR directors on 16th April 1868. For whatever reason, a four-year hiatus, followed, and it was not until 6th June 1872 that an application was made to the Board of Trade to inspect and sanction the siding. On the eleventh of that month the well-travelled and well-known Railway Inspector Col. Yolland made his inspection of the installation. His report to the Board was admirably concise by prevailing standards: "The Points leading out of, and into this Siding are properly interlocked with the Signal and the sanction of the Board of Trade for its being used for traffic may at once be given". The signal referred to was a large disc mounted above the point capstan. It was painted black with a white outer ring, and swivelled when the point was changed to indicate the route set. Sanction was given three days later, transmitted to the South Devon Railway Company, who from 1st July were formally to absorb the M&SDR.

The siding, approximately 80 yards long, was able to hold twelve standard wagons. There was also a short spur leading from the points towards the station. It had little operational value, although as the points were left set in its direction, it protected the main line from 'unauthorised' wagon movements in the siding. The connection with the main line faced trains from Newton Abbot. Company timetables contained instructions/information relating to this siding, as well as to Granite and Pottery Sidings south of Bovey; as for example in this extract from 1887:

"When the Signals which protect the .... Sidings stand at danger, Detonators (fixed on an iron rod attached to the base of the Signals) will be placed on the Line of rails, which the Signals govern. When Drivers run over the Detonators they must stop their Trains as speedily as possible. The Head Guards are responsible for the working of these Points and Signals, and for leaving the Points locked for the Main Line, and Signals turned to show "All Right"."

Following the gauge conversion of May 1892, the platform was lengthened by 52 feet in the Newton direction; this time faced with brick. Shortly after this, a signal box was installed at the north end of the platform. Of wooden construction, it was little more than a cabin, housing an 11-lever frame (8 'working'; 3 'spare'). It controlled a 'distant', 'home' and 'starting' signal in either direction, and also the points to the siding. Not being a 'block post', it could neither accept nor refuse trains, but only superintend their passage through, and shunting manoeuvres at, the station. The layout did not remain fully signalled for long, for the introduction of the electric train staff system of signalling in November 1901 rendered it redundant. The box was not so

No. 1466 waits at the halt with the 5.10pm from Moretonhampstead. As this is the last 'up' service before dark, the guard has hung a single hurricane lamp above the waiting shelter entrance. The loco will shortly propel the single trailer (W241W) the final 2¼ miles to Newton Abbot, keeping in close contact almost all the way with the long-disused Stover Canal - whose heavily overgrown bed lies on the far side of the boundary fence. 21.2.59.

Peter W. Gray

much closed as reduced in status. The signals were indeed removed, but it seems that the nearby siding points continued to be operated from the cabin for the next twenty years, with the levers being unlocked by the key-like attachment on the end of the train staff. In early 1921 this arrangement was superseded by the installation of an open two-lever stage near the foot of the platform ramp, nearer the turnout from the running line. Station staff were kept informed of train movements by a 'crossing indicator' with bell, fixed on a wooden bracket above the office telephones (the associated batteries being kept in a cupboard beneath). Adjoining the Heathfield end of the platform was 'Occupation Hut No.3': a timber-built shed used by the Newton-based permanent way gang. It contained the 'Ganger's Key' instrument and telephone, whose ten large dry-cell batteries were kept in a covered box on the floor of the hut.

With statistical data only being available from 1925, the volume and nature of traffic in the preceding period cannot be assessed, but the location retained the post of station master until that very year. Benjamin Taylor was still the incumbent in the late 1870s and early '80s, to be followed by Charles Squire and James Elliott Towillis. The last-named was still 'in-post' when, as a wartime economy measure, the station was closed on

and from 1st January 1917. It was not until 1st May 1919 that it reopened, with Sidney George Stevens occupying the revived post of station master for the next six years. His duties terminated on Saturday 9th May 1925, from which date the supervision of Teigngrace passed to the station master at Heathfield. A porter, however, was retained for another fourteen years; his annual wage in the mid 1920s being a mere £76.

The majority of passengers boarded trains for Newton Abbot, but the numbers for this and other destinations showed a steady decline from the mid 1920s. With the exception of 1932, every year between 1925 and 1939 saw a progressive diminution in the number of ticket sales and revenue. Thus in 1925 the number stood at 3,518 with a value of £97; while in 1930 it was 1,415/£52; and 1936, 918/£36. In every case the figures are for single/return tickets only; no season tickets were issued in those, or most other, years. By the last date, the total revenue collected at the station was exceeded by the porter's annual wage, and as the situation continued to decline, the station was reduced in status to that of an unstaffed 'halt' on and from 8th May 1939.

Parcels traffic was fairly low-key, with more items being

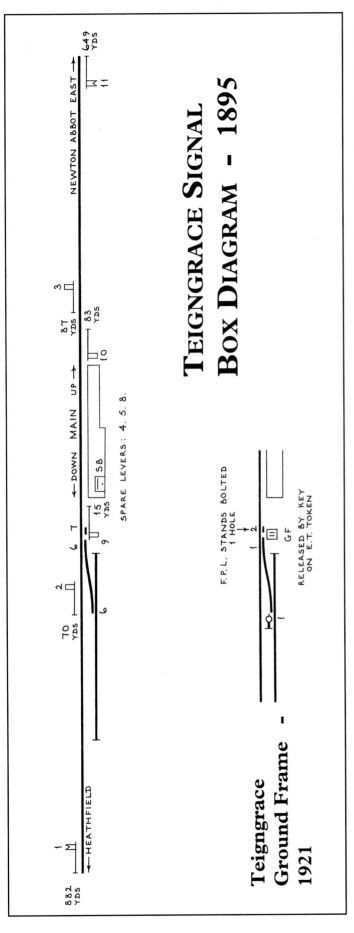

TEIGNGRACE SIGNAL BOX DIAGRAM – 1895

649 YDS

NEWTON ABBOT EAST →

11

3

87 YDS

83 YDS

10

← DOWN MAIN UP →

SB

SPARE LEVERS : 4. 5. 8.

15 YDS

9

7

6

2

70 YDS

6

HEATHFIELD

882 YDS

Teigngrace Ground Frame – 1921

F.P.L. STANDS BOLTED
1 HOLE

1
2

GF

RELEASED BY KEY
ON E.T. TOKEN

received than despatched, and the revenue earned fluctuating between £12 and £31 per annum. The despatch of milk churns to Newton Abbot each weekday morning was a feature of the station for many years, and though not large, continued after it had ceased at all the other stations on the Branch. From exactly 500 cans in 1925, the figure jumped to a peak of 623 two years later and remained above 600 to, and including, 1930. After that the traffic fell away, and 1936 was its last year (248 cans).

The unstaffing of the station in 1939 brought about the end of the parcels facility. All trains continued to call after this date, despite the low level of patronage, including the summer Sunday trains when they were restored in 1949: which was quite a concession given that there had been no Sunday provision at Teigngrace since 1917. The station building was retained as its waiting recess or 'alcove' continued in use as a shelter, avoiding the need to put up a separate structure. All matters relating to the halt passed to Heathfield, the station master there being responsible for seeing that timetables were written out and posted in the waiting recess. A porter made occasional visits to check that everything was in order, although inevitably the previous good condition of the station suffered in the absence of resident staff. Away from the building environs the platform succumbed, first, to encroachment by moss, and then grass; while the wooden fencing became increasingly shabby and in poor repair - so much so, that much of it had to be ultimately replaced with post-and-wire. The suffix 'HALT' was added to the original name board, while the attractive oil lamps were supplanted by plain, hooked metal posts on which hurricane lamps were hung. The provision of lighting was a daily duty of staff at the supervising station, and was necessary for all but the mid-summer weeks. As lighting-up time varied, cognisance had to be taken of the 'up' train service to enable the lamps to be in position by dusk. In practice, only one hurricane lamp was usually provided; this being hung up on a hooked bracket above the entrance to the 'alcove'. The late-turn porter at Heathfield filled and trimmed the lamp, lit it and left it on the platform for collection by the guard of the next 'up' train. The guard of the last train to call at Teigngrace - a 'down' service - was required to turn the lamp out. It was left in position until the next morning, when the guard of the first train from Newton collected it and returned it to Heathfield for a repeat performance.

The most fundamental change in Teigngrace's relegation to halt status was the inability of intending passengers to buy

The posts supporting the station name board consist of lengths of old rails. The name is formed of cast iron letters screwed to the face; the subsidiary board denotes the reduced 'halt' status acquired in 1939. Notice the simple lamp post to the right of the board, designed to hold the hurricane lamp which replaced the original oil standards. 1959.
S. J. Dickson

tickets prior to their journey. The guards on the Moreton Branch did not carry sets of tickets as they did on the neighbouring Teign Valley Line, so that they had to be purchased at the next staffed station. In the case of 'up' trains this was Newton Abbot, where the fare would be paid to a porter waiting at the exit from the Bay platform (No. 9). Details were made out in duplicate on an Excess Fares pad, one copy being given to the passenger and the other, along with all monies, being taken to the booking office. Newton was the chief destination, the third class cheap day return fare in the mid 1950s being 9d. Passengers travelling down the line would briefly leave the train at Heathfield to purchase pre-printed card tickets from the booking office there; quite an inconvenience, as it involved crossing the tracks to the opposite platform and walking almost to the far end of that. Where trains did not wait for long, or people did not feel like a walk, they could always buy a ticket at their destination - providing it was not another halt!

Goods traffic was occasional and generally small-scale, consisting in the main of the odd wagon or two of coal being taken in and later removed as 'empties'. However, there were interesting variations (see Table 11). After a number of years when all traffic had been 'inwards', there was suddenly an outward consignment of 956 tons in 1935, which produced an income of £335: a figure that made up almost 84% of the station's total from all sources for that year! This was accounted for by a short-lived, one-off despatch of minerals, principally ball clay, from the Stover Estate, a road-to-rail loading ramp having been provided at the siding. Although the 'passenger parcels' facility was withdrawn in 1939, the freight provision was retained - indeed, a new loading ramp faced with reconstituted stone blocks was installed in 1947. As the traffic returns now went in with those of Heathfield, the supervising station, any differentiation is impossible; although the new loading ramp seems to have had minimal use. The post-war years saw very little activity in the small yard, with a daily goods train continuing to call by request rather than having a scheduled stop (this tending to be the Teign Valley goods rather the Moreton goods as before). In the absence of a run-round facility, the siding had to be shunted by 'up' trains, any 'inward' wagon/s being taken through to Heathfield in the morning and brought back later in the day, coupled next to the engine. Following the withdrawal of passenger trains from the Branch in 1959, it was permissible for the siding to be worked by means of an out-and-back trip from Heathfield, the loco propelling the vehicles on the return journey. It is unlikely that this new arrangement was called upon. By the early 1960s the siding,

although officially still open, was becoming badly overgrown through lack of use, but in spite of this, it was not lifted until 1971.

If its days under British Railways were ones of decline, Teigngrace Halt did have a sudden burst of activity that brought passengers back in plenty. In 1952 the Royal Show came to Devon. This was a 'moveable feast', having been hosted in the previous three years by, sequentially, Shrewsbury, Oxford and Cambridge. Now it was Teigngrace's turn to host this prestigious event: in the extensive grounds of Stover Park. The highlight of the four-day show was to be a visit on the second day (Wednesday 2nd July) of the newly acceded but as yet uncrowned Elizabeth II; which doubtless increased the number of visitors that day. Although she travelled down to Newton Abbot on the 10-coach, plum-liveried Royal Train from an overnight stop at Thorverton on the Exe Valley Branch, the journey to Stover was made by road. However, for the duration of the show an augmented service between Newton and Teigngrace was provided, slotted in between the scheduled Branch trains, which themselves ran to a revised timetable. Because it was not possible to run the engine round at Teigngrace - and to maximise flexibility and frequency - an auto (push-pull) train was allocated. Rather than use one of Newton Abbot's 0-4-2 Collett tank engines, an auto fitted '64xx' class 0-6-0 Pannier Tank was loaned specially to cover this job: namely, engine No. 6406. Sent up from Laira motive power depot, Plymouth, the loco was kept in smart 'exhibition' condition for the special shuttle service to and from Teigngrace.

Following the closure of the halt to passengers in February 1959, the station building became for a short time the headquarters of the South Devon Railway Society. A keen and active pressure group, its founder was Richard Cottrell of Wellington (Somerset), while one of the prime-movers, as well as chairman and holder of the station keys, was Canon Jones, Rector of Teigngrace. Its aim was the restoration of passenger services to the Branch, to which end it engaged in feasibility studies, petitioning British Railways, and organising 'Specials' to keep the Line in the public mind (these are referred to in more detail in the Postscript). Permission was granted for the Society to lease the station building for an annual rental of £5, and by July 1961 a small amount of essential preliminary restoration work had begun; a discreet notice on the fence by the gate proclaiming it to be the Society's headquarters. Its events and special excursions over the Line were well patronised and the case for the introduction of diesel multiple units cogently argued; but BR was just not interested: they seemed to be locked into closure or rationalisation mode in the early 1960s. It soon became evident that the Society's cause was lost, and members' enthusiasm and efforts were diverted to the exciting developments connected with the reopening of the Dart Valley Branch as a steam railway. The building at Teigngrace lasted for several more years, but ultimately succumbed to the destructive intentions of the demolition men.

Table 11. Selected Traffic Returns : Teigngrace

| YEAR | PASSENGERS | | | | PARCELS | | | MILK | | GOODS | | |
	Tickets (Single & Return)	£	Season Tickets	£	No. Sent out	No. Rec'd	Total Value £	No. of cans	Total Value £	Tons Sent out	Tons Rec'd	Total Value £
1925	3518	97	-	-	19	39	3	500	16	4	482	64
1926	2640	71	1	1	27	36	1	596	20	7	440	57
1927	2452	70	5	1	29	34	4	623	20	1	570	65
1928	2099	65	-	-	50	40	7	592	17	1	369	80
1929	1869	60	8	2	48	42	5	615	14	-	441	55
1930	1415	52	1	-	26	39	5	602	12	-	350	31
1931	1316	49	4	1	27	26	2	310	12	-	18	17
1932	1425	52	-	-	13	53	2	495	21	-	26	25
1933	1234	40	-	-	6	123	7	562	24	1	9	15
1934	1193	40	-	-	8	114	2	311	12	-	130	21
1935	1101	36	1	-	12	70	-	312	12	956	35	353
1936	918	36	-	-	11	83	4	248	10	2	41	24
1937	845	34	-	-	4	57	-	-	-	9	45	44
1938	774	31	-	-	7	61	-	-	-	-	34	25

Chapter Ten

HEATHFIELD

Heathfield station, circa 1909. One of the recently built 'small Prairie' tank engines is entering the single 'through' platform with a train from Moretonhampstead. Although the track was narrowed from broad to standard gauge in 1892, it still retains the former Brunelian design of rails affixed to longitudinal sleepers. The signal box was constructed by the Teign Valley Railway Company as an independent undertaking, its standard gauge line of 1882 exclusively using its own bay platform (obscured by the large goods shed). The whole scene is dominated by Candy & Co.'s 'Great Western Pottery, Brick & Tile Works', which contributed much valuable revenue to the Branch for nearly eighty years.
National Railway Museum

Between Ventiford and Bovey Pottery, a distance of some 2½ miles, the Line traversed an extensive tract of heathland shared between, and named after, the neighbouring parishes of Teigngrace and Bovey. The heath was in its natural state until the arrival of the Moretonhampstead Branch, from which time large sections were enclosed and 'improved' (predominantly for woodland). The boundary between the two parishes more or less corresponded with the line of the Exeter, Chudleigh and Plymouth turnpike road (now the A38), which made a crossing of the nearby River Bovey at Jews Bridge: the name by which the location was known during the Line's planning and construction.

In spite of local representations, no station was provided here initially; the single-track broad gauge line passing beneath the road bridge and proceeding in a straight line north-westwards across Bovey Heath. Financial difficulties and a less than anticipated growth in traffic, dictated a policy of retrenchment on the part of the M&SDR. The Company endeavoured to persuade the South Devon Railway, who were operating the Line on their behalf, to expand the services - especially freight - but to no avail. However, soon after the SDR had formally absorbed the smaller company in July 1872, it began looking for

ways to increase traffic. The river crossing at Jews Bridge acted as a nodal point, the turnpike gathering to itself traffic from a scattering of settlements on both sides of the valley and beyond. Those in the general vicinity were mostly farmsteads or tiny villages, although three miles to the northeast was the small town of Chudleigh, with just over 2,000 inhabitants. In between was the village of Chudleigh Knighton, which was to become a significant ball clay producing centre. Collectively, this promised to be a worthwhile investment for the Railway, and in 1874 plans were drawn up for the building of a station and siding next to the road bridge, on what was then classed as the 'down' side of the track (but changed to 'up' fifteen years later).

Known as Chudleigh Road, the station opened on 1st July 1874, and consisted of a single platform 200 feet in length, reached by a long approach from the main road near Jewsbridge Cottages. Its orientation and length were dictated by the embankment built to keep within the gradient and clearance parameters set by Parliament for over-bridges. To save foot passengers from south of the Line having to make a long detour, a flight of steps was added by the bridge. With the exception of a masonry base, the neat station buildings were entirely of timber construction, comprising horizontal rebated cladding

HEATHFIELD – 1935

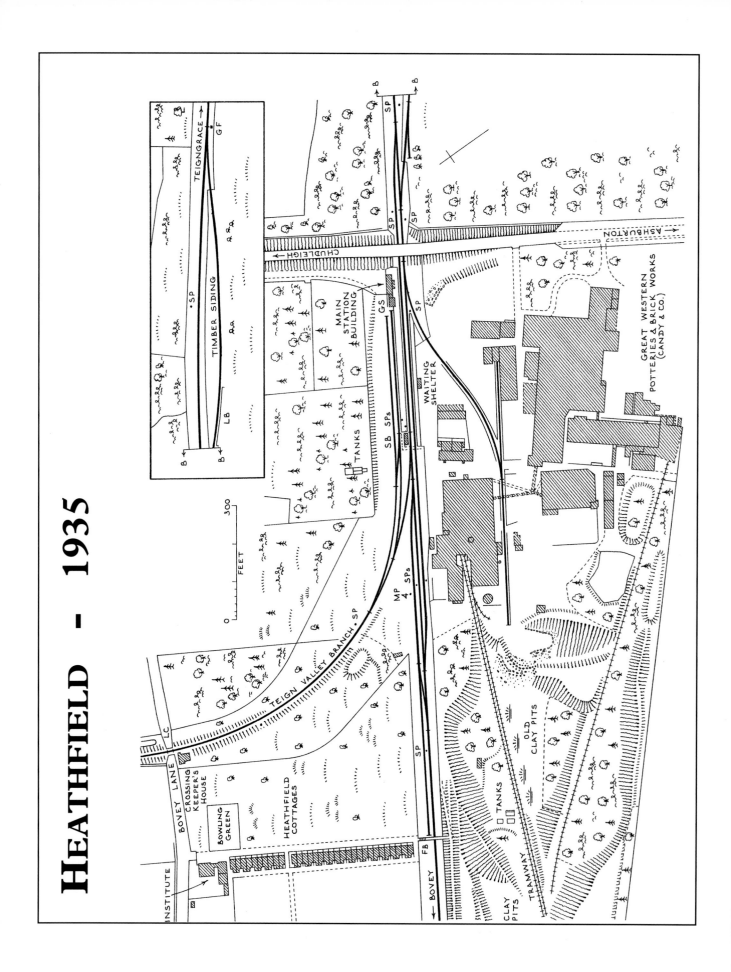

Looking north west along the wide Moretonhampstead Branch platform in the early 1920s. The three-way signal in advance of the junction controlled entry into the following lines: left arm to the Moreton Branch; centre arm to the goods loop/siding; right arm to the Teign Valley Branch. One of Churchward's 'small Prairies' stands in the 'through' platform with a Paignton to Moretonhampstead train, while an Armstrong '517' class 0-4-2 tank engine waits in the bay with the Teign Valley connection, its destination board proclaiming 'TIVERTON' (on the Exe Valley line). In 1923 - the year of this photograph - a single Heathfield to Tiverton through train was introduced, coinciding with the first appearance of auto (push-pull) trains on the Teign Valley (five years before they were to be seen on the Moretonhampstead Branch).   *L&GRP*

above a deep plinth. The hipped roof was of grey slate and the chimney-stacks of brick. Passenger access to the building was solely via the platform, which was lit by large square-tapered oil lamps. The small platform-mounted goods shed, situated a little to the north of the main building, was of the same design, though lacking chimneys and windows.

The major development in the 'passenger' scene came about with the opening of the Teign Valley Railway in 1882. The Devon Central's plan to build a standard gauge branch line down the Teign Valley was outlined in Chapter 2. Though its bill had been thrown out by Parliament in May 1861, its chief protagonist and former chairman, Sir Lawrence Palk, was still determined to pursue his railway adventure, and on Saturday 5th October that year was extolling the virtues of his 'revised' line at a promotional meeting at Ashburton. This scheme would meet with the proposed Moretonhampstead Railway at Chudleigh Road. Plans for a Teign Valley Railway had an on-off existence for the next two decades, with several Acts of Parliament, litigation and boardroom dissension, but the persistence of Sir Lawrence finally bore fruit when the line opened on 9th October 1882. (A detailed exposition of this fascinating branch line may be found in Peter Kay's book 'The Teign Valley Line'.) The fact that the TVR provided a station much nearer Chudleigh than the existing Chudleigh Road, caused the latter to be renamed Heathfield eight days before the new line opened for traffic.

As long as the Teign Valley Railway remained independent - there had once been a threat of London & South Western Railway involvement - its presence could only benefit the Moretonhampstead Branch. In the discussions over the shared use of Heathfield station, the Great Western Railway - who

from 1876 had absorbed the SDR - insisted that the cost of all the necessary work to be undertaken in enlarging the layout be borne by the TVR. This included the provision of a brick and timber signal box and the enlarging of the goods shed. Built to match its antecedent, it approximately doubled the floor space. A 227 foot-long bay platform was added. As this was longer than the Moreton Branch 'through' platform - and had to stop short of the main station building - it gave the platform a pronounced 'stagger' at the 'junction' end. The term 'interchange' rather than 'junction' may be more appropriate when describing the arrangement at Heathfield in these early days, for the difference in gauge meant that there was no physical connection between the two branch lines. For ten years the standard gauge TVR remained a 'land-locked' affair, isolated from the rest of the local railway network.

The single track Teign Valley Railway was open for all traffic for 6¼ miles to Ashton, with a 'goods only' continuation for a further 1½ miles to Teign House (later Christow). Here, and at Trusham, there were great expectations of mineral traffic, but the break of gauge and consequent transhipment at Heathfield may well have been the reason for the slow development of the quarries and mines. A rather sparse service operated between Heathfield and Ashton, timed to connect with trains on the Moreton Branch. The TVR possessed its own rolling stock and tank engine, which was kept overnight in the small engine shed at Ashton. By the time it arrived on the scene, the progressive abandonment of the seven-foot broad gauge was well underway: all new lines were being built to the 4' 8½" standard, while mixed gauge had already reached Exeter from the north. When the Moreton Branch was eventually 'narrowed' in May 1892, a connection was provided between the two lines - but it faced

Bovey, via the Up Siding, rather than the 'through' direction towards Newton Abbot. A direct link was subsequently installed in 1916, by which time the 'Exeter Railway' of 1903 had made an end-on junction with the TVR at Christow and boosted Heathfield's own role as a junction. A new, larger signal box was provided in connection with this wartime remodelling, situated a little 'down line' from its predecessor. Of standard GWR design, it was built of brick: appropriately using the distinctive buff-coloured products of Candy & Co. just across the line.

The layout and fortunes of Heathfield show more variation than anywhere else on the Branch. On the 'passenger' side this was principally due to its status as a junction rather than to any significant growth in the indigenous population. Candy & Co.'s 'Great Western Pottery, Brick & Tile Works' drew in a workers from around the area, while in the days before road transport became a serious rival, it continued to act as a railhead for the locality. In spite of its junction status, and the possibilities afforded of connections/interchange between the two branch lines, a second Moreton platform line was not put in until June 1927. Until that date, passenger trains were only able to 'cross' at Bovey, the half way point on the Line; although following the track alterations of 1916, the timetable rubric explained that:

"When absolutely necessary two Goods Trains, or a Passenger and a Goods Train may cross at Heathfield on the understanding that the Passenger Train is always kept on the Running Line, and that if the Passenger Train has to stop at Heathfield it must stop at the Platform."

The new 'down' platform of 1927 was 320 feet long and 12 feet wide, with a centrally-positioned prefabricated corrugated iron waiting shelter as the only structure. It had a slight 'stagger' in relation to the original platform by virtue of the siding leading to Candy's brick and tile works. The original 1874 structure was cut back to allow for the provision of the new 470 yard-long 'down' passenger loop and at the same time extended at the junction end to bring it in line with the end of the bay. This more than doubled its length - from 200' to 413' - and provided a width of 25' throughout that part shared with the Teign Valley bay line. The narrowing of the platform led to a reduction in size and relocation of the goods shed. Returning to its 1874 dimensions, it was moved right up to the main station building and further back on the platform, bringing its rear elevation in line with that of the adjacent lavatory block. Electric lighting was installed at this time; quite an innovation for the Branch! The only loss was the flight of steps near the road bridge. The two through platforms were signalled for both 'up' and 'down' trains, with workings to and from the Teign Valley using the 'up' loop. This gave the layout a dramatically improved operating capacity. As if to acknowledge the grander scale of operations now in evidence, the station was smartened up with a general repainting in August 1929.

The final alterations to the layout took place during the Second World War, when the Teign Valley Branch was used not only as a useful diversionary route for main line services, but also for hospital trains - both of which had substantially more coaching stock than was normally the case on the two branches. The works involved in the revision were authorised by the Ministry of Transport in October 1942, at an estimated cost of £12,000. The two 'through' platform loops were extended by 176 yards in the Newton direction, while a double junction with the TVR was installed. The new layout was brought into use in May 1943, with both Moreton and 'through' Teign Valley trains thereafter running on mutually exclusive 'up' and 'down' platform lines. Curiously, the works were not officially inspected until 16th August 1946.

Personnel

Though a staffed station in its existence as 'Chudleigh Road', there is no mention of a station master until the late 1880s; namely, John Waldron. He later moved on, in the same grade, to Lustleigh; to be succeeded at Heathfield by William James Reed. By the early 1920s the staff payroll numbered six: station master (Sidney Honeywill); clerk; two signalmen and two porters. Sidney Honeywill's earlier career had been on the Teign Valley Branch, as had that of Alfred William Brooking who was station master at Heathfield for most of the 1930s - having transferred from the same grade at Chudleigh when the post there was abolished in October 1930. At the end of the decade and into the war years, the incumbent was Ernest Davey; to be followed by Harry Hughes, R.H. Thomas and Frank Pill in the early, mid and late 1950s respectively.

Accommodation was often provided by the GWR for their station masters in the form of Company houses. Frequently this was in purpose-built houses adjoining the station; in other cases by purchasing a convenient property nearby. Thus, in March

(Traffic Department)' - acted as booking-cum-parcels-cum-goods clerk, generally assisting the station master, like whom he was classified as 'supervisory' and as such was salaried (as was an additional, junior, clerk employed at the station between 1928 and 1931). Although there was a good deal of overlap in the turns of duty worked by the two men, the 'margins' were covered by working alternating shifts with an 'early' and 'late' bias. The clerk was also required to cover the station master's half-day off, as well as short periods of absence - longer periods were dealt with by a relief station master provided by Division. With no separate office in the goods shed on the platform, the clerk dealt with the freight administration, as well as his other duties, in the main station office. In the mid 1930s the clerk was

1947 - a surprisingly late date - the Company bought No.38 Devon Square for the Newton Abbot station master W.C. Dawe, who paid the princely rental of £1 a week! Conveniently close to the station, the impressive linked gable villas and Italianate terraces arranged around the wooded grounds of St. Paul's Church, must have been felt to be in keeping with Newton's status. Out at Heathfield meanwhile, the station master lived in far more modest surroundings at 'Western Villa'.

Unlike Bovey and Moretonhampstead, there was no separate post of goods clerk. The Heathfield man - designated 'Clerk

Above: Rear, or approach road, elevation; summer 1959. The sliding door in the back wall of the goods shed permits direct handling to and from road vehicles.
                                                                S. J. Dickson

Right: The station building seen in the summer of 1957. The main, central, structure - measuring approximately 24 feet x 15 feet - houses, from right to left, the station master's office, booking hall-cum-general waiting room, and ladies' waiting room. Of the 'wing' buildings - about 12 feet long and 13 feet wide - that on the right is the 'passenger parcels' room-cum-store, while the other is the lavatory block. No. 1427 waits in the 'up' platform with a Moretonhampstead to Newton Abbot service.
                                                                G. Howells

A busy scene at Heathfield: Moretonhampstead Branch trains cross in the through platform loops, while the Teign Valley connection waits in the Bay. The 'down' train is the 10.05am from Paignton, comprising non auto-fitted 'small Prairie' 2-6-2T 4568 and trailers 224 and 234. The 3-coach 'up' train, the 10.15 from Moretonhampstead, is in the charge of 'large Prairie' 4145. Exeter Shed's long-stay 0-4-2 tank engine No. 1405, with trailer 215, waits for passengers to entrain prior to departure at 10.45. 10.6.57.

E. R. Shepherd

Bill Margetts, while by the middle of the next decade it was Leslie Poolman. Leslie is a good example of how, in climbing the ladder of seniority, a Railway career could take a man far and wide. In 1933 he began as a junior clerk in the parcels office at Torre. The following year he was posted one station up the line, to Kingskerswell, to become acquainted with general station accountancy. In 1935 he transferred to Bovey to assist the goods clerk in the busy goods department there. Ten years later he was at Heathfield in the post of clerk. As a man with obvious ability, he was chosen to be a 'Special Trainee', a privilege which involved spending time at 'headquarters' at Paddington. He subsequently became yard master at Moreton Cutting near Didcot; then station master at Wolverhampton (Low Level); and finally assistant area manager at Newton Abbot, this last post bringing him 'home'.

Two of the best-known members of staff at the station, by virtue of their very long service, were signalmen Tom Baker and Bert Hopkins. In the 1950s another man employed in the box was Stanley Yendall. He had transferred from the post of porter-signalman at Bovey, where his brother Arthur was station master; and subsequently moved on to Newton Abbot as 'relief' signalman. The years between 1932 and 1949 saw the largest number of employees on Heathfield's payroll, namely ten. This figure included the gatekeepers at Bovey Lane and Chudleigh Knighton level crossings on the Teign Valley Branch and, until May 1939, the porter at Teigngrace. The making up of the weekly wage packets was one of the responsibilities of the station master, who took them in person out to the crossing keepers. In spite of its extensive track layout - by Moreton Branch standards at least - there was no permanent way gang based at Heathfield. Apart from the extreme south end, any requisite work was dealt with by the men from the Bovey gang, who also covered the Teign Valley out to, but excluding, Bovey Lane crossing, where the Christow-based gang took over.

The Traffic

A selected breakdown of the station's accounts from 1925 is given in Table 12. On the passenger side, it is important to remember that they include revenue deriving from Chudleigh Knighton Halt from autumn 1930 and Teigngrace Halt from

Passengers on the Moretonhampstead Branch were left in no doubt as to the connectional destinations available at Heathfield. It was cheaper to travel to Exeter via the Teign Valley than the main line via Dawlish, though by no means always quicker! The facility was designed to favour Teign Valley passengers, with connections generally being arranged between their line and trains to and from Newton Abbot. 0-6-0 Pannier Tanks were occasionally diagrammed for the Moreton Branch Goods duty from the Second World War. One of the members of the enormous generic '57xx' class of engine, No. 3796, stands in 'up' platform with a southbound working. 13.8.57. *R. E. Toop*

As one of the few through passenger workings between the Moretonhampstead and Teign Valley Branches, the 4.35pm Newton Abbot to Dulverton train 'has the road' to the latter line. As with the points at the ends of the platform loops, an upper speed limit of 15mph was imposed over the junction in both directions. The loco, No. 3606, is one of Exeter Shed's long-stay '57xx' Pannier Tanks. Another member of this class waits for 'line clear' in the Long (or Up) Siding with the return leg of the Moreton Goods: 5 o'clock off Heathfield. 27.5.58. *R. A. Lumber*

Having arrived from Exeter and run round its two corridor coaches, No. 1429 waits in, the 'up' platform, to make a connection with a Newton to Moretonhampstead service (seen arriving in the charge of 'large Prairie' No. 5196). The lamp hut, seen at the rear of the yard, was relocated here as a result of the platform alterations of 1927. 13.8.57.

R. E. Toop

Table 12. Selected Traffic Returns : Heathfield

YEAR	PASSENGERS				PARCELS			MILK			GOODS			LIVESTOCK	
	Tickets (Single & Return)	£	Season Tickets	£	No. Sent out	No. Received	Total Value £	No. of cans	No. of cases	Total Value £	Tonnage Despatched	Tonnage Received	Total Value £	Wagon Loads	Value £
1925	14,567	646	59	127	628	666	122	909	-	40	13,138	10,806	17,677	-	-
1926	11,930	529	55	125	628	524	133	137	-	5	11,200	11,534	16,431	-	-
1927	15,561	587	69	142	780	600	146	-	-	-	11,134	9,222	18,401	-	-
1928	23,284	828	61	135	711	465	138	-	-	-	9,495	17,750	17,380	2	6
1929	22,379	783	51	113	941	460	171	-	-	-	9,195	11,984	16,960	-	-
1930	21,676	713	43	38	963	521	178	-	-	-	8,584	7,510	15,535	-	-
1931	21,610	710	63	49	855	650	170	-	-	-	8,775	6,861	14,951	-	-
1932	20,072	724	65	48	836	966	145	-	-	-	7,659	8,025	14,683	-	-
1933	20,719	790	84	64	822	1160	151	-	-	-	8,373	7,344	16,968	-	-
1934	21,984	743	80	74	823	1163	158	-	-	-	9,643	9,147	19,587	-	-
1935	20,739	714	58	39	596	953	104	-	-	-	11,618	8,919	19,939	-	-
1936	19,271	718	51	34	488	970	74	-	-	-	11,343	10,093	19,603	-	-
1937	16,240	641	70	42	976	927	85	-	-	-	12,177	10,896	19,758	-	-
1938	13,595	547	68	44	507	716	67	222	-	8	8,880	9,614	14,847	-	-
1939	11,576	479	118	64	514	604	60	554	-	N/D	7,965	8,984	11,932	-	-
1940	11,975	483	69	54	385	438	41	744	-	30	8,330	8,429	N/D	-	-
1941	19,014	931	62	63	N/D	N/D	53	928	-	37	6,517	19,276	N/D	-	-
1942	21,397	1208	104	98	N/D	N/D	78	595	-	19	8,853	7,700	N/D	-	-
1943	18,181	1256	240	183	N/D	N/D	150	-	-	-	8,459	36,487	N/D	-	-
1944	20,818	1345	295	224	N/D	N/D	85	-	-	-	28,879	17,722	N/D	-	-
1945	20,834	1335	283	210	N/D	N/D	160	-	-	-	11,138	7,096	N/D	-	-
1946	17,125	1090	236	147	N/D	N/D	83	-	-	-	17,510	9,684	N/D	-	-
1947	14,476	1020	191	102	N/D	N/D	120	-	-	-					
1948	12,739	899	168	109	N/D	N/D	152	-	-	-					
1949	14,055	938	110	93	N/D	N/D	129	-	-	-					
1950	11,039	704	47	50	N/D	N/D	167	-	-	-					
1951	9,027	653	54	61	320	613	148	-	-	-	Goods Zoned at Newton Abbot 1.3.47				
1952	9,687	618	19	30	328	543	159	-	-	-					
1953	9,905	686	18	22	373	666	207	-	-	-					
1954	10,560	646	10	11	376	730	194	-	-	-					
1955	11,578	753	23	17	350	705	184	-	-	-					
1956	11,869	768	39	57	324	818	224	-	-	-					
1957	12,278	794	32	36	419	879	319	-	-	-					
1958	7,894	543	18	45	747	780	302	-	-	-					

NB Passenger revenue includes Chudleigh Knighton Halt from Oct. 1930; and Teigngrace Halt from May 1939.

N/D = No Data available

spring 1939. The former location was relatively well-patronised until the late 1940s, and although Heathfield was the supervising station following the withdrawal of the post of station master from Chudleigh, separate figures were not recorded in the Divisional traffic returns. Unlike the tourist-boosted areas further north on the Branch, which showed a falling away in the number of passengers, Heathfield experienced an up-turn in traffic, with ticket sales (excluding 'seasons') exceeding 20,000 per annum between 1928 and 1935. The ensuing decline was arrested, as everywhere else, by the war years; there being an enormous military presence in the area: notably the American fuel dump on Knighton Heath and the hospital at Ilford, near Stover Park; both only about a mile away. Proximity to, and direct road communication with, Newton Abbot made the Devon General buses a growing threat from the late 1940s. It is significant, however, that the severe fall in passenger traffic recorded for 1958 corresponds with the withdrawal of passenger services on the Teign Valley Branch.

The general merchandise side of the goods traffic was multifarious, both in type and variety of origin and destination; being conveyed by general-purpose box vans. This traffic was referred to as small freight - or 'smalls' for short - and was handled in the goods shed on the 'up' platform. A sliding door front and back gave access both to the platform and station approach road. In the absence of its own 'dedicated' siding, goods had to be dealt with during the attendance of freight trains. Thus, while the engine was occupied with shunting duties, the staff set about manhandling traffic to or from the 'station trucks', which had been conveniently drawn up at the platform immediately in front of the shed. There were three of these wagons; one each from Paddington, Bristol and Newton Abbot. This method of handling changed with the introduction of the Newton Abbot 'Goods Zoning Scheme' on 1st March 1947 (see Chapter 3). Under this, Heathfield lost its rail-borne general merchandise facility, with the traffic being transferred to the Newton-based zone (or 'trunk') lorry, which either called at the station as required or went to the customer direct. Full load

and private siding traffic was not affected, and which in any case made up most of Heathfield's freight.

Long (or Up) Siding

The plans for Chudleigh Road Station submitted to the Board of Trade on 16th June 1874 included the provision of a siding running parallel with the main line, with which it was connected immediately beyond the Bovey end of the platform; facing trains travelling from Newton Abbot. On his examination of the installation on behalf of the Board, the Inspector found no problem with the siding itself, but the signalling arrangements associated with it produced lengthy exchanges between the Board and South Devon Railway Company; the former refusing to sanction the siding until the situation was to its liking. The recorded correspondence ended in early September with the situation still unresolved. However, differences must have been satisfactorily sorted out, as the Company's working timetables from early the following year make reference to its existence. It was to be shunted as required by the 6pm Bovey to Newton goods train - at this time referred to as travelling in the 'down' direction - a generous allowance of 35 minutes being allocated to allow for the work. The opening of the Teign Valley line regularised the stop here. Although it was only possible to shunt the siding on the return, that is southbound, leg of the journey, the goods train was scheduled to call in both directions: the 5pm from Newton calling briefly some fifteen minutes later, with the 6pm from Bovey calling as before. Following the extension of the weekday goods from Bovey to Moretonhampstead in 1882, the starting time of the service was moved to earlier in the afternoon. The difference in gauge between the two branches necessitated the transfer of goods at Heathfield. Small goods were most likely to have been dealt with at the platform rather than the siding - the Teign Valley trains running as 'mixed' when required. The siding might have been used for the transfer of heavier goods, although in the absence of an 'exchange platform' and yard crane, this would have been cumbersome in the extreme.

In the summer of 1959 an unidentified 0-6-0 PT engages in a spot of shunting at Heathfield, now a freight-only location. Candy's Siding is seen curving away to the left while assorted wagons, variously, pick out 'Long Siding' (beyond the junction), the 'Bay Platform Line' and 'Bay Siding'.

S. J. Dickson

In 1889 the 'up/down' nomenclature on the Moreton Branch was reversed, so that from now on the siding found itself on the 'up' side. Following the narrowing of the broad gauge in 1892, the siding was much reduced in length to little more than a long spur. This was due to the connections installed between the bay platform and Moreton Branch in the Bovey direction. The presence of the Teign Valley line itself, curving in from Bovey Lane level crossing, blocked vehicular access to the siding from the station approach road, although it seems that an 'occupation' style crossing of ballast or timber existed for a time. The 1916 revision of the track layout mentioned earlier in the chapter saw the siding extended by around 110 yards, which placed the new buffer stops immediately in front of the footbridge connecting Heathfield Cottages with the path alongside Candy's clay pits. The crossover linking the siding with the main line was correspondingly moved from its former location by Mile Post 4 to a position near the previous stop blocks. Together with the removal of the connection to the bay platform, this arrangement created both a dead-end siding able to accommodate 15 standard-length wagons, and a loop able to hold 20 wagons (both these figures excluding an engine and brake van).

The alterations of April 1943 also affected the siding. The 'down-end' loop connection was removed and the siding extended by a further 11 chains (242 yards), taking it almost to the Little Bovey road bridge. Associated with the work was the incorporation of a wagon weighbridge into the siding, the metalwork bearing the inscription: TO WEIGH 30 TON. H. POOLEY & SON LTD. BIRMINGHAM & LONDON. The adjoining, sizeable weigh-house comprised a corrugated iron superstructure on a brick base. The siding extension itself is of interest due to the unusual track formation. Instead of the conventional 7 foot-long wooden sleepers to support the chairs, square concrete slabs were used, with metal tie-bars between; the ties being bolted to the slabs. A loading gauge was provided at the 'station end' of the siding. The siding was now able to accommodate 56 standard wagons in addition to an engine and brake van. It was of sufficient length not only to act as a 'refuge' siding for goods trains, but also to play host to surplus coaching stock awaiting a turn of duty, repair or scrapping. These vehicles were pushed to the inner portion of the siding in order to leave the remainder clear for the regular goods functions.

As a holiday area, traffic levels on the South Devon main line were greatly boosted at summer weekends, requiring extra coaches - often of 8, 9 or 10-coach sets. Until the expansion of carriage berthing facilities at Goodrington Sands in 1957, the existing facilities there and also at Newton Abbot were not always sufficient to cope with all the extra peak-time stock, and consequently the siding was pressed into service during the week. In the summer of 1955 for example, there was to be found a 'condemned' 70 foot-long corridor third-class coach, which had actually been there for some time. In the first week of August it was joined by a nine-coach set of assorted vehicles - including one from the Southern Region - stabled prior to weekend service. This 'holding' function continued intermittently beyond the busy years of the 1950s. As late as the spring of 1981, only about two years before the siding was lifted, it was occupied by a large number of empty wagons.

Bay Siding

As its southern terminus, the Teign Valley Railway had need to provide means of enabling the engine, after arrival, to change ends (or 'run round' its train in railway terminology). To facilitate this, a 'loop' line running parallel with the Bay platform line was laid in. It continued beyond the points at either end to form a short dead-end siding or spur: that nearest the station building holding just 3 goods wagons, and the other, 8 (allowing of course for adequate clearance at the crossovers). The loop section of this line could accommodate 6 wagons. The track alterations of 1916 saw the north-western extremity of the siding connected into the TVR and the 'engine release' crossover moved back from the buffer stop end of the Bay to the opposite end of the platform. This created an inner siding of much more useful length, able to hold sixteen wagons; and referred to as the Bay Siding. This capacity was increased a little more in the layout changes of 1927, when the engine release crossover by the signal box was reversed in direction: from left-hand to right-hand. Further track alterations (in May 1943) saw the removal of the engine release crossover, which further increased the length of the siding: in spite of the fact that the west-end connection was moved closer to the station.

Although the Bay Siding had the advantage of direct access to the station approach road, it did not have the benefit of either a goods loading dock or public weighbridge. Even a three-ton yard crane that had once existed at the site seems to have been removed as early as 1905. This probably reflects the degree to which private siding traffic dominated both the station's own goods scene, as well as highlighting the need for siding accommodation to marshal and/or berth vehicles in connection with the Branch freight trains.

In the early 1960s, Heathfield was occasionally used as a 'holding' point for 'off-line' wagons and sundry bulk materials. This was due in part to its underused siding capacity at this time, and partly to its convenient proximity to the main line. Granite setts, for example, were sent by the hundred from Millbay Docks, Plymouth, and stockpiled on the 'up' platform, while

Geest Ltd.'s banana ripening/distribution building under construction in the summer of 1960. When complete, the 'Bay Siding' will be slewed to pass through the nearest, shorter, shed. 7.9.60. *C. L. Caddy collection*

Looking south east from the A38 road bridge across the heathland towards Teigngrace in the summer of 1959, the Line passing between the two Brock Plantations: 'Lower' on the left and 'Higher' on the right. Timber Siding, with its clay loading ramps, is in the centre of the picture. A double slip point connecting the siding with a spur and additional, shorter, siding was originally positioned a few yards beyond the gate, but was removed in the late 1920s.   *S. J. Dickson*

lengths of track - much of it concrete sleepered - were stacked in the yard alongside the Bay Siding, and also in the angle of land between the two Branches. In order to give road vehicles access to, and room to manoeuvre between, the Bay platform line and Bay Siding, the latter was slewed by several yards towards the shallow embankment at the rear of the Railway's property. This was carried out early in February 1961, and it was on the site behind the Bay Siding that Geest Industries Limited built a banana ripening, storage and distribution depot (on what had formerly been an enclosure of mixed woodland and scrub). The formal private siding agreement between Geest and BR was signed on 9th April 1963. Following the closure of the remaining section of the now goods-only Teign Valley Line to Trusham (in 1968), the short length out to Bovey Lane level crossing was retained as a headshunt for the two sidings. During the manhandling of the bananas between the railway box vans and warehouses, some inevitably fell off the bunches. This was noted, indeed watched for, by eagle-eyed train crews. If men simply helped themselves to this booty and were seen by the manager, very serious consequences could follow, so they always approached him to ask if, as these bananas were now 'damaged stock', they might have them. He always acceded to their request! The Geest establishment produced regular rail-borne traffic for over ten years, but in December 1975 the private siding agreement was terminated and the siding itself was subsequently removed when the junction layout was rationalised around eight years later.

Candy's Siding

Geological and geographical processes have combined to richly endow the 28 square-mile Bovey Basin with mineral wealth: ball clay, lignite, sand and gravel. The coarse, white silica-rich ball clay is the premier resource, and had a history of commercial exploitation well before the Moretonhampstead Branch appeared on the scene. The later development of the deposits at Heathfield was due to the business acumen of a certain Frank Candy, who arrived in the area in the early 1870s. Noting the clay's quality, versatility and abundant reserves, and with the Railway literally in his back yard, he realised the great potential waiting to be developed. Having found backers for his project, the firm of Candy & Co. was established in 1874: the same year the station opened; on the opposite side of the Line. By the end of the decade the firm was producing a wide range of products: bricks, tiles, heavy-duty pipes of various kinds, paving blocks and stoneware pottery. The scale of operations continued to grow at the grandly-named 'Great Western Pottery, Brick & Tile Works', but it was not until October 1887 that an arrangement was made to provide a direct rail link into the complex.

The siding made a connection with the running line at the south-east (Newton Abbot) end of the platform, immediately in front of the road bridge and facing trains from Newton. The absence of a run-round facility at Heathfield imposed constraints at the location in broad gauge days: Candy's Siding and Long Siding could only be 'conventionally' shunted by trains travelling from Bovey. To partially offset this inconvenience, the GWR issued the following characteristically precise, if verbose, instruction:

"To save time in shunting at Heathfield trucks for Bovey may be pushed by the Engines of Goods Trains from Heathfield, but the speed of the Trains between the two places must not exceed 8 miles per hour, and the Second Guard must

Timber Siding in more recent times, dominated by the loading sheds of ECC Ball Clays Ltd. *Author*

preferred. In any event, drivers had to take care in working the siding; the squealing from the wheel flanges against the track audibly recording the progress of the shunt. The doubling of the track through the station in 1927 did not affect the siding, as the new line was laid in on the 'up' side. The only alteration was the removal of the ground frame which controlled the points; these now being mechanically operated directly from the signal box.

Not surprisingly, Candy's distinctive buff-coloured bricks found a wide variety of uses locally: and were used to build the waiting room on the 'down' platform at Bovey - although Heathfield itself had to make do with a basic corrugated iron affair. The firm's large-diameter drain pipes were to be seen at the station - along with Bovey and Lustleigh - where they were pressed into service as supports for flower arrangements in the summer months: in which regard competition was intense. The siding saw steady use until the late 1950s, particularly in the despatch of truck-loads of glazed bricks, tiles and pipes. In addition, there was a regular 'coal inwards' traffic for the kilns and other, more general, purposes. In 1964 the pipe-making side of the business was sold to the Newton Abbot clay firm of Watts, Blake, Bearne & Co., but by this date the siding's use had become infrequent as road haulage was taking a rapidly

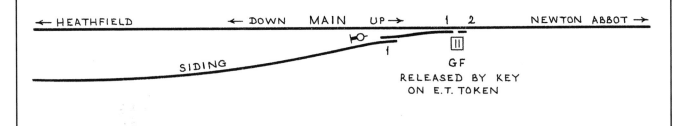

TIMBER SIDING GROUND FRAME

← HEATHFIELD   ← DOWN   MAIN   UP →   1   2   NEWTON ABBOT →

SIDING

GF
RELEASED BY KEY
ON E.T. TOKEN

ride on the front vehicle (unless it be a bonnet-end truck, in which case he may ride on the first low sided vehicle from it) to keep a good look-out, and be prepared to give any signal to the Engine Driver that may be required, and by night he must show a white light ahead. No trucks must be pushed unless there is a Guard in the rear vehicle of the Train."

A few yards in from the connection with the main line, a gate across the track marked the boundary between 'private' and 'railway' territory. As the owner of the land, but client of the Railway, Candy's paid an annual 'siding rent' to the GWR, in return for which the latter undertook to provide both a service and to maintain the track - in connection with which the Bovey-based permanent way ganger periodically inspected the siding. Inside the gate - which was supposed to be kept locked across the track in between shunting duties - there was a sharp reverse curve. The tightness of the curve was such that, in later years, a 'stop board' was installed in advance of the gate, restricting access to the siding to certain classes of locomotive. In 'British Railways' years, the instruction proclaimed: "No engines to pass stop board, except uncoloured, yellow and blue W.R. tank engines and B.R. Standard Class 3 (2-6-2T)." This ruled out the 94xx 0-6-0 Pannier Tank class (route availability 'red') to which Newton Shed was host for a while, and although technically it permitted the 'large Prairies' (classed as 'blue'), their smaller '45xx' cousins with their shorter wheel-base were

increasing share of the traffic. Indeed, by the summer of the following year, Candy's Siding was all but disused. The private siding agreement was ended in 1966 and the connection with the running line removed in March 1967. The business, however, carries on and in spite of take-overs and restructuring, maintains the name of their founder in the present title 'Candy Tiles Ltd.'

Timber Siding

This siding was installed by the Great Western Railway in 1913 on behalf of the Stover Estate, the 'Granite Lodge' entrance to which is only some 400 yards from the bridge which carries the A38 over the railway. Actually, it was a long 'loop', situated on the 'down' side of the Branch, the connections with which were initially controlled by ground lever frames released/locked by the electric train staff used between Newton Abbot and Heathfield at this time. As a private siding, the line was gated at either end, the distance between the two gates being just over 280 yards.

Opened as 'Stover Siding', its original purpose was to despatch sawn timber from the Stover Estate. This traffic caused the siding to be known colloquially as the 'Timber Siding', and this name stuck despite something of a chequered history in which it was periodically out of use or dealing with other products. Indeed, the appellation even passed into official railway terminology. Timber continued to be the main feature of the early years, although by the end of the decade the siding's ownership had passed to the Devon Ball Clay Company. It would seem that expected levels of clay traffic did not materialise, for in September 1921 the firm made an offer to sell the siding to the GWR for "the purpose of stabling coaching stock". The Railway declined the offer. Its ownership changed hands three times between then and the Second World War, with timber once again becoming the principal feature of the traffic. In the track expansion of 1927 the siding points nearest the station came directly under the control of the signal box, although the 'far' connection (nearest Teigngrace) continued to be worked by a ground frame as before. It was the war years, and those immediately following, which saw the most intensive use of the siding. The former were characterised by regular consignments of pit props. The timber was obtained locally and sawn into lengths of 4' 6", 6' 6" and 9' 6". The latter were too long to be loaded flat into the high-sided ('Open C') wagons used for the other lengths, so were stacked on a slant and then secured to prevent movement during transit. Their destination was the South Wales coalfield, but because of the mode of stowage, the 'long timber' was not permitted through the Severn Tunnel, and had to go instead the 'long way round' via Gloucester.

Even before the Second World War ended, it was apparent that Britain was heading for a serious fuel shortage; indeed, during the war years the siding had been used to bring in and stockpile supplies of coal. In an effort to forestall a post-war crisis, the President of the Board of Trade, Sir Richard Stafford Cripps, promoted a search for viable alternatives. This caused the spotlight to fall on the substantial lignite deposits of the Bovey Basin. The soft brown, rather woody lignite was inter-bedded with the clay in various parts of the locality. Known somewhat euphemistically as 'Bovey Coal', there had been some exploratory production back in the 1860s, with further interest shown in its possible industrial potential in the years immediately before the Great War. However, when burned it gave off clouds of unpleasant sulphurous smoke and consequently could only be considered as a domestic fuel in extremis. In 1945 samples were sent away to London for analysis, and work began to pump out the large flooded lignite pit of Blue Waters near Bovey Pottery. With estimated reserves of around 400 million tons - some occurring in seams up to 40 feet thick - ambitious plans for its utilisation were drawn up, including a miners' village. As the post-war fuel crisis deepened, exacerbated by the atrocious winter of 1946/7, it was time for plans to be translated into action, and a private company was set up to promote and exploit the resource: British Lignite Products Limited. Work began in earnest in 1947, with machinery being brought in, principally, from collieries in South Wales, along with small four-wheeled trucks to carry the lignite on an internal narrow gauge tramway system to the briquetting plant, where the material was compressed into ovoids. From there, they were taken by road the short distance to Timber Siding, to be railed away on a regular basis to a wide variety of destinations. One of the more exotic uses was as a coal substitute in the glasshouse boilers of the extensive Channel Islands market garden industry.

The enterprise became of such significance that it warranted a visit by Sir Richard, now Minister for Economic Affairs, but the initial enthusiasm and prosperity were short-lived. The cost of opencast working was proving inordinately expensive, so the decision was taken to mine the lignite by driving adits into the seams from the sides of the pit. This was not to the liking of many of the local workers, who promptly left the enterprise to work in other extractive industries nearby. This plunged the company into crisis, forcing them to advertise for miners in South Wales. Concurrently, in 1948, the Devon House of

Extensive opencast lignite excavations underway at Blue Waters, near Bovey Pottery, in 1947. This 'Bovey Coal' was taken, in briquette form, to Timber Siding for distribution by rail.

Bovey Tracey Heritage Trust

Mercy at Bovey was converted into flats in readiness to receive the newly recruited men. As the decade drew to a close, coal supplies nationally were already beginning to improve, and in 1950 lignite production at Blue Waters came to an end; the mining equipment being sold for scrap.

The most notable post-war traffic handled at Timber Siding was ball clay. Through a process of mergers, the number of clay firms operating in the Bovey Basin reduced to just two 'giants': Watts, Blake, Bearne & Co. (WBB) of Newton Abbot, and English China Clays (Ball Clays) Ltd. At Heathfield it was the latter which gained the ascendancy, and with it the ownership of Timber Siding; taking over from the Pochin Ball Clay Company - part of ECC - and before that the locally based firm of Hexter & Budge. The clay was loaded into railway wagons from a platform near the station end of the siding, which was reached by a new road put in through the thinned-out wood, brush and furze at the edge of Higher Brock's Plantation. Following the closure of the signal box in October 1965, the connections with the running line were fitted with hand-operated levers at the points. By the end of the decade, the high, ramped loading dock was handling considerable clay traffic. During the next few years, the platform was extended and a covered loading shed provided.

In more recent times, a new clay works and loading complex was built by ECC in association with the fleet of new air-braked 'Tiger' PBA bogie vehicles brought in from 1987 to replace the ageing 'tented' tarpaulin-covered open wooden wagons which had given sterling service since the 1950s. The conveyor-fed filling of the PBAs took place inside the loading shed at the 'up' end of the platform. Bagged clay was loaded into long wheel-base continental Ferry Vans for export via Dover. In 1990, the siding was serviced on most, if not all, weekdays; the train typically consisting of one or two 'Tigers' and an occasional Ferry Van. (Other, shorter wheel-base, PGA hopper vehicles seen in the formation from time to time were destined for WBB's siding at Newton Abbot.) A shunter rode on the locomotive to attend to the necessary duties at the siding and operate the gates at Teignbridge level crossing. This lucrative traffic ceased abruptly in the early part of the decade, although the firm has not, at the time of writing, decided whether or not the cessation will be permanent.

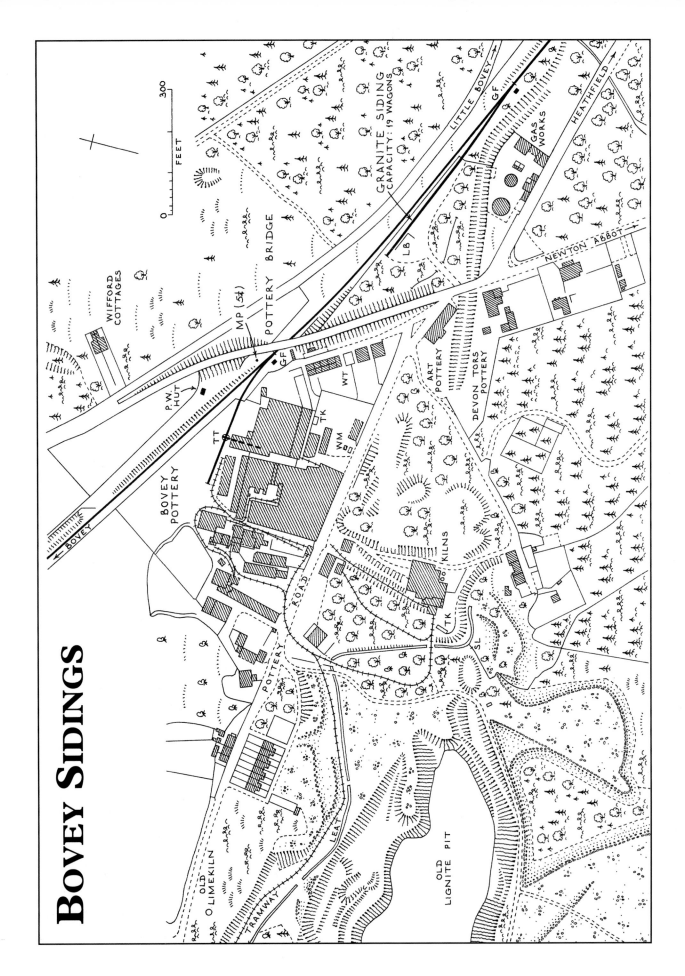

BOVEY SIDINGS

Chapter Eleven

BOVEY SIDINGS

Near Mile Post 5, the Moretonhampstead Branch parted company with the course of the old Haytor Granite Tramway. The tramway had been used as a 'bench-mark' by the M&SDR all the way from Ventiford, and had largely been obliterated by it. Now towards the twin-arched, skew bridge carrying the Newton to Bovey road, the line of the tramway struck off to the west to pass near the Pottery of Messers. Divett, Buller & Co. on its climb to the granite quarries on the edge of Dartmoor.

Two of the key players in the history of the Moretonhampstead & South Devon Railway had interests hereabouts: the Duke of Somerset and John Divett of Bovey Pottery. As the owner of the tramway since 1829, the Duke sought to capitalise on his strong bargaining position over the sale of the southernmost 2½ miles or so, by insisting that the Railway Company provide a siding, loading dock and crane at the junction between the two transport modes, hoping it might revitalise the Haytor quarries. John Divett was the senior partner in the Pottery enterprise, and a long-time supporter of the M&SDR (and before that the Newton & Moretonhampstead Railway scheme). He was one of the Company's first directors, and he too wanted a siding. The two sites were so close together that the M&SDR considered installing just one to serve both requirements. As the construction of the Line progressed, and both money and time were getting short, the siding project was not considered an immediate priority, and the Branch opened minus the feature.

Needless to say, the two men were not pleased, and made urgent representations to the Company. At a meeting of the M&SDR Directors at Newton Abbot station on Monday 13th August 1866, some seven weeks after the Line had opened, it was reported that:

"....the Haytor Granite Quarry was now being worked, and that the Duke of Somerset had called upon the Company to construct the Siding, near the Bovey Potteries, in accordance with the agreement; and also that Mr. Divett was desirous of having a siding into the Potteries. Mr. Margary submitted plans and Estimates which he had had prepared after careful examination and explained the grounds upon which he had arrived at the conclusion that it would be advisable to construct two sidings instead of one for the purposes of both parties as had been suggested by the Duke of Somerset's Agent."

It was not just this location that was missing out on the provision of sidings. As bad weather over the winter of 1865-66 had put the work behind schedule, all the last minute efforts had gone into getting the stations ready for passenger use. Goods trains did in fact start running between Newton Abbot and Bovey in the autumn, but with no intermediate stops. At the first General Meeting of 1867, held on Wednesday 27th February, it was stated that;

Coming up the grade through the shallow wooded cutting on the north west side of White Hill is Pannier Tank No. 3796, on the return working of the daily pick-up Goods. It is just possible to make out the connection to 'Granite Siding' diverging to the left in the middle distance; whilst in the far distance is the twin-arch, skewed 'Pottery Bridge' on the outskirts of Bovey Tracey. 27.2.59.   *Peter W. Gray*

"A Siding has been made near to the Bovey Pottery to facilitate the conveyance of granite from Hay-Tor to the ports of Dartmouth or Teignmouth."

While the Duke now had his siding, John Divett did not. This state of affairs must have been galling for him to accept at the meeting, seeing that he was the chairman on that occasion. Matters were in hand, however, and on Saturday 31st August that year came the terse report from the engineer to the assembled persons that: "A siding has been opened into Mr. Divett's Pottery at Bovey."

Both sidings were installed on the south of the running line: with Hay Tor Siding connected to it at a distance of 5 miles and 6 chains from Newton Abbot, and Pottery Siding 14 chains further on, by the 5 ¼ mile post. Both faced trains from Newton, the points when not in use being padlocked to protect the main line. Following the 'narrowing' of the Branch in 1892, this arrangement continued, although by now in addition to the padlock key carried by the goods guards, spares were held by the station master at Newton Abbot to cover special workings or the absence of the regular guard. To permit access to, or inspection of, the sidings by the Engineering Department, a key was also kept at Bovey station. Following the introduction of the electric train staff in 1901, the sidings were worked from lever frames (housed initially in wooden cabins) which were unlocked - or 'released'- by means of the keyed attachment at the end of the staff.

Granite Siding

The Haytor Granite Tramway was a remarkable enterprise, the brain-child of George Templer of Stover House. The advantages of granite as a building stone had long been recognised; it was both hard and durable, though also able to be cut and dressed. Used extensively in the locality, its wider exploitation had been severely curtailed by a lack of bulk transport facilities. The Stover Canal, built by George's father James, had opened to Ventiford in June 1792. Although the granite massif of Dartmoor was not far away, any connection between the two had to contend with the constraining matter of topography. The land around Haytor belonged to the Duke of Somerset, from whom Templer leased that portion of the moor between Haytor Rocks and Holwell Tor to open up quarries.

To get the stone from quarries above 1,300 feet to the canal basin a mere 30 feet above sea level was quite a challenge. It was met by constructing a tramway of granite setts, laid to a gauge of 4' 3". The centre of the quarry complex was 6 miles from Ventiford in a straight line, but in order to provide gradients capable of use by horse-drawn waggons, a circuitous route was necessary: though even this added only

a little over a mile to the distance.

The tramway opened on 16th September 1820, amidst much local rejoicing. Five years later, Templer formed the Devon Haytor Quarries Company, and new workings were started to meet increased demand; each new quarry being connected to the tramway. At Ventiford the stone was transferred to barges to be taken thence to Teignmouth Quay. Despite his great achievements and the prosperity of both transport modes, Templer's own finances were in a mess, and in 1829 he sold not only the canal and tramway but also his Stover Estate to the Duke of Somerset. Slump followed boom, and by the mid 1850s the quarries were no longer working, and the tramway was disused. It is no surprise therefore that the Duke hoped the M&SDR might bring new life to his moribund asset.

Having wound its way down from the Moor, the tramway ended its sojourn in a triangular plot of land into which the railway siding was laid. There was a long 'lead-in' from the main line, fitted later with a catch point, before the siding gate. As an additional protection of the running line, one of the rails was fitted with a hinged, padlocked wheel-stop, which was dealt with either by the guard or the shunter who travelled with the Branch goods train. The siding itself was about 290 feet long: assigned a capacity of 19 wagons in GWR days. Towards the buffer stop end was a 50 foot-long loading bank, intended to despatch large quantities of stone from the Duke's tramway. The siding was variously referred to as 'Hay Tor Siding' or 'Bovey Granite Siding', but was always known locally and in timetables simply as 'Granite Siding'. In the event, the title came to be a misnomer, for granite was the one commodity not handled there! In spite of the Duke's assertion of August 1866 that the Haytor quarry was in production, any traffic can only have been sporadic and small-scale. A 'Haytor Granite Company' certainly existed well beyond the Moreton Line's opening, as it is referred to in December 1878 when the lease of the tramway is being terminated, but it does not seem to have brought any business to the Railway.

If the non-realisation of the intended traffic was a blow, the siding came to be put to other uses, and by the time of the gauge conversion had sufficient merit to be included in that exercise. In the early days the most regular traffic was coal: loaded inwards/empties outwards. In 1884 Bovey Gas Works opened on the southern flank of the siding site - alongside the 'old road' to Heathfield. Although it was close to the railway, there was no physical connection between the two, by virtue of a deep intervening gully. However, the proximity of the siding was doubtless a major factor in locating the gas works there. The coal was first railed into the siding and then carried the short remaining distance by road waggon: horse and cart for most of the time this operation continued. Other coal received in the siding was destined for Bovey Pottery. In addition to that used in the kilns, smaller consignments for general heating and other purposes were regularly required. The paucity of siding accommodation at the Pottery itself caused the nearby Granite Siding to be pressed into service; the fuel being conveyed over to the works by waggon. During the 1920s the long-established Bovey Pottery was joined, a little to the south, by two much smaller concerns: Devon Tors Pottery and Art Pottery. They too collected their very much more modest deliveries of coal from Granite Siding. Providing firms had their own transport, they arranged the carriage away from the site. When this was not the case, and truck-loads arriving at the siding required delivery, the supervising station (Bovey) asked Newton Abbot Goods Department to send a lorry.

Between Granite Siding's loading dock and the terminal basin of the Stover Canal at Ventiford, the Branch closely followed the route of the Haytor Granite Tramway, obliterating its carefully dressed formation of granite setts. However, above the Siding, stretches of the 4 foot 3 inch gauge tramway remain, as here in Yarner Wood in the summer of 1986.   *Author*

Less regular was the handling of basic slag, for agricultural use. Resembling coal dust, it was packed in tough paper bags and received in several wagon-loads at a time. Due to poor handling, careless loading, or damage in transit, the bags often arrived split, causing considerable spillage during unloading (not a popular job). When this happened, the merchants left the damaged bags behind and put in a claim to the GWR for the appropriate reimbursement. This, along with the coal, was classed as 'Mileage Traffic'; that is to say, 'full loads' as opposed to miscellaneous items of general merchandise (or 'smalls') traffic. All the paperwork connected with the siding was dealt with at Bovey.

Under Great Western ownership, the boundary fence between the main line and siding site comprised wooden posts and wire. A stop board just in front of the gate barred locomotives of all classes from passing beyond it. Thus in order to work wagons to or from the inner end of the siding, a certain

October 1965; and it was not until September 1967 that the 'lead-in' connection was removed. The heavily overgrown dock remained discernible into the 1980's, to be swept away finally in 1987 as a result of road works at the southern end of the Bovey by-pass.

Pottery Siding

Bovey Pottery was already well-established by the time the siding was opened in 1867, although the original premises dating back to 1776 had been in nearby Indio. The establishment was purchased in 1836 by Messrs. Divett, Buller & Co., and subsequently much enlarged at its new location. As with the granite quarries on Dartmoor, transport considerations were important if the industry was to prosper on any significant scale. Associated with the thick deposits of ball clay which had given rise to the industry in the first place, were bands of lignite: a soft carbonaceous material known locally as 'Bovey Coal' (and

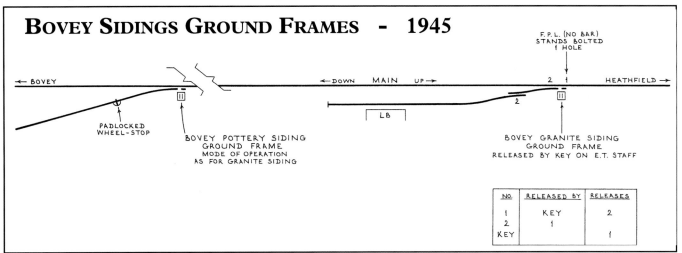

BOVEY SIDINGS GROUND FRAMES - 1945

procedure had to be followed. With no run-round facility, the shunting of the siding was performed on the return leg of the freight train's roster (that is, southbound). Wagons destined for Granite Siding were left at Bovey on the outward stage of the trip to Moreton and collected on the return, being marshalled near the front of the formation. If, on arriving at the siding, there was no 'outward' traffic to be collected, the engine simply propelled the loaded trucks as far along the siding as required - the other wagons between it and those being shunted acting as 'spacers' to prevent the engine passing the stop board. These were then returned to the rest of the stock parked on the main line (the brake van ensuring that they did not run away). When there was 'outward' traffic only, this was collected again using the 'spacer' principle, although sometimes the empty wagon/s would have been manually pushed to the gate ready for collection. If there was traffic to be both attached and detached, a longer variation on this theme was necessary. Once wagons had been positioned in the siding, their brakes were pinned down and the siding gate closed and locked before the points at the ground frame were reset to allow the train to resume its journey. The nature of the traffic dealt with here was such that trains were not booked to call on a scheduled basis, but only 'as required'.

In the late 1930s the gas works traffic ended when the production of town gas ceased at Bovey, the gas-holder then being connected by pipeline to the plant at Newton Abbot. The loss of this regular coal traffic was followed some ten years later by increasing road competition for the smaller consignments. From the early 1950s the loading dock began to fight a losing battle with encroaching vegetation, but in spite of this lack of use, the siding was not officially declared redundant until

referred to in the previous chapter). For a time it was used in the kilns, although its physical advantage of being 'on-site' was offset by its inferior quality and reliability as compared with the harder and more expensive 'extra-district' coal.

Prior to the arrival of the railway, obtaining the growing requirement for coal at the Pottery was a cumbersome affair. Brought by coastal colliers to the quay at Teignmouth, transport thence by road was painfully slow. The roads were rock-hard with deep-set ruts in dry weather, and a sea of sticky mud after rain - especially in the clayfields, where the ground was particularly tenacious. Even before the increasing clay and coal traffic began churning up their surfaces, the roads of the district had acquired a poor reputation. From the 1770s the Teign estuary had been used by barges, while the Stover Canal of 1790-92 pushed water-borne transport into the southern part of the Bovey Basin. Barges could carry the accumulated loads of many horse-drawn waggons, but the canal never progressed beyond Ventiford. Even with Templer's later Tramway, transhipment had to take place here, and also at Teignmouth. The products of the Pottery had to be despatched by the same tedious means in the reverse direction. By the middle of the nineteenth century this was not only inconvenient for existing needs, but militated against expansion. With the prospect of more reliable delivery, greater capacity and reduced transport costs, it is no wonder that John Divett was an enthusiastic supporter of local railway schemes.

The need for improved and cheaper transport became even more acute in the period of financial uncertainty which afflicted the industry in the early and mid 1860s. Recovery coinciding with the provision of a railway siding saw the Pottery prosper. About 300 people were employed there in 1870, with truck-loads of earthenware goods for home and abroad being railed direct to the quay at Teignmouth (where a siding had been put in as early as 1851, with an expansion of the layout following in 1884). After Divett's death in 1885 Bovey Pottery experienced a serious slump in its fortunes, which lasted for the next ten years; but by the end of the century it was flourishing once again.

Pottery Siding was worked in the same manner as Granite Siding nearby. Other features in common were the stop board by the gate, and the covered ground frame: a small, timber-clad cabin, whose two levers were unlocked by the key-like attachment at the end of the staff (later token) used on the Heathfield to Bovey section of the Branch. Unusually, however, Pottery Siding did not have a catch point to protect the main line from 'runaways' although, like Granite Siding, it did possess a wheel-stop.

The Pottery complex was substantial, and possessed a narrow gauge tramway network to serve the disparate parts of the site: one branch leading ultimately to the 'Upper Mill' and another to the 'Lower'. Fixed to wooden sleepers and built to a gauge of two feet, the tracks were used by wooden-bodied wagons which were manhandled from place to place. On the 'inward' side of the rail-borne traffic came coal and flints. The coal was needed only for the kilns, as all the machinery in the plant was worked by water power. The trucks were propelled along the outer part of the siding by the 'up' goods engine, uncoupled and manhandled individually along the siding, straight across the wagon turntable at the end of the packing shed, and on to the 'inner spur'. Here the coal was transferred to tub-like trucks waiting on the adjoining tramway, to be taken thus to the kilns. The flints were imported from Northern France via Teignmouth. As a producer of earthenware, flint was required in large quantities, as it made up about a third of the composition of the finished products. After transfer to the tramway, the flints were taken to be calcined at high temperature before being added to the clay, and then fired. From the kilns the various items were ultimately taken to the packing shed. Here they were crated up and loaded into open railway trucks by means of an overhead crane. When full, they were covered with tarpaulins. Box vans were less frequently used for this traffic. The loaded wagons were pushed, one at a time, by the workers along the track which ran from the shed to the wagon turntable on the main arm of the siding. They were turned through a right angle and moved along the siding towards the gate, ready for collection by the afternoon goods train.

A producer of plain white earthenware, the Pottery provided the Railway with steady revenue, the trains calling here 'as required': down to the late 1940s this in practice meant virtually every weekday. The main customers were institutions such as hospitals and various Government ministries. One regular and substantial order was from the Ministry of Defence for N.A.A.F.I. crockery. Truck-loads were despatched, much of it bound for the Royal Ordnance factory in Plymouth. This received a boost during the Second World War, with products being sent all over the country. One sizeable and unusual order came from Northern Ireland. It was requested that the crockery be packed in galvanised tanks as they wanted both (the tanks were made in Wolverhampton and railed down to Bovey). With the exception of the Ulster traffic, the crockery was skilfully packed in straw-filled crates, made of local wood.

One of the perks of the Branch goods duty was that the train crew could often obtain separate items of crockery, or even full tea-sets, during the 'Pottery shunt'. All the considerable paperwork relating to this traffic was dealt with at Bovey as the supervising station, and in whose accounts the revenue featured. From the end of the 1940s the Railway's share of the transport began to diminish, partly because of road competition but also because production at the Pottery began to fall away. Use of the siding declined rapidly in the next few years, and in 1956 the Private Siding Agreement between the Pottery Company and British Railways was terminated (and on 24th June that part of the siding between the running line and the siding gate was lifted). Financially, the loss of the Pottery traffic was a blow to the Branch, but in the event it was inevitable, for the Pottery itself closed down the following year.

Bovey Pottery sprouts a veritable forest of brick-built bottle-shaped kilns in this 1908 view. This was a time of welcome prosperity after a serious slump in the mid 1890s. At its height, there were up to 16 kilns in use, and considerable traffic was handled by the Moretonhampstead Branch. The Pottery complex possessed its own internal tramway, a section of which is seen in the foreground.

Lance Tregoning Collection

Chapter Twelve

BRIMLEY

The 1920s and '30s saw an extensive programme of halt building throughout the Great Western network, either to meet new needs or in response to the growing threat of bus competition, or both. The scattering of houses on the Heathfield and Ashburton roads, and to the west of Bovey Pottery, was deemed adequate to warrant one of these 'unstaffed' stations. It opened on Monday 21st May 1928 as Brimley Halt, 5 miles 46 chains from Newton Abbot, and half a mile away from Bovey station. The name was taken from the hamlets of Higher and Lower Brimley about a mile to the south-west. Situated a few yards south of Ashburton Road bridge, on the 'up' side of the line, and in the deepest part of 'Cricket Field Cutting', the platform was reached by a cinder footpath sloping down from the road at the corner of the recreation ground. The platform itself was just 72 feet long, although with the addition of the ramps this was increased to just over 110 feet. Though of humble status, it was a substantially-built structure, with a fascia of reconstituted-stone blocks, 4-inch thick concrete edging slabs measuring 4 feet by 2 feet; and an 8-foot-wide metalled surface (that is, rolled, broken stone). The accommodation on the other hand was pretty basic, consisting of a centrally-positioned 12-foot by 8-foot waiting shelter. Formed of horizontal timber cladding above a shallow concrete plinth, and with a backwardly-sloping corrugated iron roof, it was fitted out with a plain wooden bench. Two platform benches, two concrete lamp-posts and a name board completed the list of fixtures.

Engine drivers found this an awkward place at which to stop with the precision required by the short platform. Just prior to the opening of the halt, auto trains were introduced to the Branch. The one-class carriages (or 'trailers') were built on the open, or saloon, principle with a single doorway in the guard's vestibule. Varying in length from 60 to 70 feet, one trailer could be accommodated at the platform with room to spare. The difficulty arose with the 2-coach auto trains, which were commonly in use. To the coach body length had to be added the distance over the buffers between the trailers, and so drivers had to develop considerable skill in stopping the train so that both doors were drawn up at the extreme platform ends! Not all the trains, however, were autos. Some continued to be made up of non-corridor stock, especially in the summer months - which included the popular Sunday trains, a couple of which ran through to the Torbay resorts in 'British Railways' (ie. post 1948) days. In these cases the driver would stop the brake-coach at the platform to enable the guard to step out and superintend the boarding and alighting of passengers, and make sure that doors were secure before flagging the train away. People joining the train could get into any of the compartments of the coaches that stopped alongside the platform. The guard had already ascertained which of the passengers already on board were for Brimley, and had directed them into the compartments nearest his own, to enable them

to alight at the halt without the time-consuming inconvenience of the train having to 'pull forward' or 'set back'. Regular passengers of course knew of these arrangements!

The expertise that drivers had to exercise here was especially tested by virtue of the fact that the halt was right at the summit of the climb from both Pottery Bridge and Bovey. Also, being on the inside of the curve through Cricket Field Cutting, it was unsighted until almost the last minute. At night, the blackness of the cutting was an added complication, the glow from a single oil lamp on the platform serving only as a general marker. Whilst the stop was unpopular with drivers, from at least some passengers' point of view it proved advantageous at apple-harvest time. It is reliably reported that occasionally one of the Fat Parks allotment holders threw surplus fruit from the top of the cutting. Passengers with eager, outstretched arms thrust through carriage windows gratefully caught as much of the bounty as possible!

Brimley Halt was placed under the supervision of Bovey. The station master there was responsible for writing out the train time information for posting up at the halt - on the board at the top of the access path - while one of the porters made periodic visits to sweep out the waiting shelter and check that everything was in order. Bovey's permanent way gang passed the halt at regular intervals - indeed, the length had to be walked every day that trains were running - and were able to keep an eye on it from the structural/maintenance point of view. The gang was responsible for keeping the approach path and platform in order, such as cutting back grass or clearing snow. The provision of lighting followed the same regime as that described for Teigngrace. The original arrangement consisted of two square-sectioned concrete posts, sited mid-way between the ramps and waiting shelter. They were capped with a shallow circular metal tray, with three claw-like attachments equally arranged around the circumference. The base of a hurricane lamp fitted exactly into the tray, being secured by means of an adjustable screw in the front 'claw'. At a later date, cylindrical

Looking south through Brimley Halt in 1955.
I. D. Beale

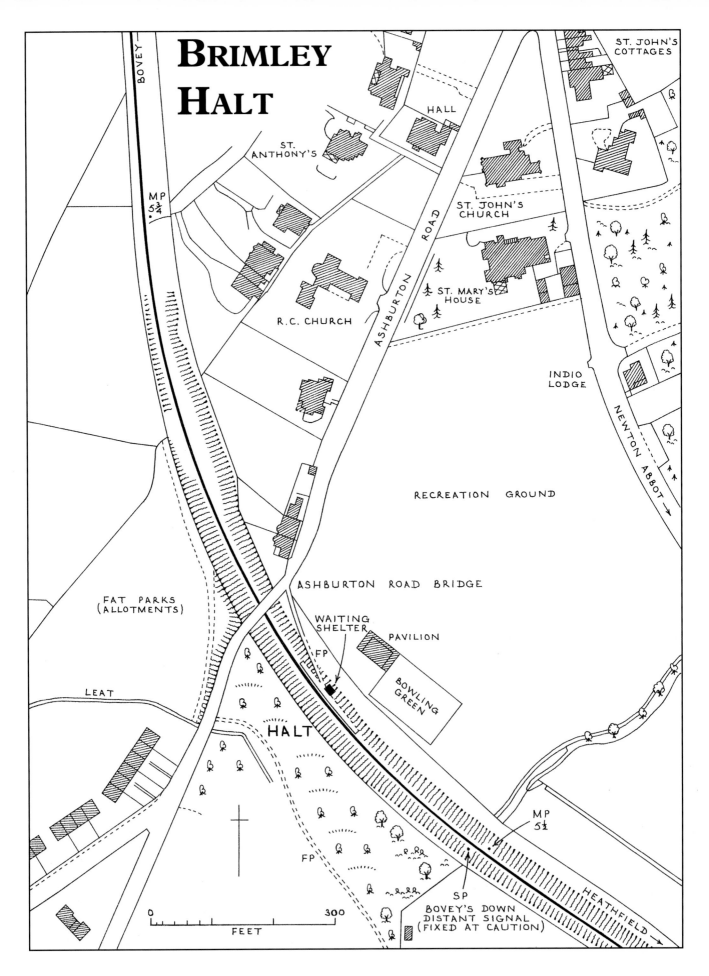

BRIMLEY HALT

BOVEY

ST. JOHN'S COTTAGES

HALL

ST. ANTHONY'S

MP 5¾

ST. JOHN'S CHURCH

R.C. CHURCH

ASHBURTON ROAD

ST. MARY'S HOUSE

INDIO LODGE

NEWTON ABBOT

RECREATION GROUND

FAT PARKS (ALLOTMENTS)

ASHBURTON ROAD BRIDGE

WAITING SHELTER

PAVILION

FP

BOWLING GREEN

LEAT

HALT

MP 5½

FP

SP

BOVEY'S DOWN DISTANT SIGNAL (FIXED AT CAUTION)

HEATHFIELD

0   300

FEET

118

metal posts were installed: one at the bottom of the path, adjoining the shelter, and one to the left of the name board. The tops of these posts ended in hooks for the handles of the lamps, while a flat metal ring to support the base was bolted to the post about 18 inches below. As a rule only one lamp was sent out to the halt, and this was hung on the pole at the foot of the path.

The use of the halt increased as residential development took place in the triangle of streets to the west of the Pottery. The first phase of building, in the late 1930s, was halted by the War, but resumed soon afterwards. This added to the halt's existing 'catchment', and it received a good measure of patronage. As an unstaffed station, and in the absence of 'conductor-guards', passengers had to obtain their tickets at the next station - Bovey or Heathfield - in the manner described for Teigngrace. The revenue originating at Brimley was credited to Bovey in the Divisional annual traffic returns, so that it is not possible to ascertain factually the degree of passenger usage. Certainly, subjectively, the best-supported services were those in the morning to Newton Abbot, the principal destination for most of the halt's patrons on weekdays (with increased numbers on Wednesdays, this being Newton's market day, and Saturdays). There was a 'balancing' return flow in the late afternoon/early evening. During the mid 1950s, the third class single fare to Newton was one shilling (5 pence) and the cheap day return 1/5. A sample of other cheap day returns is as follows:

Above: Looking north through Brimley Halt in 1955. *I. D. Beale*

Exeter* (via Newton Abbot)	5/9	Paignton	3/3
(via Christow)	4/3	Teignmouth	2/6
Heathfield	0/6	Torquay	2/9
Lustleigh	0/11	Torre	2/6
Moretonhampstead	1/8	Totnes	3/6
(*St Thomas or St. David's stations)			

Below: 'Small Prairie' 4547 climbs the last few yards of the bank from Bovey to the summit near Brimley Halt with the 10.15am from Moretonhampstead. The prefabricated concrete permanent way hut was the only one of its kind on the Branch. 30.8.54. *R. C. Riley*

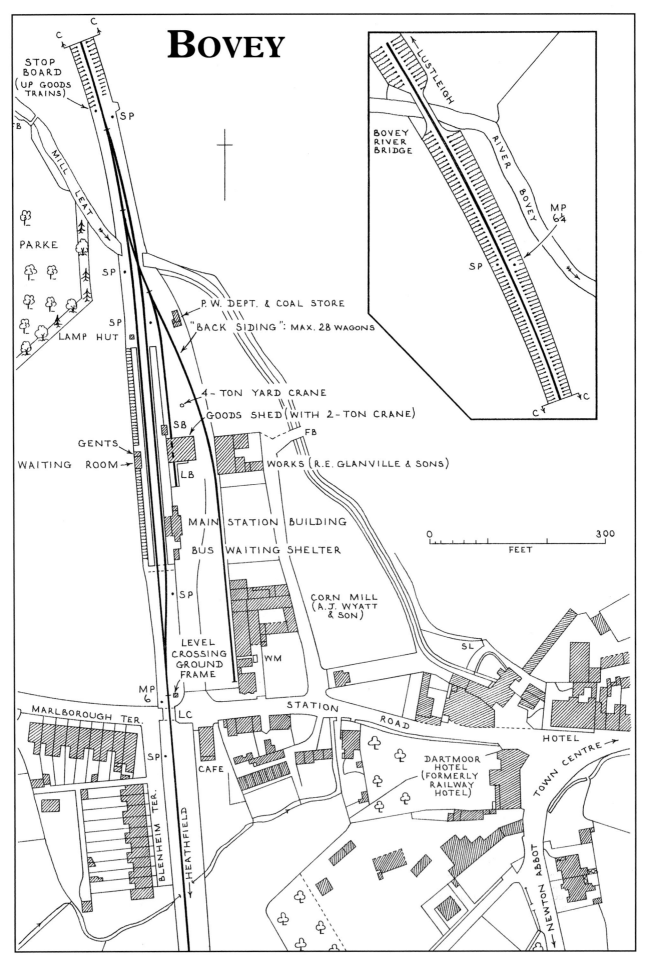

BOVEY

STOP BOARD (UP GOODS TRAINS)

C C C

SP

B

MILL LEAT

PARKE

SP

SP

LAMP HUT

P.W. DEPT. & COAL STORE

"BACK SIDING": MAX. 28 WAGONS

4 - TON YARD CRANE

GOODS SHED (WITH 2-TON CRANE)

SB

FB

GENTS

WAITING ROOM

LB

WORKS (R.E. GLANVILLE & SONS)

MAIN STATION BUILDING

BUS WAITING SHELTER

CORN MILL (A.J. WYATT & SON)

SP

SL

LEVEL CROSSING GROUND FRAME

WM

MP 6

MARLBOROUGH TER.

LC

STATION ROAD

HOTEL

SP

CAFE

DARTMOOR HOTEL (FORMERLY RAILWAY HOTEL)

BLENHEIM TER.

HEATHFIELD

TOWN CENTRE

NEWTON ABBOT

0   300

FEET

LUSTLEIGH

BOVEY RIVER BRIDGE

RIVER BOVEY

MP 6¼

SP

C

C

Chapter Thirteen

BOVEY

The small, old-established town of Bovey Tracey marked the half way stage on the Moretonhampstead Branch, the station being situated immediately to the north of the Manaton road level crossing in the low-lying district of Pludda. One might have expected the Railway Company to use the town's full title, but this is an unusual instance where railway nomenclature followed local custom. Platform name boards throughout the station's life simply proclaimed 'BOVEY': the name by which the town was, and still is, almost universally known in and around the area.

The Station Buildings

The principal station building was situated on the 'up' (or east) platform. As the building survives virtually intact, one is in the happy position of being able to give a description in the present tense. Executed in local granite, the blocks have rough-hewn faces, with only the edges being dressed to allow matching up of adjoining blocks. Unlike some building stones, which are physically coherent but at the same time can be cut with precision, granite is less texturally consistent (there is no natural 'grain' to aid the mason). The result of this is that no two apparently similar blocks are exactly the same size. Where some greater precision is required - as with the corner strengthening blocks (quoins) and wedge-shaped sections over windows and doorways (voussoirs) - there is a higher degree of uniformity, though still not the exactitude one would find with brick or more malleable stone. No two lintels, sills, window openings or door recesses possess the same dimensions. All of this, together with slight variations in colour - ranging from grey-brown to sandy brown - give the station building a most attractive and solid appearance.

The aesthetic quality of the edifice is enhanced by the smaller details which adorn it; such as the inch-wide, hand-chiselled dressed edging found on the voussoirs which form the arches over the Gothic-style door and window recesses and on the quoins. The stepped cornices on the wings, the extension of the roof line to form a central canopy, and the carefully shaped granite corbels supporting the chamfered timber canopy

brackets are all noteworthy features. The roof is of grey slate, with plain ridge tiles. The granite chimney-stacks are elaborate: the corners of the basic square-section being trimmed to produce an octagonal shape. All in all, the building has a most pleasing appearance, a monument to its Dawlish-based designer Peter Margary and builders Call & Pethick of Plymouth. For a time, its merits were further enhanced by proximity to the huge, inelegant corrugated iron grain silos - now demolished - of the adjoining mill!

The public approach to the station was along the roadway leading from the level crossing. Walking over the paved apron in front of the building, the Booking Hall was entered through the double doors beneath the canopy, overhanging the central section of the east elevation. The booking hall also served as the general waiting room, its floor consisting of large flagstones. Turning to the left on entering was the booking office, partitioned from the hall by a panelled wooden screen, which extended the full height of the room (11' 7"). A door in the left-hand corner connected the hall with the office, while the ticket window was in the centre of the screen. On the opposite side of the hall, next to the doorway into the ladies room, was the fireplace. Above the mantelpiece, at either end, two wall-mounted brass lamp brackets supported oil lamps (although these were replaced in later years by a single Tilley lamp - that is, pressurised-vapour paraffin lamp - suspended from the ceiling). To the right of the double doorway leading to the platform, beneath the window, was a wooden seat; while to the left, high on the wall between the window and the door, was the back of the clock - or more accurately the place where the clock had been, for by Edwardian times it had been removed. The circular hole thus left was incompletely sealed and, during the 1950s, allowed a robin to get into the Booking Hall and build a nest in the flower display the station master had placed in the deep window sill above the seat.

Birds seemed to favour the station in its later years. Blue-tits nested in the letterbox attached to the fence at the street end of the approach road. Although most of the mail was delivered to

The 'up' platform; 1920. Station staff pose for the camera in front of the main building which, like the platform face, is of rough-hewn granite construction. Farther along the platform, to the north, are the goods shed and signal box. The shed doors are open, to reveal the arched entrances. A loading gauge is seen framed by the farther arch, being suspended from a metal bar inside the shed.

Courtesy James Mann

An unidentified 0-6-0 saddle tank coasts into the 'down' platform at Bovet with a train of short wheelbase clerestory coaches around the turn of the 20th century. The track, though recently 'narrowed', retains the bulk road construction characteristic of Brunel's broad gauge; while the station building has yet to aquire a canopy.   *Author's collection*

the booking office direct, some correspondence was dropped into the box - but this did not seem to worry the birds, as they returned year after year. In the early 1960s the freight handled at Bovey consisted of 'full loads' only - mainly coal and grain - so that the 4-ton yard crane was no longer used. This undisturbed location encouraged another bird to nest there; between the cogs in the winding apparatus.

The Booking Office was the station master's centre of operations. Beneath the ticket window, running the full length of the partition from the door to the window, was a solid mahogany counter. The ticket racks were fixed to the partition above the counter to the left of the window; the date-stamping machine was on the counter itself; and beneath it were cupboards and the safe. Underneath the window looking out on to the station approach were cupboards for stocks of tickets, and to the right of these was the heavy iron copying press. The fireplace was centred on the back wall of the office, and to the right of this was the station master's table. A shelf above the fireplace displayed signalling 'repeating instruments', including the two bells, by which the signalman at Bovey, Heathfield and Moretonhampstead communicated. The equipment carried the same brass label-tags as on the instruments in the signal boxes. The ringing of bells and movement of the indicators kept the station master informed as to train movements, thereby alerting him to send the porter out to the level crossing ground frame to deal with the gates. A single Tilley lamp provided the office with light, while the floor covering was the standard GWR-issue brown linoleum. This minor concession to comfort, however, did nothing to ameliorate the unpleasantness of the working conditions in the winter. The yellowish-green light issuing from the hissing Tilley lamp was not particularly easy on the eyes, casting long, deep shadows across parts of the room. The fire gave some warmth, but the coldness which permeated the stone building caused the air only a few feet from the fire to retain a distinct chill. This created a predisposition to chilblains!

Ticket sales accounted for only a small part of the station master's routine; most of his work

The approach road (east) elevation of the station building in May 1969. Disused since the beginning of 1966, the remaining goods facilities were to be withdrawn thirteen months later.   *Photomatic Ltd*

Above: View north through the station in 1920. Notice the lamp hut at the far end of the 'down' platform and the generous provision of lamp standards. Machines for dispensing sweets, cigarettes and matches stand between the seats on the 'up' platform. One of the original station name boards is currently held at the Great Western Society's Didcot Centre.   *Courtesy James Mann*

Below: The station in February 1959. From July 1927 two-way working through the 'up' platform loop was introduced, so that all passenger trains used this platform - unless they were required to 'cross'. The greater than usual clearance between the tracks (normally 6 feet) is a product of the narrowing of gauge.   *Peter F. Bowles*

Above: The level crossing and associated ground frame cabin viewed from the 'up' platform in the summer of 1949. Beyond the crossing is the 'down home' signal, the bracket arm covering movements from the 'down main' to 'up' platform line. On the extreme left is Torvue Cafe, the latter-day descendant of the 'Refreshment Rooms', whose raison d'etre was the Rail/Road Motor tourist traffic of the inter-war years.

S. J. Dickson
L&GRP

Below: Looking into the station from the level crossing in 1921, showing part of the lever cabin or ground frame.

going on unseen by the travelling public. The majority of tickets were sold in the morning, and predominantly for the first three 'up' trains. The most widely requested destination was Newton Abbot. Sometimes as much as £20 might be taken over the counter in just a few minutes on one of these services. This might not sound very much today, but bearing in mind that a day return to Newton in the mid 1950s cost 1/8d - the equivalent of about nine pence in decimal coinage - it represents a significant number of people (one could book all the way to Plymouth for 5/3d: less than 27p). In addition to these daily purchases, many of the regular users - such as schoolchildren, shop and office workers - had season tickets. These might be weekly, monthly, or quarterly or even annual, and could be purchased at leisure, avoiding the need to queue at busy times. The ticket sale par excellence was that of an annual, all-line (GWR) season ticket to a gentleman who lived at Lower Knowle, very close to Hawkmoor Halt, and who journeyed frequently and far afield. This one sale produced a huge income compared with the sums with which Bovey was usually acquainted. The first 'up' train, just after 8 o'clock, was patronised by what we now call 'commuters': although on this, as on any, service there might be a few longer-distance passengers. Between the wars schoolchildren formed a significant proportion of the clientele; there being 40-50 on board by the time the train reached Newton. When the Grammar School moved to Exeter Road, at the opposite end of town, and bus competition became more pronounced, the numbers of children travelling from Bovey dwindled. The second 'up' train, around 9 o'clock, was used by shoppers and people travelling to Newton on business; receiving extra patronage on Wednesdays, Newton's market day. Longer distance passengers favoured this service because it made good connections at Newton with main line expresses. From the summer of 1953 this train was of benefit to day-trippers to the coast as it ran through to Paignton. Those who did not want such an early start used the mid-morning train, although had to change at Newton Abbot. Teignmouth was a popular seaside destination, and at 2/9 return was 9d cheaper than Paignton and Goodrington Sands.

A door to the left of the booking office fireplace led into the Parcels Room. This occupied the south wing of the station building which, when viewed from the outside, appeared as an annex. Measuring 13' 8" by 9' 5" it had a sloping roof: joists running longitudinally at 18-inch intervals, with a single central transverse purlin. Thus, at the end adjoining the booking office the room was 11 feet high, tapering down to 8' 4" at the south end. The outside walls were surmounted by a parapet with a plain, stepped cornice; and as this was above the level of the roof, rainwater drained off through an internal downpipe (seen in the corner by the outside door). A solitary lamp, hanging from one of the joists, gave the only light; but as this did not have sufficient clearance for safety it was provided with a thick metal 'heat-hood' above.

Bovey handled a considerable amount of parcels traffic, and while the room was just about adequate for its needs, it had once been sub-divided by a brick partition. Viewed from the outside, there were two identical doorways in the end wall. That on the left had once given access to the station's coal store, while the one on the right opened into the original parcels room. The obvious need to increase the capacity of the latter led to the demolition of the brick dividing wall and the almost complete sealing up of the ex-coal store doorway. This was done with granite masonry, which carefully matched the original surrounding stonework. A small window was left below the soffit of the old doorway, and even a 3-inch sill installed. Just when this took place is not certain but it was certainly before 1920. The new coal store was transferred to the goods yard, taking the form of a sleeper-built hut.

Of ample dimensions is the waiting room on the 'down' platform. It was built at the same time as the platform was lengthened - soon after the gauge conversion of 1892. The extension at the north end, with panelled screen in front of the doorway, is a urinal, although it had been sealed off from at least the mid 1930s. *S. J. Dickson*

There was no parcels clerk as such at the station, although one of the signalmen was given the additional responsibility of assisting with parcels (his 'opposite turn' colleague helping-out in the goods office). In the main, this entailed assisting the station master with the paperwork; notably preparing accounts and the monthly summaries, working out delivery charges, and attending the cartage agent (later the Company's own Collection & Delivery vanman). Between the wars this was performed by Fred Murphy, and latterly Tom Booth, who spent around two and a half hours of his shift each day in the parcels office. The porters undertook the work of manhandling and sorting the parcels, and taking them to and from trains. Items had to be got ready for despatch by particular passenger trains; while those received needed to be sorted prior to delivery by the local cartage agent/C&D van, or collection by the customer. Some parcels were 'charged' at Bovey, while others were 'to pay': that is, charged at the receiving station. In this way, revenue was collected on both incoming and outgoing traffic - the value of the latter always being the higher. When weights required checking, the weighing machine by the north wall of the goods shed was used; this measuring up to a half a hundredweight.

The parcels themselves showed infinite variety, ranging from enormous heavy tin trunks down to hat boxes. The outward traffic may not have been particularly voluminous, but it was regular, and until the Second World War included large wicker baskets of laundry, washed by the girls at the 'Devon House of Mercy'. Rabbits were a seasonal speciality. Tied in bunches by the feet and brought thus to the station to be loaded into wicker baskets, they were destined mainly for Birmingham. Mr. Owen Willis and his brother actually made a living locally by trapping rabbits, and were regular customers of the Railway. Less regularly, a Mr. Rogers of Haytor sent live mink away for the fur trade. After the last war, cases and a few churns of milk were despatched, and although it increased in volume it was not substantial. Rather more exotic was the despatch of 'decorative vegetation'. Moss and ferns were the speciality of Henry Christophers. In spite of his advancing years Henry cycled out from Newton Abbot about twice a week to collect sacks of vegetation from the area around Lustleigh Cleave and Pullabrook. Once it had been brought to Bovey, weighed and paid for, the wily gent then saturated the contents with water to

Bovey Station Building

Plan

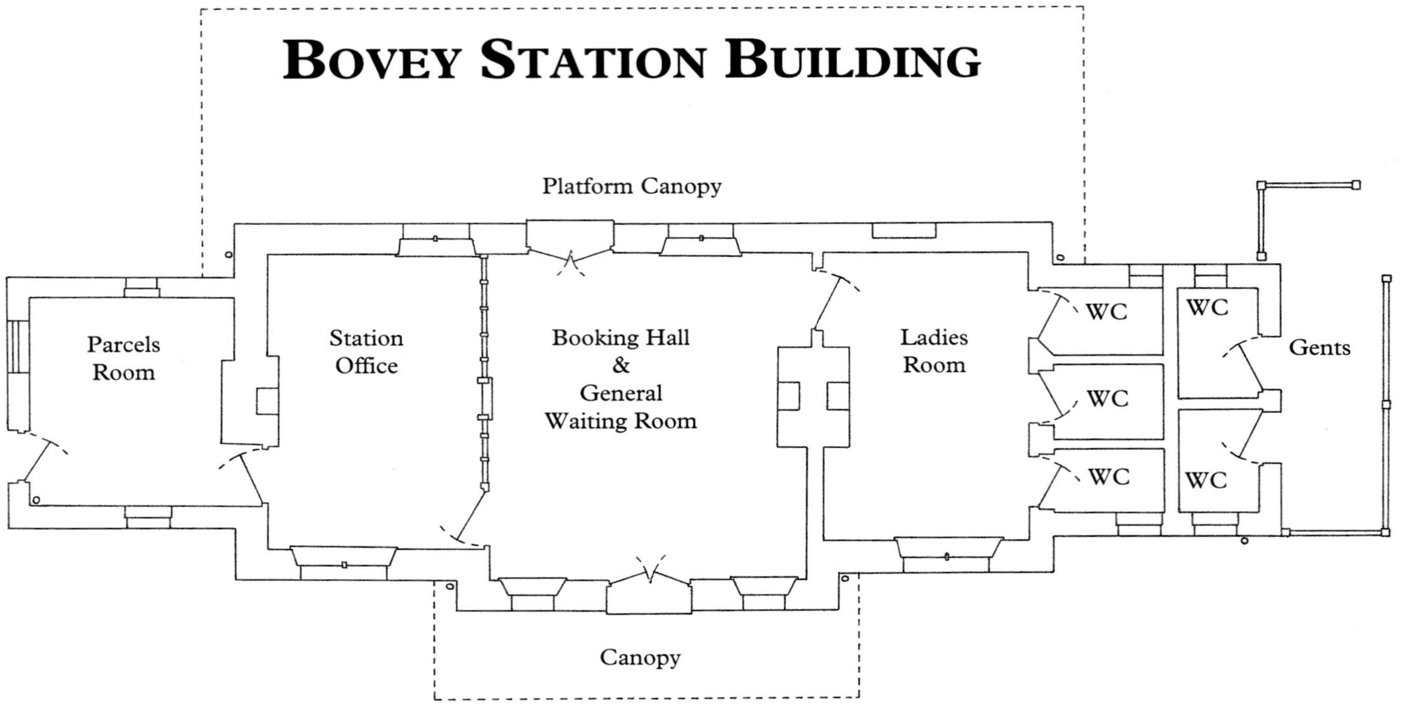
Platform Canopy
Parcels Room
Station Office
Booking Hall & General Waiting Room
Ladies Room
WC
WC
WC
WC
WC
Gents
Canopy

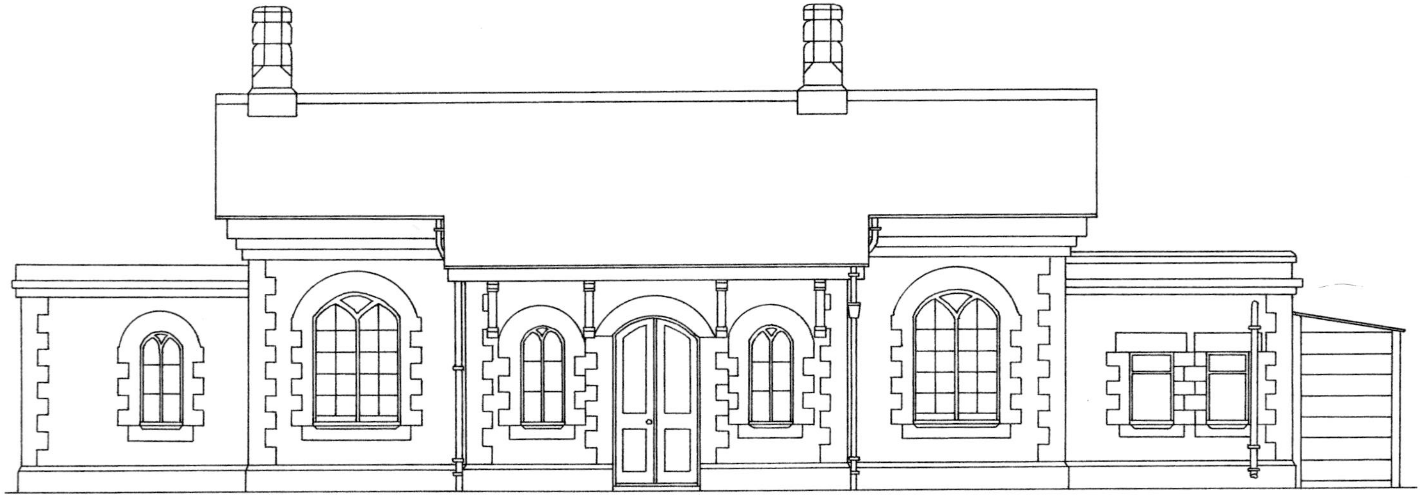

Approach Road (East) Elevation

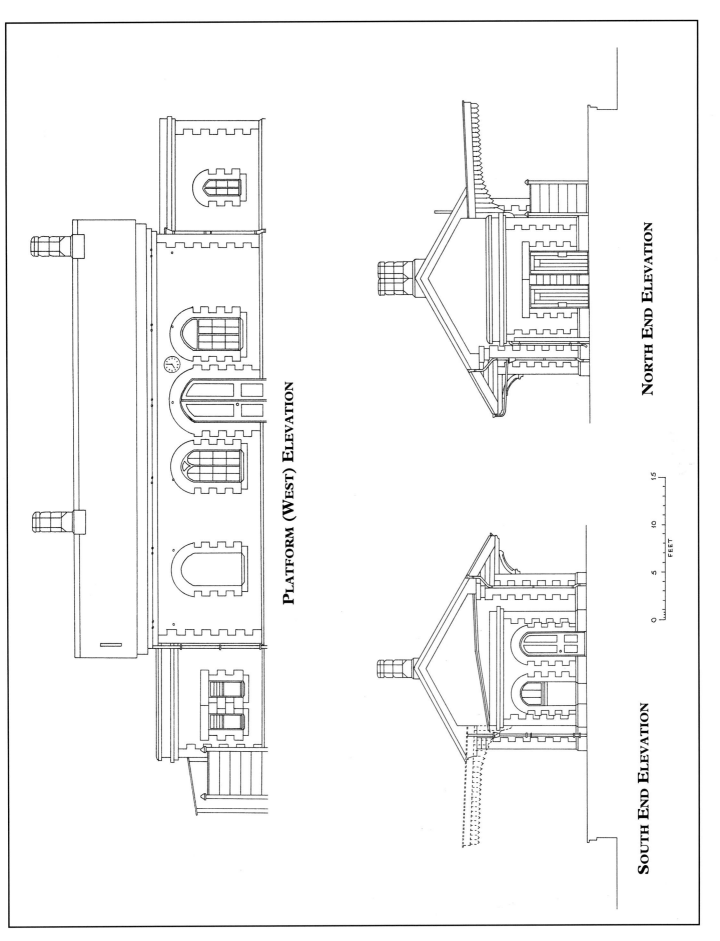

PLATFORM (WEST) ELEVATION

NORTH END ELEVATION

SOUTH END ELEVATION

FEET

0   5   10   15

preserve them during transport (thus the weight carried by train considerably exceeded that actually paid for!). Most of these unusual 'parcels' went to London for inclusion in floral or product displays at Covent Garden and other markets, as well as high-class retail establishments. In addition to the moss and ferns, eucalyptus was also sent from Bovey. Tied in sprigs and carefully packed in boxes, it was the brain-child of a local retired military man who had the business acumen to identify and cater for this incredibly specialised niche.

Pre-eminently, there was the more steady traditional 'town trade', especially in the 'parcels received' category, characterised by even greater diversity. Boxes of wet fish, packed in ice, regularly came in on the first train from Newton Abbot for delivery to fishmonger William Brooks of Fore Street. Quarters of beef and New Zealand lamb were also received: these being destined for Eastman's Ltd. of Town Hall Place. An interesting snap-shot of the incoming parcels traffic in the later years is given in a report written by the station master to the District Commercial Manager's office, Exeter, on 24th July 1956:

"Most of the parcels traffic is received on the 7.50am Newton Abbot. We have received the following traffic off the 12.44pm and 2.15pm Newton Abbot: Cans Cream, Boxes Bullion, hampers live pigeons, cartons chicks etc. Perishable and urgent traffic is frequently received after mid-day from N.A. including boxes Blood for transfusions at Hawkmoor Chest Hospital. There are no P.O. mails dealt with at this station under normal circumstances."

On the north side of the booking hall, occupying the equivalent space to the station master's office on the south, was the Ladies Room. While fitted out with some seating, and with a mirror over the fireplace, this room served essentially as an anteroom for the lavatories; these, along with the 'gents', being in the northern wing of the building (equivalent to the parcels room in the southern). Three lavatory cubicles were attached to the ladies room; quite a generous provision for a branch line station! The two lateral ones were lit by small frosted glass side windows, with louvres above; the central cubicle possessing a small rectangular roof-light (the height of the ceiling being 9' 2"). Additional light was admitted through frosted glass in the upper panels of the doors. Behind the back wall of the lavatories was the Gents: two water closets, and beyond them the urinal. This latter was a lean-to prefabricated structure. The roof of the toilet block was flat, made of sheet lead; while the lean-to was built of horizontal concrete slabs and vertical supports, with a sloping corrugated roof. A non-drinking water tap was to be found on the short end wall of the urinal; this being used, amongst other things, to top-up the rack of fire buckets fixed to the outside of the structure. All the lavatory doors were fitted with the usual rectangular brass coin-in-slot locks. Periodically, the station master emptied these of their collection of pennies: quite a tricky operation if one wished to avoid coins falling to the floor, as it required the simultaneous turning of two keys - the aim of this being to make the machines thief-proof. The annual revenue from the closets averaged just over £4, and although this figure may seem small, it doubtless represents a considerable amount of passenger relief!

Rabbits featured regularly in the 'traffic despatched' regime of Bovey. In this late 1920s scene one such consignment is being loaded into baskets by a local trapper, thought to be Owen Willis. The activity is being overseen by Station Master Haywood and is also being observed by one of the white-capped GWR 'road motor' bus drivers in the background.
Courtesy 'Mid-Devon Advertiser'

In the mid 1950s a new silo was constructed for the firm of Wyatt & Bruce between the station approach road and 'Back Siding'. Its foundations are in the process of excavation and the eventual towering, angular corrugated iron structure joined its predecessor in dominating the locality. In the centre background is Torvue Cafe, between which and the level crossing is a 'British Railways' notice board. *A. W. Yendall Collection*

To the south of the main station building was the former Bus Waiting Shelter. 'Road Motor' tours of the Moor began a few years before the outbreak of the First World War, the Bovey-based service being operated by Messrs. Hellier & Lee. After a break during the war, the developing tourist industry was given a boost by the Great Western Railway's own fleet of Road Motors (see Chapter 5). Designed to connect with the Branch trains during the summer months, they and their private-owner successors featured at Bovey for many years. To provide waiting accommodation for bus passengers, a large corrugated iron shelter was provided on the approach-road side of the 'up' platform, directly across the path in front of the parcels room. Built in readiness for the 1922 season, it was fitted out with wooden bench-like seats.

The buses were joined on the station approach by taxis operated by a couple of local garages: namely, Aggett and Moir & Davie. In the tourist hey-day, they conveyed many people to and from the station, and found it worth their while to rent a space on the station approach to wait for incoming passengers. Annual cab rents in the mid and late 1920s yielded £23 or £24, but thereafter only intermittently featured in the station's accounts.

The reduction in the volume of bus traffic in the early 1930s, precipitated the Great Western's decision to withdraw the Road Motors. Their routes were now taken over by the Western National Omnibus Company: with service WN 122 running from Bovey to Haytor, with an extension to Widecombe-in-the-Moor in the summer months; and WN 123 from Bovey to Manaton. This was a short-lived arrangement, for in 1935 both these routes were transferred to J. Potter & Sons of Tor Garage, Haytor. The ending of the Railway's direct involvement with road tours removed the need for a waiting facility. The seats were taken out of the shelter to enable it to be converted into the station's new oil store and lamp room. Previously, the oil drums had been kept in a much smaller corrugated iron structure - the 'standard' type used on the GWR - a few yards from the north end of the 'down' platform. This was now removed. The proximity of the oil to the station building led to the installation of a substantial metal baffle-plate at the station end of the hut as a fire precaution.

If the courtesy of shelter had been afforded to bus passengers virtually from the outset, rail users were not so comprehensively catered for in 'broad gauge' days and beyond. That is to say, the main station building was not fitted with a platform awning. True, there were the waiting rooms, but a canopy over the platform would be an added convenience. The continued absence of this amenity prompted the Rector of Manaton to complain to the GWR in July 1903; but in their reply, the Company intimated that there was little probability of one being provided in the near future. Someone, somewhere obviously had a change of mind, for the central portion of the main building came to be adorned with a requisite canopy very much sooner than such a non-committal answer might lead one to expect. A wide, elegant structure, supported on six massive, ornamented wrought iron wall brackets, the fascia boards displayed the 'classic Great Western' dog-tooth serrations. It is

unclear precisely when it was installed, but it was certainly in situ by the summer of 1910. Beneath the canopy, against the wall, were two chocolate dispensing machines; features, literally, of long-standing. Their servicing came under the remit of the station master, who was actually paid a small commission on sales. It was his responsibility to order the chocolate bars, keep the machines topped-up, and empty the cash trays.

The 'down' platform was reached by way of a boardwalk at the south end of the station. The only structure on the platform was a substantial 'general waiting shelter' with a flat roofed gents' lavatory built on to the north wall (the entrance to this was sealed off in later years). The distinctive vitreous buff-yellow local brick was used in its construction, the waiting room being provided with seats and a hearth; although as the provision of a fire in winter was too much of a luxury for the station's precious coal resources, it was never lit - apart from which, most passengers using this platform were alighting from trains than waiting for them.

For almost thirty years after the station opened, the 'down' platform was the shorter of the two: 190 feet to the 'up' side's 300 (the lengths including ramps). In the event of the last carriage of a train 'overhanging' the rear of the platform, the point rodding leading away from the ramp was boarded over for a few yards to allow passengers to alight. (The broad gauge, and early standard gauge, coaches were provided with an upper and lower set of wooden steps or running boards that extended the length of the vehicles and permitted boarding from low platforms or even the ground.) The point rodding here was actually depressed below its normal height to accommodate this; a feature which remained until the very end. As the length of trains increased from the early 1890s, the shortness of the platform became an inconvenience; and so in 1894 or thereabouts, it was lengthened at the north end by 110 feet to literally bring it into line with the 'up' side. Both platforms had originally been built with masonry faces and metalled surfaces. The surface of the 'down side' extension was also metalled, but as its face was built of local brick, it was easy 'see the join'. Though rendered unnecessary, the wood cladding over the point rodding at the other end of the platform remained for another thirty years or so.

Throughout its life the station was lit by oil lamps, despite numerous written requests in later years for electric light. Heathfield was granted electric lighting, while Moreton had its gas lamps; but Bovey had to soldier on in the time-honoured way. In the late 1920s the old-style square-tapered, glass-cased lamps on the platforms were replaced by the much less attractive hurricane lamps. A single tall concrete post with a lamp-hoist was positioned midway along either platform, while the other concrete posts utilised for lighting were of the type described at Brimley Halt. The rooms in the station building, together with the signal box and goods shed/office were lit by Tilley lamps, which could be 'pumped up' to give a brighter light than the hurricanes, but with a shorter duration. It was the responsibility of the 'late turn' porter to attend to the filling, trimming, lighting and placing of the lamps - which included preparing a single hurricane lamp each for Brimley and Hawkmoor Halts. When the lamps were turned out after the last train, they were left in position until the morning, when the 'early turn' porter collected them and returned them to the oil store-cum-lamp room. After the Second World War, no passenger trains 'crossed' at Bovey during the hours of darkness, so that all services used the 'up' platform: this having been signalled for bi-directional working from July 1927. This removed the need to provide lighting on the 'down' platform.

As the signalmen were additionally involved with other, clerical, duties, the porters were required to attend to the signal and level crossing lamps, a time-consuming duty that came round, fortunately, only once a week. The 'home' and 'starting' signals had a relatively close proximity to the platform but, by definition, the 'distants' were more remote: that for 'down' trains was a few yards beyond Brimley Halt, and for 'up' ones out by Parke Wood; just under half a mile and three quarters of a mile respectively from the lamp hut. Trudging out to the 'distants' with a full lamp-case of oil (white paraffin), the man clambered up the ladder attached to the rear of the signal post, and lifted out the existing case. He then lit the new lamp and lowered it into place. If necessary, the amber spectacle lens was given a wiping over, together with the small white backlight. If the light went out for any reason, the signalman was alerted by a bell in the signal box, while the 'distant signal lamp indicator' on the instrument shelf above the levers changed to 'LAMP OUT' (white letters on a red background). This was facilitated by the simple expedient of the careful positioning of two metal strips near the top of the lamp case, with only a minute gap between them. The heat from the burning paraffin caused the metal to expand, thereby coming into contact and completing an electrical circuit. This registered 'LAMP IN' on the signal box indicator (white letters on a green background). When the lamp went out the metal cooled, contracted and consequently broke the circuit, causing the warning. When this happened, the signalman first notified his colleague in the adjoining box, so that the driver of the next train could be informed. The porter would then be sent out to the signal to attend to the problem.

The signal box was situated against the platform elevation of the goods shed. Of wooden lap-board construction, with a hipped slate roof and tall brick chimney stack, its platform-level operating floor measured 15' by 8' 6". There were insufficient train movements at Bovey to warrant the staffing of the signal box with full-time signalmen, so both the 'early' and 'late' turn men were partly employed on other duties. Technically referred to as 'porter-signalmen' - a higher grade than 'porter' - the work which they undertook was considerable and varied, and is detailed elsewhere in the chapter. When the station master was not on duty they were required to issue tickets, answer the telephone and deal with enquiries from the public.

The level crossing at the south end of the station layout carried the road leading from the town to the popular Dartmoor tourist spots of Haytor Rocks, Widecombe and Becky (or Becka) Falls - amongst others. As at Teignbridge, the crossing possessed two sets of gates: the single 18-foot hand-operated road gates, and the side pedestrian (or 'wicket') gates. The

wickets were on the south, or Heathfield, side of the road. Being a public highway, the gates were kept open for road traffic until a train was due, being locked in place by means of a bolting mechanism. An oil lamp showing a red light was fixed to the top of the gates during the hours of darkness. The posts on which the gates were hinged consisted of 10-inch square wooden stanchions, ending in a pyramidal capping; while those on the opposite side (right) of the road, and which carried the locking mechanism, were 7-inch diameter cast iron uprights, surmounted with an acorn-shaped capping. The wicket gates were left unlocked.

As it was too far from the signal box to be directly worked from there, the crossing was controlled by a ground frame, which was housed in a small wooden hut to the north the crossing on the 'up' side of the track. In addition to the two-lever frame, the hut also contained a stove; but this was not so much to provide warmth for the occupant as to prevent the frame freezing in periods of exceptional cold. The hut was kept locked at night when the trains were not running, but during the day it was left open - but even if anyone attempted to interfere with the levers, the built-in safety measures would thwart them. Until the frame was 'released' from the signal box, its important road 'gate bolt lever' was securely locked in place. When a train was due, the porter walked out to the hut. Meanwhile the signalman pulled the brown-painted 'ground frame release' lever (no.8) in the signal box. This moved the metal rodding that connected the two frames, and thereby mechanically unlocked the gate bolt lever in the cabin. Through the system of interlocking beneath the signal box frame, this action concurrently locked those levers that operated the signals on either side of the crossing. In this way a train could not be given the 'all clear' while the gates were in the process of being closed against traffic. Pulling the gate bolt lever released the locking mechanism at the 'free' end of the gates. The porter then left the hut to swing the gates across the road. Returning to the hut, the lever was pushed back to bolt the gates in position, and a bell-plunger pressed to let the signalman know that the manoeuvre had been completed, and that he could regain control of his signals. The signalman duly pushed lever no.8 back into the 'normal' position, freeing the signals. Although the road gates were closed, pedestrians were still able to cross the track by means of the wicket gates. As a 'down' train approached from Brimley, or an 'up' train was ready to start from the platform, the porter pulled the wicket gate lever, which locked them and so prevented anyone making a risky last-minute dash across the track. Once the train had passed, the whole process was repeated.

Attendance at the level crossing made up only a fraction of the work performed by the two porters. The duties of a porter were manifold; he was a sort of general factotum. Some of the work was heavy, some mundane, but at least there was variety; and all of it was essential to the smooth running of the station. Inevitably the work involved much contact with the public. This was generally amicable, friendly even; although in 1912 an incident occurred which was both unfortunate and uncharacteristic. When a non ticket-holding passenger was challenged by the duty porter, a violent altercation ensued, which ended with the porter striking the man. The question of provocation was not entertained by the Railway Company, and the porter was summarily dismissed. An insight into the nature of their duties may be gained from the following extract of a letter written by Bovey's station master in answer to an enquiry from Divisional headquarters in Exeter. Dated 3rd January 1957, it reads:

"In reply to your letter of the 11th ulto, the work of the 2 Porters is rather varied and an estimate of the time occupied on the work is as follows:

Early turn. Attending to Passenger trains. Crossing gates &

general Passenger Station duties: 3 hours. Parcels work: 50 minutes. Goods work: 3 hours 30 minutes.

Late turn. Attending to Passenger trains. Crossing gates & general Passenger Station duties: 4 hours 20 minutes. Parcels work: 30 minutes.

Goods work: 2 hours 30 minutes.

Their duties consist of the following:- Attending to Crossing gates and trains. Loading and unloading parcels. Cleaning and lighting Tilley lamps, signal lamps and Hurricanes for Halts. Cleaning station and Halts. Attaching and detaching vehicles. Record inwards and outwards wagons in the yard and visit Granite siding daily for this purpose. Obtain signatures for Yard, Shed and Bovey Pottery traffic.

Assist unloading and loading trunk motor and Bovey Vehicle. Prepare Goods Delivery and station sheets. Record ret. empties for Devonmoor Art Pottery. Unload wagons. Cranage. Daily and weekly wagon returns. Labelling. Issue tickets in absence of Stationmaster and Signalman. Sort and tie up collected tickets and assist generally. Billposting."

If the porters were kept pretty busy all year round, a seasonal feature for which Bovey Station was justifiably renowned was its summer time floral displays. This tradition was pursued by each station master in turn, often resulting in the winning of prizes. Flower baskets were hung beneath the canopy; pots and tubs decorated the platform in front of the main building; and the strip of land between the 'up' platform and level crossing was a blaze of colour. There was no greater enthusiast than the last station master, Arthur Yendall. Roses were his speciality and he put a lot of effort into the displays. Each year the Railway ran its own competition - organised in various categories - and Bovey was regularly awarded 'Garden Certificates'; the prize money being 'ploughed back' (pun intended), and new plants and cuttings bought to put on different displays the following year: roses perhaps giving way to rhododendrons. One summer, one of the prepared 'competition' flower baskets was too heavy to be safely hung from the canopy, so one of Candy & Co.'s earthenware drains was commandeered and used to provide a platform-mounted show instead. The displays so impressed Henry Bentinck of Indio that he sent various bedding plants to the station every May in readiness for that summer's competition.

The Goods Department

In spite of the limited accommodation at Bovey - there were just two sidings - its Goods Department conducted considerable business. In 1925, the first year for which detailed records are available, goods traffic made up just over 53% of the revenue earned at the station. By 1930 this had risen to 60%, and in 1935 stood at almost 79%: but as the actual value of the traffic remained almost the same, its increased importance is only relative, explained by the fall in passenger receipts as road competition bit deeper (see Table 13).

The 'centre of operations' in the Yard was the substantial Goods Shed. Measuring 50 feet by 39 feet, its walls were built of local stone, but contained more brown and grey metamorphic rock ('shillet') and less granite than the station building. As a structure with a less public function, the blocks of masonry were also less regular in shape and size than at the station, and consequently gave a more rough-hewn appearance: although all the corner strengthening blocks were of dressed granite. The original roof was of slate, but in the early years of the 20th century the slates were replaced by sheets of asbestos. In more recent times, this was in turn superseded by corrugated iron. The roof was supported by a central joist running between the gable ends, with two cross-members.

The goods siding passed right through the shed (to serve a loading dock beyond). The arched entrances were 14' 9" wide, with the masonry of the walls being succeeded by boards in the arched section and remaining height to the roof. The road entrance, centred in the east wall, was 16 feet wide. All three openings were provided with heavy, sliding double doors, which were hung from a guide rail above and ran on another below. The upper rail was protected by a bracketed wooden cowl, while the lower one was terminated by a door-stop. Lengths of old railway line were used for the runners, one of them being inscribed 'Rhymney Railway' and another 'M&SDR 1865'. When the shed doors were closed, the building was lit by day by two large windows in the west wall (station side). These were unlike all the other windows at Bovey in that they possessed no rebate in the stone. In the days when the shed had a slate roof, sky-lights also existed; but these were blanked-off later. During the hours of darkness, an oil lamp was hoisted into the roof space, the winding handle being located on the south wall, by the entrance. A metal heat shield above the lamp protected the roof timbers. A loading platform ran right through the building, accompanying the siding, from door to door. Predominantly built of masonry, it was 'decked out' with a 16 inch-thick timber lattice, consisting of three courses of joists arranged at right angles, and surmounted by inch-thick floorboards. A 2-ton crane was located half way along the platform. The back/centre part of the platform was cut away to form a well, or bay, into which road vehicles would back for loading and unloading goods. A 'Type B' loose-screw wagon coupling was permanently kept in the shed in the event of a breakage occurring on the daily goods train; a similar provision existing at Heathfield and Moreton.

In the south-east corner of the shed was the Goods Clerk's Office. This had overall measurements of 13' 7" by 9' 6", with the height of the flat roof also being 9' 6". A fireplace occupied the outer corner of the room, and daylight was admitted through three windows: one looking out on to the station approach, and the other two in the wooden partition that made up the inner walls, and looking into the central well of the shed. Running the full length of this inner screen was a wide, solid wooden desk, with cupboards and drawers beneath, and shelves and sorting racks attached to the partition above. The clerk's table was beneath the outer window, next to the fireplace; and the remainder of the wall space was filled with cupboards and shelves to house the multiplicity of paperwork handled in the office. The clerk was assisted in his daily routine by one of the signalmen, who spent around two hours a day dealing mainly with the invoicing and abstracting in between his bouts if activity in the signal box. As required, he helped out with the loading and unloading of wagons with the yard crane, and also gave assistance with the securing of wagon doors, sheets and roping. Bert Payne, for example, put in many years in this capacity. The porters undertook most of the manual work in the shed or loading dock, and this made up a sizeable part of their duties. Indeed, so busy were they, that when they were summoned by the signalman to attend the level crossing, they could not always immediately leave what they were doing, and consequently had to make a last minute dash out to the ground frame hut.

Down to the 1930s working conditions in the goods shed office were pretty unpleasant. Although one of the windows in the partition had a small inwardly-opening top-light, the outside window could not be opened as it had externally-fitted vertical iron bars. Given the confined space of the office, it became stifling and airless in hot weather. In winter, the fire gave some warmth, but the spacious goods shed with its oft-opened three huge doorways, was bound to be a cold place. Draughts were an unavoidable reality, and with the frequent coming and going through the office door, it was a hard job to keep much warmth in the place. The outer walls of the room, like the rest of the goods shed, were unlined; consisting, rather, of whitewashed rough-hewn stone that readily collected dust and cobwebs.

Bovey Goods Shed

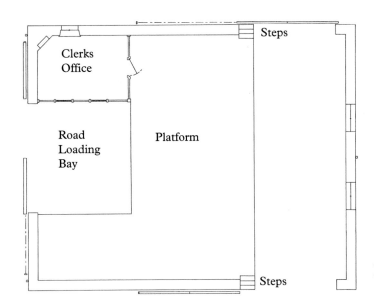

Clerks Office

Road Loading Bay

Platform

Steps

Steps

PLAN

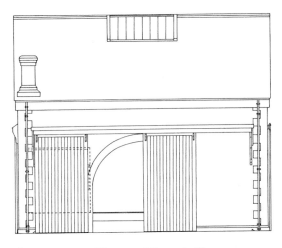

APPROACH ROAD (EAST) ELEVATION

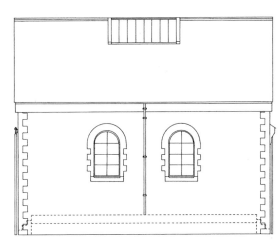

STATION (WEST) ELEVATION

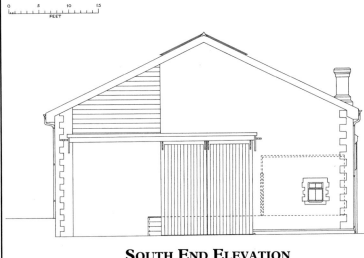

SOUTH END ELEVATION

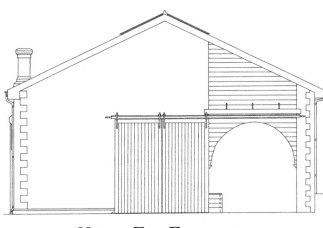

NORTH END ELEVATION

0 5 10 15
FEET

When the porter came in to sweep the floor, he created clouds of dust, which simply settled somewhere else. It was more an exercise in relocating rather than removing the dirt! In 1935 the long-standing incumbent Bill Teague was succeeded by Arthur Yendall who, dismayed at the conditions, began a drive to improve matters - only to find the Railway hierarchy totally unsympathetic. After repeated requests for better ventilation fell on deaf ears, he took matters into his own hands. Removing the metal bars on the outside window, the top-light could now be opened outwards. Next came a campaign for the provision of electric lighting, as working in the winter months by the light of a single Tilley lamp was a taxing business. Once again, in spite of a number of written requests, the pleas were ignored and the office, indeed the whole station, continued to the very end devoid of any electric light.

With the literal exception of the lighting, not everything was gloom, as the clerk scored a couple of successes in spite of bureaucracy. Following complaints about the state of the walls, they were eventually plastered, thereby lessening the dust problem. Next came the floor. The rough bare boards were unpleasant underfoot and difficult to keep clean. Despite numerous requests for a linoleum covering, the GWR showed no intention of obliging. In an effort to further his campaign, Arthur consulted a local firm and got them to quote an estimate for the job, to prove to the powers-that-be that it would not plunge the entire Railway network into insolvency. The information was conveyed to Division, and although they deprecated the initiative - for having dared to go outside established channels - they agreed to provide some sort of floor covering. Eventually a requisition was sent to the Great Western's central stores at Swindon, and they responded by despatching a piece of linoleum. A triumph indeed - except that when it was laid, it was not actually big enough to cover the whole floor!

The outbreak of the Second World War caused a shortage of manpower on the Railway, as elsewhere. The usual level of recruitment of younger staff fell away, which put an increased premium on more experienced members. To fill the short-fall, women were brought into a much wider variety of railway work than had been the case before. So it was that two ladies were employed at Bovey to cover the work of the goods clerk: namely, Misses Kelly and Edwards. Once they had been taught the job, the clerk was moved around as requested either to cover other depots or undertake various administrative duties. Actually, Miss Kelly spent more time in the booking office than the goods office, as 'opposite turn' to the station master. Miss Edwards had the shortest distance to go to work of any of the station staff as her mother, Muriel, was the proprietor of the cafe near the level crossing. The job description of goods clerk disappeared altogether from Bovey in the 1947 Zoning Scheme (which is described in Chapter 3). Responsibility for the paperwork now passed to the station master, although as before one of the signalmen continued to assist - and in fact took on a greater share of the clerical work (latterly, this person was Derek Aggett). The data regarding type, quantity and value of goods was passed on to, and recorded under, Zone headquarters - Newton Abbot - and consequently reference to Bovey ceases in the Annual Traffic Returns for Goods.

Immediately south of the goods shed was a 37-foot long Loading Dock. With both side and end-loading provision, it was put to a variety of uses; and in the absence of a separate cattle dock, fulfilled that purpose as well. From the rear of the dock, a

Table 13. Selected Traffic Returns : Bovey

| YEAR | PASSENGERS | | | | PARCELS | | | MILK | | | GOODS | | | LIVESTOCK | |
	Tickets (Single & Return)	£	Season Tickets	£	No. Sent out	No. Received	Total Value £	No. of cans	No. of cases	Total Value £	Tonnage Despatched	Tonnage Received	Total Value £	Wagon Loads	Value £
1925	25,547	3040	178	217	3276	8078	404	-	-	-	1474	12,701	6878	3	4
1926	17,677	2188	94	111	2877	7260	1036	-	-	-	1244	10,106	6295	1	2
1927	20,673	2626	157	116	2738	8032	1029	-	-	-	1366	13,913	8312	7	14
1928	19,634	2155	167	88	2691	8058	1031	-	-	-	1624	13,017	8174	8	11
1929	16,397	1838	187	94	2558	7354	920	-	-	-	1430	13,029	7094	7	9
1930	15,023	1692	281	119	2587	7413	901	-	-	-	1373	12,328	6854	1	2
1931	14,949	1458	183	75	2422	7856	857	-	-	-	1378	11,311	7148	3	5
1932	15,166	1470	207	75	2347	8323	835	-	-	-	903	11,031	6164	2	6
1933	14,546	1581	180	79	3371	9021	853	-	-	-	1028	10,535	5986	6	30
1934	13,961	1551	165	79	2160	8906	789	-	-	-	1031	11,256	6925	13	31
1935	14,749	1335	148	72	2000	8582	200	-	-	-	969	11,357	6359	9	20
1936	13,493	1365	190	98	2078	8203	207	-	-	-	925	10,932	5216	8	15
1937	12,548	1412	244	119	1935	7899	200	-	-	-	1009	11,868	6241	4	21
1938	11,952	1227	253	106	1877	8144	210	38	-	N/D	869	12,187	7207	7	39
1939	9,969	1188	271	102	1697	7613	172	30	-	N/D	1119	11,516	6482	3	15
1940	11,647	3201	77	28	1652	6204	201	-	-	-	2662	14,451	N/D	1	-
1941	16,749	2767	92	67	N/D	N/D	295	-	-	-	3280	13,401	N/D	-	-
1942	20,784	2409	148	84	N/D	N/D	312	-	-	-	6584	13,418	N/D	-	-
1943	20,052	2724	182	74	N/D	N/D	504	-	-	-	5085	11,626	N/D	-	-
1944	19,516	2576	398	146	N/D	N/D	322	-	-	-	4904	10,369	N/D	-	-
1945	18,534	2938	163	103	N/D	N/D	456	-	-	-	2820	9,747	N/D	-	-
1946	13,259	2499	170	134	N/D	N/D	476	-	-	-	2551	11,745	N/D	4	-
1947	10,218	1969	127	141	N/D	N/D	590	1442	37	70					
1948	9,824	2073	110	138	N/D	N/D	561	1532	81	68					
1949	11,217	2230	259	174	N/D	N/D	609	980	65	45					
1950	10,432	1763	250	180	N/D	N/D	502	2	67	6					
1951	7,351	1583	163	110	1482	6241	538	-	77	7	Goods Zoned at Newton Abbot				
1952	9,308	1652	91	80	1717	4581	471	-	79	12	1.3.47				
1953	10,521	1700	79	72	1878	5925	537	-	94	11					
1954	9,677	1461	125	78	1657	6221	490	-	114	16					
1955	9,417	1451	109	99	1352	5631	441	-	128	13					
1956	7,541	1334	105	122	1505	5154	462	-	123	16					
1957	9,878	1740	154	110	1722	5590	500	-	127	11					
1958	7,078	1199	229	144	1541	5340	511	--	142	14					

NB Passenger revenue includes Brimley Halt from May 1928; and Hawkmoor / Pullabrook Halt from June 1931

N/D = No Data available

long sliding gate gave access to the 'up' platform. At the opposite (north) end of the shed, centred against the wall, was a drinking-water tap, and near it a weighing machine (calibrated to take loads up to half a hundredweight). In the yard beyond, adjoining the 'Goods Siding', was a platform-mounted 4-ton crane; while next to the 'Back Siding' was a sleeper-built store for 'station coal' (supplies for which were sent down from Swindon once a year). Here also was the 'base' of the Bovey Permanent Way Gang: a platelayers' hut and tool store.

In terms of the Goods Traffic itself, Bovey always received more than it despatched; both in terms of tonnage and value. In the case of the former, the ratio was from 8-10 times as much, while for the latter it was lower: 2-3 times. One of the most enduring rail-users was the firm of grain millers and seedsmen, A.J.Wyatt & Son (later Wyatt & Bruce). The firm originated in the Old Town Mills, about 200 yards further along Station Road (a site later occupied by Dartmoor Garage). Albert John Wyatt took over the family business in 1889 and in the early years of the next century abandoned the old premises straddling the mill leat and moved to a new location adjoining the station approach. Not only was this a more spacious site, with room for expansion, but was also about as near to the source of transport as possible. The recently installed second, or 'back', siding then ended in a loading dock close to the goods shed. Following negotiations with the GWR, it was extended by 100 yards. This took it almost to Station Road, and right past the front of the mill, thereby providing it with direct unloading facilities. The mill received regular shipments of wheat, barley, maize, oats and molasses, together with proteins. The grain came down from Avonmouth Docks in sack-loads. These were initially of the two-hundredweight size, and were very heavy and awkward for staff to manhandle off the wagons. The finished products were all various types of animal feedstuffs, with a certain amount of flour in the early years, but this was all distributed by road - with the exception of local deliveries made between the wars to the firm's store in the station yard at Moretonhampstead. Large quantities of fertiliser were also brought to the mill by rail, but this too was subsequently forwarded by road. In the mid 1950s, the firm, now known as Wyatt & Bruce, erected an enormous corrugated iron grain silo at the extreme inner end of the 'back siding'. This new structure was served by both road and rail vehicles, the rail-borne bulk grain being delivered in twenty-ton capacity covered hopper wagons.

Another old-established firm providing steady revenue for the Railway was R.E.Glanville & Son, 'Agricultural Merchants & Engineers'. They operated from an attractive building, made of local stone, which was put up at about the same time as Wyatt's mill relocated. Situated right alongside the 'back siding', opposite the goods shed, the building possessed a short loading platform at wagon level, with a crane hoist from a projecting loft above to winch heavy items directly to the upper floor. The firm specialised in the manufacture of farm implements, and at one time railed-in imported tractor parts from the Syracuse Company of America. Ploughs were sent out by rail to North Wales - notably to Bala and Dolgellau - while a range of other agricultural equipment had a wide distribution: notably round-topped galvanised animal pens. Measuring some 8 to 10 feet in length and 4 feet in height, they were loaded into wagons by means of the yard crane. Another local agricultural engineering firm which received large machinery by rail was E. Bowden & Sons of Town Hall Place. Plough-shares were a particular feature of this traffic.

Coal formed the most common 'full load' traffic, being destined for a number of merchants in the town, chief of whom were the Co-operative Society; Frank Harris & Co.; and Wakeham & Jeffrey. The last-named firm possessed Bovey's one-and-only 'private owner' wagon - though not for long. Soon

after they proudly took delivery of it, with their names printed in large white capital letters on the sides, the Second World War broke out and it was soon requisitioned, taken into common stock and consequently lost to the Branch. Shipments of domestic coal were received almost every weekday, coming principally from collieries in Staffordshire. Some coal also came in for Wyatt & Bruce, but this was for re-sale and not for use in the mill.

A housing development near Brimley Halt in the early 1950s saw the London Brick Company rail in large quantities of bricks to the yard at Bovey. These came from Calvert near Bicester, one of the large rail-connected brickworks in the Oxford Clay belt in Buckinghamshire/Bedfordshire. A much less bulky, but regular, cargo was beer from the Bass brewery of Burton-on-Trent. The barrels were sent to one or two hostelries in the town and to the Moorland Hotel near Haytor. This last-named location was outside the area covered by the Railway's delivery van, and so the station master arranged for the beer to be forwarded by wagon from a nearby garage; or by one of the coal merchants if they happened to be going that way. The fee for this service was 4/9d (about 24p), the payment being charged to the 'Bass Account' - an entry which always educed raised eyebrows and questions from the auditor on his annual visitation.

Another regular feature, but this time before the Second World War, was the arrival of calves from other parts of the country for fattening - a practice widely seen in Devon. As Bovey did not possess cattle pens, the animals were dealt with at the loading dock. When only one or two calves were involved, they were transported in sacks that had been cut in such a way as to allow their head and legs to protrude through. They arrived by passenger train, tied up in the luggage compartment. While this was once quite a common feature, a celebrated 'one-off' event involved another four-legged creature: a ram. This too arrived in the luggage compartment of a passenger train, and was tied up in the corrugated iron former bus shelter, while the farmer was phoned to come and collect it. In the meantime, however, the ram became restless and broke free of its tether. As the animal obviously decided that the only way out of the shelter was via the window, it duly jumped through it and careered off across the field opposite the station. The sound of breaking glass alerted the staff en masse, who chased after the liberated animal. After being given a literal run-around, they managed to capture it - a sort of ram-raid in reverse! In comparison, the despatch of livestock from the station was negligible, and it was rare for the number of wagons sent out per year to reach double figures. Other animals handled at the station in the 1920s and '30s were the horses of the Dartmoor Hunt. During the season, horse boxes attached to service passenger trains arrived in the morning, were shunted into the loading dock, and the horses ridden up to the Moor. They returned in the evening.

The 'Goods Outwards' traffic was mainly of the 'smalls' variety; namely, a wide range of general merchandise mostly between a half and three hundredweight. This was loaded in the goods shed. Of the bulkier items railed from Bovey were iron-ore, copper, timber and pottery. Down to the 1920s iron and copper ores were brought down to the station from the mines in the Haytor Vale and Yarner areas respectively, just a few miles away on the edge of Dartmoor. The Haytor Iron Ore Company in particular sent away many truck-loads by rail, the ore being conveyed from the mine by a Sentinel steam wagon owned by Newton Abbot haulage contractor Frank White. At the station it was transferred to railway trucks at the loading dock. With extensive woodlands nearby, the timber traffic remained a feature of the goods scene into the 1950s. The sawn timber was brought the short distance from the forestry plantations to the west of the town. It principally took the form of pit-props destined for South Wales, so that empty mineral wagons could be used rather than the long wheelbase bogie bolster vehicles. The timber was lifted into the trucks by the 4-ton yard crane. Pottery was received - packed in barrels and crates - from the Devonmoor Art Pottery Co. Ltd. of Liverton.

For most of the station's existence, the fetching and carrying of the general merchandise - the 'town traffic' - was performed not by the GWR itself, but by a Cartage Agent or 'Carrier' appointed by the Company. He worked on a commission basis, being paid between a halfpenny and threepence (old pence!) a package, depending on size and distance carried. Both the agent and goods clerk kept records of all deliveries, and at the end of every month the two men met to compare their respective registers. Sometimes they would not quite balance, the Railway owing the Agent a little more money than had been calculated - or vice versa. However, this was always settled amicably, as discrepancies were small. In the early days, the carrier had been one Jonas Holmes of Fore Street, while between the two world wars the agent was George Lang; his delivery waggon, pulled by an attractive chestnut mare called 'Girlie', being part of the everyday scene in Bovey and district. As part of the Zoning Scheme instituted in 1947 the Railway took over the collection and delivery of 'smalls'. The sphere of operation remained much as before due to the continued large 'inward' traffic, although it was extended to the north to take in Lustleigh and district. A 1946 Y-series Morris van (HYR 548) performed the work at the outset, being replaced by a larger Bedford van in the mid 1950s. The 'collection and delivery' driver was Jack Heale; often simply referred to as the 'vanman'. Even though there was some diminution in both quantity and variety of freight handled in the 1950s, there was still plenty of work to keep the porters and 'vanman' busy; indeed, the goods function at Bovey outlasted the passenger, albeit in a rationalised form.

Personnel

Bovey's first station master was Jonas Parnell. He remained in the post for a good many years, residing at No. 1 St. John's Park on the road to Heathfield. Only very much later did the Great Western Railway buy one of the houses (No. 6) in Marlborough Terrace, by the level crossing, as the station master's residence. During the early years of the 20th century, the station master was William Tucker; while another of the 'long-stay' incumbents, centred on the 1920s, was George Haywood: whose brother, Fred, was station master at Lustleigh at the same time. George had the distinction of being the first station master at Christow when, in 1903, the Exeter Railway opened to meet up with the existing Teign Valley Branch from Heathfield. After many years in the post, he moved away to live in retirement at Brixham. He was followed by C.V. Williams who, in 1935, also moved on to Brixham; but in this instance as station master. His successor was Harry Vowles, who came to Bovey from his previous job as chief parcels clerk at the busy

Newton Abbot office. His erstwhile colleagues marked his departure with the presentation of an armchair; but as a thorough professional, Harry was very far from becoming an 'armchair railwayman' as a consequence of his promotion. After a short stay he moved away to Paignton, to be followed by John Henry ('Jack') Margetts. In the early 1940s Jack transferred to Silverton, on the main line some seven miles north of Exeter. His replacement, Bill Teague, was no stranger to Bovey; indeed, he had begun his railway career there, working his way up from lad-porter, through porter and porter-signalman, to goods checker in 1920, when he took over from Geoffrey Chubb. In addition to his duties as checker, he undertook a considerable amount of purely clerical work for a number of years and, as a result, successfully applied for regrading as 'clerk': a salaried post. In 1935 Bill took up his first appointment as station master at Uffculme, on the Culm Valley Branch between Tiverton Junction and Hemyock; and it was from there that he returned to Bovey in the same grade. After just a few years at his 'home' station, he took the post of station master at Langport in Somerset, and then moved out of the Exeter Division completely: first to the rural junction of Leominster in Herefordshire, and finally to the busier location of Wellington in Shropshire. The post at Bovey was then occupied by Richard ('Dick') Platt, formally of the goods department at Goodrington; and finally, for what proved to be the last years of passenger services on the Branch, by Arthur Yendall.

Arthur's family had strong railway connections. His paternal grandfather had worked on the building of the Exe Valley Railway (opened in 1885); his maternal grandfather had been a permanent way ganger; and his father an engine driver, so that he and his three brothers were automatically put to the same profession. Work on the Railway was after all regular, even if in the lower grades the money was poor. When Arthur started as a junior clerk on the Culm Valley Line in 1923, his weekly lodging expenses came to more than his wage, and he had to be subsidised from home (in Exeter). Of his three brothers, one became an engine driver like his father; another began as porter-signalman at Bovey before moving on to Heathfield and elsewhere as full time signalman; while the third worked as a clerk, ending up in the busy Control Office at Bristol. Arthur meanwhile had been moving up through the grades, gaining a wide variety of experience in a number of locations. From his

The station staff in 1920. Seated left to right are: W. Teague (checker), F. Murphy (signalman), J. Roberts (lad porter), E. Hexter (lad porter) and A. Miller (relief porter/signalman). Standing behind is station master George Haywood. Fred Murphy was in charge of the parcels department as well as his signalling duties. Mr. Miller was sent down from Exeter to cover the vacancy created by the promotion of Bill Teague from porter/signalman to goods checker - a vacancy which was subsequently filled by lad porter Hexter. *Courtesy James Mann*

position as parcels clerk at Torre, he undertook relief duties at several places, before moving, in 1934, to Kingskerswell as acting station master. The following year, he transferred to Bovey as goods clerk (taking over from Bill Teague). During the Second World War he was moved to Exeter to work in the booking office. After the war, he was employed for a short time at Teignmouth before moving back to Exeter, where he worked in the District Manager's office; commuting to and from Bovey every day. Finally, in 1952, he applied for, and was granted, the position of station master in his home town.

Also with strong railway connections was the Tanton family. Born in Eastleigh near Bideford, John Tanton moved to South Devon in 1901 to work as a permanent way lengthman (or 'packer') on that part of the Moretonhampstead Line covered by the Newton Abbot Branch Gang. From Newton he lived for a time at Teigngrace before moving to a semi-detached GWR 'Company' house alongside the main road (A38) at Heathfield. Now sub-ganger, or 'second man', his next-door neighbour was station master Sidney Honeywill. In 1921 he was promoted to the post of ganger at Bovey, where he remained until retirement. That event should have taken place in 1944, but due to manpower shortages caused by the war, he was asked to stay on. He finally hung up his key hammer and heavy boots in 1948, releasing him to spend more time in his beloved garden.

Not only did his brother follow a career on the Railway - in the works at Newton Abbot - but so too did all three of his sons. The eldest, William, began as a lad-porter at Teigngrace, before transferring to Heathfield as porter. Moving away from the Branch to take up the post of porter-signalman at Montacute on the Taunton to Yeovil Line, Bill later worked as signalman at Kingskerswell and Swimbridge before promotion took him to Barnstaple in 1937, where he remained until ill health forced an early retirement 25 years later. Born in 1907, John ('Jack') Tanton started out as a lad-porter at Bovey in the early 1920s. As with so many of his colleagues on the Branch, he had a varied career. Being a versatile sort of chap, Jack was called on in the summer months of the early '30s to help out with duties at Paignton parcels office, where holiday makers vastly swelled the 'luggage in advance' traffic. In 1936/7 he was appointed 'checker' at Moretonhampstead, though continued to live in Bovey: next door to his parents in Heathfield Terrace. He remained at Moreton until the withdrawal of freight services in 1964, whereupon he was transferred - in the same grade - to Newton Abbot Goods Department who stationed him at Teignbridge to deal with the clay traffic there until his retirement in 1972. In 1935 his younger brother Geoffrey also started out at Bovey as 'lad-porter'. Following a six-year break for service in the Armed Forces, he returned to his 'home' station as signalman. Destined to go far, Geoff began a fourteen-year stint as a relief signalman at Newton Abbot before being appointed assistant district inspector at Yeovil Junction in 1964. Three years later he moved to Exeter Central in the same grade, before transferring to Plymouth. Covering an extensive area, he was closely involved with operations at Laira motive power depot and latterly as 'traffic assistant signalling' to the area manager. Geoff retired in 1982.

One of the best-remembered members of staff, by dint of his long service in the inter-war years and beyond, was signalman Fred Murphy. He was on duty the evening in 1937 that the Royal Train passed through on its way to Moretonhampstead. Not only was he required to turn out smartly in full uniform, but even to stand in a particular place for the train staff exchange. Fred wore his prized gold tie-pin specially for the occasion and, on calling in to the Railway Hotel afterwards, it

Under the Newton Abbot Zoning Scheme road vehicles played a greater role in small goods/parcels distribution. In this scene at Bovey, the Zonal 'Collection & Delivery' lorry - an Austin 'K series' vehicle No. HUL 90 - is parked alongside Bovey's own Bedford van in the station yard in February 1959. Maurice Stoyle, the Newton Abbot lorry driver (resting his arm on the Bedford's bonnet) stands next to Station Master Yendall. On the other side of Arthur Yendall is Jack Heale, Bovey's van driver. Signalman Derek Aggett (left) and porter Cecil Fowden are also pictured. *A. W. Yendall Collection*

provoked much comment. Seeing the opportunity for a good yarn, he steadfastly maintained that it had been presented to him by the king himself. Some fell for it!

Another of Bovey's well-remembered characters was Sidney Medland. He came to the station as a porter in the late 1930s. A Newton man, his father worked as a lineman in the Signal & Telegraph Department. Incomers who were not so welcome, however, were the rats and mice emanating from A.J.Wyatt's mill across the yard. The feed grain handled there inevitably attracted the rodents in large numbers, and in an ever-widening quest for food or shelter, some found their way into the goods shed nearby. Working at his table in the quiet of the late afternoon, the clerk would often hear the patter of tiny feet as one of these visitors scampered into the office. A mouse could be tolerated, but large rats were another matter. Work stopped until the clerk and the 'late turn' porter, armed with brushes or other implements, drove the rat out. Sidney proved to be adept at this task, and his services were frequently called upon. He set about designing all sorts of ingenious devices for harmlessly trapping the creatures, all of which entertained the staff enormously. He later became a signalman at Starcross, on the Exe estuary section of the South Devon main line, where fish rather than rodents were the order of the day! Moving through the seniority league, he eventually became signalman at Aller Junction box to the south of Newton Abbot.

Of Bovey's two porters, one or both might sometimes have the designation of 'lad-porter'. Working for a very low wage, a proficient youngster would progress to the post of 'porter'. Many men subsequently moved up through the grades to attain senior positions, as illustrated in preceding paragraphs. A couple of other examples may serve to illustrate this trait. In 1920 John Roberts and Edward Hexter were lad-porters at Bovey. John worked his way up the ladder to ultimately become signalman at Dawlish Warren on the main line; while his colleague ended up in the prestigious Newton Abbot East Signal Box (though sadly did not live to enjoy a well-earned retirement). One of the porters in the last war was John Nekola. While using the hand-operated yard crane to unload some heavy machinery from a wagon - a risky operation at the best of times - the clutch slipped and he received a nasty wound to the face caused by the spinning handle. Another wartime porter was Eddie Holmes, who cycled over from his home in Chudleigh Knighton. His brother Victor worked as a porter at Heathfield. The last occupants of the post were Cecil Fowden and Horace Heale; the former having previously been one of the station's permanent way lengthmen for many years, and the latter having transferred 'on loan' from Christow on the neighbouring Teign Valley Branch.

While it was common for sons to follow fathers into railway service, the reverse was unusual in the extreme: especially so when both were employed at the same place. This rare event happened at Bovey in the mid 1940s. As one of the coalmen for the local Co-operative Society, Ronald Rowe was a regular visitor to the station, and in 1944 learned of a vacancy for a clerk there. He mentioned it to his sixteen year-old son Stan, who duly applied for, and was offered, the post; beginning duties as 'junior clerk' in July. Less than twelve months later, another vacancy arose; this time for a porter. Stan passed this information on to his father who, having hurt his back in the relentless handling of heavy coal sacks, was contemplating a change of occupation. His application was successful, and so father and son worked together. In 1946 Stan moved to

Moretonhampstead as signalman, while Ron remained for another five years or so before transferring to Lustleigh as leading porter. It was while travelling to that place one day in 1952 that he was involved in an incident which led to his receiving a prestigious First Aid award. This was in recognition of his prompt treatment of a lady who, while alighting at Hawkmoor Halt, missed her footing and fell from the train, sustaining a badly broken leg. (Stan's predecessor as junior clerk, Stan Dart, moved onwards and upwards to ultimately work in the demanding environment of Reading Control.)

Permanent Way Gang

The Bovey Gang had responsibility for the Branch between the 3¾ and 7¾ mile posts: from near Heathfield's 'up advanced starting' signal to, but excluding, Hawkmoor Halt. They also covered a quarter-mile stretch of the Teign Valley Line as far as, but excluding, Bovey Lane level crossing. Originally, five men made up the team: ganger, sub-ganger and three lengthmen. By the early 1930s, the gang had been reduced to four, under the direction of ganger John Tanton and sub-ganger Bill Twose. Bill took over as ganger on John's retirement, while a later occupant of the post was G. Reynolds. Other members of the gang, at various times, included the following: W. Eggerton, C. Fowden, H. Heale and S. Raisey. The inspection trolley used by the men was a really antique-looking three-wheeled velocipede. The seat and two larger wheels were on the 'offside' rail, with the balance being achieved by the heavy brake strut leading to the smaller 'nearside' front wheel. It was motivated by manually pushing a handle in a back-and-forth motion, while at the same time working pedals with the feet. In addition, the Gang also had a low-slung, four-wheeled deck-type unpowered trolley for conveying materials and tools to a job. The widespread adoption of the 'motor trolley system of maintenance' on many other routes passed the Moretonhampstead Branch by (although, interestingly, was used on the neighbouring Teign Valley Line). The Permanent Way hut and tool store was at the north end of the goods yard, while there was a post-box for PW letters by the booking office window on the 'up' platform.

With closure imminent, station staff are photographed for posterity. From left to right they are: Horace Heale (porter), Tom Booth (signalman), Cecil Fowden (porter), Jack Heale (vanman) and Arthur Yendall (station master). The picture was probably taken by Derek Aggett (signalman), as he features in other 'last day' line-ups at Bovey.
A. W. Yendall Collection

HAWKMOOR / PULLABROOK HALT

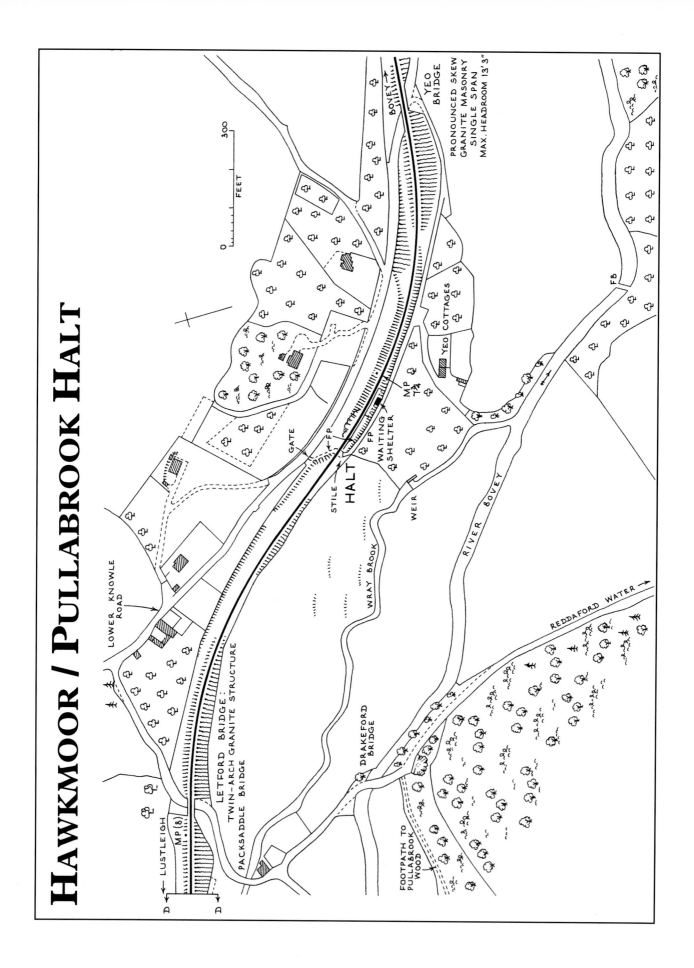

YEO BRIDGE

PRONOUNCED SKEW
GRANITE MASONRY
SINGLE SPAN
MAX. HEADROOM 13'3"

BOVEY →

300

FEET

0

YEO COTTAGES

FB

MP 7¾

WAITING SHELTER

GATE

FP

STILE FP

HALT

WEIR

RIVER BOVEY

WRAY BROOK

REDDAFORD WATER →

LOWER KNOWLE ROAD

LETFORD BRIDGE:
TWIN-ARCH GRANITE STRUCTURE

PACKSADDLE BRIDGE

DRAKEFORD BRIDGE

FOOTPATH TO PULLABROOK WOOD

← LUSTLEIGH

MP (8)

D

D

Chapter Fourteen

HAWKMOOR/PULLABROOK

At the seven and three-quarter mile post, the Line was just over 50 feet above the level of the nearby River Bovey, and close to a handful of large houses which collectively constitute Lower Knowle. The location is reached by narrow serpentine lanes, which are mostly steeply graded and bordered by high, thick-set hedges. The notable paucity of settlement did not warrant the provision of a station when the Branch was built, and so begs the question as to what caused the change in policy 65 years later, when the Great Western Railway installed a halt here. The location was certainly convenient for walkers, picnickers and day-trippers, as the lanes and tracks gave access to footpaths threading their way through Houndtor Wood to Becky (or Becka) Falls and Lustleigh Cleave. But the traditional starting point for these rambles was Lustleigh. The provision actually had more to do with gentlemen than geography, for although there might be only a few houses in the vicinity, many of their well-heeled occupants were regular users of the Railway, but were forced to make the journey by road to and from Bovey. One particular resident who travelled a great deal in connection with his work found this necessity irksome, and was instrumental in forming a small but influential pressure group with the aim of securing a halt. They obviously had considerable 'clout', as the GWR acceded to their request. Perhaps one of the factors which helped their cause was the recent expansion of Hawkmoor Hospital, the county's sanatorium for tuberculosis sufferers. Opened in 1913, and enlarged three years later, a special section for children was added in 1927 and this increased the number of visitors. It was in fact from this institution that the halt took its name.

Hawkmoor Halt opened on Monday 1st June 1931. Located on the 'down' side of the track, 7 miles and 61 chains from Newton Abbot, it had the distinction of being the smallest and most basic station on the Branch. The platform face was built out of old sleepers, whose dimensions (nominally 8" x 10" x 5") determined the details of its construction. Thus its six 'panels' of longitudinally-laid sleepers gave a length of just over 48 feet, the projecting edging boards being supported by truncated sleeper baulks positioned at the ends of the panels. Its overall length was increased by the ramps, that at the 'down' (Lustleigh) end being longer, and thus more gently inclined, as it was the one used to gain access to the platform. With a width of around 8 feet the platform surface was metalled; the low grassy bank at the back being surmounted by an eight-strand wire/wooden post boundary fence. At the extreme 'up' (Bovey) end of the platform, the bank was breached to provide space for a waiting shelter: of the same shiplap construction and dimensions as that at Brimley. A wooden bench next to the shelter, a name board and two metal posts for hurricane lamps - one next to the shelter, and one at the foot of the access ramp - were the only other accoutrements.

From the 'access' ramp, a narrow metalled footpath ran alongside the line for approximately twenty yards, separated from it by a 4-strand wire and concrete post fence. At the end of the path, the principal exit from the halt was by means of a boardwalk over the track and up the sloping path to an iron gate on Lower Knowle Road. The gate-posts here were made from old rail lengths, while the gate itself opened away from the adjoining road. The alternative way out was to turn left at the end of the path, and climb the stile into the long lane which ran at the back of the halt and led to the public road at Yeo Bridge.

Before the war, the majority of trains called at Hawkmoor; and after it, they all did: even though by then few passengers made use of it. A survey carried out by BR over a week during 1957 recorded a daily average of only eight people joining trains, with the same number alighting. With a rising gradient of

1:53 commencing at the halt for 'down' trains, drivers did not appreciate having to stop there, as it meant they had to begin the climb from a cold start - made all the more annoying by the almost certain knowledge that, on most services at least, no-one would be leaving or joining the train. The difficulty was compounded in wet weather for, with greasy rails, the engine was liable to a bout of slipping when moving off. The flow, if that is the right word, of patronage was to Newton Abbot in the morning, and back in the afternoon. As guards did not issue tickets on the train, passengers boarding at the halt would briefly alight at Bovey and purchase their tickets at the booking office there. In the mid 1950s a third class cheap day return to Bovey and Lustleigh cost 6d; to Moretonhampstead the fare was 1/2 and to Newton Abbot 1/9. Hawkmoor, like Brimley, was supervised by Bovey station, so that the same general administrative arrangements applied.

The linking of the name of the halt with the sanatorium had

Above: Isolated Hawkmoor Halt viewed from the 'down' (Lustleigh) end. What it lacked in amenities was more than compensated for by the beauty of its surroundings. 10.10.50.   *E. R. Shepherd*
Below: A trackside view of the location in its later guise as Pullabrook Halt. 2.5.56.   *E. R. Shepherd*

The 2.15pm auto train from Moretonhampstead sets off from the halt, the single trailer being propelled by No. 1466. The 7¼ mile post stands out clearly to the right of the coach, while the sinuous nature of the Line hereabouts is also evident. 31.1.59. *Peter W. Gray*

0-4-2T No. 1466 makes an energetic start from the halt, en route with trailer W240W to Moretonhampstead. The narrow road to Knowle, Wrayland and Lustleigh is behind the boundary fence by the telegraph poles, far left. 31.1.59.
E. R. Shepherd

halt. The name had a nice ring to it, and was certainly unique, and consequently it was forwarded to Division (in Exeter) where it found favour. Matters were soon put in hand, and from Monday 13th June 1955 the halt carried the revised designation. Unfortunately, the arrival of the new name board was not matched with the arrival of new passengers, and although all trains continued to call, patronage remained meagre. Indeed, the seclusion of the locality imparted a sense of tranquillity in which large numbers of people would seem out of place. Its remoteness was reinforced by the ethereal mixture of birdsong drifting on the wind, and the babbling murmur of the combining waters of the River Bovey and Wray Brook. At merely brief intervals through the day was this peace punctuated by a shrill whistle and the bark of a locomotive's exhaust as it started away from the halt; serving as a fleeting reminder of a world outside.

unforeseen repercussions. Some visitors to the hospital did use the train to the halt - or at least they did for their first visit. The name, after all, implied reasonable proximity; indeed, the two places were only three-quarters of a mile apart when measured in a straight line. That is not an inordinate distance when seen on a map, but the actual distance was over twice that, along narrow, hilly roads and rough lanes, all unsigned. People were not pleased at being dropped off in the depths of the country in their best clothes, with no idea of how to reach the hospital. Guards soon latched on to this problem, and advised these passengers to leave the train at Bovey and catch the Moretonhampstead bus, which went right past the end of the hospital drive. The GWR actually received occasional complaints from the public about the inappropriateness of the name, as visitors came from well outside the area and were unacquainted with local geography.

Rather late in the day, the authorities decided to do something about it. Members of staff along the Branch were asked to suggest a new name for the halt. 'Knowle' understandably was a favourite, after the nearby hamlets of Knowle and Lower Knowle. However, whenever possible, the Railway (now British Railways, Western Region) preferred to give stations an 'individual' nomenclature to avoid possible confusion. So although the name 'Knowle' was geographically appropriate, there was already another place with the same name on the Western Region network (near Solihull in the West Midlands), so it was rejected and further suggestions invited. The 'Collection & Delivery' van driver at Bovey, Jack Heale, was well-acquainted with the area by the very nature of his work, and he mentioned to the station master that 'Pullabrook' might be acceptable. This was the name of a sizeable farmstead and tract of woodland on the opposite side of the river to the

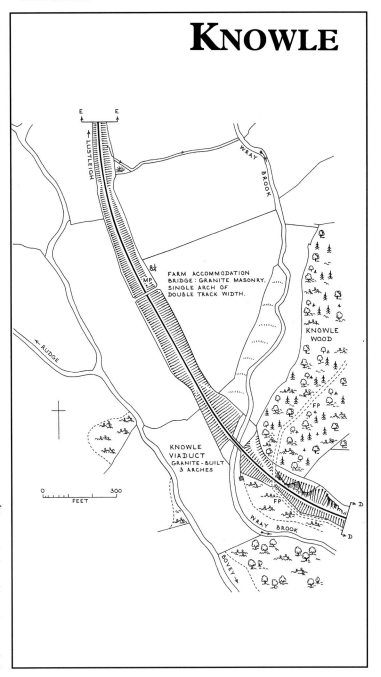

KNOWLE

FARM ACCOMMODATION BRIDGE: GRANITE MASONRY. SINGLE ARCH OF DOUBLE TRACK WIDTH.

KNOWLE WOOD

KNOWLE VIADUCT GRANITE - BUILT 3 ARCHES

WRAY BROOK

BOVEY

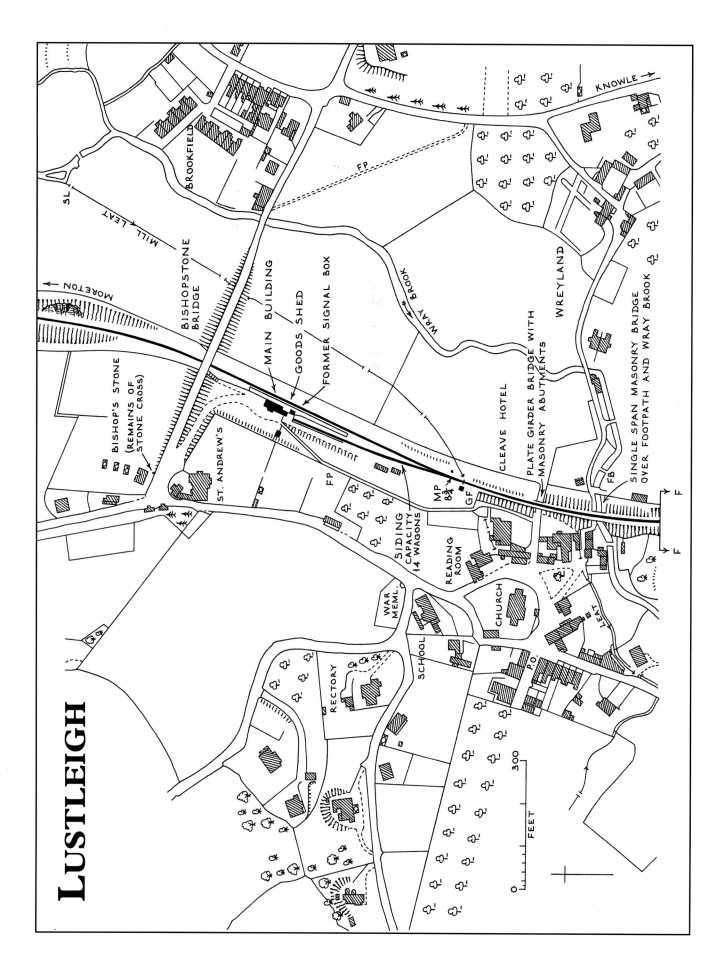

LUSTLEIGH

KNOWLE

BROOKFIELD

FP

WREYLAND

MILL LEAT

SL

MORETON

BISHOPSTONE BRIDGE

MAIN BUILDING

GOODS SHED

FORMER SIGNAL BOX

WRAY BROOK

BISHOP'S STONE (REMAINS OF STONE CROSS)

ST. ANDREW'S

FP

SIDING CAPACITY 14 WAGONS

MP 83

GF

CLEAVE HOTEL

PLATE GIRDER BRIDGE WITH MASONRY ABUTMENTS

SINGLE SPAN MASONRY BRIDGE OVER FOOTPATH AND WRAY BROOK

FB

F

F

READING ROOM

WAR MEML.

CHURCH

P.O.

LEAT

SCHOOL

RECTORY

300

FEET

0

Chapter Fifteen

LUSTLEIGH

Centred on the 'official' rail distance of 8 miles 66 chains from Newton Abbot, the Lustleigh station site marked the only level stretch on the long climb from Woolford (or Wilford) Bridge, south of Hawkmoor Halt, to the outskirts of Moretonhampstead. The station itself - a 245 foot-long masonry-faced platform - and the single goods siding were built on the 'down' (west) side of the single track. Just a matter of yards beyond the north end of the platform was Bishopstone Bridge. This granite-built structure had, as elsewhere on the Branch, been constructed with an arch sufficient to span two broad gauge lines, although a second track never materialised. The bridge was the means by which the small settlements of Brookfield/Wreyland and Lustleigh/Caseley - respectively east and west of the Line - were connected. A flight of steps led down from the roadway to the station.

Two of the aforementioned places highlight a problem pertaining to this locality more than any other on the Line; namely, variation in place-name spelling. The Wray Brook in whose valley the places lie, has given its name to many locations and settlements, and yet even ones which are contiguous adopt different spellings, such as: Wreyland/Wrayland Barn; East Wray/Eastwrey Barton; and Casely Cottages/Caseley Court. Others have changed over the years, generally to a simpler form: Sandduck becoming Sanduck; Kelley telescoped to Kelly. However, as the largest of all the scattered settlements, it was the village of Lustleigh that gave its name to the station. Already a 'showpiece' village when the Railway arrived, property developers saw the possibility of cashing-in on its new-found accessibility to the outside world. Plans were drawn up for extensive villa-style housing on the slopes around the village, with the intention of turning it into a sort of Victorian 'Torquay of the Moors'. In the event, the exposed location combined with the often bleak winter weather, put paid to this, and only two of the planned houses were built; allowing Lustleigh to escape wholesale gentrification and retain its quiet rural charm.

Having had the same designer and builder as Bovey station, it is not surprising that there are marked similarities in both style and construction between the two places. However, there are also significant differences. The symmetry possessed by Bovey is lacking here, by dint of there only being one 'wing' building: the lavatory block on the southern end-elevation: and

even here, there is only a single door leading to the 'Gents'. As if by way of partial compensation, the west (approach road) elevation was punctuated by a narrow, pitched-roof extension. A large open-fronted, lean-to style bicycle shed of horizontal timber cladding was appended to its south side at a later date, further spoiling the clean lines of the solid granite building. The absence of canopies is another obvious difference. The lack of a platform awning in particular made the main station building look somehow unfinished, especially when compared with the fine structure at Bovey and the substantial train-shed at Moretonhampstead. A clock, however, was present - for much of the station's existence at least - located between the booking hall door and window voussoirs. The only access to the building was via the platform. The lamp room/oil store - latterly a rather basic breeze-block affair - was set back from the foot of the wide fenced footpath which led to the centre of the village (to the rear of the Cleave Hotel).

The village had the smallest population of the three settlements originally provided with stations by the Moretonhampstead & South Devon Railway Company. Even as late as 1925 for example, the population was only just over 500, and even by incorporating the tiny satellite hamlets and farmsteads nearby, could not rival the 2,800 souls of Bovey or 3,500 of Moreton and Chagford combined. In spite of this demographic disparity, the station provided remarkable passenger income for the Branch. Before the Second World War, the revenue figures were not much below Bovey's, and even overtook Moreton's for a while in the mid 1930s. In

The Moreton-based permanent way gang stand clear of the longitudinally-sleepered track as an 0-6-0 saddle tank locomotive coasts into the station with a train of short-wheelbase coaches. The recently decommissioned wooden signalbox is prominent in this early Edwardian picture.   *I. D. Beale Collection*

1930 itself for example, Lustleigh sold 15,223 tickets to Bovey's 15,304 and Moreton's 15,914: although in terms of cash value the ranking was more disparate. It was the only station on the Branch where annual ticket sales never fell below 10,000. A selection of traffic and revenue data may be seen in Table 14.

The Railway provided an invaluable, even essential, service to the communities hereabouts in all sorts of ways. It was, in the modern jargon, 'user-friendly'. The following instances may serve by way of illustration. A baker from Bovey had a bread round in the village and its outliers two or three times a week. Often accompanied by his daughter, he arrived at his 'home' station by taxi armed with baskets crammed full with loaves to

143

catch the train out to Lustleigh. They were such regulars, that if they were not on the platform when the train arrived, it would wait for them. Coming from the opposite direction, a doctor in Moretonhampstead found the Railway a reliable means of getting prescriptions to his patients in and around Lustleigh. After he had finished his surgery and visits on a Saturday, he telephoned through the requirements to the practice dispensary, enabling the prescriptions to be made up and taken to the station in time for the evening train. If he was late in phoning through the details, his secretary rang the station to ask them to hold the train - which they always did! A lady who lived near Lustleigh station, and who kept goats, found the train a convenient way of transporting the animals to market. Periodically, she turned up at the station on a Wednesday - Newton Abbot's market day - paid the necessary 'livestock' charge and duly secured the animals in the luggage compartment of a passenger train for the 8¾ mile journey.

In addition to the regular, year-round custom, Lustleigh also had considerable seasonal traffic: namely, as the destination for off-line day-trippers. Tourism was very much in evidence during the summer months throughout the station's life. Walkers, hikers, cyclists and sightseers arrived by train prior to setting off to enjoy the picturesque scenery of the locality. For Torbay residents, for example, who had the sea on their doorstep, the Branch offered a complete contrast. Large numbers travelled out to the village, notably on Sundays and bank holidays; many walking thence to the nearby beauty spots in and around Lustleigh Cleave. The Cleave was already a tourist attraction before the arrival of the Railway in 1866. The growing reputation of Dartmoor generally was given a boost by the publication (in 1902) of Arthur Conan Doyle's 'Hound of the

Baskervilles'. One of his most enduringly popular Sherlock Holmes novels, it further enhanced - if also exaggerated - the Moor as a great wilderness and place of mystery. With the rise of the film industry, the book was a prime candidate for adaptation. The Islington-based Gainsborough Pictures organisation was the first to jump in, filming 'on location', with Lustleigh station taking on the name of 'Baskerville' for the duration. Little is known now of this early 1931 film, except that Robert Rendel played Holmes; Frederick Lloyd, Dr. Watson; an innominate Great Dane the Hound; and 'small Prairie' 2-6-2 tank engine No. 5530 the Paddington Express!

In addition to the grandeur of the general environs, the village itself has a great deal of charm. Thus when the Great Western Railway took the decision to introduce holiday Camping Coaches to the system, Lustleigh was an obvious choice. Old carriages were adapted for use for short-stay family holidays, offering something half way between conventional camping and lodging in a boarding house, but without the disadvantages of either. A number of these vehicles first appeared in South Devon in the summer of 1934, the single coach allocated to Lustleigh being berthed at the buffer-stop end of the goods siding, alongside the low platform. The camping coach quickly proved to be a popular concept, the only condition of booking being that the holidaymakers had to travel to the location by train. During the winter the coaches were taken to Swindon for general maintenance and any necessary refurbishment. With various types of vehicle in use, and with dispersal from a centralised pool at the start of each new season, there was much interchange between locations from year to year. Thus in 1935 for example, the coach allotted to Lustleigh was an ancient 31 foot long, 6-wheeled, former 5-compartment

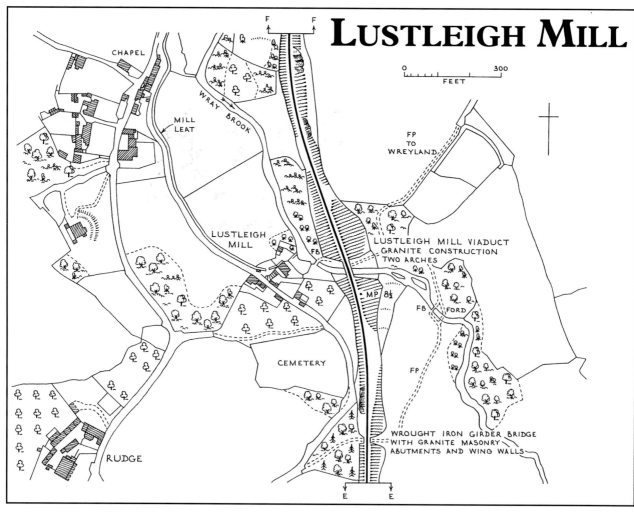

A charming view of Lustleigh station in 1921. The very epitome perhaps of the Great Western wayside station between the wars, with everything neat and tidy and obviously well cared for. The gardens occupying the space set aside for a possible second track were tended by the station staff and were a feature for a large part of the station's existence. Notice also the floral displays on the platform and main building. *L&GRP*

vehicle, painted in the neat 'chocolate-and-cream' livery of the period. After an absence during the Second World War, the coach was back; a more modern type now generally being supplied. In 1952 for instance, it was converted 'top-light' carriage No. W9927W, while in 1954 it was another of the same type: W9934W (which had been at Chudleigh the previous year). In 1958, as if to buck the trend to modernity, an antique ex-Cambrian Railway clerestory coach turned up for what was to be the last season. On change-over day (Saturday), the hectic chore of inspecting, cleaning and generally servicing the coach, as well as changing the linen, in readiness for the next family fell to the station porter.

If revenue connected with the camping coach was seasonal, that produced by the traffic in parcels was regular. Conveyed by passenger train, it was manifold in nature, with more items being received than despatched. They were dealt with and/or stored at the back of the station office; which location was also the repository for all the general paperwork. This office - at the north (Moreton) end of the main building - served a number of functions: from station master's office, to booking office, parcels office and porters' room. The post of station master was relatively short-lived at Lustleigh. In the early, 'broad gauge', years the station was placed under the supervision of a clerk-in-charge, and only around the turn of the century was a station master appointed: this being John Waldron, who had previously been at Heathfield. During the 1920s, if not before, the post was held by Frederick John Haywood, brother of George, Bovey's station master at the same period. Fred turned out to be the last incumbent, for the post was abolished early in 1930, with the station's supervision passing to the station master at Moretonhampstead. The latter made regular visits; always on pay day with the wage packets, and otherwise as required. The

daily routine at Lustleigh was now covered by two porters, on early turn/late turn alternating shifts. One of these was Bill Bishop, who soon afterwards moved to St. Thomas station, Exeter, as parcels porter. The staff took great pride in, and care of, their station; at one time even keeping a visitors' book in the waiting room. The station garden was a particularly noteworthy feature. Occupying the spare strip of land on the 'up' side of the line that had been laid aside for a possible second track, it was tended with loving care. Indeed, it won Garden Certificates in the Railway's annual competition every year between 1931 and 1940, and again between 1947 and 1951. It was in this last year, 1951, that further rationalisation took place, when the staffing was reduced to just one leading porter working a split shift. Initially this was Arthur Fleet and, from the following year, Ronald Rowe, who transferred from the post of porter at Bovey.

In these last years, the porter opened up the station in plenty of time for passengers to purchase tickets for the first train of the day: the 7.50am from Moretonhampstead - a very well used service. With the departure of the 11.35 from Moreton, the booking office was closed for almost two hours; reopening in readiness for the next 'up' train: the 1.35pm ex Moreton. On the intervening 'down' service, the 12.45 from Newton Abbot, the guard was required to collect tickets from passengers alighting at Lustleigh while anyone joining the train had to purchase their ticket at the terminus. The goods train latterly was scheduled to call only in the 'up' direction, by which time the leading porter was back on duty to assist with the 'smalls' traffic. He remained until the clearance of the 5.15pm from Moreton, following which the station building was locked until the following morning - the platform oil lamp having been attended to if and when required. As earlier in the day, the guard collected tickets from passengers leaving the remaining

The compact, granite station building at Lustleigh viewed from the garden in 1955. To the left is seen part of the wooden goods shed and, beyond, the end of the camping coach berthed for the season in the goods siding.
Both, *I. D. Beale*

The approach road view of the station building, showing the projecting 'back room' and adjoining bicycle shed. Among the posters is one advertising a cheap day return fare of 2/6 to Goodrington Sands Halt by any train after 9.30am - the usual cost was 4/- (20p).

trains: two 'down' and one 'up', and turned out the lamp on the last service.

One of the most celebrated 'members of staff' in earlier days was Jumbo, the station cat. Quite a character, and oblivious to the human imperative to 'beware of trains', the fearless feline had a number of close calls over the years. He so endeared himself to passengers that on his death he was buried in the station garden, complete with inscribed headstone: "Beneath this slab, and stretched out flat, lies Jumbo, once our station cat." His successor, Jemima James, had a less charmed life. Perhaps caught up in a gender crisis over his ambivalent name, he seemed less aware of reality. Learning the hard way that trains are heavier than cats, he soon joined his illustrious predecessor in the garden - though without commemoration. A proposal in 1936 to install a second line and so convert Lustleigh into a crossing place, came to naught, enabling the two meritorious moggies to continue to rest in peace.

Of extremely short duration was the station's signal box. In broad gauge days, the Line was worked by block telegraph, the instruments being housed in the station office. There were no signals, while the siding points were worked by a capstan (kept locked when not in use). In spite of the low level of service in those days the GWR decided to provide a fully signalled layout

The station name board. *S. J. Dickson*

here (as at Teigngrace), and in June 1892 - just one month after the conversion of gauge - placed an order for a signal box. Of wooden lap-board construction, with a hipped slate roof, it was sited on the platform a little to the south of the main building, the line of its roof ridge being slightly behind the line of the platform fence. The operating floor, measuring 15' by 8' 6", contained a 13-lever frame: 11 working and 2 spare levers. It was not a block post - that is, could only supervise the passage of trains en route between Bovey and Moreton - and could be 'switched out' when not in use. References are made to the signal box in official publications for the next few years, sometimes even specifying opening times, but the introduction of the 'electric train staff' on the Branch in November 1901 rendered it unnecessary. The new goods siding ground frame of two levers (one 'facing point lock' and one 'point' switch) was unlocked by the key-like attachment on one end of the staff. Though redundant, the cabin remained in situ for very many years, probably being used as an additional storeroom.

During the few years that the signal box was in use, the layout was fully signalled - even to the provision of a 'shunt' signal beneath the arm of the 'up advanced starting' signal. The arms of the 'down starting' and 'up home' signals, near Bishopstone Bridge, were also mounted on a single post, though unlike the previous arrangement were for trains travelling in opposite directions. When the signal box was switched out, the signals were left to show 'all clear'. This attracted the attention of Cecil Torr, the unofficial local chronicler, who confessed that: "Seeing both arms lowered for trains to come both ways, I felt a little uneasy, there being only a single line. But the station-master said:- "Well, there isn't an engine up at Moreton; and, if a truck did run away, it wouldn't stop because the signal was against it." Trucks do sometimes run away, but have never yet done serious damage." This shared, bi-directional arrangement was an uncommon feature of Great Western signalling, although was to be found again on the Moreton Line near the junction at Newton Abbot, where the combination was that of 'branch advanced starting' and 'branch intermediate home' signals.

Of much greater permanence was the timber-built goods shed. This abutted the lavatory block of the main station building, and was set well back on the platform. With sliding doors front and back, it was a smaller version of the one seen at Heathfield, though with vertical cladding. It was designed for small goods traffic - that is, up to three hundredweight - which was unloaded from the Station Truck conveyed by the 'down' goods train and transferred straight into the shed. The Goods was generally allowed a five minute stop to effect this work, calling for a couple of minutes longer on its return to deal with 'full load' traffic in the yard siding. A request for a loading dock in this siding was submitted to the M&SDR Company on 29th September 1866, a few weeks after the Line had opened. A low platform, some 135 feet long, was eventually provided at the inner end of the siding. If it was too low to serve the usual role of loading dock, it was later to be of benefit to the camping coach (as outlined above). Sometimes goods trains called at the station 'as required'; while at other times were given a booked stop - although in practice if there was no traffic to be dealt with the train continued to the next station.

Freight contributed about a third of the total revenue at Lustleigh down to the Second World War, from which time data is not available due to the centralised way of recording under the Goods Zoning Scheme. The 'traffic received' dominated the total goods handled here. In 1925 it amounted to over 73% of the total volume by weight; and of this 65% (1,253 tons) was coal and coke. By 1935 the respective figures had risen to over 92% and 77% (1,194 tons), and in 1946 to over 97% and 99% (1,400 tons). The principal coal merchant for very many years was W.H. Bartlett and also, between 1947 and 1961, W.C. & D. Waldron. The substantial stone building near the village end of the siding was used as a coal store. Supplies for W.H. Bartlett arrived in their own 'private owner' vehicle: a 10-ton, 7-plank coal wagon built by the Gloucester Carriage & Wagon Company in 1907. Private owner wagons were exclusively reserved for use by the firm concerned; a fact which had to be taken into account in the marshalling of freight trains, as they had to be in the correct sequence for shunting en route. They were also charged differently from railway-owned vehicles when stabled in sidings. In the late 1930s for example, there was a 'siding rent' of 6d (2½p) a day payable on wagons occupying Railway Company, as opposed to private, sidings - the former being the case at Lustleigh.

A significant exception to the 'loaded in/empties out' trend was the interesting appearance of entries in the 'other minerals' section of the annual traffic returns (that is to say, traffic other than coal or coke). Discontinuous in time and generally small-

Signs of the times! Doubtless fulfilling a legal requirement, such signs were a commonplace feature all over the network. The GWR evidently expected the general public to have both the required level of literacy and the time to read them! The wicket gate to the right of the smaller sign is at the top of the flight of steps to which the notice applied, and which provided pedestrians with a short-cut to the station.

S. J. Dickson

scale in nature, it is probably linked with output from the nearby Kelly iron ore mine. The ore, of a type known as haematite, was particularly rich in the mineral mica, and found an important use in the production of grey-coloured, rust-retarding paint. It barely featured in the accounts after 1926 - when only 176 tons were sent out - ceasing altogether in the early and mid 1930s. It reappeared again during the war years, albeit at low levels, to cease completely from 1946.

Because the yard possessed no run-round facility, freight trains could only perform shunting duties in the 'up' direction. Thus 'full load' wagons for the village were taken through to Moreton and marshalled next to the engine on the return leg of the journey. The crew of the goods train appreciated the stop at Lustleigh on the south-bound journey, if they were running ahead of time, as it gave an opportunity for the driver and guard to slink off to the Cleave Hotel for a drink, or perhaps even a cream tea in summer; leaving the train in the charge of a doubtless envious fireman. Another perk of the stop here, was that the men were always able to obtain milk and cheese from a nearby farm.

LUSTLEIGH SIGNALLING DIAGRAM - 1895

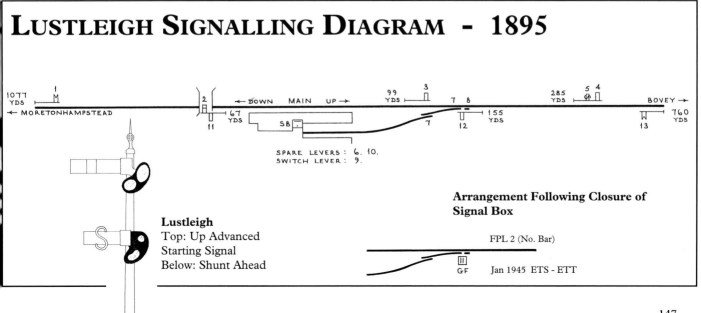

Lustleigh
Top: Up Advanced
Starting Signal
Below: Shunt Ahead

Arrangement Following Closure of Signal Box

FPL 2 (No. Bar)

Jan 1945 ETS - ETT

With the exception of the years 1940-51, a camping coach was located at Lustleigh each summer from 1934. It was housed at the buffer-stop end of the siding, in the loading dock; converted 'top-light' corridor coach W9934W being in residence in 1954. 16.8.54.   *National Railway Museum*

Table 14. Selected Traffic Returns : Lustleigh

YEAR	PASSENGERS				PARCELS			MILK			GOODS			LIVESTOCK	
	Tickets (Single & Return)	£	Season Tickets	£	No. Sent out	No. Received	Total Value £	No. of cans	No. of cases	Total Value £	Tonnage Despatched	Tonnage Received	Total Value £	Wagon Loads	Value £
1925	19,386	1561	75	107	1230	1521	182	-	-	-	695	1924	864	-	-
1926	16,945	1367	53	76	1095	1599	122	-	-	-	619	1445	797	-	-
1927	17,746	1382	59	79	1004	1689	176	-	-	-	492	1690	927	-	-
1928	17,669	1351	121	77	959	1845	186	-	-	-	462	2500	1336	-	-
1929	16,461	1281	80	51	841	1782	156	-	-	-	436	1526	778	-	-
1930	15,137	1178	86	44	750	1542	140	-	-	-	531	1657	730	-	-
1931	14,587	1146	102	52	574	1384	91	-	-	-	262	1545	565	-	-
1932	13,947	1017	103	52	511	1352	81	-	-	-	217	1549	557	-	-
1933	13,458	1005	126	67	628	1754	78	-	-	-	278	1733	718	-	-
1934	12,662	918	199	112	676	1682	79	-	-	-	195	1475	556	-	-
1935	12,919	943	200	122	505	1804	41	-	-	-	125	1541	552	-	-
1936	13,055	947	175	114	362	1667	25	-	-	-	82	1484	475	-	-
1937	12,795	960	201	129	475	1523	37	-	-	-	117	1501	613	-	-
1938	13,084	855	119	97	585	1387	52	-	-	-	99	1527	691	-	-
1939	11,820	954	129	86	763	1589	76	-	-	-	122	1556	543	-	-
1940	10,793	975	115	83	840	1849	102	-	-	-	2745	1440	N/D	-	-
1941	15,394	1359	81	75	N/D	N/D	104	37	-	2	1933	1556	N/D	-	-
1942	15,816	1423	116	87	N/D	N/D	105	-	-	-	1717	1376	N/D	-	-
1943	17,943	1651	101	96	N/D	N/D	104	-	-	-	858	1281	N/D	-	-
1944	19,073	1735	125	101	N/D	N/D	117	38	-	N/D	91	1187	N/D	-	-
1945	17,858	1903	95	101	N/D	N/D	143	-	-	-	68	1389	N/D	-	-
1946	17,776	1997	170	154	N/D	N/D	192	-	-	-	33	1523	N/D	-	-
1947	15,139	1659	212	189	N/D	N/D	171	-	-	-					
1948	14,266	1892	230	221	N/D	N/D	222	60	-	8					
1949	14,367	1802	112	176	N/D	N/D	236	34	-	5					
1950	13,425	1373	114	258	N/D	N/D	173	121	-	9					
1951	10,814	1251	213	258	465	1609	147	348	-	14	Goods Zoned at Newton Abbot from 1.3.47				
1952	12,257	1290	164	195	574	1925	153	193	-	13					
1953	10,968	1115	137	183	320	1359	107	-	-	-					
1954	10,666	1156	115	137	364	1032	70	-	-	-					
1955	11,006	1286	86	97	184	1077	68	-	-	-					
1956	10,317	1190	65	55	218	1005	73	-	-	-					
1957	11,933	1258	103	107	267	966	65	-	-	-					
1958	10,789	1063	81	67	252	856	77	-	-	-					

N/D = No Data available.

Sanduck Siding

The Earl of Devon was an important landowner in the large moorland parishes of Lustleigh and Moretonhampstead, and until the end of the 19th century was the latter's Lord of the Manor. This fact, together with his leading role in the promotion of the M&SDR had been of enormous assistance to the Railway. Now it could be of assistance to him. A mile and a half or so north of Lustleigh, the Line passed Sanduck Wood, the property of the Earl. In the early 1870s he decided to exploit the commercial value of the timber by clearing the wood. With the railway to hand, the removal of the timber would be made easy. Having discussed the matter with the South Devon Railway who now fully owned the Line, it was arranged to provide a siding for the duration of the clearance (situated near the 10¼ mile post below Willoway Farm). Indeed, the siding was already in place and available for use even before the SDR sent the plans and request for inspection to the Board of Trade. Considering our Victorian forebears did not have the instant telecommunications systems we enjoy (or endure?) today, events moved remarkably fast. The initial letter left the Company's Plymouth offices on 28th May 1873. It arrived at the Board of Trade's Railway Department later the same day; was read, considered and passed for inspection; a reply drafted; proper copy written out and posted; and the Inspector contacted all within 'office hours' on 28th!

The inspection took place just two days later; the omnipresent Col. Yolland arriving to carry out the task. The siding proper - that part of it inside the gated entrance - was 120 feet long. Outside the gate was a catch point, or 'throw off switch' as it was called in the plan, to deflect trucks away from the running line should they somehow 'run away'; followed by a 600-foot radius connection leading into the main line. A signal was provided 325 yards from the connection, in the Lustleigh direction, as this was the direction of possible - though highly improbable - conflicting train movements. In his report of 30th May to the Board, Yolland says of the siding that it is to be "used for the clearance of Sanduck Wood, and then to be removed .... the Siding is to be worked exclusively from and to Moretonhampstead Station. It is provided with a catch point and the facing Points towards a down train, are properly interlocked with a Signal." It should be remembered of course that the

Top left: Having commandeered the office chair to help the two lady visitors into their transport, station master Fred Haywood and Hugh Chudley make sure they are safely seated and their luggage secure. The horse and trap belonged to Hugh's brother, A. H. Chudley, of Ellimore, an arrangement having been made to meet the travellers at the station and convey them to one of the farms in the locality. Circa 1920. *I. D. Beale Collection, courtesy Mike Jacobs*

Top right: A smartly dressed young porter poses nonchalantly at Lustleigh station around 1920. The only other member of staff at this date was the station master. *I. D. Beale Collection, courtesy Mike Jacobs*

Below: As usual, a Newton-bound train is assured of passengers at Lustleigh. The vehicle next to the engine - an unidentified 'Prairie' - is 57 foot corridor full brake van W269W. Built in 1945, it carries the lined maroon livery applied to such vehicles from 1957, while the two carriages are of the non-corridor 'suburban' type.

I. D. Beale Collection, courtesy Mike Jacobs

designations 'up' and 'down' were swapped round in later years. The Colonel recommended that the siding be sanctioned. The SDR was notified of this decision on 4th June. Reference to Sanduck Wood Siding - sometimes referred to as Sandrick - continued through the mid 1870s, but by the end of the decade had gone: like the trees.

'Large Prairie' No. 4117 rattles over Kelly Embankment with the 'last day' 3.15pm working from Moretonhampstead. The tree-studded hillside below Lower Elsford forms the backdrop to the train. Indeed, the lower slopes on both sides of this broad moorland valley are extensively wooded hereabouts, with individual plantations frequently coalescing to form more continuous tracts. 28.2.59.   *Peter F. Bowles*

Chapter Sixteen
MORETONHAMPSTEAD

For topographical reasons, the Branch terminus at Moretonhampstead was situated a quarter of a mile outside the town, at a lower elevation, and was reached by means of Station Road, running from the town centre to the old turnpike road (now A382) near King's Bridge. Just past the well-proportioned houses of Courtenay Terrace - built three years after the opening of the Railway - a notice board and gas lamp marked the position of the wooden gate at the top of the sloping path which gave foot-passengers direct access to the station building. Vehicles gained entry to the site through a wide gated entrance further down Station Road.

The Station Building

The architectural style of the main station building followed that of the other two original Moretonhampstead & South Devon Railway stations: what might be termed 'Dartmoor Gothic'. Unlike the others, however, it was built as a single unified block, with a straightforward rectangular plan. The absence of differentiated 'wings' or annexes gave it a solid austerity, enhanced by the exclusive use of the local, predominantly grey, granite masonry for the walls and grey slate for the roof. It possessed the same overall measurements as Bovey - a nominal 59 feet by 17 feet - but by virtue of its geometrical regularity, had a larger total floor area.

Of larger dimensions than the building was the adjoining train shed (or overall roof) covering the platform and tracks. Measuring some 80 feet by 40 feet, it was entirely of timber construction, except for the supporting open-arched masonry wing walls projecting beyond the end of the station building on its platform elevation. It certainly provided shelter against the wind and rain in this exposed location although, being on the south side of the building, greatly reduced the daylight in its various rooms. At night, the gloom beneath the train shed was relieved by three gas lights, Moreton being the only station on the Branch to be so provided: a benefit of being near the town's gas works. There was little in the way of 'platform furniture' beneath the train shed: just a couple of wooden bench seats, a few notice boards, a weighing machine and, for a number of years, a Nestle's chocolate dispensing machine (located between the scales and booking hall door). Although large edging slabs were used for the full length of the platform, it was only beneath the roof that its width was flagged, the remainder being metalled.

If there were few accoutrements beneath the train shed, there were even less beyond: a gas lamp and seat near the station name board, and another lamp at the extreme end of the platform. Another seat or two sometimes appeared by the goods shed wall, but they seemed to be moveable features! The platform was backed by standard 'dog-tooth' GWR wooden fencing, although by the early years of the twentieth century, the

Moretonhampstead. Its journey from Newton Abbot over, 1466 and trailer W241W stand quietly at the terminus in the summer of 1957. This saloon coach was regularly used on the Branch trains at this time, being one of the 'early BR' 64 foot all-steel bodied varieties fitted out with plastic interior panelling and green upholstered bus-type seats. The station staff's vegetable garden is much in evidence in the foreground.
G. Howells

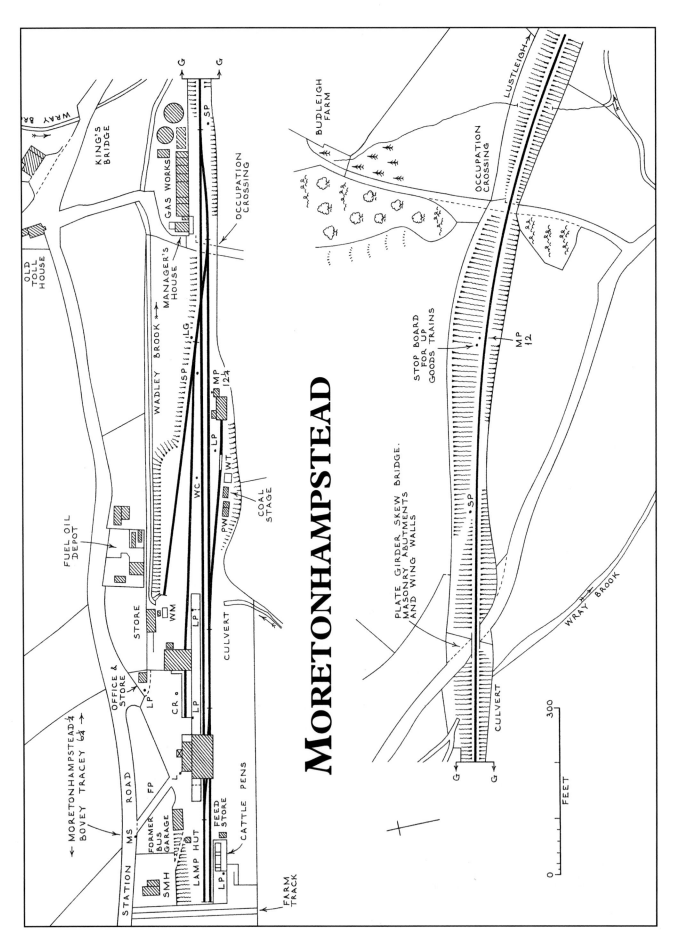

MORETONHAMPSTEAD

length between the goods shed and train shed had been replaced with iron railings, along with a metal gate next to the train shed instead of the former wooden one. At one time, the fence was almost completely covered with enamel advertisement boards. In Edwardian times these included: Anglo-Bavarian Ales, BDV Tobacco, Callard & Bowser's Butter Scotch, Epps' Cocoa, Mazawattee Tea and Pears' Soap.

The station building was constructed more or less on an east-west orientation. Its central portion consisted of the Booking Hall-cum-General Waiting Room. With a floor area of approximately 290 square feet, it was lit by a single large window front and back, and illuminated at night by a gas lamp, with a modicum of winter warmth provided by a small cast-iron fireplace. Ingress was through double doors from both forecourt pavement and platform. Leading off from the east side of the hall was the Ladies Waiting Room, with lavatories off that room in turn. The Gentlemen's lavatory/urinal was reached by way of the arch in the wing wall at the end of the train shed and a doorway at the far corner of the end wall. The door was concealed from view from the forecourt by a substantial wooden screen. This corner of the station was enclosed by railings, against which were a number of fire buckets and a standpipe. A doorway leading directly into the Gents from the pavement outside the station was filled in with masonry almost at the end of the station's life.

Adjoining the booking hall on the west (town) side was the Station Office, the domain of the station master. Most of his time was taken up with a plethora of paperwork relating to the 'passenger' side of operations at the station as well as its general administration. One of the daily routines involved the despatch of monies to the Divisional Treasurer's Office. Unlike all the other Traffic (later Operating) Department administration, which was dealt with at Exeter, the money went to Plymouth;

Above: The station viewed from the road entrance in 1913. The Brunel-style train shed covers the platform and two tracks beyond. A GWR-operated Milnes-Daimler omnibus waits on the forecourt, providing a link with the village of Chagford three miles away: a service which began in 1906 and was currently running seven journeys each way on summer weekdays.   *L&GRP*

Below: The station seen from the footpath - at the town end of the layout - on a drizzly, moorland day in the mid 1950s. At the beginning of the decade the roof of the train shed was renewed; the slates were removed and replaced by heavy-duty roofing felt secured to the boards below by battens. The glazed skylights were taken out and sheets of corrugated iron used to cover over the aperture - all that is except for a narrow strip on either side of the central ridge, which thus acted as a smoke ventilator. The doorway to the booking hall lost its canopy at the same time. In addition to the two wall-mounted gas lights seen here, there was also a lamp standard by the wicket gate at the top, Station Road, end of the footpath.   *OPC/BR*

conveyed in a travelling safe. The day's takings were totalled and recorded by the station master as one of his last duties of the day. The money, along with the accompanying return slip, was placed in a leather pouch, which displayed the name of the station engraved on a brass plate. This was then locked overnight in the safe. Next morning, it was dropped into the travelling safe in the charge of the guard, who recorded its receipt. This same procedure was repeated at Lustleigh, Bovey and Heathfield. The safe was a large, solidly-built wooden chest, with metal reinforced corners. It had an ingeniously designed thief-proof hinged lid that could only open one way: inwards. It bore in bold black-edged gold lettering the inscription 'Moreton to Plymouth' beneath the initials G.W.R., later B.R.(W). At Newton Abbot the safe was transferred to a main line service to Plymouth. Here, it was unlocked, the

A general view of the station and its environs in February 1959. To the left of the goods shed the 6-ton yard crane stands on the loading dock, being a replacement for the original 4-ton version. Above the left hand end of the train shed is the station master's residence and, across Station Road, the attractive houses of Courtenay Terrace. New residential development is underway in the adjoining field, leading the eye up to the 15th century tower of the parish church of St. Andrew.

Peter F. Bowles

monies checked against the docket, the figures written up in the Divisional records, and then added to the global figure before being sent to Paddington. The empty safe and pouches were returned in the afternoon. Every now and again auditors paid an unannounced visit to the Branch, having travelled down from 'head office': namely the audit office at Paddington. Such visits were not popular, more for the demeanour of the officials than for any errors they might uncover. Their manner was somewhat aloof, even intimidating, and station masters found the experience something akin to an inquisition. They checked the petty cash and then minutely examined the entries in the station ledgers.

In addition to keeping the books in order, the station master also had to ensure that the Station Inventory was up to date. Every single item had to be listed: from ticket cases to desks and chairs. If replacements were required for any reason, a requisition would be made out and sent to the central stores at Swindon. The replacement would be sent out in due course, but the worn or damaged item had first to be handed in before the new one was issued - even if it was just a fragment of a signalman's duster for example. Bureaucracy was rampant and all-pervasive! Requisitions for stationery went to Paddington.

Circulars required the station master's attention almost daily. Some were simply for information, but others requested data on a myriad of subjects related to the station's running. This ranged from obvious things like passenger, parcels and goods traffic returns, to the state of the platforms, condition of seats and number of fire buckets. The officials responsible for checking on the fittings and fixtures were based at Swindon.

They too made periodic visits to the Branch - though less frequently than the auditors - checking items against the inventory. The Railway hierarchy seemed to have an insatiable appetite for statistics, and the resulting paperwork became quite a chore. Some of the requests seemed of doubtful value, especially as regular returns were made in any case: the weekly revenue return for example was sent to Division every Monday. This was generally filled in by the station master on the previous Saturday, and then despatched with the takings the following Monday morning. The demand for data rose to a particularly, and ominously, high level in what proved to be the period leading up to the withdrawal of passenger services.

The station master was also responsible for paying the employees' wages. The staffing at Moreton was quite large for a rural branch line: the Traffic Department personnel alone stood at nine from at least 1925 down to closure in 1959 - rising in fact to eleven between 1952 and 1955. They included a goods clerk, checker, porters, signalmen, guards and town delivery van driver. In addition, other men were also based at the terminus, although did not show on station payroll accounts; namely, two sets of locomen (until 1947) and, of shorter duration, an overnight shedman. Between 1906 and 1932 a GWR bus driver was retained at the station (with an additional man being taken on for the summer months in many of these years). The largest single group employed at Moreton was the Engineering Department's permanent way gang. These men were paid at the station office, where they were supposed to present their brass pay checks to the station master as proof of identity. Such formality was dispensed with given the almost 'family atmosphere' that prevailed amongst the staff - unless word was received that the auditors or district inspector were about. The 'global sum' required at each of the Branch stations was made up at Plymouth according to the wage sheets sent in by the station masters, and forwarded to Newton Abbot. Where large sums were conveyed on certain trains within the Division, a railway policeman at one time accompanied the guard, in whose charge the money was assigned. The Moreton Branch wages travelled out on the mid-morning train from Newton, secured in 'personalised' canvas bags for each location. The station master signed for the bag on receipt and then made up the individual sums. Only much later were the wages sent ready packaged in sealed envelopes.

By the very nature of the job - rising through the ranks as it were - station masters did not generally have the same longevity at Moretonhampstead as other grades, and often originated from beyond the immediate locality. For much of the Line's existence, they lived at private addresses. Thus Henry Lambert Gorwyn, the first incumbent - whose occupancy lasted through the 1870s - resided at Cross Street. It was only in the 1920s that the GWR built a 'Company house' on an existing piece of Railway land between the cattle dock access path and Station Road, suitably adjacent to, and overlooking, the terminus. At the turn of the century, the station master was John Mugford, who actually had a relatively long tenure, having been 'in post' from at least the mid 1880s. By 1910 he had been replaced by Albert John Bradridge, who was still 'in post' at the outbreak of the First World War. His successors, down to the 1930s, included Messrs. Banbury and Harman. During the Second World War the position was held by Jack Hawkes. He cut a distinctive figure: though short in stature, he was always dapper - complete with bow tie. A Bradninch man, he had previously worked as goods clerk at Hele & Bradninch station on the main line, about eight miles north of Exeter. He had strong musical interests, singing in the church choir and playing in Bradninch Town Band. He had married a local girl, but when the Moreton job came up, he decided to apply for it and was duly appointed. It became evident after a while that he missed his 'roots', reinforced by the fact that as he tended to do everything strictly 'by the book', he was not overly popular with his colleagues. When a vacancy was advertised at Silverton - the next station to Hele & Bradninch - he put in for, and got, the job. However, just prior to his moving, the station master's job at the more important location of Cullompton came up (this being the next station to Hele in the other direction!). In the event, it was directly to there that he removed. He was succeeded at Moreton by Bob Tooley and, after an occupancy of just a few years, by Edgar ('Eddie') Valentine. Moving from Acton in West London, he stayed for only a few years before receiving promotion to a new post. The ensuing brief interregnum in the early part of 1956 was filled by relief station master T. Granville from Exeter. The final incumbent was Ray Thomas, who came to Moreton from his native Wales.

For almost its entire history, the regular Branch passenger guards were based at Moretonhampstead: one covering the 'early turn' and one the 'late'. The station office served as their 'base', where they booked on and off duty and wrote up their journals. In 1935 these were Messrs. Bailey and Dyment. Already

The station site from the 'gas works end'; summer 1955. Just beyond the 'engine release road' exit ground signal, a gated occupation-type level crossing gave access to a long lane serving fields on the hillside to the south of the Line. *I. D. Beale*

by that date, Alf Dyment had been a guard on the Branch for fifteen years, and was so to remain until passenger services were withdrawn some two and a half decades later. Guard Bailey was soon succeeded by Bill Horrell who, apart from a break during the Second World War, also remained until closure. (Bill's son Lloyd also worked on the Railway, initially as a clerk at Newton Abbot and later Plymouth.) Even when the engine shed closed towards the end of 1947 - which required the loco to return to Newton Abbot at the end of the day - the carriages were stabled overnight at the terminus, enabling the guards to remain there. From the summer of 1956, however, the entire train was booked to run back to Newton as 'empty carriage stock', which meant that the guards' rosters were thenceforth transferred there also.

Beyond the booking office, and accessible to it by an interconnecting door, was the Parcels Office. It boasted no less than four external doors; two of these being side by side in the end wall - a legacy of the time when a coal store was

A 1959 view through the train shed to the cattle dock and buffer stops. *S. J. Dickson*

incorporated in a corner of the room. The office was somewhat gloomy, although had the benefit of gas light; while a fireplace on the inner wall provided some warmth in cold winter weather. A weighing machine for lighter parcels was housed in the office, while heavier ones were dealt with by the scales on the platform. With a population of only 1,500 - 1,600 throughout the station's existence, Moretonhampstead sustained a large volume of parcels traffic, reflecting its importance as a railhead for a sizeable part of north-eastern Dartmoor (most notably Chagford). The number of items received always substantially exceeded those despatched, although the totals handled over the 34 years for which records are available held up at a healthy level throughout. Thus the number received annually between 1925 and closure fluctuated between 8,000 and 10,000, and occasionally rose higher; while those despatched never rose above the 5,000 mark, and in fact showed a general downward trend (but still only once, in 1956, falling below 2,000). A breakdown of the figures is provided in Table 15.

In Great Western days, parcels requiring collection or delivery were dealt with by the Company's local cartage agent (or 'carrier'). Following the introduction of the GWR's own motor omnibus service to Chagford in 1906 - replacing the earlier horse-drawn bus - small parcels were also conveyed by this means; the traffic being entered in the station accounts as 'Road Motor Parcels'. In 1925, the last year in which this was a feature, the number of parcels so carried was 3,677, and produced an income of £107. This was essentially local traffic, for the 4,980 parcels sent out by rail that year were worth £1,171; this being a per capita increase of 800% over the road motor figure.

The trade was steady all year round, but in the busier summer months the parcels office became very congested. Variety was the keynote. Amongst the mass of general merchandise, certain items stood out. Some of the most constant traffic was connected with the Manor House Hotel, a little to the west of the town, above the show-piece village of North Bovey. This impressive pile, formerly the residence of the Lord of the Manor, had along with 193 acres been bought by the GWR in 1929 and converted into a hotel (see Chapter 5). As a 'Railway Hotel', in fact if not in name, its supplies reached Moreton by train. These included cases of wine and spirits from the stock cellars at Paddington; sides of smoked bacon; churns of milk; chests of tea; large boxes or crates of cheese and general groceries; and wicker baskets of clean linen (this originally

having been laundered at Devon House, Bovey). Other prominent traffic included a large amount of mail and 'luggage in advance'. The latter comprised a huge variety of cases, trunks and boxes, all of which arrived at the station bearing large coloured labels with the legend: "Manor House Hotel, Moretonhampstead, NORTH BOVEY, DEVON" and the Company's motif. Other 'regulars' included cans of film for the Rex Cinema, owned by Messrs. Howell and Curtis. The former Drill Hall in the town had been converted into a picture house in 1938, and continued until 1957. The reels of film were despatched by passenger train and travelled in the charge of the guard. The morning papers came out from Newton on the first train of the day. Tied in bundles, they were collected promptly, and taken to the newsagent in the town.

Traffic of a more seasonal nature consisted of rabbits and bilberries. The proliferation of rabbits in the area produced a great demand for the services of the town's rabbit catcher. Up until the mid 1930s this was George Northcott, who lived in Mount Pleasant. He was succeeded by the Yeoman Brothers and Lester Crump. Some people, incidentally, when buying rabbit would insist on an animal that had been trapped rather than shot, to avoid possible problems with lead contamination in the meat. The trapped rabbits were hung up in crates or wicker baskets and sent off to markets in London, the Midlands and North of England. In hot weather this particular traffic impressed itself on the senses of all those who went near the baskets, and it continued to feature until around 1953. Bilberries, or whortle-berries, were collected in considerable quantities around the town. The sweet-tasting blue berries were packed into drums and brought to the station for despatch to London, where their juice was extracted for the production of dyes.

Supervision of the parcels office, including all the paperwork, devolved upon the station master, although most of the actual routine was the responsibility of the parcels porter. Longevity of tenure was the rule rather than the exception for many Branch personnel, and is exemplified by Moreton's last parcels porter, Reg Moore. A well-respected member of staff, his career at the station began in 1920, and he was still there when the parcels facility was withdrawn almost forty years later. A Moretonhampstead parish councillor from the late 1930s, he later became a Justice of the Peace. The sorting of parcels either ready for the train or for collection by the road delivery vehicle/customer formed a major part of his work, along with left luggage and the weighing of items brought for despatch, or of those thought to be under-charged (namely, 'excess luggage'). His colleague, porter Harry Yeoman - also of long service at Moreton - assisted in the office as required; although his work was principally to help out in the goods yard.

In this 1963 close-up view of details at the west end of the building, the carefully chiselled dressing on the door edging blocks and plinth are seen to good effect. The panelled door leading to the parcels office/cloak room retains its enamel identification plate, and next to it is the door which formerly gave access to the station master's office.
S. J. Dickson

Road Motors

The hoped-for continuation of the Branch to Chagford so eagerly sought at the time of the Line's planning never materialised, although the Light Railways Act of 1896 briefly raised the possibility once again. The Act sparked a new wave of interest in railway schemes across the country, for with less rigid constraints on construction and operation, lines could be built more cheaply. Amongst those in the West Country were the Lyme Regis and North Devon & Cornwall Junction (ie. Torrington to Halwill) branch lines. With the Exeter Railway currently under construction - linking that city with the Teign Valley line - interest was generated in the old Devon Central scheme of the early 1860s. Indeed, there was already a plan to link the new line at Leigh (or Lea) Cross with Chagford via Dunsford and Fingle Bridge. In 1897 plans were drawn up for a line from Moretonhampstead through Chagford to Okehampton: the 'Mid Devon Light Railway'. Largely an 'outside' initiative with doubtful economic potential, it did not really capture the local imagination, and the following year both it and the Chagford Branch of the Exeter Railway were abandoned - to join the great list of railway 'might-have-beens'. (The year 1897, incidentally, also saw the promotion of a 'Brent, Ashburton & Heathfield Railway' which, in connection with the Teign Valley and Exeter Railways, was designed to provide an alternative route between Exeter and Plymouth. This, too, was dropped the following year.)

Chagford, therefore, continued to rely on its road connection with the Moretonhampstead Branch. A good hour's walk away, a horse and trap was doubtless available for those wishing for more rapid, if not particularly comfortable, travel between the two places. A horse-bus also ran twice a day between the station and Chagford. This of course provided passengers with a service to Moretonhampstead town centre; while the White Hart and White Horse Hotels also provided transport to meet the trains. The long-established Chagford service provided its operator with an annual retainer of £133 by the GWR in the early years of the twentieth century. On 9th April 1906 the horse-bus was replaced by the Railway Company's own motor omnibus. Between October and June it ran four times in each direction on weekdays, increasing to six in the summer months. Four years later, the service was increased by an additional round trip for all but the mid-winter months. In 1912 it was joined by a

Above: The Great Western Railway's 'Chagford to Moreton' horse-drawn omnibus pictured in the 1890s at Half Way House, the mid-point of the journey. *Dartington Rural Archive*
Below: The GWR's motor omnibus grinds along elm-lined Station Road, Moretonhampstead, circa 1908. The road was built to coincide with the arrival of the Railway; previously, all traffic from the Bovey direction came to the town from Gales Sawmill to Dillon Corner and up Exeter Road. *Dartington Rural Archive*

Below: Rival and Usurper. Devon General service 16 operated between Newton Abbot, Chagford and Okehampton, providing the replacement mode of transport following with withdrawal of passenger trains. In the early 1970s AEC 'Reliance' (985 MDV) in traditional red and cream livery waits for passengers opposite the Union Inn, Moretonhampstead, for Chagford.
The late David Fereday Glenn (Miles Barber Glen collection)

summer-time 'tourist' service across the Moor to Princetown; again phased in with train times.

In 1925 the number of 'Road Motor Car' tickets issued by Moretonhampstead station and the GWR's Chagford agent combined, amounted to 24,446 (worth £643). Already numbers were on the decline, and four years later the regular service was taken over by the Western National Omnibus Company, although the Railway Company continued to run the summer tourist bus until 1932 - when that season's ticket sales stood at 11,138; worth £196. The types of vehicle used on these Road Motor services varied over the years, with Milnes Daimler, Maudsley and Thornycroft all being represented. They were kept in a wooden garage at the buffer-stop end of the station layout. The Exeter-based Western National company ran the Moreton to Chagford link, as service number 121, until 1934, when mutually agreed operating area changes transferred the route to the Torquay-based Devon General bus company.

Goods Department

The goods yard was situated on the north side of the layout. There were just two sidings: the 'Goods Shed Road' and the 'Back Road'. These two lines did not possess a 'headshunt' or direct connection to the main line, facing points on running lines being avoided wherever possible. Shunting thus necessitated the cumbersome procedure of drawing wagons over the diamond crossing on the main line, to the engine release loop and thence out on to the running line before setting them back. The site was dominated by the granite-built goods shed, built to the same specifications and internal layout, and by the same contractor, as that at Bovey. Likewise, it housed a 2-ton crane. The yard crane was located on the loading dock, between the shed and station building. With a length of 78 feet, the dock was able to accommodate three standard wagons. The original yard crane had been of the 4-ton variety, but around the time of the First World War was superseded by a steel lattice-built version with a 6-ton capacity, to better handle the heavy sawn timber from George Brimblecombe & Sons. At the inner end of the 17-wagon Back Siding was a Henry Pooley & Son weighbridge, with associated corrugated iron weigh house.

Although only a small yard, it handled a considerable volume of traffic, and warranted the employment of both a goods clerk and checker. The goods clerk, along with the station master, was classed as 'supervisory', and as such was salaried. Unlike the latter, however, his work went on largely unseen by the travelling public, from his small office in a corner of the goods shed. His first duty each morning was to collect the invoices for any incoming traffic from the station office. These came in daily by passenger train. Wagon labels then had to be prepared for outward-bound wagons, and goods weighed and charged as necessary. With these tasks complete, the invoices then had to be 'abstracted'; that is, their details transferred to ledgers, from which the accounts would later be prepared. Regular customers' accounts were drawn up once a month, the clerk being responsible for collecting any monies outstanding. Sometimes, several invoices piled up before the customer appeared in the office to sign for goods already received and to pay up. The matter of payment was made more contentious by the varied system of charges levied by the GWR, and even further complicated by the mixture of 'private owner' and Railway Company wagons in use.

Where customers used Railway Company wagons, they were liable to a 'demurrage charge'. After three 'free' days, demurrage was charged at around three shillings a day. Coal merchants in particular complained about these charges, even though three days would seem ample time to unload the contents. However, they liked to use the wagon itself as a 'store' - transferring the coal directly to their carts or lorries, and

In the summer of 1955, the goods shed - with the Railway's C & D lorry in attendance - is viewed from the station site's road entrance. The goods office is to the left of the loading bay, with its corrugated iron external extension of 1910 beyond. The grounded coach body was used as a store by animal feed merchant Silcock, while the wooden gas meter shed is in the right foreground.   *I. D. Beale*

thereby cutting out the need for stock-piling and reloading. If they continued with this practice, it cost them after day-three! All these details had to be recorded by the goods clerk: the dates of the wagons' arrival and subsequent departure entered in ledgers, and details of any demurrage charges calculated and charged-up to the customer. Although the clerk had got to know each client personally over the years, there were a few who seemed reluctant to pay promptly, or disputed the amount billed, and having to deal with this was not a task he relished.

Goods to be railed away from Moretonhampstead were, in the first instance, brought to the yard either by the customer or the cartage agent. Computing the rate to be charged was no easy matter; it depended upon the type of traffic, the cost per ton-mile - calculated on a sliding scale - plus, in some cases, handling charges and/or the provision of coverings (such as tarpaulins). Fortunately, the clerk had recourse to the Board of Trade's 'Railway Rate Book', which enumerated some 1,400 articles. (When the compilation began in 1852 the number of articles stood at a mere 748, but quickly grew to around 4,000 by 1890!) Once the rate had been established, the customer was issued with a receipt. Details were entered in a ledger, recording either the 'amount paid' or 'to pay'. Given the diversity of goods, customers and handling arrangements, this generated a considerable amount of paperwork. Invoices were prepared and taken to the station office for despatch by passenger train to the various receiving stations. As goods accumulated in the shed and yard, the clerk had to arrange for wagons to remove them. As the type and quantity were never the same any two days running, this was not always a straightforward affair - although

From the earliest days of the Railway, a cartage service linked station and town, with carrier John Parker additionally operating to Exeter direct on Tuesdays and Fridays (William & James Garrish providing a similar facility at Chagford). The longest association with the GWR was that of Henry James Osborne, one of whose lorries is seen here (date unknown).   *I. D. Beale Collection, courtesy Mike Jacobs*

The newly painted water tank stands out clearly in the bright winter sunshine. Engines on non-auto workings were obliged to run round their coaches at the terminus, and took on water before setting back into the platform: the procedure being followed here by 'large Prairie' No. 4150. Immediately behind the engine is the 'Goods Siding' and, beyond, several wagons occupy the 'Back Siding', at the end of which is the corrugated iron weighbridge hut. The large, pitched roof building behind it is a local coal merchant's store. 19.2.59.   *Peter W. Gray*

Table 15. Selected Traffic Returns : Moretonhampstead

YEAR	PASSENGERS				PARCELS			MILK			GOODS			LIVESTOCK	
	Tickets (Single & Return)	£	Season Tickets	£	No. Sent out	No. Received	Total Value £	No. of cans	No. of cases	Total Value £	Tonnage Despatched	Tonnage Received	Total Value £	Wagon Loads	Value £
1925	27,309	3896	153	191	4980	8,898	1189	290	-	15	3,114	12,279	7797	420	559
1926	24,130	3349	88	549	4265	11,080	1211	9	-	-	3,599	9,360	7724	385	604
1927	23,907	3097	87	125	4070	9,515	1176	-	-	-	2,680	11,361	7927	346	658
1928	20,830	2730	105	123	4460	8,877	1239	N/D	-	14	2,612	12,050	10363	316	803
1929	18,687	2421	118	127	4014	8,341	1096	63	-	3	2,673	11,063	7806	263	580
1930	15,756	2169	158	148	4018	9,550	1082	-	-	-	3,436	9,987	7033	187	379
1931	14,214	1856	150	167	3676	9,372	977	-	-	-	1,945	10,424	6474	104	273
1932	13,517	1746	179	168	3334	9,927	822	-	-	-	1,487	8,939	5506	85	254
1933	12,099	1435	212	159	3233	10,329	732	11215	-	193	1,496	9,063	5977	116	301
1934	11,990	1376	170	126	3233	10,764	831	-	-	-	1,034	8,801	5741	139	287
1935	13,671	1513	117	118	2873	10,559	542	-	-	-	603	10,541	7360	184	424
1936	13,052	1365	137	153	2938	10,155	579	-	308	7	364	10,011	5565	174	318
1937	12,550	1387	146	136	2904	9,340	601	-	-	-	374	10,350	5366	111	353
1938	10,445	1153	131	126	2916	8,718	589	-	-	-	284	9,437	5193	57	193
1939	9,078	1077	262	176	2781	8,548	577	-	-	-	427	10,723	5264	66	242
1940	7,880	1864	122	134	2624	8,275	556	-	-	-	2,419	10,479	N/D	38	N/D
1941	14,155	3238	234	216	N/D	N/D	889	94	-	6	4,079	11,551	N/D	40	N/D
1942	19,720	2589	333	303	N/D	N/D	777	29	-	2	6,317	9,453	N/D	30	N/D
1943	18,439	3401	399	386	N/D	N/D	853	39	-	2	7,561	8,645	N/D	56	N/D
1944	17,645	3371	632	524	N/D	N/D	792	-	-	-	5,050	8,311	N/D	44	N/D
1945	16,536	3401	467	375	N/D	N/D	829	817	-	32	3,446	6,988	N/D	61	N/D
1946	12,278	2816	463	394	N/D	N/D	814	1395	-	58	1,452	6,949	N/D	74	N/D
1947	10,308	2307	451	463	N/D	N/D	919	349	-	26	1,255	7,562	N/D	69	N/D
1948	8,145	1985	330	480	N/D	N/D	1082	621	-	53	1,912	7,336	N/D	64	N/D
1949	9,115	1746	591	609	N/D	N/D	757	940	19	63	2,320	7,342	N/D	82	N/D
1950	8,680	1330	582	643	N/D	N/D	880	1256	17	86	1,683	6,600	N/D	108	N/D
1951	7,281	978	502	605	3093	8,757	925	-	-	-	1,767	7,270	N/D	66	N/D
1952	10,173	1197	800	785	2467	9,026	883	47	-	8	1,538	6,833	N/D	38	N/D
1953	11,899	1534	866	877	2889	9,474	932	50	11	10	1,577	6,481	N/D	27	N/D
1954	10,818	1487	1012	928	2658	10,343	834	-	-	-	1,430	5,644	N/D	22	N/D
1955	9,927	1352	1133	919	2856	9,086	708	88	102	21	900	4,946	N/D	25	N/D
1956	9,953	1285	1085	766	1856	9,654	554	27	100	17	845	4,305	N/D	15	N/D
1957	13,351	1707	834	634	2359	9,736	597	-	101	12	963	4,566	N/D	19	N/D
1958	11,766	1554	723	682	2035	10,302	520	-	98	12	674	4,481	N/D	7	N/D

N/D = No Data available.

The 'Goods Department' personnel in 1958, on the occasion of Ern Berry's retirement. Pictured from left to right are: George Burgess (goods clerk), Jack Tanton (checker), Ern Berry (vanman) and Wilf Wright (signalman, with additional 'goods' duties).

Courtesy Valerie Huish

about when he inadvertently locked himself in a cupboard in the goods shed, remaining in uncomfortable incarceration until liberation two long hours later. Arthur was followed after the last war by Jane Tooley, wife of station master Bob; and then for much of the 1950s by George Burgess. George moved away to work as a clerk at Newton Abbot, to be replaced briefly and finally by relief clerk George Dennis.

Working in close association with the goods clerk was the checker. This job was at a grade above that of basic 'goods porter', and was held by Jack Tanton from 1936/7 until the freight operation ceased in 1964. His duties were many and varied. A large proportion of his time was concerned with the checking of goods to be forwarded against the relevant consignment note made out by the customer, inserting weights where appropriate ready for charging by the clerk. All 'traffic received' was likewise checked against invoices. This was not always as simple as it sounds, for the goods sometimes arrived several days ahead of the paperwork, so a record of the consignment had to be made. Similarly, records were kept of goods that had failed to arrive within a reasonable time after receipt of the invoices. All this created extra work for the clerk. The checker also recorded the wagon numbers 'in' and 'out', and the dates on which wagons were unloaded, to enable the clerk to compute demurrage charges. This involved dealing with wagon labels. Each truck was fitted with a metal label holder on the sole-bar; a sprung metal clip keeping the stiff paper label in place. The label showed the origin and destination of the wagon and the class of traffic it carried. All this, too, was recorded in a ledger by the goods clerk. Finally, the checker superintended the loading of goods on to road delivery vehicles.

The 'Collection and Delivery' service in the area had for a great many years been undertaken by the GWR's cartage agent, or 'carrier'. The Moreton-based carrier in the early years of the twentieth century was Harry Friend; his horse-drawn waggon being commonly seen in and around the town. The Company's parcels and goods agent in Chagford was Henry James Osborne of Rock House. Originally doing the rounds with a horse and cart, a motor lorry was employed on this work from around 1920. Following the implementation of the Newton Abbot Goods Zoning Scheme on 1st March 1947, the C&D service changed in practice if not in principle. The handling of the merchandise now passed to the Railway Company's own motor vehicles. The level of traffic at Moreton was such that it continued to receive rail-borne goods and parcels from Newton Abbot as before. Other locations on the Branch had their 'small'

in many cases he had prior notification (such as Brimblecombe's timber traffic). Wagons that had arrived earlier in the week and were now empty could be used, providing they were suitable. If no such wagons were on hand for originating traffic, the clerk submitted a request to Divisional Traffic Control at Exeter for the appropriate stock to be provided, and as a rule something could be found at Newton Abbot.

During the years that Arthur Dymond was goods clerk, the exacting and busy routine was interspersed with lighter moments. Arthur was something of a comedian, his antics and practical jokes giving rise to much mirth amongst his colleagues. Work in and around the goods shed was invariably accompanied by considerable leg-pulling, but one of the biggest laughs came

goods dealt with by the Zone 'trunk' lorry, this travelling out from Newton to the terminus each weekday, bringing 'smalls' from Heathfield and Bovey. Later, the lorry also called at Lustleigh, which had previously been covered by the vehicle based at Bovey. Another vehicle was actually based at Moreton, and it was this that delivered both rail and road borne small goods and parcels to the station's 'hinterland'. A familiar sight around the district in the early 1950s was the distinctive, slab-fronted Thornycroft 'Bantam' vehicle in its eye-catching red and cream livery with prominent banner emblem - irreverently referred to by some as a 'flying hot dog' - proclaiming in white letters 'BRITISH RAILWAYS'. Later in the decade

A 'Brimblecombe Timber' Sunday special of round timber - probably destined for use as pit props - moving carefully down the steep gradient near Sanduck Wood (date unknown).
Dartington Rural Archive

the depot took delivery of a brand new BMC lorry, which found some of the bridges on the country lanes quite a tight fit.

From 1952 the C&D lorry was driven by Ernest Berry. As a youngster of fourteen, Ern had started work with H.J. Osborne, back in the days when the delivery waggon was horse-drawn. He came to know the locality like the back of his hand, and was highly spoken of by the large number of customers he met over the years. He retired in the summer of 1958, after over fifty years service. Other 'vanmen' in the later years included porter-drivers Stan Bickham, Jim ('Backy') Bennett, Bill Westlake and Ron Holland. The goods operation continued for a few years after the closure of the Line to passenger services, and although goods trains continued to run until April 1964, it was not until the last day of that year that the lorry was withdrawn; the work being transferred to the Zone.

The goods traffic itself was substantial and varied. Minerals formed a major part of the traffic dealt with at the yard, and virtually all of this was of the loaded in/empties out variety, although a little gas works coke was sent away. Thus, in 1925 7,913 tons of mineral traffic was railed into Moreton, with only 83 tons despatched. Of the first figure, just under 64 % was coal. By way of comparison, the data for 1935 were: 6,712 tons/41 tons/71%; and for 1955 3,401 tons/149 tons/98%. An

tons, this had to be unloaded and weighed until the correct amount had been measured out.

Grain and animal feedstuffs formed another prominent type of traffic. The Bovey firm of A.J. Wyatt - later Wyatt & Bruce - established a sub-depot at Moreton, their office being near the goods yard gate. Some of the traffic received by this firm was railed-on from 'headquarters' at Bovey. Other seedsmen and agricultural merchants were Silcock's, Leavers and J. Bibby - the last-named eventually taking over Wyatt & Bruce. Large hipped-roof prefabricated extensions appended to the east wall of the goods shed facilitated the unloading of merchandise directly from railway wagons; sacks of cattle cake being especially prominent in this regard.

More occasional in occurrence was the despatch of sawn timber on behalf of George Brimblecombe & Sons. From their timber and saw mills near the gas works, the wood was brought to the yard and loaded into mineral wagons. The weight of these trains, combined with the steep down-grade to Bovey, required the provision of extra brake vans in the formation. (All freight trains leaving the terminus were required to pull up at a Stop Board 100 yards beyond the 'advanced starting' signal, by Mile Post 12, to allow brakes to be pinned down; this minimising the danger of a 'runaway' by retarding its speed. A pause was made

A 'last day' group photograph of station personnel. From left to right: George Dennis (relief goods clerk), Dave Evans (signalman), Ray Thomas (station master), Wilf Wright (signalman), Jack Tanton (checker), Jim Bennett (porter) and Reg Moore (parcels porter).   *Courtesy Valerie Huish*

important and long-term customer of the Railway was the town's small gas works. Opened in 1868, the two were virtual contemporaries, the latter being facilitated by the former. The first manager, Edward Chave, lived at Ivy Cottage, although some time later a house was built on the edge of the gas works site. Although it was located alongside the Line, near the occupation crossing at the east-end of the layout, the works did not possess its own siding. Coal was unloaded in the goods yard - generally in the back siding - and then taken the short distance by road. Domestic coal was brought in for local coal merchants, notably Messrs. Neck & Son and Moretonhampstead Co-operative Society (later taken over by the larger Newton Abbot Society). Generally, the wagons were made up as 'full loads' for one customer, so that their unloading was straightforward. However, if a merchant wanted a consignment of just a few

before the 'home' signal at Bovey to allow the brakes to be 'picked up' again.) The time necessary to load these trains, plus the sheer amount of timber involved, meant that they were run as 'specials' on a Sunday. During the Second World War trees were felled in Sanduck Wood to be used for pit-props, while other timber was sent to J.W. & A. Upham Ltd., the Brixham shipbuilder, for the construction of wooden minesweepers. After the War, until closure, sawn timber continued to be regularly despatched by rail, with Swindon being one of the regular destinations. Of particular note was the consignment of local oak sent out in 1957, again to Upham's, to be used in the making of the replica of the 'Mayflower'.

In years when there was major over-production of potatoes, surplus stock was taken away for dumping. Once loaded into mineral wagons, the Ministry of Agriculture, Fisheries & Food

A tall, distinguished lamp standard stands sentry over the cattle dock in 1921. The pens and associated fencing are built out of bridge rail. Bottom left is the oil store and one of the two lamp huts, and beyond the pens the slate-roofed, brick-built straw and sawdust store. Above the 'Toad' brake van is the local office of the Bovey-based miller and feedstuffs merchant A. J. Wyatt; while to the left of the van is the large timber-built garage for the GWR's road motor vehicles. *L&GRP*

required the contents to be soaked in blue dye to render them unfit for human consumption. Surplus of another, saleable, kind (namely scrap metal) was railed away by local merchant Sam Harris.

Cattle Dock Siding

Before the First World War, livestock played an important part in the goods traffic handled at Moreton. Of this, cattle were pre-eminent. A regular market was held in the town on the fourth Tuesday of the month - on which day an extra train was run to and from Newton Abbot for a number of years. Chagford also held a market day once a month, the animals being moved 'on the hoof' to the station afterwards. In addition, there were the famous cattle fairs at Moreton. These events took on a festive atmosphere, with wrestling tournaments - for which the town was noted - being held to entertain the crowds. The fairs were annual events, fixed by the ecclesiastical calendar; and were thus held on St. Margaret's Day (20th July), St. Michael's Day (29th September) and St. Andrew's Day (30th November). In addition, the 'Great Market' was held on the Saturday before Whitsun. Despite the prominence of the traffic generated by these fairs, the station was not initially provided with a cattle dock, the animals being dealt with at the loading platform adjoining the goods shed. This situation persisted beyond the gauge conversion of 1892 and into the twentieth century. Eventually, a dock with pens was installed at the dead-end continuation of the engine release road, which had been extended to come into alignment with the buffer stops at the end of the platform line. The siding was able to hold five standard-length wagons.

The provision of the cattle dock would appear to date from

the alteration of the Brunelian-style of track to the Great Western 'standard' type. The former consisted of iron bridge-rail on longitudinal sleepers, with well-spaced transoms: some of the track bore the stamp 'S.D.R. 1875'. Sometime between the autumn of 1910 and the spring of 1912 this was replaced with steel bull-head rails in cast iron chairs, fixed to closely spaced transverse pine sleepers. The fact that the cattle pens were made of bridge-rail - utilising a ready source to hand perhaps - gives at least an approximation of the date of installation, for from photographic and map evidence, the dock was not present in 1909 but was certainly in situ by early 1913.

The dock was reached by way of a fenced track constructed alongside an existing farm lane running behind the buffers from Station Road to fields on the south side of the tracks. Adjoining the end of the dock was a brick building used initially as a store for hay and sawdust. In later years it was used as the 'office' in which the station staff made out the labels for the cattle wagons. A water point, with hose, was provided near the front centre of the pens, to allow the dock to be washed down after use. The amount of slush produced by this process caused the track in front of the pens to be anchored to a concrete base with drainage sump. From the two large pens, individual animals were driven along the gated 'alleys' leading to the cattle wagons. The trucks were fitted with moveable wooden partitions, giving large or small floor areas as desired. Cattle specials were a feature early in the century, running 'as required' on Wednesdays only. Typically, an engine and brake van arrived from Newton Abbot at 7.50am, to leave with the 'special' at 8.15; crossing at Bovey with the first 'up' and 'down' passenger trains respectively. The cattle wagons were also used to rail out sheep and ponies.

The end of the Great War saw the demise of the large-scale movement of animals from Moreton. While the cattle fairs were no more, the station continued to handle the bulk of the Branch's livestock, although road transport began to make an ever-increasing impression. The advent of the cattle lorries did not initially take too much of the long distance trade, however, with the animals in fact being brought by road to the station from Chagford market instead of being herded as before. This continued until the early 1950s, when the service was provided by Lustleigh coal merchant W.C.& D. Waldron, whereafter the cattle were transported throughout by road. Thus from the figure of 420 wagons despatched in 1925, the volume fell away to a mere seven wagons in 1958 (see Table 15).

The siding was also involved in the handling of 'station coal'. Moretonhampstead received its annual allocation of coal in the autumn. This was made up at Swindon and sent to Newton Abbot to be forwarded to each station in turn along the Branch. It had to last a full twelve months, supplying the needs of the booking, parcels and goods offices, waiting rooms and signal box. When winters were exceptionally cold, like that of 1946-7, or spring came late, it was a struggle to eke out the supplies; and supplementary requisitions were definitely not encouraged! The sleeper-built coal store was near the foot of the path leading from the station master's house. The 'station coal' wagon arrived attached to the goods train, and was positioned in the cattle dock siding, where it was out of the way of other shunting movements and conveniently opposite the store hut. Unloading the truck was the duty of the porters, who also had to attend to the various fires in the station during the winter.

Engine Release Siding

Travelling out of the cattle dock to the cover of the train shed, a set of points operated from the signal box brought in a connection, or crossover, from the running line which enabled engines to run round their stock in the platform. This length of track ran parallel with the main line to the extreme east-end of the layout, thus serving as an engine release siding. It was on this siding, beneath the train shed, that the Branch coaching stock was stabled at the end of the day's services. At a position more or less in line with the end of the platform, a siding led off to the engine shed, its hand-operated points being switched in that direction once the stock had been berthed, as a safeguard in the event of the unattended vehicles running away.

Engine Shed Siding

At the station end of the siding was the small depot belonging to the Permanent Way Gang. Their 'base of operations' consisted of a moderately-sized whitewashed granite building, with a forwardly-sloping roof and furnished with a small fire-grate. Abutting this on the east was an almost equally sized timber-built structure which served as a store for the variety of tools and equipment used by the men. Their territory, or 'length', extended from the buffer stops at the station to the 7¾ mile post at Hawkmoor Halt. The inspection trolley assigned to the Gang was one of the three-wheelers, as at Bovey. It may only have been hand-operated, but it could be got up to quite respectable speeds on the steeply graded section between Budleigh occupation crossing and Lustleigh. Rattling down the 1:49 bank at Caseley, the 16-chain curve there frequently caused the 'nearside' single wheel to lift momentarily and disconcertingly off the rail. Fortunately the vehicle, though flimsy to look at, was extremely stable!

As the 'boss', the ganger was responsible for prioritising, organising and superintending the daily work schedule for the five-strong team; the hours being from 7.30 in the morning until 5pm. A name frequently heard in relation to the permanent way

Below: Looking east from the end of the platform in 1949. From left to right, the tracks are: 'back (or mileage) siding', 'goods shed siding', 'platform (or running) line', 'engine release road' and 'engine shed siding'. *S. J. Dickson*

Above: Under the watchful eye of the fireman, 0-6-0 Pannier Tank No. 3796 takes on water - capacity 1,200 gallons - at the column prior to working back to Newton Abbot in the summer of 1957. Built in 1938, the engine spent most of its B.R. days at Newton, moving for its final two years' service to South Wales before withdrawal in March 1965. *G. Howells*

Left: This picture taken in the summer of 1959 shows the lineside accoutrements of the engine shed siding. The water crane below the elevated water tank is clearly seen; the limited clearance here dictating its attachment to the underside of the tank. Next comes the simple timber-built coal stage, its purpose being to service the Branch locomotive shedded overnight. The whitewashed granite masonry hut served as the 'home-base' for the Moretonhampstead Permanent Way Gang, the timber-built structure adjoining its east wall being their equipment store.
S. J. Dickson

gang is that of Jim Wright. Jim began his railway career the day after his fourteenth birthday. Working as a lengthman at Starcross, he daily walked the mile and a half from his home in Kenton. He later became sub-ganger, or 'second man', and in 1919 moved to Moreton as ganger. During his long 'reign', the day traditionally began with an egg and bacon breakfast in the P.W. hut; indeed, Jim was justly renowned for his early morning fry-ups! Eggs were easy to come by, as chickens were kept on part of the railwaymen's allotments on the south side of the station layout. Alternatively, they could, along with the bacon, be bought from local farmers. Following good Railway tradition, the meal was cooked on a shovel. Although it was thoroughly cleaned off before being put to this use, an old well-used shovel was better than a newer one - the latter tending to cause the contents to spit a lot and cook less evenly. Jim also managed to acquire the occasional rabbit, which he gladly sold to train crews for sixpence each; while locomotive coal bunkers would periodically play host to bundles of bean sticks which had also been procured through his good offices. (Sometimes the footplatemen on the daily goods train were able to supply their own sticks. The crew would make enough time to stop the train - usually in a cutting where they could not be seen - clamber off the footplate and pick the sticks from a favoured line-side spot noted on an earlier trip.) Jim should have retired early in the

Second World War, but was asked to stay on. When his railway career ended finally at the age of seventy, the long years of arduous and dedicated service to the GWR were rewarded with a miserly pension of four shillings a week.

Jim's three sons all worked for the GWR: Victor and Bob became engine drivers (Bob having previously spent time as a fireman on the Branch). Wilfred worked in a different department, including a few years in the signal box at Moreton - as did his sister Edna during the Second World War. Jim's sub-ganger was Frank Rice, whose son Fred also worked on the Railway: as a goods guard based at Newton Abbot. Jim Wright and Frank Rice were joined by various lengthmen over the years, including: Messrs. Snow, Langworthy, Yeo and Gilham. Following Jim's retirement at the end of the war, Frank Rice was promoted ganger and George Snow 'second man'. Their lengthmen were Bert Gilham and Albert Treen. When Bert Gilham left the gang, his place was taken by Bill Westlake. Stan Winsor joined the team for the last few years, having previously been a member of the Christow-based Teign Valley gang. Later, George Snow succeeded to the position of ganger, the last person to hold that post at Moreton, while Bill Westlake left the gang to work in the station's goods department.

Next to the permanent way depot, on Engine Shed Siding, was the coal stage. A timber-built, open deck-like structure measuring approximately 20' x 10' it served as the coal store for the Moreton-based Branch engine. Wagons of 'loco coal' arrived, as required, attached to the goods train. Engines would generally only top-up their bunkers during the overnight stop, the major coaling taking place at Newton Abbot during the working day. The 0-4-2 Collett tank engines, incidentally, had a coal capacity of 2 tons 13 cwt; and a 'small Prairie' 3 tons 14 cwt.

The quality of the coal was often unpredictable, which could result in the fireman having a hard time. This was especially the case when the supplies took the form of briquettes or ovoids. The first problem with the former was to break them into sizes that could be shovelled up easily. They were often so hard that this was not as straightforward as it might seem. Bringing down the point of pick axe with all his force, a man often found that instead of the block breaking, the axe lodged firmly and was difficult to work free. Even when the briquettes had been reduced, their sheer hardness was a problem, for they tended to settle and lie in the fire as a solid mass. So although the fire might look good and bright on top, it was in fact going out underneath, and required urgent attention. The oval-shaped nuggets, widely known by locomen as 'egglets', were as bad, though in a different way. Superficially they burned very well, but had a tendency to settle into a tar-like mass on the bottom of the firebox, where they would stick to the firebars and drip with a treacle-like viscosity into the ash pan. In time, the presence of this tacky veneer over the bars reduced the air supply, which did not do the fire any good - while it was also possible for the contents of the ash pan to catch fire.

Some coal produced a great deal of ash, so much so that the ash pan became full to the brim before the end of the turn of duty. This increased the likelihood of damage to the lugs by which the firebars were fitted into the grate. Contact with the hot ash, especially when the bars were already old, sometimes resulted in a lug or lugs burning through, which caused the bar/s to drop. Once back on shed it was necessary to shovel out the contents of the firebox in order to replace the bars. The fitter at Newton Abbot responsible for this was the 'fire-dropper', and it was an extremely unpleasant duty. Once the fire had been removed, and while the firebox was still very hot, he manoeuvred himself into it through the stoke-hole to replace the bars by hand. He worked stripped to the waist, so hot was it inside the firebox.

If the quality of the coal was unpredictable, that of the water supply was a known entity. An elevated tank alongside the engine shed siding, next to the coal stage, supplied the water crane beneath, the non-drinking water requirements at the station and, later, a water column situated between the running line and goods shed siding. This was installed in response to the introduction of auto trains over the full length of the Branch in the mid 1930s. It removed the inconvenience of the locomotive having to uncouple from the coaching stock and transfer to the water tower. A 'fire-devil' - brazier with long stove-pipe - was provided at the column as much to keep the leather hose supple in bitter winter weather as the water from freezing. As a preliminary to the earthworks involved in laying out the site at Moreton, the tiny Wadley Brook had to be diverted and culverted to run beneath the railway property in the shortest distance. Rising a mile and a half away at Bughead Cross, the constancy of supply was adequate to meet the Railway's needs, but would have involved pumping up to the header tank. To avoid this expense, the M&SDR looked for a source with a sufficient natural 'head' to allow gravity feeding of the tank. This condition was fulfilled by the stream that drained the northern and western slopes of Hingston Down. At Budleigh Farm the tiny tributary entered the main valley, about 40' above the track level at the station. Fortunately for the Company the land was owned by the Earl of Devon and worked by a tenant, John Harvey, who had been an enthusiastic supporter of the Railway from the beginning. Water was drawn off from near the farmhouse and piped the half-mile or so through the Earl's land to the tank; the M&SDR having to pay an annual rental of £5 for the privilege. The water meter was housed in a manhole by the occupation crossing at the gas works, its reading being one of the occasional duties of the ganger.

The 'Shore to Moor' nature of the Branch was clearly reflected in the matter of water supply. Engines could only take on water at either end of the Line; there were no intermediate facilities. Geography played the key role in determining the quality of the water. The layout at Newton Abbot was supplied from the River Teign, just above its confluence with the River Lemon. From an intake on the river's right bank, at the brick-built pumping station, the Teign water - with perhaps a dash of Lemon! - was fed to the elevated tank near the Moretonhampstead Bay platform and to another at the motive power depot. From these it was gravity fed to various locations around the layout: the water column for Branch trains being situated at the north end of the Bay, between the 'No.9 platform' and 'up through' roads - permitting use by either. The system itself was fine; the problem lay in the quality of the water. Though at the head of the Teign estuary, the river was still tidal and thus somewhat brackish. Its lack of purity was further aggravated by silting - as witnessed by the expanse of mud flats at low tide - and by the presence of extremely fine clay particles carried in suspension from the works a little way upstream. The water was pumped from the river when the tide was on the ebb, for then the ratio of river water to brackish water was in the former's favour. Even so, the water was still 'dirty', in spite of filtration. Sometimes it was necessary to pump water when the tide was rising to maintain supplies; as the regime at the MPD had to function irrespective of tide times. The situation was particularly acute during the 'thirsty' summer weekends, when the depot played host to an increased number of locomotives involved with the holiday excursion traffic.

The problem with dirty water was its tendency to induce 'priming', especially with a full boiler. The increased concentration of dissolved salts sometimes caused the water to effervesce vigorously, with the result that instead of steam alone being fed to the cylinders and exhausted through the chimney, it was accompanied by scalding water. When this happened, footplate crews could expect problems, not only with the performance of the engine, but also to their own safety as boiling water rained down on the cab. An indication that a loco was priming was a profusion of hazy white smoke pouring from the chimney.

In marked contrast, the water available at Moretonhampstead was excellent. The granite mass of Dartmoor produced naturally soft water, while the short distance from the source to the intake at Budleigh gave little chance for contamination. With an annual rainfall total twice that of the sheltered coast just a few miles away, there was an abundant supply of pure water. The climb from Bovey to the terminus demanded some hard work from the tank engines employed on the Branch. The '1400' class of 0-4-2 tank engine used extensively from the end of the 1930s only had an 800-gallon capacity, and consequently could not avoid taking on 'Teign water' at Newton during their turn of duty. The policy was to fill up with clean moorland water at Moreton before travelling to Newton; a journey which was predominantly on falling gradients and thus relatively easy on water consumption. At the main line destination the tanks would just be topped up. The other widely represented class of engine used on the Branch - the 'small Prairie' - had a larger capacity: 1,000 gallons in the case of the first series with straight tank tops; and 1,300 in the later ones with sloping tops. In the last years, the B.R. Standard Class 3 '82xxx' tank engines and 'large Prairies' had capacities of 1,500 and 2,000 gallons respectively. The principle, however, remained the same: fill up at Moreton, top up at Newton. Thus when the larger capacity engines left Newton with full tanks at the beginning of a tour of duty on the Branch, the driver would divest his charge of as much 'Teign water' as was safely possible before reaching the moorland terminus. This was generally done on the final steep climb above Lustleigh. Water was fed from the tanks to the boiler by means of injectors, requiring the opening of both water and steam valves (the loco's steam created a vacuum that drew the water into the boiler). By turning the steam cock off, but leaving the water valve open, water drained away via a pipe beneath the coal bunker.

The siding continued beyond the water tower to end at the engine shed: a solid granite building measuring approximately 43 feet by 22 feet. Four round-arched windows in both side walls admitted plenty of light, although the positioning of the signal box against the north wall cut this down a little. The major feature of both the end elevations was a large arched entrance. That at the front was provided with heavy timber sliding double doors. The rear arch was boarded up, although the fact that it existed might suggest that there was an intention to continue the siding beyond the shed. The ridge line of the low-pitched slate roof was surmounted by a louvred, hip-roofed smoke vent. The track inside the shed was provided with an inspection-cum-maintenance pit, while a little way in front of the building was an ash pit. Between these two there once existed a turntable. Surprisingly perhaps, this survived the narrowing of gauge in 1892 and was still present in the first few years of the twentieth century, although had gone by 1913 (the turntable pit being filled in).

For the quarter century or so before 1946, a shedman was employed to look after the Branch engine overnight and attend to various shed labouring duties. Throughout the period, this post was the province of Billy Mears. Though not a member of the footplate grades, he was authorised to move the engine within 'shed limits' as required by its servicing needs: such as out to the ash pit, water crane or coal stage. His main job was to attend to the fire and check the water level; dispose of ash, cinders and clinker ('smokebox char') from the site; unload loco coal from wagons at the coal stage; and generally keep the engine clean. This latter duty involved using a ball of cotton waste and paraffin jelly - and plenty of elbow grease! By the end of his shift, Billy had the engine nicely simmering in readiness for the arrival of the 'early turn' crew, who would then attend to the finishing touches before taking it off shed to collect the carriages for the first service of the day to Newton Abbot. This regime dictated that the shedman worked permanent nights. As the Branch loco was not required on Sundays - the summer Sunday trains were covered by Newton Abbot shed - it was the job of the fireman on Saturday night to 'drop' the fire, thereby giving Billy a night off.

Offset from the north-east corner of the shed was the small locomen's cabin. Also of granite construction, with low-pitched slate roof and brick chimney-stack, it measured some 17 feet by 11 feet. It served as the base for Moreton's two sets of enginemen. In the inter-war years, the drivers had been J. Williams, Walter Aplin and Sam Pearce; while firemen included B. Sanders, Reg Harris and Jim Farr. The last-named moved as a boy to Moretonhampstead from Brixham in 1919. Occupying the post of 'cleaner', he lodged in the town. The work was by its very nature dirty and hard, while the hours were 'unsocial' - and the wages minimal. Soon afterwards, these duties passed to the newly created post of 'shedman' as described above; although at Moreton it generally continued to be referred to as that of 'cleaner'. Meanwhile, Jim Farr had passed the examination on basic rules, and moved up a rung as it were to become a fireman on the Branch. During the 1920s and '30s he fired to Walter Aplin and Sam Pearce, men with very different temperaments. This stood Jim in good stead when, as a driver himself, he came to pass on his knowledge to others. Married in 1924, he and his wife Mary opened their home to other railwaymen, providing bed and breakfast for men who had to lodge at the terminus overnight. Principally this involved those on relief duties, covering for regular personnel who were on leave or rest days. It was around 1941 that Jim was promoted to driver; again on the Branch. To help young firemen gain the necessary knowledge to similarly progress, he held impromptu instruction sessions in his home. In these homely 'classes', Jim enlisted the aid of a blackboard, posititioned near the old black coal-fired range in his kitchen. His first 'pupil' was Bob Wright - son of ganger Jim Wright - followed by Frank Radcliff and then, in 1945/6, Des Lock. Once 'passed', Frank moved away to Exeter, while Des had begun his railway career as a cleaner at Taunton. Following promotion to fireman, the expectation of men generally was of a move away from the 'home' shed. Reporting to the office, proudly in possession of his newly-acquired registration number, Des was told to report to Moretonhampstead the following Monday. There could hardly be a greater contrast between the busy shed with which he was familiar and the one-engine/two-shift location of which he had never even heard. Duly taking up lodgings in the Farr household, Des spent a hardworking but pleasurable time at the tiny depot, gaining familiarity with the working of auto trains, in which the fireman was left alone in the loco's cab when in 'propelling mode'. He soon moved on to gain wider footplate experience, as indeed did his mentor Jim, who eventually rose to become a locomotive inspector at Bristol.

The 'early turn' locomen booked on duty at around half past six, to attend to the final stages of preparation. The driver oiled around the engine and conducted a thorough check to ensure that everything was in order; while the fireman ascertained the water level, built up the fire and generally 'cleaned around the cab'. Finally, he checked the sandboxes and collected the lamps. Upon completion, the engine moved off shed to collect the coach or coaches on the engine release siding, a good twenty minutes before departure in order to allow time for the steam heating in the carriages to take effect. At the other end of the day, the 'late turn' crew brought the engine back to the shed for 'disposal'. On Mondays to Fridays, when the loco would be booked out again the following morning, its fire simply required 'cleaning' rather than being 'dropped'. To aid this, the fireman endeavoured not to have a large fire in the box on the final stage of the journey out from Newton Abbot. Once on shed, the remaining live coal was pushed to the front of the firebox with a fire-iron, separating it from the burnt coal and clinker, which was shovelled out through the stoke-hole and thrown down on the ground. The live fire was then drawn back and spread, to keep the engine in light steam. Only on a Saturday night was the fire 'dropped', that is, removed completely.

In 1946 the post of shedman was abolished. This of necessity changed the regime at the shed. On a Monday morning the fireman arrived for work about three hours earlier than usual to get the engine ready from cold. A small amount of coal was shovelled into the firebox, along with a number of wooden firelighters and/or paraffin-soaked rags distributed within the fire. As it began to build up, the through draught between chimney and firebox via the boiler tubes helped to intensify the blaze and so allow more coal to be added. Periodic checks were made on the steam pressure gauge, until there was sufficient to move the engine out to the water crane to fill up the tanks. Coaling now took place at Newton Abbot, saving the need to transport loco coal out to the terminus and thereby rendering the coal stage redundant. When the first 'up' train of the day - the 7.50am from Moretonhampstead - arrived at Newton, the engine was transferred to the motive power depot to take on coal. With its sizeable allocation of locomotives, the operation was on a carefully organised scale. Seven or eight trucks of loco coal were generally marshalled on the coal stage road, being moved as required by a 'spare' engine. The coal was shovelled out of the trucks and into tub-like wagons, which were wheeled on tracks over the stage floor and tipped into the tenders/bunkers of locos waiting below. Each engine's allocation was logged in the coalmen's book. It was hard, unremitting, backbreaking work, made worse by the wooden plank wagons of Great Western days, when shovels caught in the battered and splintered timbers of the wagon bottoms. With the advent of all-steel wagons, this became less tedious, as shovels slid easily over the smooth wagon floors.

Above: The signal box and engine shed (GWR No. 103) in 1960. For some ten years past, the shed - and purpose-built brick bunkers by the entrance - had been let to the local branch of the Newton Abbot Co-operative Society. *BR/OPC*

Below: The signal box and engine shed/enginemen's cabin from the east end. *BR/OPC*

The following year, 1947, a further change took place. By the autumn, concern was growing over the condition of the engine shed: a couple of large cracks had appeared above the arched entrance and, more urgently, part of the louvred smoke vent seemed in danger of imminent collapse. This may well have contributed to the decision to run the engine back 'light' to Newton after the last 'down' working of the day and back the following morning. On 22nd November the shed was officially closed. Given the fact that the roof was eventually repaired, the closure was probably due more to considerations linked with operational and financial expediency. The advertised Branch train services, however, adhered to

the old pattern, starting and finishing at the terminus, although the overnight stabling of the engine at Newton (and from 1956 the whole train) took direct involvement with locos and locomen away from Moretonhampstead for the first time since the Line opened in 1866. In 1949, when the necessary roof repairs had been carried out, the Co-operative Society leased the disused engine shed as a coal store; the large sliding front doors being removed at this time.

The Signal Box

With its operating floor at rail level, the small non-standard design signal box was built as a lean-to structure against the north wall of the engine shed. Of neat brick and timber construction, with sloping slate roof and tall brick chimney

stack, it dated almost certainly from the time of the gauge conversion of 1892, when the Branch was fully signalled. A 'gong' type bell on the instrument shelf provided coded communication with the signal box at the other end of the section (Bovey), with a repeating bell in the station office to keep staff there informed of train movements. The periodicity and nature of the work undertaken in the box meant that it was only assigned a 'Class 5' status, the lowest on the Branch (Bovey was a Class 4 box and Heathfield a Class 3). Technical details of the signalling arrangements are given in Chapter 6.

Signal box personnel exemplify both the 'family' and long-service tradition so prevalent at Moretonhampstead. Signalman Robert ('Bob') Sawyer spent much of his working life at the terminus. His earlier career had taken him, at the age of nineteen, to a signal box at Newport Docks, where he was caught up in a short-lived but extremely bitter strike, requiring constant police protection for a time. In 1921 he arrived at Moreton, where he remained until retirement at the age of 65. He took great pride in his work, and kept the signal box in immaculate condition. As at Bovey, signalmen were required to undertake other duties; consequently Bob spent a considerable proportion of his time assisting with the work in the goods yard. Unlike Bovey, however, the Moreton men had to attend to their own signal lamps. Because this had to be undertaken in between trains, it was a job that took two days: one to deal with those at the station, and another with that out at the distant signal, almost half a mile from the box. Sometimes the ganger would very obligingly attend to the latter as he walked by on his inspection of the length.

In 1931 Bob was joined on the opposite turn by Jack Cornish, who transferred from the same grade at Longdown on the Teign Valley Branch. During the Second World War, men were often moved to other places, and the shortfall in new manpower caused by conscription to the Armed Forces was made up for by the recruitment of women. Understandably, Railway families were a prime source of these much-needed new employees, and with its strong tradition in this regard, Moreton-hampstead was no exception. Thus Marjorie Yeoman was employed in the signal box for three and a half years, between 1942 and 1945. Her father-in-law, Harry Yeoman, was a long-serving porter at the station. Edna Wright, daughter of ganger Jim Wright, also worked in the signal box; additionally undertaking occasional guard's relief duties. (Another lady guard, Ellen Perrott, was the aunt of Mary Farr, driver Jim Farr's wife.) Edna was something of a practical joker, helping to relieve the gloom of the war years. On one occasion, she generously undertook to provide packets of cheese sandwiches for the train crew's meal break - except that the cheese was actually soap. This produced some choice rejoinders, but at least the men had

no difficulty in washing their mouths out! They got their own back not long afterwards by soaking her with water as she walked past the water column.

Another member of the Wright family worked in the signal box in its last few years: Wilfred. He had started his railway career at the beginning of the War as a lad-porter at Heathfield. Following a short time as booking boy at Newton Abbot East Signal Box, he moved to Lustleigh as porter. In December 1946 he transferred to Minehead, before returning to Devon to work in the signal box at Dawlish Warren. This was followed by relief signalling duties in the Newton Abbot area, a role that occasionally brought him 'home' to Moretonhampstead to provide cover for the regular men. After a brief spell in the Midlands, he returned to Moreton in 1952/3 as one of the 'resident' signalmen. In the post-war years, there was a succession of mostly young, short-stay signalmen, beginning with Bert Rowell - who eventually became an inspector at Newton Abbot station - and continuing with Stan Rowe, Bernard Cann, Cliff Pearce, and Gordon Vowden, before the final partnership of Welshman Dave ('Taff') Evans and 'local lad' Wilf Wright in the period leading up to the closure of the box in 1959. With homes many miles away, both Bernard and Cliff lodged in Moreton, the latter with the Pike household, whose son Edward also embarked on a railway career: as clerical officer in the Locomotive Department at Newton Abbot and then, following its closure, at Exmouth Junction (Exeter). When a vacancy arose in the signal box at Kingskerswell, conveniently near his Torquay home, Cliff moved there, and later to Torquay itself. Stan and Gordon transferred to other 'branch line' boxes - Trusham and Bovey respectively - before moving on to main line locations. Both men eventually came back to work as relief signalmen in the busy boxes in and around Newton Abbot (and in Gordon's case, the 'high-tech' panel box at Exeter that superseded them).

Engine shed and enginemen's cabin seen from the south east in the summer of 1955.
I. D. Beale

Postscript

THE AXE AND AFTER

The first service trains of the day cross at Bovey for the very last time. The 7.50am from Newton Abbot, in the charge of 0-4-2T No. 1466, waits for 'large Prairie' No. 5196 with the 'up' service to clear the single line section to Moreton. Being the last day of passenger operation, both trains comprise 3 non-corridor coaches instead of the usual two on the 'up' train and single auto trailer on the 'down'. 28.2.59. *Peter W. Gray*

"The British Transport Commission hereby give notice that they propose, subject to the approval of the South Western Area Transport Users' Consultative Committee to whom the matter has been referred, to withdraw the passenger train service between Newton Abbot and Moretonhampstead." Such was the ominous opening sentence of the notice issued from Paddington on Saturday 12th July 1958. The axe was poised.

For a few years previously there had been rumours of possible closure. Moreton Branch station masters had received a missive from the Railway Executive's Western Region, dated 30th July 1952, which spoke of the need "to ascertain what staff will be necessary to cover the work at your station in the event of it being decided to withdraw the Passenger Train Services." Though extremely disconcerting at the time, the threat receded for a while, only to resurface four years later when the Princetown Branch across the Moor was axed (in March 1956). Even more menacing was the phrase "unremunerative railway passenger services" which now began to be used in correspondence and questionnaires emanating from 'Division' in Exeter.

The news, in 1958, that the neighbouring Teign Valley and Dart Valley branch lines were to close - on 9th June and 3rd November respectively - set alarm bells ringing in the communities served by the 'Moorland Railway'. An anxious Moretonhampstead Parish Council urgently petitioned British Railways for a definitive statement on the future of their line. They received what seemed to be a reassuring reply, in the short-term at least, namely, that: "....its future was merely under consideration, together with that of many other lines." This information was relayed to councillors at their July meeting: it was safe to assume that there was no immediate threat. In the light of this, it is hardly surprising that the publication of the closure proposal the same month came as something of a bombshell. While it remained as a declaration of intent, perhaps there was hope that the Line might be saved, but there was a strong feeling that the Council had been deliberately misled, and clarification was urgently sought. In response, a BR spokesman at Exeter, Mr. L.W. Perry, stated that the Council had evidently misinterpreted the original reply, for "....it is a fact that it is the intention of the Railway Executive to withdraw passenger trains from the Moretonhampstead line." It transpired that on the very day the Council had been told that there was no immediate threat, the decision to close the Line had already been taken and the Branch personnel informed.

If the Moreton Council felt deceived and worried, grave concern was also felt by the other civic bodies along the Line: Lustleigh Parish Council, Bovey Tracey Town Council and

Newton Abbot Urban and Rural District Councils. Each of them hurriedly called meetings to discuss the closure proposal, spearheaded by Bovey on Monday 14th July. Time was of the essence, for the BTC was clearly intent on pruning the Branch from the railway network, their assertion being that annual losses were running at £17,000. No serious investigation had been undertaken into how operating costs might be reduced, nor was any desire shown to engage in a meaningful process of consultation. It was an undeniable fact that both passenger and goods revenue was declining, but compared with many other branch lines it was not a hopelessly uneconomic proposition. Given some good will and serious thinking by management with regard to cost-cutting exercises, many believed that the downward trend could be turned round, and traffic won back. Central to this belief was the replacement of steam traction with new, cheaper to run diesel railcars; rationalisation of signalling; and the provision of a timetable more responsive to the needs of the travelling public. There was uncertainty and frustration in the locality as just how to go about registering objections. At a meeting of Newton Abbot UDC, Mr. D.W.C. Shute commented on the elusive nature and workings of the TUCC: "We do not know the members of the Transport Users' Consultative Committee. We do not know who to put pressure on." Significantly, railway employees were barred from sitting on, or giving evidence to, the regional Transport Users' Consultative Committees on the grounds that they had a vested interest. These committees had been set up by the Transport Act of 1947, but it was not until 1964 that this proscription on personnel was lifted. It was no wonder that the 'railway town' of Newton Abbot felt so aggrieved.

There were serious misgivings generally about the whole way the case for closure had been prepared. Many local railwaymen were critical of the way that data had been collected, and suspected that British Railways were somewhat selective in the statistics they quoted in support of their case. Thus the daily average number of passengers joining and alighting from trains at each station and halt were "based on a count taken during a week in 1957." The question was: which week? During the summer months and on Bank Holidays the Branch trains were very well patronised, providing average daily totals greatly in excess of those quoted by BR, which led to the belief that the census must have been taken at the quietest time of the year. In any case, could figures from a single week be sufficient to permit an extrapolation into a representative overall picture? Many doubted that this could be so. Also, a great deal of new paint was suddenly in evidence in the period leading up to the closure announcement. It seemed strange that it was so urgently and expensively required in so many places at the same time: especially on non-essential features like the water tower at Moretonhampstead or the little-used waiting shelter at Pullabrook Halt, which were otherwise in a sound state of repair.

Petitions against the proposed closure were organised throughout the area, and evoked an enormous response from the public. Further meetings were called in an urgent endeavour to stave off the impending disaster; one such on Thursday 31st July bringing together the councils of Moretonhampstead, Lustleigh and Bovey. Unfortunately all this activity was to no avail. The bureaucrats of the British Transport Commission were unsympathetic and unyielding. In their eyes the case for retaining the Line's passenger services was weakened by the existence of a virtually parallel bus route. Only the handful of dwellings with proximity to the isolated Pullabrook Halt did not have, or would be unsuitable for, an alternative bus service. This reduced any arguments put forward against closure on the grounds of hardship - in its broadest sense - despite the fact that the bus took over half as long again as the train to complete the journey. On a more important level, however, was the fact that,

even with double-deckers, buses had a greatly reduced capacity for both passengers and small parcels. There was also the concern that the narrow, winding A382 between Bovey and Moreton, along with the already considerable volume of traffic in the Newton - Heathfield area, would disrupt timetable schedules in the summer and be liable to restrictions in the winter caused by bad weather. Such vital considerations cut no ice with the Commission, who made arrangements for the replacement bus services and staff redeployment or redundancy with almost indecent haste.

The body charged with looking after the interests of rail users, the TUCC, seemed to be content to rubber-stamp the plans although, rather unrealistically, did recommend that the position be reviewed following the introduction of diesel railcars in the area (which was not officially scheduled until 1961). Thus it was a matter of only a few months after the closure was proposed that the intention was formally confirmed. Notices to this effect were posted at stations and halts along the Line: the axe was to fall on Monday 2nd March 1959. As there was no Sunday service in the winter months, the last day of operation would be Saturday 28th February. For many people, it just did not seem possible that this could happen; they seemed to have been railroaded - if that is not an unfortunate use of the colloquialism! Last-ditch hopes were pinned on a deputation to the Minister of Transport, Harold Watkinson. Led by Ray Mawby, MP for Totnes, it was hoped that the minister could be convinced of the viability of the Line, especially if diesel railcars could be used. The group went with a well-argued case, based on economic reality rather than sentiment, but were coldly informed in no uncertain terms that there would be no reprieve. Not willing to let the Line die without a fight, Mr. Mawby made further representations to the ministry, but returned from Westminster to his home in Kingsteignton on 27th February with the disappointing, but not really unexpected, news that he had received no further word from Mr. Watkinson. The fate of the Moretonhampstead Branch was thus sealed: the next day was to be the last for passenger trains after 92 years of continuous service.

The Last Day

The last day would be a memorable event in its own right, but the weather that year was to make it more so. The whole of February had been unusually dry and mild. In the final week, locals and enthusiasts alike had been able to take their last journeys on the Branch in perfect spring-like weather. By Friday, the penultimate day, the temperature had reached an unseasonal 62 degrees Fahrenheit, and was expected to rise over the weekend. Before dawn on 28th, the two tank engines diagrammed for the early turns of duty were prepared at Newton Abbot Shed: 0-4-2 number 1466 and 'large Prairie' number 5196. As large numbers of people would inevitably be travelling on the Line on this special, if sad, day, the normal carriage allocation was augmented, with both sets used on the morning services consisting of three non-corridor coaches. At five minutes to seven, the 'Prairie' set off with its empty first and second class carriage stock to the terminus ready to work the 7.50 'up' departure (and subsequently the 9.20am from Newton Abbot, and the 10.15 return from Moretonhampstead). Normally, 1466 would have collected a single auto-trailer and left Newton at the same time to run as an advertised service to Totnes, from where the first 'down' Moreton service of the day originated. On this day, however, the turn of duty was to begin at Newton Abbot with three non-corridor coaches (numbers 6837, 2642 and 4289), though with the usual departure time from there of 7.50am.

After returning from Moreton with the 8.40 service, 1466 made two more round trips; the last of these being the 12.50pm from Newton, and 1.35 return from Moretonhampstead. The driver was dismayed to find that the loading for this train had been increased by the addition of an extra carriage to cater for the increasing number of passengers wishing to travel over the Line. (People were coming not just from the local communities, but from all over the South West and even as far afield as London and the Midlands.) Indeed, the four coaches were already well-filled. Fearing that his engine would be unable to cope with this load unassisted on the steeply graded northern half of the Line, he flatly refused to take the train out. After an altercation with officialdom, in which the driver remained intransigent, it was decided to remove the extra coach, its occupants transferring to the others. Thus, when it finally left Newton Abbot the train was full and standing. The run to Bovey was uneventful, but then 1466 really had her work cut out to pull the heavy train up the bank to the moorland terminus. With regulator wide open, and a sharp, barking exhaust raising the echoes, the little Collett tank engine struggled valiantly up the testing gradients. The powerful blast from the chimney and draught through the boiler tubes was such that not only did the loco's fire burn fiercely, but ash, cinders and even pieces of live coal were drawn from the firebox and forcibly expelled in the exhaust. Given the lack of recent rainfall, the ground had become tinder-dry and there was a very high fire-risk in the area generally, as attested-to by large heath fires on the Saturday near the roads from Manaton to Bovey and Haytor. Thus in its pyrotechnic progress northwards it is not surprising that the loco started a number of fires, a few of which continued to burn for some time afterwards.

The late turn loco, 'large Prairie' number 4117, worked the remaining trips, beginning with the 2.15pm from Newton. This comprised four well-filled non-corridor coaches: the same three that had been assigned to 1466, plus number 7087. The next 'down' train was the 4.25pm, which left, six minutes late, from the main line station rather than the Moretonhampstead Bay (Platform 9). The earlier complement of four coaches had now been joined by a fifth (number 821) which had been chartered for the round trip by the South Devon Railway Preservation Society, a group officially inaugurated that very day with a view to reinstating services on the Branch. Boys from Exeter School secured a wreath to the locomotive's smokebox. The sun continued to shine, though by now rather low in the sky; and as the last train to leave in daylight it was full: as was the 6.05 and, finally, the 8.15pm. If the atmosphere throughout resembled something of a carnival, the occasion it marked was none-the-less deeply felt. Whole families had turned out in the course of the day to take a very last ride on, or simply watch, the trains, and bid farewell to a Line which had meant so much to their communities for so long. But now the end had almost come, and crowds gathered on the Bay platform at Newton Abbot to await the very last Branch passenger train. When the end came, there were not many people left on the platform to wave the train off, as most were on it! On normal occasions, the 8.15 returned from Moretonhampstead as empty carriage stock, leaving the terminus at 9 o'clock. To enable people to make a return journey, this very last train was re-timed to depart at 9.15 as an advertised service - though calling only at Bovey and Heathfield.

The four-coach train was packed with around 250 people, some of them standing. Slogans had been chalked on some of the compartment windows, one of which - "Sack Sir Brian Robertson" (the chairman of the British Transport Commission) - though humorous in expression, portrayed a widely-held feeling of anger that the Commission had needlessly sacrificed the Branch. As the train pulled out of the platform, three minutes late, it was accompanied by a loud eight-shot volley of fog detonators which had been placed on the track. The Line was not going to die quietly. The 64 year-old driver, himself coming towards the end of his railway career, sounded 4117's whistle in a prolonged series of 'crows' as the train moved parallel with the main line towards East Signal Box, these being answered by other engines in the vicinity. There was much whistling as the train approached Teigngrace Halt, but there were no passengers or sightseers here. As the guard took down the hurricane lamp from the post by the station name-board, someone on the train with an ironic sense of humour yelled out, "Change here for Crewe!" At Heathfield and Brimley Halt small crowds were waiting to see the train off, with a few boarding to take their last ride. At Bovey there was a much bigger reception committee, with a number of people joining the train. With whistle blowing, the train stormed off into the darkness for Pullabrook Halt, whose tiny platform required the train to 'pull up' to make sure that passengers could alight from any of the compartments of the non-corridor stock. At Lustleigh, which had always given the Line good patronage, a small crowd was present; a few of whom waited on to wave their valediction as the train ran through non-stop on its return to Newton Abbot. The largest crowd was reserved for Moretonhampstead, where people thronged the platform to await the arrival of the train. Their numbers were swelled as people left the train, and there was much taking of photographs. As the engine ran round the carriages in readiness for the return, Jim Fursden of Widecombe began to play "Auld Lang Syne" on a trumpet, to be taken up in song by the assembled by-standers, passengers and railway staff. Those making the final journey piled back into the compartments, and just before the guard waved the train out, Jim very poignantly sounded the "Last Post".

At 9.17pm on Saturday 28th February 1959 the last public passenger train pulled out of the Moretonhampstead terminus. The engine's farewell whistle was answered by motorists sounding their horns, while the explosion of some two dozen detonators drowned out the cheers of the waving crowd on the platform. Detonators had been placed on the track at frequent intervals after the 'down' train had passed to give the last train a noisy departure from the Branch. The engine's shrill whistle regularly pierced the balmy air as it made its way south, the waves of the people standing by the line-side going unseen in the blackness of the night. Nobody was waiting at Pullabrook Halt to see the train pass, but the driver whistled-up in a final salute to the halt. In complete contrast, at Bovey there was quite a crowd waiting on the platform, with both the arrival and departure of the train being accompanied by a fusillade of detonators. The approach to Brimley Halt was heralded by much whistle blowing, reciprocated by animated waves from the small knot of people gathered on the platform to see the train run through. At Heathfield around half a dozen souls were waiting to greet the train. A large number of people alighted here, but as the train was running ahead of time, stayed around a while to watch its departure. As on the outward trip, nobody was at Teigngrace to witness this piece of local history, but at least at Teignbridge level crossing the keeper was present to acknowledge the engine's whistles. Almost as if to extend the last rites for as long as possible, the train was held at signals at Newton Abbot East for almost ten minutes before it made the final slow run into Platform 1, coming to a halt at one minute to ten.

So the end had come. After the last train had passed through, or pulled away from, the stations along the Branch, those who had travelled on it or turned out to say good-bye, drifted home. Platform lights were turned out and buildings locked: a long, unbroken chapter in the Line's history had come to an end.

After the Axe

It continued to be a widely-held belief by both members of the public and railwaymen that the Line could be a viable proposition, and it was this that lay behind the formation of the

South Devon Railway Preservation Society (the 'preservation' part of the title was soon dropped). The inaugural meeting took place in the Queens Hotel near Newton Abbot station on the very day that passenger services were withdrawn. Possessed of a vigorous membership, the Society set about publicising their case in the locality, hoping to harness enough support to press for the reinstatement of the service. To this end, an excursion was organised on Whit Monday 1960 (6th June). Given the title the 'Heart of Devon Rambler', the train began its journey at Paignton. The six corridor coaches making up the Special were in the charge of 'large Prairie' 4174. The engine was in a grimy condition, so a group of enthusiasts set to work to clean the side drawn up at the platform. When they asked for permission to go on to the track to deal with the other side, this was refused and thus remained dirty until the train reached Moretonhampstead, where officialdom was more relaxed. Leaving at 12.25pm, the train called at Torquay, Torre, Kingskerswell and Newton Abbot to pick up passengers, the final tally being a very respectable 225. Large numbers of people turned out along the route to greet the 'Rambler', thereby demonstrating their support of the Society's aims. At Lustleigh, the train received a particularly rousing welcome. The village and surrounding hamlets had felt the closure badly, having maintained a good level of patronage of the Branch right up to the end.

The SDRS continued to press its case and seek publicity, and on Saturday 4th March 1961 organised a 'brake van special' from Newton Abbot to Trusham. This had originally been arranged for the previous autumn - Saturday 8th October - and to run to Christow, but had to be postponed due to serious flood damage in the East Gold Marshes and in the Teign Valley between Ashton and Christow. The damage at the latter location was such that, in the event, the Special had to stop short of its intended destination. Once again, 4174 was the allocated engine - this time running bunker-first from Newton - with eight vans containing 50 people for the three-hour round trip. Events like this were important to keep the Line in the public eye, especially as the Transport Users' Consultative Committee back in 1958 had recommended the Line might be suitable for an experimental service with diesel railcars to test its viability (a type of train increasingly in evidence in the new decade). Given the climate prevailing in the higher echelons of management at the time, any move for restoring a service was resisted - indeed, the 'Beeching Axe' had not yet really started to swing into action.

Undaunted, the Society continued with their campaign from their new headquarters at Teigngrace Halt, and planned a further major publicity Special for the following Whit Monday (11th June 1962).

To advertise and promote the event, the SDRS held a competition to find a suitable name for the excursion; the winning title of 'South Devon Phoenix', suggested by a lady in Kingskerswell, being most appropriate given its intention. The 'Phoenix' left Newton Abbot at 1.18pm, with motive power being provided by 'large Prairie' 5153, and the six carriages carrying 200 or so occupants - one of whom was W.N. Ayliffe, chairman of Newton Abbot Rural District Council. Stops were made at all the stations and halts along the Line, the train again receiving a particularly enthusiastic welcome at Lustleigh, the villagers having decorated the station as they had done two years previously. At the terminus, a 'pilgrimage' was made to the granite memorial stone inscribed with the names of the original M&SDR directors. After a stop-over of an hour and a quarter, the excursion set off for the leisurely amble back to Newton Abbot - there being a 15mph speed limit in force over the Branch - arriving there at 5.30pm. Although the trip had been an undoubted success in terms of attracting local publicity and interest, not to mention a pleasantly nostalgic day out in its own right, this well-supported hint to the Railway Authorities once again fell on deaf ears and unseeing eyes. With the exception of a Sunday School Special run just two months later, the 'Phoenix' proved to be the swan-song for passenger-carrying trains over the full length of the Branch. It also marked a change in direction for the SDRS, which soon switched its attention to developments taking place in the Dart Valley.

The activity of the early 1960s was underpinned by a real enthusiasm and dynamic optimism, but sadly proved to be a fast-fading dream. By this time the Beeching Axe was being honed in readiness to wreak its merciless destruction of much of the rail network in the South West: the Teign Valley and Moreton closures were mere preludes of what was to come. With the exception of the Devon & Somerset Line from Taunton to Barnstaple, all the former Great Western branch lines in Devon had been closed to passenger traffic by the autumn of 1964 - and even the D&S suffered the same fate just two years later. In such bleak times for rural railways, any hopes of reopening the Moretonhampstead Branch were doomed to failure. Although the Branch remained open for goods traffic, even this service succumbed to rationalisation and retrenchment. The daily goods train was cut back to Mondays, Wednesdays and Fridays only, although Bovey was served additionally by a 'request' service

The 'South Devon Phoenix' approaching Teignbridge level crossing, hauled by 'large Prairie' No. 5153. Despite the 'express' lamp headcode, the train was not permitted more than a sedate 15mph. 11.6.62. *Peter W. Gray*

from Heathfield on Tuesdays and Thursdays (as part of the Teign Valley duty, which ran on these days and Saturday morning).

Following the withdrawal of passenger services there was an inevitable reduction in, and reorganisation of, personnel. Overall responsibility for the Branch was given to the station master at Heathfield (Frank Pill), with the equivalent posts at Bovey and Moretonhampstead being abolished. Ray Thomas, the last incumbent at Moreton, transferred to Starcross on the main line. He remained there for about five years, but as rationalisation made relentless inroads into traditional staffing patterns, unfortunately had the distinction of being the last station master at that place as well. His colleague at Bovey, Arthur Yendall, remained at his 'home' station on a protected salary, but redesignated as 'depot clerk'. His duties included winding up the passenger business not only at Bovey but also Lustleigh and Moreton. This involved the sad task of burning masses of posters, old notices, circulars and the like, and disposing of fixtures and fittings. Thereafter he dealt with the administrative work associated with the continuing goods traffic, and general day to day affairs.

Then came the announcement that the section north of Bovey was to close to all traffic on and from Monday 6th April 1964 (although small goods continued to be taken by road to the goods shed at Moreton until the end of December). Track lifting began the following year. The rails were lifted on to railway low-loaders and taken away for temporary storage before final despatch to the blast furnaces of South Wales for recycling. The contractors finished the task on 21st June, with the Branch now terminating at buffer stops by the 6¼ mile post immediately south of Bovey Bridge. Exactly one week before, on 14th June, the Newton Abbot Goods Concentration Scheme came into operation. Under this, facilities for handling parcels and general merchandise were withdrawn from Bovey, so that only 'full loads' for Wyatt & Bruce and Messrs. Vono Ltd., along with coal, continued to be received. The goods trains by this date were commonly in the charge of Class 22 (D63xx) diesel-hydraulics, the steam operation at Newton Abbot having ceased in June 1962. (The withdrawal of the Class 22s from the end of 1971 saw motive power pass principally to the more powerful Class 31 Brush-built diesel-electrics.) Depot clerk Arthur Yendall was transferred to Heathfield early in 1965 to assist Frank Pill with the greater workload at that location. After about six months, Arthur left the Railway to enjoy a long and fruitful retirement.

It was in 1965 that the next administrative changes came about, with the implementation of the 'station manager' scheme at Newton Abbot. Mr. L.J. Saunders was the last person to exclusively hold the venerable title of 'station master' at Newton. He removed to take up the equivalent post at Bristol (Temple Meads), and was replaced on 5th April 1965 by Alec Bath. However, exactly three weeks later, the coldly-utilitarian designation of 'station manager' was

instituted at Newton, which not only gave the incumbent supervision of the main line between Hackney and Aller Junction inclusive, but also the surviving sections of the Moreton and Teign Valley branches. The term 'station manager' was superseded at the beginning of the following year by that of 'area manager': a concept which fundamentally altered the time-honoured, station-specific mode of supervision. The amount of work left for the sole surviving porter at Bovey to deal with made his retention unviable, and on the same day that the area manager scheme began - Monday 3rd January 1966 - Bovey station finally closed, in what was its centenary year. At the same time, Frank Pill finished at Heathfield, leaving the work there to be covered by a single 'person in charge' (the single-shift signal box manned by a porter-signalman having closed in October 1965). After the re-grading exercise of 1967/8, the designation 'person in charge' became 'leading railman'. The man who had the distinction of being the very last member of staff at Heathfield was Ossie Biddiscombe. However, on 5th June 1972 this post was withdrawn, and any remaining work transferred to the leading railman at Teignbridge, until even that post was abolished a little later. Sometime within the next five years, the attractive wooden station buildings at Heathfield were demolished, to leave its gaunt platforms as the only structural reminders of this once-busy junction.

Goods traffic was further reduced by the closure of Candy's Siding on 10th March 1967, although it had been disused for several months. In November that year the surviving, intermittent traffic over the remaining four-mile stub of the Teign Valley Line to Crockham Sidings ceased: latterly coal and gas oil to Chudleigh and stone and concrete pipes from Crockham. The line was not officially closed until 1st July the following year. Hard on the heels of this was the opening of a large coal concentration depot at Exmouth Junction (Exeter) on 4th December 1967. This saw all of Devon served from that place by road, and consequently the end of coal traffic on the Moreton Branch. The next blow was the ending of rail-borne grain traffic for Wyatt & Bruce, from 1st May 1970. The formal declaration of closure to Bovey and likelihood of subsequent track removal, prompted the organisation of a 'farewell special'. On Sunday 5th July - the day before formal closure - a five-car diesel multiple made four round trips between Newton Abbot and Bovey. Comprising a 3-carriage set and 2 single rail cars, the train worked from the old Moretonhampstead bay platform

To mark the complete closure of the Heathfield to Bovey section of the now goods-only Branch, a special 'farewell' diesel multiple unit shuttle service between Newton Abbot and Bovey was arranged for the official last day: Sunday 5th July 1970. Consisting of cars 51312, 51327, 51329, 55016 and 59481, the second of four round trips run that day - the 12 noon from Newton - is seen entering Bovey station. *R. A. Lumber*

at Newton, and carried somewhere in the region of 500 people at ten shillings a head. It was only a matter of weeks before the track lifting contractors moved in, the exercise being completed on 8th September. Evidence of this could still be seen in the former yard at Bovey the following spring, where the dismantled track remained in stock-piles prior to its cutting into shorter lengths for transport to a buyer in West Germany. Buffers were installed at the 4¾ mile post, although the Line was cut back by some 300 yards nearer Heathfield on 21st August 1974: to 4 miles 46 chains from Newton Abbot - which remains the end of the Line to this day.

The track-bed and structures on the section north of the buffer stops on Bovey Heath remained remarkably intact for many years after abandonment. A few girder over-bridges were removed for reasons of height clearance and/or visibility, and in places vegetation began its predictable staged invasion. Following the complete closure of railway operations at Moretonhampstead in 1964, the local agricultural buildings manufacturer Mootels Ltd acquired the station site and buildings. After having been a familiar landmark for so long, the main station building was demolished in November 1968, although fortunately the goods shed and engine shed were spared - and still stand. In 1976 local haulier B. Thompson & Sons (Transport) Ltd. took over the site for use as a transport depot. Ten years later, work commenced on the Bovey by-pass. This brought about the most extensive post-closure upheaval to date, with 1½ miles of the track-bed north of Pottery Bridge being utilised by the new road. The cutting at the former Brimley Halt site was widened, and the Ashburton Road bridge rebuilt (the old M&SDR structure being demolished in November 1986). Mercifully its construction did not require the sacrifice of the main station building or goods shed at Bovey, which remained in use as a store and workshop respectively. The road opened on Friday 16th October 1987. A mile-long section of trackbed through the Parke Estate beyond Bovey station is now a public footpath, the estate having been bequeathed to Dartmoor National Park in 1974. It is still possible to see the wooden platform of Pullabrook Halt amongst a tangle of vegetation, whilst the station building at Lustleigh also remains, with additions, as a private house.

Parallel with this depressing catalogue of decline, dereliction and demolition, there were encouraging developments in other sectors, which seemed to assure the future of at least the southernmost part of the Branch. The opening of Geest Industries' banana warehouses at Heathfield in 1961 generated a considerable amount of traffic over the next few years, but sadly it was relatively short-lived, and the traffic ceased in 1975. The handling of ball clay on the other hand had long been a staple of the freight scene, and from the mid 1960s underwent something of a renaissance. There were substantial and regular shipments from the loading platforms at Heathfield, Teignbridge and East Gold (Newton Abbot), and by the mid 1980s the Branch was carrying about 30,000 tons of clay a year. In December 1986 BR's 'Railfreight' sector announced that £4 million were to be earmarked for the provision of 124 new air-braked wagons to replace the open wooden plank wagons which had been in use for the previous thirty years. Thus from the following year the clay was conveyed principally in either PBA bogie wagons or PGA hoppers, with smaller amounts of bagged clay loaded into Ferry Vans.

One event of great importance was the opening of a rail-served oil distribution depot on a four-acre site north of Heathfield station. Proximity to the busy A38 trunk road, and ample room for possible future expansion, made this an attractive site to the oil company: Gulf Oil (Great Britain) Ltd. Following negotiations between the company and BR in June 1965, two sidings were installed on the site immediately beyond the substantial three-arch granite-built bridge carrying the minor road to Little Bovey. Known as Gulf Sidings, their connection with the running line - trailing to 'down' trains - was at 4 miles 36 chains from Newton Abbot. Following the necessary inspection, block trains of tank wagons were accepted over the Branch to the depot on Monday 17th January 1966 (although the official opening was much later in the year). The lack of a run-round facility necessitated the empty, outward-bound tankers being propelled back to Heathfield to allow the locomotive to change ends before continuing to the main line. Following the withdrawal of freight traffic between Heathfield and Bovey in 1970, a section of line was left by way of a head-shunt for the sidings. Even though this was cut back by 14 chains (308 yards) four years later, it still left a very generous length of 220 yards. The loaded oil tankers made the long journey from Gulf Oil's refinery at Waterston, Milford Haven. From only once a week in the summer, the frequency rose to two or even three during the winter months. The empties were returned to Briton Ferry near Swansea.

In more recent times, the variety of work handled at the sidings increased. Enclosed by high fences and perused by security cameras, a large notice at the road entrance proclaimed: HELTOR LTD. RAIL FREIGHT TERMINAL. In addition to fuel oil and lubricants

Literally the end of the Line. Some twelve months after the withdrawal of goods trains between Bovey and Moretonhampstead (6th April 1964), contractors moved in to lift the track north of the 6¼ mile post. The bogie low-loaders, seen here not far from that mile post, conveyed the rails to Heathfield for stockpiling prior to their despatch to South Wales. Spring 1965.
A. W. Yendall Collection

brought in 4-wheeled and bogie tank wagons, there was considerable traffic in animal feedstuffs and fertiliser (commonly carried in long wheel-base Ferry Vans). During these settled years, the Branch was targetted by a number of enthusiasts' excursions (and also by the Royal Train, as related in Chapter 5). The Railway Correspondence & Travel Society's 'Devon Rambler' tour of 20th April 1974 included a trip from Newton Abbot to Heathfield and back as part of its visits to certain 'goods only' lines in the county (the Torrington and Meldon branches being the others). Originating in Bristol, the excursion comprised a 3-car, Swindon-built, cross-country diesel multiple unit. By the time of the next 'special', the layout at Heathfield had been reduced to the two platform lines and Timber Siding loop. The latter was retained for ECC's clay traffic and the former as an engine run-round facility. This facility was used by Class 47 number 47583 *County of Hertfordshire* which brought the heavy 11-coach 'Torbay Express' rail-tour to the station on 16th May 1987. The following year, on 4th September, a 2-car diesel unit chartered by the Cornwall Railway Society ran over the Branch, while two years later the 'Taw Retour' made a visitation. Run on 16th September 1990, and organised by 'Pathfinder Tours', the substantial train worked over the Branch with a Class 50 at both ends: 50032 *Courageous* at the Heathfield end and 50031 *Hood* at the other. These provided the motive power on the trip to and from Gulf Sidings respectively.

At the beginn-ing of the 1990s the future of the attenuated Branch looked bright, with regular appearances of Class 37, 47 and 50 locomotives hauling viable payloads. The loss soon afterwards of the general freight to Heltor was unfortunate, but more serious was the cessation of the regular ball clay traffic. Suddenly the Line was experiencing a collapse. By 1995 the block oil trains had dropped back to only one a week, and then came Gulf's decision to modify its fuel distribution in the region, switching to a direct sea-borne facility at Plymouth. The last train of twelve empty 20,000-gallon oil tank wagons left

Heathfield at 11.40am on 17th January 1996 in the charge of a Class 37 locomotive (37141) and with it went the prospect of a secure future for the Line. Concerned at this development, Teignbridge Council's transport working party sought a statement from Railtrack on the future of the Line. History seemed to be repeating itself. In August they received the reply that "....there is a possibility freight operations might be resumed in the near future (and that there was) no intention at the present time to dismantle the line".

On New Year's Eve 1996, the Branch played host to another 'Special'. It ran in connection with 'Rail 150 Newton Abbot', which marked the 150th anniversary of the opening of the South Devon main line to the town. Entitled 'The Newton Abbot 150', the train began its trip in Bristol, and made three well-patronised round trips between Newton and Heathfield; taking 25 minutes each way. Running now in the era of privatisation era, the excursion was a joint operation between 'South Wales & West Railway' and 'Railtrack', with motive power being provided by EWS ('English, Welsh & Scottish Railway'). With the future of the Line increasingly precarious, further excursions were arranged for Easter and mid December 1997. The train on both occasions was an HST Inter City 125. It was neither high-speed nor did it link any cities on its slow trundle over the four and a half-mile trip out to the end of the Line near Gulf Sidings (which had already been removed), but was quite an event none-the-less!

At the end of 1998 the remnant of the Line stood rusty and disused, its future uncertain. There are serious and sustained calls for it to fulfil a 'park-and-ride' function to relieve traffic congestion in, and north of, Newton Abbot. Passengers would be shuttled to and from a car park at Heathfield. Others suggest a steam-operated 'tourist' line, after the fashion of the Torbay and Dart Valley Railways; while still others hope to see regular freight traffic restored (encouragingly, occasional clay trains were to be seen early in 1999). In the unfortunate event of the track being lifted, some people would like the route to be turned

Modern motive power on the Branch. In pouring summer rain Class 50 No. 50149 (in Rail Freight livery) with two loaded PBA clay wagons, pulls clear of the level crossing at Teignbridge to allow the shunter to close and padlock the gates before continuing to St. Blazey with the 10.45am working from Heathfield. Class 37s and 47s were also used at this time on both this and/or the block oil trains to and from Heathfield. 28.7.88. *Hugh Ballantyne*

into a 'linear park': an all-weather path to provide recreation for walkers, cyclists and horse-riders. Another group simply hope the track-bed will be abandoned to nature. Of recent interest in the post-closure scene was the appearance of a steam-hauled 'special' on the evening of Easter Monday (April 5th), 1999. Organised by 'Past Time Rail' of Lichfield, and advertised as the 'Heathfield Mule', the train originated at Exeter. Consisting of seven carmine and cream coaches hauled by Stand-ard Class 4 2-6-4T No. 80079, it made its visitation to the Branch upon completion of a highly successful afternoon shuttle service between St. David's station and Newton Abbot as the 'Dawlish Donkey'. In the new millennium, as part of the Newton Abbot 'Festival of Transport', steam 'specials' worked to Heathfield and back on the weekend of 13th/14th May 2000, hauled by ex-GWR Pannier 0-6-0PT No. 9600.

While trains can never again run all the way from 'Shore to Moor', it is unquestionably the case that the story of the Moretonhampstead Branch is not yet over.

Newton Abbot Clay Siding, with its revamped loading facilities. 1.2.91. *Author*

Having taken a block train of oil tankers to Gulf Sidings, north of Heathfield, Class 47 No. 47197, returning 'light engine', draws up at Teignbridge level crossing for the shunter to open the gates. 1.2.91.

Author